BUSINESS ISSUES, COMPETITION AND ENTREPRENEURSHIP

SMALL BUSINESS

FUNDING, MANAGEMENT AND MENTOR PROGRAMS

BUSINESS ISSUES, COMPETITION AND ENTREPRENEURSHIP

Additional books and e-books in this series can be found
on Nova's website under the Series tab.

BUSINESS ISSUES, COMPETITION AND ENTREPRENEURSHIP

SMALL BUSINESS FUNDING, MANAGEMENT AND MENTOR PROGRAMS

ANGEL BECKER
EDITOR

snova
New York

Copyright © 2019 by Nova Science Publishers, Inc.

All rights reserved. No part of this book may be reproduced, stored in a retrieval system or transmitted in any form or by any means: electronic, electrostatic, magnetic, tape, mechanical photocopying, recording or otherwise without the written permission of the Publisher.

We have partnered with Copyright Clearance Center to make it easy for you to obtain permissions to reuse content from this publication. Simply navigate to this publication's page on Nova's website and locate the "Get Permission" button below the title description. This button is linked directly to the title's permission page on copyright.com. Alternatively, you can visit copyright.com and search by title, ISBN, or ISSN.

For further questions about using the service on copyright.com, please contact:
Copyright Clearance Center
Phone: +1-(978) 750-8400 Fax: +1-(978) 750-4470 E-mail: info@copyright.com.

NOTICE TO THE READER

The Publisher has taken reasonable care in the preparation of this book, but makes no expressed or implied warranty of any kind and assumes no responsibility for any errors or omissions. No liability is assumed for incidental or consequential damages in connection with or arising out of information contained in this book. The Publisher shall not be liable for any special, consequential, or exemplary damages resulting, in whole or in part, from the readers' use of, or reliance upon, this material. Any parts of this book based on government reports are so indicated and copyright is claimed for those parts to the extent applicable to compilations of such works.

Independent verification should be sought for any data, advice or recommendations contained in this book. In addition, no responsibility is assumed by the Publisher for any injury and/or damage to persons or property arising from any methods, products, instructions, ideas or otherwise contained in this publication.

This publication is designed to provide accurate and authoritative information with regard to the subject matter covered herein. It is sold with the clear understanding that the Publisher is not engaged in rendering legal or any other professional services. If legal or any other expert assistance is required, the services of a competent person should be sought. FROM A DECLARATION OF PARTICIPANTS JOINTLY ADOPTED BY A COMMITTEE OF THE AMERICAN BAR ASSOCIATION AND A COMMITTEE OF PUBLISHERS.

Additional color graphics may be available in the e-book version of this book.

Library of Congress Cataloging-in-Publication Data

ISBN: 978-1-53615-969-1

Published by Nova Science Publishers, Inc. † New York

CONTENTS

Preface vii

Chapter 1 The Small Business Lending Fund (Updated) 1
Robert Jay Dilger

Chapter 2 Small Business Loans: Additional Actions Needed to Improve Compliance with the Credit Elsewhere Requirement 57
United States Government Accountability Office

Chapter 3 State Small Business Credit Initiative: Implementation and Funding Issues (Updated) 103
Robert Jay Dilger

Chapter 4 SBA Assistance to Small Business Startups: Client Experiences and Program Impact (Updated) 171
Robert Jay Dilger

Chapter 5 Small Business Management and Technical Assistance Training Programs (Updated) 203
Robert Jay Dilger

Chapter 6	Small Business Mentor-Protégé Programs (Updated) *Robert Jay Dilger*	**265**
Index		**309**
Related Nova Publications		**319**

PREFACE

Congressional interest in small business access to capital has increased in recent years because of concerns that small businesses might be prevented from accessing sufficient capital to enable them to start, continue, or expand operations and create jobs. Chapter 1 focuses on the Small Business Lending Fund (SBLF). It opens with a discussion of the supply and demand for small business loans then examines other arguments presented both for and against the program. Chapter 2 discusses how SBA monitors lenders' compliance with the credit elsewhere requirement, the extent to which SBA evaluates trends in lender credit elsewhere practices, and lenders' views on the credit elsewhere criteria for 7(a) loans.

Chapter 3 examines the State Small Business Credit Initiative (SSBCI) and its implementation, including Treasury's response to initial program audits conducted by the U.S. Government Accountability Office (GAO) and Treasury's Office of Inspector General (OIG). Chapter 4 discusses small business startups' experiences with the SBA's management and technical assistance training programs, focusing on Small Business Development Centers (SBDCs), Women Business Centers (WBCs), and SCORE (formerly the Service Corps of Retired Executives); the SBA's 7(a), 504/CDC, and Microloan lending programs; and the SBA's Small Business Investment Company (SBIC) venture capital program.

Chapter 5 examines small business startups' experiences with the SBA's management and technical assistance training programs, focusing on Small Business Development Centers (SBDCs), Women Business Centers (WBCs), and SCORE (formerly the Service Corps of Retired Executives); the SBA's 7(a), 504/CDC, and Microloan lending programs; and the SBA's Small Business Investment Company (SBIC) venture capital program. Chapter 6 provides an overview of the federal government's various small business mentor-protégé programs.

Chapter 1 - Congressional interest in small business access to capital has increased in recent years because of concerns that small businesses might be prevented from accessing sufficient capital to enable them to start, continue, or expand operations and create jobs. Some have argued that the federal government should provide additional resources to assist small businesses. Others worry about the long-term adverse economic effects of spending programs that increase the federal deficit. They advocate business tax reduction, reform of financial credit market regulation, and federal fiscal restraint as the best means to assist small businesses and create jobs. Several laws were enacted during the 111th Congress to enhance small business access to capital. For example,

- P.L. 111-5, the American Recovery and Reinvestment Act of 2009 (ARRA), provided the Small Business Administration (SBA) an additional $730 million, including funding to temporarily subsidize SBA fees and increase the 7(a) loan guaranty program's maximum loan guaranty percentage to 90%.
- P.L. 111-240, the Small Business Jobs Act of 2010, authorized the Secretary of the Treasury to establish a $30 billion Small Business Lending Fund (SBLF), in which $4.0 billion was issued, to encourage community banks with less than $10 billion in assets to increase their lending to small businesses. It also authorized a $1.5 billion State Small Business Credit Initiative to provide funding to participating states with small business capital access programs, numerous changes to the

SBA's loan guaranty and contracting programs, funding to continue the SBA's fee subsidies and the 7(a) program's 90% maximum loan guaranty percentage through December 31, 2010, and about $12 billion in tax relief for small businesses.
- P.L. 111-322, the Continuing Appropriations and Surface Transportation Extensions Act, 2011, authorized the SBA to continue its fee subsidies and the 7(a) program's 90% maximum loan guaranty percentage through March 4, 2011, or until available funding was exhausted, which occurred on January 3, 2011.

This chapter focuses on the SBLF. It opens with a discussion of the supply and demand for small business loans. The SBLF's advocates claimed the SBLF was needed to enhance the supply of small business loans. The report then examines other arguments presented both for and against the program. Advocates argued that the SBLF would increase lending to small businesses and, in turn, create jobs. Opponents contended that the SBLF could lose money, lacked sufficient oversight provisions, did not require lenders to increase their lending to small businesses, could serve as a vehicle for Troubled Asset Relief Program (TARP) recipients to effectively refinance their TARP loans on more favorable terms with little or no resulting benefit for small businesses, and could encourage a failing lender to make even riskier loans to avoid higher dividend payments. The report concludes with an examination of the program's implementation and a discussion of bills introduced to amend the SBLF. For example, during the 112th Congress, S. 681, the Greater Accountability in the Lending Fund Act of 2011, would have limited the program's authority to 15 years from enactment and prohibited TARP recipients from participating in the program. H.R. 2807, the Small Business Leg-Up Act of 2011, would have transferred any unobligated and repaid funds from the SBLF to the Community Development Financial Institutions Fund "to increase the availability of credit for small businesses." H.R. 3147, the Small Business Lending Extension Act, would have extended the Department of the Treasury's investment authority from one year to two years. During the

113th Congress, H.R. 2474, the Community Lending and Small Business Jobs Act of 2013, would have transferred any unobligated and repaid funds from the SBLF to the Community Development Financial Institutions Fund.

Chapter 2 - SBA's 7(a) program is required to serve creditworthy small business borrowers who cannot obtain credit through a conventional lender at reasonable terms. The Joint Explanatory Statement of the Consolidated Appropriations Act, 2017 includes a provision for GAO to review the 7(a) program. This chapter discusses, among other things, (1) how SBA monitors lenders' compliance with the credit elsewhere requirement, (2) the extent to which SBA evaluates trends in lender credit elsewhere practices, and (3) lenders' views on the credit elsewhere criteria for 7(a) loans. GAO analyzed SBA data on 7(a) loans approved for fiscal years 2007–2016, the latest available, and reviewed literature on small business lending; reviewed standard operating procedures, other guidance, and findings from SBA reviews performed in fiscal year 2016; and interviewed lender associations and a nonrepresentative sample of 7(a) lenders selected that concentrated on larger lenders.

Chapter 3 - Congressional interest in small business access to capital has increased in recent years because of concerns that small businesses might be prevented from accessing sufficient capital to enable them to start, continue, or expand operations and create jobs. Some have argued that the federal government should provide additional resources to assist small businesses. Others worry about the long-term adverse economic effects of spending programs that increase the federal deficit. They advocate business tax reduction, reform of financial credit market regulation, and federal fiscal restraint as the best means to assist small businesses and create jobs. During the 111th Congress, P.L. 111-240, the Small Business Jobs Act of 2010, provided the Small Business Administration (SBA) additional funding and enhanced several SBA lending programs in an effort to assist small businesses access capital. The act also authorized the Secretary of the Treasury to establish and administer a $1.5 billion State Small Business Credit Initiative (SSBCI). Treasury's role in administrating the program ended on September 27,

2017. The SSBCI provided funding, allocated by formula and distributed in one-third increments, to states, territories, and eligible municipalities (hereinafter referred to as states) to expand existing or create new state small business investment programs, including state capital access programs, collateral support programs, loan participation programs, loan guarantee programs, and venture capital programs. In most instances, the initial round of funding (called a tranche) took place in FY2011. Most states received their second tranche during FY2013. As of December 31, 2016, 98% of total allocated funding had been disbursed to the states and all 57 participants had received their first tranche, 56 had received at least two tranches, and 53 had received their third and final tranche. SSBCI participants were expected to leverage their SSBCI funds to generate new small business lending that is at least 10 times the amount of their SSBCI funds. As of December 31, 2016, SSBCI participants had leveraged $8.95 in new financing for every $1 in SSBCI funds. Forty-seven states; American Samoa; the District of Columbia; Guam; the Northern Mariana Islands; Puerto Rico; the U.S. Virgin Islands; Anchorage, Alaska; two consortiums of municipalities in North Dakota; and a consortium of municipalities in Wyoming participate in the program. The Obama Administration recommended in its FY2015, FY2016, and FY2017 budget requests that another $1.5 billion round of funding take place, with $1 billion competitively awarded to states and $500 million awarded "by a need-based formula based on economic factors such as job losses and pace of economic recovery." Legislation with provisions similar to the Obama Administration's proposal was introduced during the 113th Congress (H.R. 4556 and S. 2285), the 114th Congress (S. 1901, H.R. 5144, and H.R. 5672), and the 115th Congress (S. 1897). This chapter examines the SSBCI and its implementation, including Treasury's response to initial program audits conducted by the U.S. Government Accountability Office (GAO) and Treasury's Office of Inspector General (OIG). These initial audits suggest that SSBCI participants generally met the statute's requirements but that there were some compliance problems. They also indicate that Treasury's program oversight could have been improved and that performance measures are needed to assess the program's efficacy.

Chapter 4 - The Small Business Administration (SBA) administers several programs to support small businesses, including loan guaranty and venture capital programs to enhance small business access to capital; contracting programs to increase small business opportunities in federal contracting; direct loan programs for businesses, homeowners, and renters to assist their recovery from natural disasters; and small business management and technical assistance training programs to assist business formation and expansion. Congressional interest in these programs, and the SBA's assistance provided to small business startups in particular (defined as new businesses that meet the SBA's criteria as small), has increased in recent years, primarily because these programs are viewed by many as a means to stimulate economic activity and create jobs. Economists generally do not view job creation as a justification for providing federal assistance to small businesses. They argue that in the long term such assistance will likely reallocate jobs within the economy, not increase them. In their view, jobs arise primarily from the size of the labor force, which depends largely on population, demographics, and factors that affect the choice of home versus market production (e.g., the entry of women in the workforce). However, economic theory does suggest that increased federal spending on small business assistance programs may result in additional jobs in the short term. Congressional interest in assistance to business startups is derived primarily from economic research suggesting that startups play a very important role in job creation. That research suggests that business startups create many new jobs, but have a more limited effect on net job creation over time because fewer than half of all startups remain in business after five years. However, that research also suggests that the influence of small business startups on net job creation varies by firm size. Startups with fewer than 20 employees tend to have a negligible effect on net job creation over time whereas startups with 20-499 employees tend to have a positive employment effect, as do surviving younger businesses of all sizes (in operation for one year to five years). This chapter examines small business startups' experiences with the SBA's management and technical assistance training programs, focusing on Small Business Development Centers (SBDCs), Women Business Centers

(WBCs), and SCORE (formerly the Service Corps of Retired Executives); the SBA's 7(a), 504/CDC, and Microloan lending programs; and the SBA's Small Business Investment Company (SBIC) venture capital program. Although data collected by the SBA concerning these programs' impact on economic activity and job creation are somewhat limited and subject to methodological challenges concerning their validity as reliable performance measures, most small business owners who have participated in these programs report in surveys sponsored by the SBA that the programs were useful. Given the data limitations, however, it is difficult to determine the cost effectiveness of these programs. The report also discusses the SBA's growth accelerators initiative, which targets entrepreneurs looking to "start and scale their business" by helping them access "seed capital, mentors, and networking opportunities for customers and partners," and the recently sunset SBIC early stage debenture program, which focused on providing venture capital to startups.

Chapter 5 - The Small Business Administration (SBA) has provided technical and managerial assistance to small businesses since it began operations in 1953. Initially, the SBA provided its own small business management and technical assistance training programs. Over time, the SBA has relied increasingly on third parties to provide that training. Congressional interest in the SBA's management and technical assistance training programs ($226.7 million in FY2019) has increased in recent years, primarily because these programs are viewed as a means to assist small businesses create and retain jobs. These programs fund about "14,000 resource partners," including 63 lead small business development centers (SBDCs) and more than 900 SBDC local outreach locations, 121 women's business centers (WBCs), and 320 chapters of the mentoring program, SCORE. The SBA reports that more than 1 million aspiring entrepreneurs and small business owners receive training from an SBA-supported resource partner each year. The Department of Commerce also provides management and technical assistance training for small businesses. For example, its Minority Business Development Agency provides training to minority business owners to assist them in obtaining contracts and financial awards. Some have argued that the SBA could improve program efficiency by eliminating duplication of services across federal agencies and improving cooperation and coordination among the SBA's resource partners. Congress has also explored ways to improve the SBA's measurement of these programs' effectiveness. This chapter examines the historical development of federal small business management and technical assistance training programs; describes their current structures, operations, and budgets; and assesses their administration and oversight and the measures used to determine their effectiveness. It also discusses legislation to improve program performance, including P.L. 114-88, the Recovery Improvements for Small Entities After Disaster Act of 2015 (RISE After Disaster Act of 2015), which, among other things, authorizes the SBA to provide up to two years of additional funding to its resource partners to assist small businesses located in a presidentially declared major disaster area and authorizes SBDCs to provide assistance outside the SBDC's state, without regard to geographical proximity to the SBDC, if the small business is in a presidentially declared major disaster area. This assistance can be provided "for a period of not more than two years after the date on which the President" has declared the area a major disaster; and P.L. 115-141, the Consolidated Appropriations Act of 2018, among other provisions, relaxed requirements that Microloan intermediaries may spend no more than 25% of Microloan technical assistance grant funds on prospective borrowers and no more than 25% of those funds on contracts with third parties to provide that technical assistance by increasing those percentages to no more than 50%.

Chapter 6 - Mentor-protégé programs typically seek to pair new businesses with more experienced businesses in mutually beneficial relationships. Protégés may receive financial, technical, or management assistance from mentors in obtaining and performing federal contracts or subcontracts, or serving as suppliers under such contracts or subcontracts. Mentors may receive credit toward subcontracting goals, reimbursement of certain expenses, or other incentives. The federal government currently has several mentor-protégé programs to assist small businesses in various ways. For example, the 8(a) Mentor-Protégé Program is a government-wide program designed to assist small businesses "owned and controlled by socially and economically disadvantaged individuals" participating in the Small Business Administration's (SBA's) Minority Small Business and Capital Ownership Development Program (commonly known as the 8(a) program) in obtaining and performing federal contracts. Toward that end, mentors may (1) form joint ventures with protégés that are eligible to perform federal contracts set aside for small businesses; (2) make certain equity investments in protégé firms; (3) lend or subcontract to protégé firms; and (4) provide technical or management assistance to their protégés. The Department of Defense (DOD) Mentor-Protégé Program, in contrast, is agency-specific. It is designed to assist various types of small businesses and other entities in obtaining and performing DOD subcontracts and serving as suppliers on DOD contracts. Mentors may (1) make advance or progress payments to their protégés that DOD reimburses; (2) award subcontracts to their protégés on a noncompetitive basis when they would not otherwise be able to do so; (3) lend money to or make investments in protégé firms; and (4) provide or arrange for other assistance. Other agencies also have agency-specific mentor-protégé programs designed to assist various types of small businesses or other entities in obtaining and performing subcontracts under agency prime contracts. The Department of Homeland Security (DHS), for example, has a mentor-protégé program wherein mentors may provide protégés with rent-free use of facilities or equipment, temporary personnel for training, property, loans, or other assistance. Because these programs are not based in statute, unlike the SBA and DOD programs, they generally rely upon preexisting authorities (e.g., authorizing use of evaluation factors) or publicity to incentivize mentor participation. See Table A.1 for a summary comparison. P.L. 111-240, the Small Business Jobs Act of 2010, authorized the SBA to establish mentor-protégé programs for small businesses owned and controlled by service-disabled veterans, small businesses owned and controlled by women, and small businesses located in a HUBZone. P.L. 112-239, the National Defense Authorization Act for Fiscal Year 2013, authorized the SBA to establish a mentor-protégé program for all small businesses, and generally prohibits agencies from carrying out mentor-protégé programs that have not been approved by the

SBA. Based on the authority provided by these two laws, the SBA published a final rule in the *Federal Register* on July 25, 2016, modifying the 8(a) Mentor-Protégé Program and establishing, effective August 24, 2016, "a government-wide mentor-protégé program for all small business concerns, consistent with the SBA's mentor-protégé program for participants in the SBA's 8(a) Business Development program." The all small business Mentor-Protégé Program began accepting applications on October 1, 2016. The SBA noted in the final rule that because the new all small business mentor-protégé program applies to all federal small business contracts and federal agencies, "conceivably other agency-specific mentor-protégé programs would not be needed." Since then, several federal agencies have ended their mentor-protégé programs and encouraged interested parties to consider the SBA's all small business Mentor-Protégé program.

In: Small Business
Editor: Angel Becker

ISBN: 978-1-53615-969-1
© 2019 Nova Science Publishers, Inc.

Chapter 1

THE SMALL BUSINESS LENDING FUND (UPDATED)[*]

Robert Jay Dilger

SUMMARY

Congressional interest in small business access to capital has increased in recent years because of concerns that small businesses might be prevented from accessing sufficient capital to enable them to start, continue, or expand operations and create jobs. Some have argued that the federal government should provide additional resources to assist small businesses. Others worry about the long-term adverse economic effects of spending programs that increase the federal deficit. They advocate business tax reduction, reform of financial credit market regulation, and federal fiscal restraint as the best means to assist small businesses and create jobs.

Several laws were enacted during the 111th Congress to enhance small business access to capital. For example,

---

[*] This is an edited, reformatted and augmented version of Congressional Research Service, Publication No. R42045, dated February 7, 2019.

- P.L. 111-5, the American Recovery and Reinvestment Act of 2009 (ARRA), provided the Small Business Administration (SBA) an additional $730 million, including funding to temporarily subsidize SBA fees and increase the 7(a) loan guaranty program's maximum loan guaranty percentage to 90%.
- P.L. 111-240, the Small Business Jobs Act of 2010, authorized the Secretary of the Treasury to establish a $30 billion Small Business Lending Fund (SBLF), in which $4.0 billion was issued, to encourage community banks with less than $10 billion in assets to increase their lending to small businesses. It also authorized a $1.5 billion State Small Business Credit Initiative to provide funding to participating states with small business capital access programs, numerous changes to the SBA's loan guaranty and contracting programs, funding to continue the SBA's fee subsidies and the 7(a) program's 90% maximum loan guaranty percentage through December 31, 2010, and about $12 billion in tax relief for small businesses.
- P.L. 111-322, the Continuing Appropriations and Surface Transportation Extensions Act, 2011, authorized the SBA to continue its fee subsidies and the 7(a) program's 90% maximum loan guaranty percentage through March 4, 2011, or until available funding was exhausted, which occurred on January 3, 2011.

This chapter focuses on the SBLF. It opens with a discussion of the supply and demand for small business loans. The SBLF's advocates claimed the SBLF was needed to enhance the supply of small business loans. The report then examines other arguments presented both for and against the program. Advocates argued that the SBLF would increase lending to small businesses and, in turn, create jobs. Opponents contended that the SBLF could lose money, lacked sufficient oversight provisions, did not require lenders to increase their lending to small businesses, could serve as a vehicle for Troubled Asset Relief Program (TARP) recipients to effectively refinance their TARP loans on more favorable terms with little or no resulting benefit for small businesses, and could encourage a failing lender to make even riskier loans to avoid higher dividend payments.

The report concludes with an examination of the program's implementation and a discussion of bills introduced to amend the SBLF. For example, during the 112th Congress, S. 681, the Greater Accountability in the Lending Fund Act of 2011, would have limited the program's authority to 15 years from enactment and prohibited TARP recipients from participating in the program. H.R. 2807, the Small Business Leg-Up Act of 2011, would have transferred any unobligated and repaid funds from the SBLF to the Community Development Financial Institutions Fund "to increase the availability of credit for small businesses." H.R. 3147, the Small Business Lending Extension Act, would have extended the Department of the Treasury's investment authority from one year to two years. During the 113th Congress, H.R. 2474, the Community Lending and Small Business Jobs Act of 2013, would have transferred any unobligated and repaid funds from the SBLF to the Community Development Financial Institutions Fund.

SMALL BUSINESS ACCESS TO CAPITAL

Congressional interest in small business access to capital has increased in recent years because of concerns that small businesses might be prevented from accessing sufficient capital to enable them to start, continue, or expand operations and create jobs.[1] Small businesses have played an important role in net job growth during previous economic recoveries, particularly in the construction, housing, and retail sectors.[2] For example, after the eight-month recession that began in July 1990 and ended in March 1991, small businesses (defined for this purpose as having fewer than 500 employees) increased their net employment in the first year after the recession, whereas larger businesses continued to experience declines in employment.[3] During the most recent recession (December 2007-June

---

[1] The United States does not have a statutory definition for medium-sized or large businesses. A business concern can either be considered *small* or *not small* under §3(a)(1) of the Small Business Act, 15 U.S.C. §632(a)(1), which indicates that a small business concern "shall be deemed to be one that is independently owned and operated and which is not dominant in its field of operation." The Small Business Administration (SBA) has established two widely used size standards: 500 employees for most manufacturing and mining industries and $7.0 million in average annual receipts for most nonmanufacturing industries. However, many exceptions exist. For example, a small business concern can have up to 1,500 employees for certain industry categories. The SBA's size standards may be found at 13 C.F.R. §121.201. For additional information and analysis, see CRS Report R40860, *Small Business Size Standards: A Historical Analysis of Contemporary Issues*, by Robert Jay Dilger. In contrast, the European Union defines small business as those with fewer than 50 employees, medium-sized business as those employing 50 workers to 250 workers, and large businesses as those with more than 250 employees. See European Commission, "Small and Medium Sized Enterprises: What is an SME?" at http://ec.europa.eu/growth/smes/business-friendly-environment/sme-definition_en.

[2] Brian Headd, "Small Businesses Most Likely to Lead Economic Recovery," *The Small Business Advocate*, vol. 28, no. 6 (July 2009), pp. 1, 2.

[3] U.S. Small Business Administration (SBA), Office of Advocacy, "Small Business Economic Indicators for 2003: A reference guide to the latest data on small business activity, including state and industry data," August 2004, p. 3.

2009), small businesses accounted for almost 60% of net job losses.[4] From the end of the recession through the end of FY2012, small businesses accounted for about 63% of net new jobs, close to their historical average share of net new job creation.[5] Since then, small businesses have added about 65% of net new jobs.[6]

Some have argued that the federal government should provide additional resources to assist small businesses. Others worry about the long-term adverse economic effects of spending programs that increase the federal deficit. They advocate business tax reduction, reform of financial credit market regulation, and federal fiscal restraint as the best means to assist small businesses and create jobs.

Several laws were enacted during the 111th Congress to enhance small business access to capital. For example,

- P.L. 111-5, the American Recovery and Reinvestment Act of 2009 (ARRA), provided the Small Business Administration (SBA) an additional $730 million, including $375 million to temporarily subsidize SBA fees and increase the 7(a) loan guaranty program's maximum loan guaranty percentage from 85% on loans of $150,000 or less and 75% on loans exceeding $150,000 to 90% for all regular 7(a) loans.
- P.L. 111-240, the Small Business Jobs Act of 2010, authorized the Secretary of the Treasury to establish a $30 billion Small Business

---

[4] SBA, "The Small Business Economy, 2010: A Report to the President," pp. 2, 5, 21, 22, at https://www.sba.gov/sites/ default/files/sb_econ2010.pdf; and SBA, *Fiscal Year 2010 Congressional Budget Justification*, p. 1, at https://www.sba.gov/sites/default/files/aboutsbaarticle/Congressional_Budget_Justification_2010.pdf.
[5] SBA, Office of Advocacy, "Small Business Employment: Fourth Quarter 2013," *Quarterly Employment Bulletin*, February 6, 2014, p. 1, at https://www.sba.gov/sites/default/files/Quarterly_Employment_Bulletin_4q2013%20.pdf.
[6] U.S. Bureau of the Census, "2012-2013 SUSB Employment Change Data Tables, Data by Enterprise Employment Size, U.S. & states, totals," at https://www.census.gov/content/census/en/data/tables/2013/econ/susb/2013-susbemployment.html; U.S. Bureau of the Census, "2013-2014 SUSB Employment Change Data Tables, Data by Enterprise Employment Size, U.S. & states, totals," at https://www.census.gov/content/census/en/data/tables/2014/econ/susb/2014-susb-employment.html; and U.S. Bureau of the Census, "2014-2015 SUSB Employment Change Data Tables, Data by Enterprise Employment Size, U.S. & states, totals," at https://www.census.gov/content/census/en/data/tables/2015/econ/susb/2015-susb-employment.html.

Lending Fund (SBLF) ($4.0 billion was issued) to encourage community banks with less than $10 billion in assets to increase their lending to small businesses. It also authorized a $1.5 billion State Small Business Credit Initiative to provide funding to participating states with small business capital access programs, numerous changes to the SBA's loan guaranty and contracting programs, funding to continue the SBA's fee subsidies and the 7(a) program's 90% maximum loan guaranty percentage through December 31, 2010, and about $12 billion in tax relief for small businesses.

- P.L. 111-322, the Continuing Appropriations and Surface Transportation Extensions Act, 2011, authorized the SBA to continue its fee subsidies and the 7(a) program's 90% maximum loan guaranty percentage through March 4, 2011, or until available funding was exhausted, which occurred on January 3, 2011.

According to the SBA, the temporary fee subsidies and 90% maximum loan guaranty for the 7(a) program "engineered a significant turnaround in SBA lending.... The end result is that the agency helped put more than $42 billion in the hands of small businesses through the Recovery Act and Jobs Act combined."[7]

This chapter focuses on the SBLF. It begins with a discussion of the supply and demand for small business loans. The SBLF's advocates argued that the fund was an important part of a larger effort to enhance the supply of small business loans. After describing the program's structure, the report then examines other arguments that were presented both for and against the program's enactment. Advocates claimed the SBLF would increase lending to small businesses and, in turn, create jobs. Opponents contended that the SBLF could lose money, lacked sufficient oversight provisions, did not require lenders to increase their lending to small businesses, could serve as a vehicle for the Troubled Asset Relief Program (TARP)

---

[7] SBA, "Jobs Act Supported More Than $12 Billion in SBA Lending to Small Businesses in Just Three Months," January 3, 2010, at https://www.sba.gov/content/jobs-act-supported-more-12-billion-sba-lending-small-businesses-justthree-months.

recipients to effectively refinance their TARP loans on more favorable terms with little or no resulting benefit for small businesses, and could encourage a failing lender to make even riskier loans to avoid higher dividend payments.

The report concludes with an examination of the SBLF's implementation by the Department of the Treasury and a discussion of bills introduced during recent Congresses to amend the SBLF. For example, during the 112th Congress, S. 681, the Greater Accountability in the Lending Fund Act of 2011, would have, among other provisions, limited the program's authority to 15 years from enactment and prohibited TARP recipients from participating in the program. H.R. 2807, the Small Business Leg-Up Act of 2011, would have transferred any unobligated and repaid funds from the SBLF when its investment authority expired on September 27, 2011, to the Community Development Financial Institutions Fund "to continue the program of making capital investments in eligible community development financial institutions in order to increase the availability of credit for small businesses."[8] H.R. 3147, the Small Business Lending Extension Act, would have, among other provisions, extended the Department of the Treasury's investment authority from one year following the date of enactment to two years. During the 113th Congress, H.R. 2474, the Community Lending and Small Business Jobs Act of 2013, would have transferred any unobligated and repaid funds from the SBLF to the Community Development Financial Institutions Fund.

TWO INDICATORS OF THE SUPPLY AND DEMAND FOR SMALL BUSINESS LOANS

Federal Reserve Board: Survey of Senior Loan Officers

Each quarter, the Federal Reserve Board surveys senior loan officers concerning their bank's lending practices. The survey includes questions

---

[8] H.R. 2807, the Small Business Leg-Up Act of 2011.

about both the supply and demand for small business loans. For example, the survey includes a question concerning their bank's credit standards for small business loans: "Over the past three months, how have your bank's credit standards for approving applications for C&I [commercial and industrial] loans or credit lines— other than those to be used to finance mergers and acquisitions—for small firms (defined as having annual sales of less than $50 million) changed?" The senior loan officers are asked to indicate if their bank's credit standards have "Tightened considerably," "Tightened somewhat," "Remained basically unchanged," "Eased somewhat," or "Eased considerably." Subtracting the percentage of respondents reporting "Eased somewhat" and "Eased considerably" from the percentage of respondents reporting "Tightened considerably" and "Tightened somewhat" provides an indication of the market's supply of small business loans.

As shown in Figure 1, senior loan officers reported that they generally tightened small business loan credit standards from 2007 through late 2009. Since 2009, small business credit markets have generally improved, with some tightening in 2016.

The survey also includes a question concerning the demand for small business loans: "Apart from normal seasonal variation, how has demand for C&I loans changed over the past three months for small firms (annual sales of less than $50 million)?" Senior loan officers are asked to indicate if demand was "Substantially stronger," "Moderately stronger," "About the same," "Moderately weaker," or "Substantially weaker." Subtracting the percentage of respondents reporting "Moderately weaker" and "Substantially weaker" from the percentage of respondents reporting "Substantially stronger" and "Moderately stronger" provides an indication of the market's demand for small business loans.

As shown in Figure 1, senior loan officers reported that the demand for small business loans declined somewhat in 2007 and 2008, and declined significantly in 2009. Demand then leveled off (at a relatively reduced level) during 2010, increased somewhat during the first half of 2011, declined during the latter half of 2011, generally increased from 2012 through 2015, and has varied somewhat, increasing in some quarters and declining in others, since then.[9]

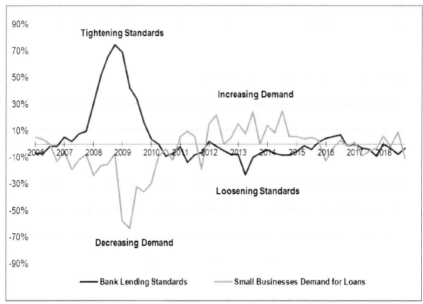

Source: Federal Reserve Board, "Senior Loan Officer Opinion Survey on Bank Lending Practices," at http://www.federalreserve.gov/boarddocs/SnLoanSurvey/; and Brian Headd, "Forum Seeks Solutions To Thaw Frozen Small Business Credit," *The Small Business Advocate*, vol. 28, no. 10 (December 2009), p. 3, at https://www.sba.gov/sites/default/files/advocacy/The%20Small%20Business%20Advocate%20-%20December%202009.pdf.

Figure 1. Small Business Lending Environment, 2006-2018; (senior loan officers' survey responses).

Federal Deposit Insurance Corporation: Outstanding Loan Balance

The Federal Deposit Insurance Corporation (FDIC) has maintained comparable small business lending data for the second quarter (June 30) of

---

[9] Federal Reserve Board, "Senior Loan Officer Opinion Survey on Bank Lending Practices," at http://www.federalreserve.gov/boarddocs/SnLoanSurvey/.

each year since 2002. Figure 2 shows the amount of outstanding small business loans (defined by the FDIC as commercial and industrial loans of $1 million or less) for nonagricultural purposes as of June 30 of each year from 2006 to 2018. As shown in Figure 2, the amount of outstanding small business loans for nonagricultural purposes increased at a relatively steady pace from June 30, 2006, to June 30, 2008, declined over the next several years, and has increased each year since June 30, 2013.

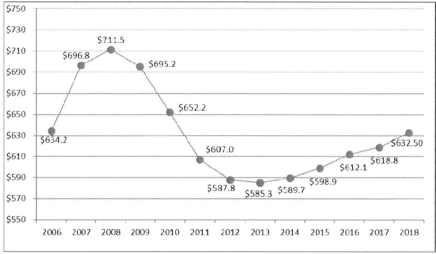

Source: Federal Deposit Insurance Corporation, "Statistics on Depository Institutions," at https://www5.fdic.gov/sdi/main.asp?formname=standard.
Notes: Data as of June 30 each year.

Figure 2. Outstanding Small Business Loans, Non-Agricultural Purposes, 2006-2018; (billions of dollars).

Although changes in small business outstanding debt are not necessarily a result of changes in the supply of small business loans, many, including the SBA, view a decline in small business outstanding debt as a signal that small businesses might be experiencing difficulty accessing sufficient capital to enable them to lead job growth.

Factors that May Have Contributed to the Decline in the Supply of Small Business Loans in 2007-2010

According to an SBA-sponsored study of small business lending, several factors contributed to the decline in small business lending from 2007 to 2010.[10] The report's authors noted that the 30% decline in home prices from their peak in 2006 to 2010 diminished the value of collateral for many small business borrowers, some of whom had relied on home equity loans to finance their small businesses during the real estate boom. The authors concluded that the absence of this additional source of collateral may have contributed to a decline in lending to small businesses.[11] They also argued that many small businesses found it increasingly difficult to renew existing lines of credit as lenders became more cautious as a result of slow economic growth and an increasing risk of loan defaults, especially among small business start-ups, which are generally considered among the most risky investments.[12] The authors argued that

- in this newly regulated market, smaller lenders are likely to be less profitable because they have fewer sales of products and services to spread out over the higher auditing and FDIC costs. Hence, they have less money to lend to small businesses and others; and
- the relative difficulty in assessing creditworthiness due to the lack of information about potential financial performance is very high in small business lending, especially in financial markets driven by factor—rather than relationship— lending. Therefore, one would

---

[10] George W. Haynes and Victoria Williams, *Lending by Depository Lenders to Small Businesses, 2003 to 2010*, SBA, Office of Advocacy, March 2011, at https://www.sba.gov/sites/default/files/rs380tot.pdf.

[11] Ibid., p. 25.

[12] Ibid., p. 26. One possible contributing factor for at least some lenders becoming more cautious is that in recent years many lenders experienced an increase in nonperforming loans and a depletion of their loan loss reserves, limiting the funds available for lending to small businesses.

expect the small business loan market to recover more slowly than other financial markets.[13]

The authors also noted that FDIC data indicated that small business lending had not only declined in absolute terms (the total amount of dollars borrowed and the total number of small business loans issued), but in relative terms as well (the market share of business loans):

> Over the eight years from 2003 through 2010, small business loans as a share of total business loans declined by more than 12 percentage points, from 81.7% in 2003 to 68.9% in 2010. Perhaps of most concern is the further decline in the ratios of small business loans to total assets and small business loans to total business loans. Small business loans constituted about 16.8% of total assets in 2005, but only 15.3% in 2010; hence, small business lending is becoming less significant for these lenders. Small business lending is also losing market share in the business loan market. In the eight-year period from 2003 to 2010, small business loans as a share of total business loans declined more than 10 percentage points from 81.7% in 2003 to 68.9% in 2010.[14]

Factors that May Have Contributed to the Decline in the Demand for Small Business Loans in 2007-2010

According to the previously mentioned SBA-sponsored study of small business lending, the demand for small business loans fell during the recession primarily because many small businesses experienced a decline in sales and many small business owners had a heightened level of uncertainty concerning future sales. The study's authors argued that given small business owners' lack of confidence in the demand for their goods and services, many small business owners decided to save capital instead

---

[13] Ibid., p. 26.
[14] Ibid., p. 25.

of hiring additional employees and borrowing capital to invest in business expansions and inventory.[15]

The responses of small business owners to a monthly survey by the National Federation of Independent Business Research Foundation (NFIB) concerning small business owners' views of the economy support the argument that declining sales contributed to the reduced demand for small business loans. From 2008 through 2011, small business owners responding to the NFIB surveys identified poor sales as their number-one problem. Prior to 2008, taxes had been reported as their number-one problem in nearly every survey since the monthly surveys began in 1986.[16]

Also, employment data suggest that small businesses were particularly hard hit by the recession. As mentioned previously, small businesses accounted for almost 60% of the net job losses during the December 2007-June 2009 recession.[17]

According to testimony by the Secretary of the Treasury before the House Small Business Committee on June 22, 2011, small businesses were especially hard hit by the recession because

> [s]mall businesses are concentrated in sectors that were especially hard hit by the recession and the bursting of the housing bubble: construction and real estate. More than one-third of all construction workers are employed by firms with less than 20 workers, and an additional third are employed by businesses with fewer than 100 employees. Just over half of those employed in the real estate, rental, and leasing sectors work for businesses with less than 100 workers on their

---

[15] Ibid.
[16] William C. Dunkelberg and Holly Wade, *Small Business Economic Trends* (Washington, DC: NFIB Research Foundation, September 2011), p. 18, at http://www.nfib.com/Portals/0/PDF/sbet/sbet201109.pdf; and William J. Dennis Jr., *Small Business Credit in a Deep Recession* (Washington, DC: NFIB Research Foundation, June 2008), p. 1, at https://www.nfib.com/Portals/0/PDF/AllUsers/research/studies/Small-Business-Credit-In-a-Deep-Recession-February-2010-NFIB.pdf.
[17] SBA, "The Small Business Economy, 2010: A Report to the President," pp. 2, 5, 21, 22, at https://www.sba.gov/ sites/default/files/sb_econ2010.pdf; and SBA, *Fiscal Year 2010 Congressional Budget Justification*, p. 1, at https://www.sba.gov/sites/default/files/aboutsbaarticle/Congressional_Budget_Justification_2010.pdf.

payrolls. More broadly, the rate of job losses was almost twice as high in small businesses as it was in larger firms during the depths of the crisis.[18]

The Congressional Response to the Decline in the Supply and Demand for Small Business Loans

During the 111th Congress, legislation designed to increase both the supply and demand for small business loans was adopted. For example, Congress provided more than $1.1 billion to temporarily subsidize fees for the SBA's 7(a) and 504/Certified Development Company (504/CDC) loan guaranty programs and to increase the 7(a) program's maximum loan guaranty percentage from 85% on loans of $150,000 or less and 75% on loans exceeding $150,000 to 90% for all regular 7(a) loans (funding was exhausted on January 3, 2011).[19] The fee subsidies were designed to increase the demand for small business loans by reducing the cost of

---

[18] U.S. Congress, House Committee on Small Business, *The State of Small Business Access to Capital and Credit: The View from Secretary Geithner*, 112th Cong., 1st sess., June 22, 2011, p. 1.

[19] P.L. 111-5, the American Recovery and Reinvestment Act of 2009, provided the SBA $375 million to subsidize fees for the SBA's 7(a) and 504/CDC loan guaranty programs and to increase the 7(a) program's maximum loan guaranty percentage from up to 85% of loans of $150,000 or less and up to 75% of loans exceeding $150,000 to 90% for all regular 7(a) loans through September 30, 2010, or when appropriated funding for the subsidies and loan modification was exhausted. P.L. 111-118, the Department of Defense Appropriations Act, 2010, provided the SBA $125 million to continue the fee subsides and 90% maximum loan guaranty percentage through February 28, 2010. P.L. 111-144, the Temporary Extension Act of 2010, provided the SBA $60 million to continue the fee subsides and 90% maximum loan guaranty percentage through March 28, 2010. P.L. 111-150, an act to extend the Small Business Loan Guarantee Program, and for other purposes, provided the SBA authority to reprogram $40 million in previously appropriated funds to continue the fee subsides and 90% maximum loan guaranty percentage through April 30, 2010. P.L. 111-157, the Continuing Extension Act of 2010, provided the SBA $80 million to continue the SBA's fee subsides and 90% maximum loan guaranty percentage through May 31, 2010. P.L. 111-240, the Small Business Jobs Act of 2010, provided $505 million (plus an additional $5 million for administrative expenses) to continue the SBA's fee subsides and 90% maximum loan guaranty percentage from the act's date of enactment (September 27, 2010) through December 31, 2010. P.L. 111-322, the Continuing Appropriations and Surface Transportation Extensions Act, 2011, authorizes the SBA to use funds provided under the Small Business Jobs Act of 2010 to continue the SBA's fee subsides and 90% maximum loan guaranty percentage through March 4, 2011, or until available funding is exhausted—which occurred on January 3, 2011.

borrowing. The 90% loan guarantee was designed to increase the supply of small business loans by reducing the risk of lending.

Congress also provided the SBA additional resources to expand its lending to small businesses. For example, ARRA included a $255 million temporary, two-year small business stabilization program to guarantee loans of $35,000 or less to small businesses for qualified debt consolidation, later named the America's Recovery Capital (ARC) Loan program (the program ceased issuing new loan guarantees on September 30, 2010); an additional $15 million for the SBA's surety bond program and a temporary increase in that program's maximum bond amount from $2 million to $5 million and up to $10 million under certain conditions (the higher maximum bond amounts ended on September 30, 2010); an additional $6 million for the SBA's Microloan program's lending program and an additional $24 million for the Microloan program's technical assistance program; and increased the funds (*leverage*) available to SBA-licensed Small Business Investment Companies (SBICs) to no more than 300% of the company's private capital or $150 million, whichever is less.[20]

Several other programs were also enacted during the 111th Congress to increase the supply of small business loans. For example, ARRA authorized the SBA to establish a temporary secondary market guarantee authority to provide a federal guarantee for pools of first lien 504/CDC program loans that are to be sold to third-party investors. ARRA also authorized the SBA to make below-market interest rate direct loans to SBA-designated "Systemically Important Secondary Market (SISM) Broker-Dealers" that would use the loan funds to purchase SBA-guaranteed loans from commercial lenders, assemble them into pools, and sell them to investors in the secondary loan market.[21]

P.L. 111-240 extended the SBA's secondary market guarantee authority from two years after the date of ARRA's enactment to two years after the date of the program's first sale of a pool of first lien position 504/CDC loans to a third-party investor (which took place on September

---

[20] P.L. 111-5, the American Recovery and Reinvestment Act of 2009, §505, Increasing Small Business Investment.
[21] Ibid.

24, 2010).[22] The act also increased the loan guarantee limits for the SBA's 7(a) program from $2 million to $5 million, and for the 504/CDC program from $1.5 million to $5 million for "regular" borrowers, from $2 million to $5 million if the loan proceeds are directed toward one or more specified public policy goals, and from $4 million to $5.5 million for manufacturers. It also increased the SBA's Microloan program's loan limit for borrowers from $35,000 to $50,000 and for microlender intermediaries after their first year in the program from $3.5 million to $5 million.[23] In addition, it temporarily increased for one year (through September 26, 2011) the SBA 7(a) Express Program's loan limit from $350,000 to $1 million. The act also authorized the Secretary of the Treasury to establish the $30 billion SBLF and a $1.5 billion State Small Business Credit Initiative to provide funding to participating states with small business capital access programs.

THE SBLF

The SBLF was designed "to address the ongoing effects of the financial crisis on small businesses by providing temporary authority to the Secretary of the Treasury to make capital investments in eligible institutions in order to increase the availability of credit for small businesses."[24] The SBLF's legislative history, including differences in the

---

[22] SBA, Office of Congressional and Legislative Affairs, "Correspondence with the author," January 4, 2010.

[23] The act also temporarily allowed the SBA to waive, in whole or in part, for successive fiscal years, the nonfederal share requirement for loans to the Microloan program's intermediaries and for grants made to Microloan intermediaries for small business marketing, management, and technical assistance under specified circumstances (e.g., the economic conditions affecting the intermediary). See P.L. 111-240, the Small Business Jobs Act of 2010, §1401. Matching Requirements under Small Business Programs.

[24] P.L. 111-240, the Small Business Jobs Act of 2010, §4101, Purpose. In 2011, there were 7,513 FDIC-insured lending institutions in the United States. Of that number, 6,846 lending institutions had assets amounting to less than $1 billion (totaling $1.42 trillion), 561 lending institutions had assets of $1 billion to $10 billion (totaling $1.43 trillion), and 106 lending institutions had assets greater than $10 billion (totaling $10.76 trillion). See FDIC, "Quarterly Banking Profile: Second Quarter 2011," at http://www2.fdic.gov/qbp/2011jun/qbp.pdf.

House- and Senate-passed versions of the program, appears in the Appendix.

P.L. 111-240 authorized the Secretary of the Treasury to make up to $30 billion in capital investments in eligible institutions with total assets equal to or less than $1 billion or $10 billion (as of the end of the fourth quarter of calendar year 2009).[25] The authority to make capital investments in eligible institutions was limited to one year after enactment.

Eligible financial institutions with total assets equal to or less than $1 billion as of the end of the fourth quarter of calendar year 2009 could apply to receive a capital investment from the SBLF in an amount not exceeding 5% of risk-weighted assets, as reported in the FDIC call report immediately preceding the date of application. During the fourth quarter of 2009, 7,340 FDIC-insured lending institutions reported having assets amounting to less than $1 billion.[26]

Eligible financial institutions with total assets of $10 billion or less as of the end of the fourth quarter of calendar year 2009 could apply to receive a capital investment from the fund in an amount not exceeding 3% of risk-weighted assets, as reported in the FDIC call report immediately preceding the date of application. During the fourth quarter of 2009, 565 FDIC-insured lending institutions reported having assets of $1 billion to $10 billion.[27]

Risk-weighted assets are assets such as cash, loans, investments, and other financial institution assets that have different risks associated with them. FDIC regulations (12 C.F.R. §567.6) establish that cash and government bonds have a 0% risk-weighting; residential mortgage loans

---

[25] Eligible institutions may be insured depository institutions that are not controlled by a bank holding company or a savings and loan holding company that is also an eligible institution and is not directly or indirectly controlled by any company or other entity that has total consolidated assets of more than $10 billion, bank holding companies, savings and loan holding companies, and community development financial institution loan funds, all with total assets of $10 billion or less (as of the end of 2009).

[26] FDIC, "Quarterly Banking Profile: Fourth Quarter 2009," at http://www2.fdic.gov/qbp/2009dec/qbp.pdf.

[27] Ibid. In the fourth quarter of 2009, 107 FDIC-insured lending institutions had assets greater than $10 billion.

have a 50% risk-weighting; and other types of assets (such as small business loans) have a higher risk-weighting.[28]

Lending institutions on the FDIC problem bank list or institutions that have been removed from the FDIC problem bank list for less than 90 days are ineligible to participate in the program. A lending institution can refinance securities issued through the Treasury Capital Purchase Program (CPP) and the Community Development Capital Incentive (CDCI) program under TARP, but only if that institution had not missed more than one dividend payment due under those programs.

Dividend Rates

Participating banks (C corporations and savings associations) are charged a dividend rate of no more than 5% per annum initially, with reduced rates available if the bank increases its small business lending by specified amounts.[29] For example, during any calendar quarter in the initial two years of the capital investments under the program, the bank's dividend rate is lowered if it increases its small business lending, as reported in its FDIC call reports, compared with the average small business lending it made in the four previous quarters immediately preceding the law's enactment, minus some allowable adjustments.[30]

---

[28] For further analysis of risk-weighted assets, see CRS Report R44918, *Who Regulates Whom? An Overview of the U.S. Financial Regulatory Framework*, by Marc Labonte.

[29] "On the Investment Date, and at the beginning of each of the next ten calendar quarters thereafter, the amount of Qualified Small Business Lending reported by the Issuer in the most recent Supplemental Report will be compared to the Baseline amount of Qualified Small Business Lending. The dividend rate will be adjusted to reflect the amount of an Issuer's change in Qualified Small Business Lending from the Baseline." See U.S. Department of the Treasury, "Small Business Lending Fund: Senior Preferred Stock," p. 4, at http://www.treasury.gov/resource-center/sbprograms/Documents/SBLF%20Refinancing%20Term%20Sheet.pdf.

[30] The FDIC defines a small business loan as a loan of $1 million or less. P.L. 111-240 specified that small business lending included commercial and industrial loans, owner-occupied nonfarm, nonresidential real estate loans, loans to finance agricultural production and other loans to farmers, and loans secured by farmland. Loans that have an original amount greater than $10 million, or that go to a business with more than $50 million in revenues, are not allowed.

Table 1 shows the dividend rates associated with small business lending increases by C corporation banks and savings associations.

Table 1. SBLF Lending Increases and Dividend Rates for C Corporation Banks and Savings Associations

Small Business Lending Increase	Dividend Rate Following Investment Date		
	1st 9 Quarters	Quarter 10 to Year 4.5	After Year 4.5 (following Q1 of 2016)
10% or greater	1%	1%	9%
At least 7.5% but less than 10%	2%	2%	9%
At least 5% but less than 7.5%	3%	3%	9%
At least 2.5% but less than 5%	4%	4%	9%
Less than 2.5%	5%	5%	9%
No increase	5%	7%	9%

Source: P.L. 111-240, the Small Business Jobs Act of 2010, Section 4103. Small Business Lending Fund; and U.S. Department of the Treasury, "Small Business Lending Fund: Getting Started Guide for Community Banks," p. 1, at http://www.treasury.gov/resource-center/sb-programs/Documents/SBLF%20Getting%20Started%20Guide.pdf.

Table 2 shows the dividend rates associated with small business lending increases by participating S corporation banks and mutual lending institutions. These rates are slightly higher than those for C corporation banks and savings associations "to reflect after-tax effective rates equivalent to the dividend rate paid by other classes of institutions participating in the Fund through the issuance of preferred stock."[31] As will be discussed later, an S corporation does not pay federal taxes at the corporate level. Any business income or loss is "passed through" to shareholders who report it on their personal income tax returns.

Community Development Financial Institutions (CFDIs) are provided funding for an initial eight years with an automatic rollover for two additional years at the issuer's option. On the 10th anniversary of the investment date the issuer repays the principal amount, together with all accrued and unpaid interest. Additionally, the dividend rate is 2% per

---

[31] U.S. Department of the Treasury, "Overview for Subchapter S Corporations and Mutual Institutions," at http://www.treasury.gov/resource-center/sb-programs/Pages/Overview-for-S-Corporation-Banks-and-MutualInstitutions.aspx.

annum for the first eight years from the investment date (payable quarterly in arrears on January 1, April 1, July 1, and October 1 of each year) and 9% thereafter.[32]

Table 2. SBLF Lending Increases and Dividend Rates for S Corporation Banks and Mutual Lending Institutions

	Dividend Rate Following Investment Date		
Small Business Lending Increase	1st 9 Quarters	Quarter 10 to Year 4.5	After Year 4.5 (following Q1 of 2016)
10% or greater	1.5%	1.5%	13.8%
At least 7.5% but less than 10%	3.1%	3.1%	13.8%
At least 5% but less than 7.5%	4.6%	4.6%	13.8%
At least 2.5% but less than 5%	6.2%	6.2%	13.8%
Less than 2.5%	7.7%	7.7%	13.8%
No increase	7.7%	10.8%	13.8%

Source: P.L. 111-240, the Small Business Jobs Act of 2010, Section 4103. Small Business Lending Fund; U.S. Treasury, "Small Business Lending Fund: Subchapter S Corporation Senior Securities," p. 4, at http://www.treasury.gov/resource-center/sb-programs/Documents/SBLF_S_Corporation_Term_Sheet_05-02- 11.pdf; and U.S. Treasury, "Small Business Lending Fund: Mutual Institutions Senior Securities," p. 4, http://www.treasury.gov/resource-center/sb-programs/Documents/SBLF%20Mutual%20Institutions%20Term%20Sheet.pdf.

Lending Plan Requirement

SBLF applicants are required to submit a small business lending plan to the appropriate federal banking agency and, for applicants that are state-chartered banks, to the appropriate state banking regulator. The plan must describe how the applicant's business strategy and operating goals will allow it to address the needs of small businesses in the areas it serves, as well as a plan to provide linguistically and culturally appropriate outreach, where appropriate. The plan is treated as confidential supervisory information. The Secretary of the Treasury is required to consult with the

---

[32] U.S. Department of the Treasury, "Small Business Lending Fund: Community Development Financial Institution Loan Funds Equity Equivalent Capital," p. 3, at http://www.treasury.gov/resource-center/sb-programs/Documents/SBLF-CDLF%20Term%20Sheet.pdf.

appropriate federal banking agency or, in the case of an eligible institution that is a nondepository community development financial institution, the Community Development Financial Institution Fund, before determining if the eligible institution may participate in the program.[33]

The act directed that all funds received by the Secretary of the Treasury in connection with purchases made by the SBLF, "including interest payments, dividend payments, and proceeds from the sale of any financial instrument, shall be paid into the general fund of the Treasury for reduction of the public debt."[34]

ARGUMENTS FOR AND AGAINST THE SBLF

The SBLF's advocates argued that it would create jobs by encouraging lenders, especially those experiencing liquidity problems (access to cash and easily tradable assets),[35] to increase their lending to small businesses. For example, the House report accompanying H.R. 5297, the Small Business Lending Fund Act of 2010, argued that the SBLF was needed to enhance small business's access to capital, which, in turn, was necessary to enable those businesses to create jobs and assist in the economic recovery:

---

[33] If the appropriate banking agency would not otherwise recommend that the eligible institution receive the capital investment, the Secretary of the Treasury was authorized, in consultation with the appropriate banking agency, to consider allowing the eligible institution to participate in the program if the eligible institution provided matching capital from private, nongovernmental sources that is equal to or greater than 100% of the SBLF investment and if that matching capital is subordinate to the capital investment from the SBLF.

[34] P.L. 111-240, the Small Business Jobs Act of 2010, §4103. Small Business Lending Fund. Using a cost-based estimate, the Congressional Budget Office (CBO) estimated that the SBLF would result in net outlays of $3.3 billion over 2010-2015 and would reduce outlays by $1.1 billion over the 2010-2020 period. Using an alternative fair-value estimate, CBO estimated that the SBLF would result in net outlays of $6.2 billion over the 2010-2020 time period. See CBO, "Cost Estimate: H.R. 5297, Small Business Lending Fund Act of 2010," June 28, 2010, pp. 3, 4, at https://www.cbo.gov/sites/default/files/111th-congress-2009-2010/costestimate/hr5297housepassed0.pdf.

[35] For further information and analysis concerning lender liquidity issues, see CRS Report R43413, *Costs of Government Interventions in Response to the Financial Crisis: A Retrospective*, by Baird Webel and Marc Labonte.

There has been a dramatic decrease in the amount of bank lending in the past several quarters. On May 20, 2010, the Federal Deposit Insurance Corporation (FDIC) released its Quarterly Banking Profile for the first quarter of 2010. The report shows that commercial and industrial loans declined for the seventh straight quarter, down more than 17% from the year before.

Many companies, particularly small businesses, claim that it is becoming harder to get new loans to keep their business operating and that banks are tightening requirements or cutting off existing lines of credit even when the businesses are up to date on their loan repayments. Treasury Secretary Timothy F. Geithner recently acknowledged the problem encountered by some banks, both healthy and troubled, which have been told to maintain capital levels in excess of those required to be considered well capitalized.

Some banks say they have little choice but to scale back lending, even to creditworthy borrowers, and the most recent Federal Reserve data shows banks are continuing to tighten lending terms for small businesses.[36]

A dissenting view, endorsed by the House Committee on Financial Services' minority members, was included in the report. This view argued that the SBLF does not properly deal with the lack of financing for small businesses:

> Instead of addressing the problem by stimulating demand for credit by small businesses, H.R. 5297 injects capital into banks with no guarantees that they will actually lend. The bill allows a qualifying bank to obtain a capital infusion from the government without even requiring the bank to make a loan for two years. In fact, if a bank reduces or fails to increase lending to small business during those first two years, it would not face any penalty. It defies logic that the Majority would support a bill to increase lending that does not actually require increased lending. A more effective response to the challenges facing America's small businesses was offered by Representatives Biggert, Paulsen, Castle,

---

[36] H.Rept. 111-499, To Create the Small Business Lending Fund Program to Direct the Secretary of the Treasury to Make Capital Investments in Eligible Institutions in order to Increase the Availability of Credit for Small Businesses, and for other purposes, p. 16.

Gerlach, and King, whose amendment would have extended a series of small business tax credits before implementing the Small Business Lending Fund.[37]

Advocates also argued that even if the SBLF were authorized "the program probably would not be fully operational for months; banks could shun the program for fear of being stigmatized by its association with TARP; and many banks would avoid taking on new liabilities when their existing assets are troubled."[38] They contended that the bill did not provide sufficient oversight for effectively monitoring the program because the Inspector General of the Department of the Treasury, who was given that oversight responsibility under the bill, "might not be able to direct sufficient attention to this task given its other responsibilities."[39] They argued that the Special Inspector General of TARP would be in a better position to provide effective oversight of the program.[40]

These, and other, arguments were presented during House floor debate on the bill. For example, Representative Melissa Bean advocated the bill's passage, arguing that the SBLF

> builds on the effective financial stabilization measures Congress has previously taken by establishing a new $30 billion small business loan fund to provide additional capital to community banks that increase lending to small businesses. This $30 billion investment on which the government will be collecting dividends and earning a profit per the CBO [Congressional Budget Office] estimates can be leveraged by banks into over $300 billion in new small business loans. This is an important investment by the Federal Government in our small business that brings tremendous returns.
>
> The terms of the capital provided to banks are performance based; the more a bank increases its small business lending, the lower the dividend rate is for the SBLF capital. If a bank decreases its small business lending, it will be penalized with higher dividend rates.

---

[37] Ibid., p. 37.
[38] Ibid., pp. 37, 38.
[39] Ibid., p. 38.
[40] Ibid.

This legislation includes strong safeguards to ensure that banks adequately utilize available funds to increase lending to small businesses, not for other lending or to improve their balance sheet. There will be oversight consistently throughout the program, plus it requires that the capital be invested only in strong financial institutions at little risk of default and the best positioned to increase small business lending.

It's important for Americans to understand that although this fund has a maximum value of $30 billion, it is estimated to make a profit for taxpayers in the long run. And the money will ultimately go not to banks, but to the small businesses and their communities that they lend to. As our financial system stabilizes and our community banks recapitalize, these funds will be repaid to Treasury with full repayment required over the next 10 years.[41]

Representative Nydia Velázquez, then-chair of the House Committee on Small Business, added that the legislation had sufficient safeguards in place to ensure that the funds were targeted at small businesses:

First, banks must apply to the Treasury to receive funds, with a detailed plan on how to increase small business lending at their institution. This language was included at my insistence that we need to make sure that small businesses will get the benefit of this legislation.

Second, this capital, repayment of the government loans will be at a dividend rate starting at 5% per year. This rate will be lowered by 1% for every 2.5% increase in small business lending over 2009 levels. It can go as low as a total dividend rate of just 1% if the bank increases its business lending by 10% or more, incentivizing banks to do the right thing. To ensure that banks actually use the funding they receive, the rate will increase—and there are penalties—to 7% if the bank fails to increase its small business lending at their institution within 2 years. To ensure that all federal funds are paid back within 5 years, the dividend rate will

---

[41] Representative Melissa Bean, "Consideration of the Small Business Jobs and Credit Act of 2010," House debate, *Congressional Record*, daily edition, vol. 156, no. 90 (June 16, 2010), p. H4514.

increase to 9% for all banks, irrespective of their small business lending, after 4 1/2 years.[42]

Representative Velázquez added "let me just make it clear ... CBO estimates that [the SBLF] will save taxpayers $1 billion over 10 years, as banks are expected to pay back this loan over 10 years, with interest."[43]

Representative Randy Neugebauer opposed the bill's adoption, arguing that

> the majority is repeating the same failed initiatives that have helped our national debt grow to $13 trillion in the past 2 years. This bill follows the model of the TARP program, minus [TARP's] stronger oversight, and it puts another $30 billion into banks in the hopes that lending to small businesses will increase. In the words of Neil Barofsky, the Special Inspector General who oversees the TARP, "In terms of its basic design," he says, "its participants, its application process, from an oversight perspective, the Small Business Lending Fund would essentially be an extension of the TARP's Capital Purchase Program." From the Congressional Oversight Panel for TARP, chaired by Elizabeth Warren, she says, "The SBLF's prospects are far from certain. The SBLF also raises questions about whether, in light of the Capital Purchase Program's poor performance in improving credit access, any capital infusion program can successfully jump-start small business lending."
>
> This bill allows for another $33 billion in spending that will be added to the government's credit card. The CBO tells us that the bank lending portion will ultimately cost taxpayers $3.4 billion when market risk is taken into account.[44]

The House passed H.R. 5297 by a vote of 241-182, on June 17, 2010.

---

[42] Representative Nydia Velázquez, "Consideration of the Small Business Jobs and Credit Act of 2010," House debate, *Congressional Record*, daily edition, vol. 156, no. 90 (June 16, 2010), p. H4518.

[43] Ibid.

[44] Representative Randy Neugebauer, "Consideration of the Small Business Jobs and Credit Act of 2010," House debate, *Congressional Record*, daily edition, vol. 156, no. 90 (June 16, 2010), p. H4515.

The arguments presented during House floor debate on H.R. 5297 were also presented during Senate consideration of the bill. Advocates argued that the SBLF would encourage higher levels of small business lending and jobs. For example, Senator Mary Landrieu argued on July 21, 2010, that the SBLF should be adopted because it "is not a government program for banks. It is a public-private partnership lending strategy for small business."[45] She added that as chair of the Senate Committee on Small Business and Entrepreneurship, she talked with her colleagues, including the SBLF's opponents, and revised the program to address their concerns. She also argued that the SBLF has

> hundreds of endorsements from independent banks, the community banks and almost every small business association in America ... makes $1 billion [according to the CBO score] ... is not direct lending from the federal government. It is not creating a new bureaucracy
> ... [It is] voluntary ... there are no onerous restrictions.... The small business gets the loans. We create jobs. People are employed. The recession starts ending.... It has nothing to do with TARP money. It is not a TARP program. It is not a bank program. It doesn't have anything to do with banks except that we are working in partnership with banks to lend money to small businesses which are desperate for money.[46]

Opponents argued that the SBLF could lose money, lacked sufficient oversight provisions, did not require lenders to increase their lending to small businesses, could serve as a vehicle for TARP recipients to effectively refinance their TARP loans on more favorable terms with little or no resulting benefit for small businesses, and could encourage a failing lender to make even riskier loans to avoid higher dividend payments. In addition, there were disagreements over the number of amendments that could be offered by the minority, which led several Senators to oppose further consideration of the bill until that issue was resolved to their satisfaction. For example, on July 22, 2010, Senator Olympia Snowe

---

[45] Senator Mary Landrieu, "Small Business Lending," remarks in the Senate, *Congressional Record*, daily edition, vol. 156, no. 108 (July 21, 2010), p. S6070.
[46] Ibid., p. S6071.

argued that although "under a cash-based estimate, CBO listed the official score for the lending fund as raising $1.1 billion over 10 years," SBLF proponents "fail to mention" that when CBO scored the SBLF using an alternative methodology that adjusts for market risk, it estimated that the SBLF could cost $6.2 billion.[47] Senator Snowe also argued that the bipartisan Congressional Oversight Panel for TARP stated in its May 2010 oversight report that the proposed SBLF "substantially resembles" the TARP and "is a bank-focused capital infusion program that is being contemplated despite little, if any, evidence that such programs increase lending."[48] Senator Snowe noted that she regretted "that we are in a position where we have not been able to reach agreement allowing the minority to offer amendments, which is confounding and perplexing as well as disappointing."[49] Senator Snowe later added that the SBLF's incentives to encourage lending to small businesses also "could encourage unnecessarily risky behavior by banks ... to avoid paying higher interest rates."[50]

Opponents also questioned the SBLF's use of quarterly call report data as submitted by lenders to their appropriate banking regulator to determine what counts as a small business loan.[51] Call report data denotes loans of $1 million or less as small business loans, regardless of the size of the business receiving the loan. As a result, the SBLF's opponents argued that "the data used to measure small business lending in the SBLF covers an entirely different set of small businesses than those that fall within the definition set out in the Small Business Act or used by the SBA."[52]

---

[47] Senator Olympia Snowe, "Small Business Lending," remarks in the Senate, *Congressional Record*, daily edition, vol. 156, no. 108 (July 22, 2010), p. S6158.
[48] Ibid.
[49] Ibid., p. S6156.
[50] Senator Olympia Snowe, "Small Business Lending Fund Act of 2010," remarks in the Senate, *Congressional Record*, daily edition, vol. 156, no. 125 (September 16, 2010), p. S7157.
[51] The act specified that the SBLF could not be used to provide loans greater than $10 million or that go to a business with more than $50 million in revenues. See P.L. 111-240, the Small Business Jobs Act of 2010, §4102. Definitions.
[52] Representative Sam Graves, "Full Committee Hearing, The State of Small Business Access to Credit and Capital: The View from Secretary Geithner," Letter to Members of the House Small Business Committee, Washington, DC, June 20, 2011, p. 19, at http://smbiz.house.gov/UploadedFiles/6-22_Memo.pdf.

The Senate's version of H.R. 5297 was agreed to on September 16, 2010, by a vote of 68-38.[53] The House agreed to the Senate-passed version of H.R. 5297 on September 23, 2010, by a vote of 237-187, and the bill, retitled the Small Business Jobs Act of 2010, was signed into law by President Obama on September 27, 2010.

THE SBLF'S IMPLEMENTATION

On February 14, 2011, the Obama Administration issued its budget recommendation for FY2012. The budget anticipated that the SBLF would provide $17.399 billion in financings, well below its authorized amount of $30 billion.[54] This was the first indication that the SBLF's implementation may not proceed as expected.[55] The second indication that the program's implementation may not proceed as expected was an unanticipated delay in the writing of the program's regulations.

Treasury's Rollout of the Program

The U.S. Treasury was criticized by some for not implementing the program quickly enough.[56] The first financing took place on June 21, 2011,

---

[53] Senator Kay Hagen, "Motion to Invoke Cloture on H.R. 5297, the Small Business Lending Fund Act of 2010," Rollcall Vote No. 236 Leg., *Congressional Record*, daily edition, vol. 156, part 125 (September 16, 2010), p. S7158; and Senator Al Franken, "Small Business Lending Fund Act of 2010," Rollcall Vote No. 237 Leg., *Congressional Record*, daily edition, vol. 156, part 125 (September 16, 2010), p. S7158.

[54] U.S. Office of Management and Budget, *Budget of the United States Government, Fiscal Year 2012, Appendix: Department of the Treasury*, p. 989, at https://www.gpo.gov/fdsys/pkg/BUDGET-2012-APP/pdf/BUDGET-2012- APP.pdf.

[55] The Department of the Treasury based its forecast on an "analysis of demand for the program." See U.S. Department of the Treasury, "FY2012 Congressional Justification, Small Business Lending Fund," p. 7, at http://www.treasury.gov/ about/budget-performance/Documents/CJ_FY2012_SBLF_508.pdf.

[56] Representative Sam Graves, "Graves Questions Treasury Secretary Timothy Geithner on Access to Capital for Small Businesses," press release, June 22, 2011, at http://www.smallbusiness.house.gov/News/DocumentSingle.aspx? DocumentID=248058; and U.S. Congress, House Committee on Small Business, *The State of Small Business Access to Capital and Credit: The View From Secretary Geithner*, 112th Cong., 1st sess.,

about nine months after the program's enactment. The delay was largely due to the Treasury's need to finalize the SBLF's investment decision process with federal banking agencies[57] and the need to create separate SBLF regulations for financial institutions established as C corporations, Subchapter S corporations, mutual lending institutions, and Community Development Financial Institutions (CDFIs).

A *C corporation* is a legal entity established under state law and includes shareholders, directors, and officers. The profit of a C corporation is taxed to the corporation when earned and then is taxed to the shareholders when distributed as dividends.[58] The majority of insured depository institutions, bank holding companies, and savings and loan holding companies are C corporations.[59] A *Subchapter S corporation* refers to a section of the Internal Revenue Code (IRC) that allows a corporation to pass corporate income, losses, deductions, and credits through to its shareholders for federal tax purposes. Shareholders of S corporations report the flow-through of income and losses on their personal tax returns and are assessed tax at their individual income tax rates. This allows S

June 22, 2011, Small Business Committee Document No. 112-023 (Washington: GPO, 2011), pp. 3, 9-11, 22, 25. Also see U.S. Government Accountability Office, *Additional Actions Needed to Improve Transparency and Accountability*, GAO-12-183, December 14, 2011, at http://www.gao.gov/products/GAO-12-183.

[57] Treasury and the federal banking agencies ultimately agreed that the banking agencies "would advise Treasury only on the financial viability of applicants and their capacity to increase small business lending, and that they would not make investment recommendations as they had for TARP. It was agreed that an applicant would be considered "viable" if it was (1) adequately capitalized; (2) not expected to become undercapitalized; and (3) not expected to be placed into conservatorship or receivership. Further, the [agencies'] validation of viability of an applicant would reflect only currently available supervisory information and rating assessments at the time the validation was made and would not predict Treasury's loss from making an investment in the institution." See U.S. Department of the Treasury, Office of the Inspector General. *Small Business Lending Fund: Investment Decision Process for the Small Business Lending Fund*, May 13, 2011, p. 8, at http://www.treasury.gov/about/organizational-structure/ig/Documents/SBLF%20Report%20(OIG-SBLF-11-001).pdf.

[58] Internal Revenue Service, "Corporations," at https://www.irs.gov/corporations.

[59] U.S. Department of the Treasury, Office of the Inspector General. *Small Business Lending Fund: Investment Decision Process for the Small Business Lending Fund*, May 13, 2011, p. 7, at http://www.treasury.gov/about/organizational-structure/ig/Documents/SBLF%20Report%20(OIG-SBLF-11-001).pdf.

corporations to avoid double taxation on the corporate income.[60] *Mutual lending institutions*, which include many thrifts, are owned by their depositors or policyholders. They have no stockholders. *CDFIs* are financial entities certified by the CDFI Fund in the U.S. Department of the Treasury and provide capital and financial services to underserved communities.

The establishment of separate regulations for each of these different types of financial institutions was largely related to issues involving whether the SBLF's financings would be counted by banking regulatory agencies as Tier 1 capital (core capital that is relatively liquid, such as common shareholders' equity, disclosed reserves, most retained earnings, and perpetual noncumulative preferred stocks) or as Tier 2 capital (supplementary capital that consists mainly of undisclosed reserves, revaluation reserves, general provisions, hybrid instruments, and subordinated term debt).[61]

The treatment of the SBLF's financings was important given that banks must maintain a minimum total risk-based capital ratio of 8% (the ratio measures bank capital against assets, with asset values risk-weighted, or adjusted on a scale of riskiness) to be considered adequately capitalized by federal banking regulators. In addition, banks must maintain a minimum

---

[60] Internal Revenue Service, "S Corporations," at https://www.irs.gov/businesses/small-businesses-self-employed/scorporations.

[61] 12 C.F.R. §325.2: "Tier 1 capital or core capital means the sum of common stockholders' equity, noncumulative perpetual preferred stock (including any related surplus), and minority interests in consolidated subsidiaries, minus all intangible assets (other than mortgage servicing assets, nonmortgage servicing assets, and purchased credit card relationships eligible for inclusion in core capital pursuant to §325.5(f)), minus credit-enhancing interest-only strips that are not eligible for inclusion in core capital minus deferred tax assets in excess of the limit set forth in §325.5(g), minus identified losses (to the extent that Tier 1 capital would have been reduced if the appropriate accounting entries to reflect the identified losses had been recorded on the insured depository institution's books), and minus investments in financial subsidiaries subject to 12 CFR part 362, subpart E, and minus the amount of the total adjusted carrying value of nonfinancial equity investments that is subject to a deduction from Tier 1 capital as set forth in section II.B.(6) of appendix A to this part."

Tier 1 risk-based ratio to assets, typically 3% for banking institutions with the highest financial ratings and 4% for others.[62]

According to Treasury officials, under Internal Revenue Service (IRS) rules, S corporations can have only a single class of stock (common shares). Consequently, these institutions cannot issue preferred stock to Treasury. As a result, Treasury had to consider purchasing subordinated debt from these institutions, which the banking regulatory agencies would likely designate as Tier 2 capital.[63] Treasury officials believed that providing Tier 2 capital would probably result in fewer S corporation participants. Additionally, because mutual lending institutions do not issue stock, Treasury officials were unable to receive preferred stock as consideration for an investment in this type of institution. Therefore, Treasury had to consider purchasing subordinated debt from these institutions as well.[64]

Treasury completed its regulations for C corporation banks first. For C corporations, SBLF funds are treated as Tier I capital and the Treasury purchases senior perpetual noncumulative preferred stock (or an equivalent). The stock pays a quarterly dividend on the first day of each quarter after closing of the SBLF capital program funding. Tier 1 capital is the core measure of a bank's financial strength from a regulator's point of view. It is composed of core capital, which consists primarily of common stock and disclosed reserves (or retained earnings) but may also include nonredeemable, noncumulative preferred stock. In contrast, S corporations and mutual lending institutions receive unsecured subordinated debentures from the Treasury, which are considered Tier 2 capital for regulatory capital requirements.[65]

---

[62] For further information and analysis of federal banking regulations, see CRS Report R44918, *Who Regulates Whom? An Overview of the U.S. Financial Regulatory Framework*, by Marc Labonte.

[63] U.S. Department of the Treasury, Office of the Inspector General. *Small Business Lending Fund: Investment Decision Process for the Small Business Lending Fund*, May 13, 2011, p. 7, at http://www.treasury.gov/about/organizational-structure/ig/Documents/SBLF%20 Report%20(OIG-SBLF-11-001).pdf.

[64] Ibid.

[65] 12 C.F.R. Appendix A to Part 3 - Risk-Based Capital Guidelines: "The following elements comprise a national bank's Tier 2 capital: (1) Allowance for loan and lease losses, up to a maximum of 1.25% of risk-weighted assets, 3 subject to the transition rules in section

The application deadline for C corporation banks was May 16, 2011. The application deadline for Subchapter S corporations and mutual lending institutions was June 6, 2011, and the application deadline for CDFIs was June 22, 2011. A total of 926 institutions applied for $11.8 billion in SBLF funding.[66]

Treasury approved more than $4.0 billion in SBLF financing to 332 lending institutions ($3.9 billion to 281 community banks and $104 million to 51 CDFIs).[67] SBLF recipients have offices located in 47 states and the District of Columbia. The average financing was $12.1 million, ranging from $42,000 to $141.0 million.[68]

Of the 332 lending institutions which received financing, 137 institutions had participated in TARP's Community Development Capital Initiative or its Capital Purchase Program. These institutions received nearly $2.7 billion in SBLF financing (66.8% of the total).[69]

Small Business Lending Progress Reports

Treasury is required to publish monthly reports describing all transactions made under the SBLF program during the reporting period. It is also required to publish a semiannual report (each March and September) providing all projected costs and liabilities, operating expenses, and transactions made by the SBLF, including a list of all participating institutions and the amounts each institution has received under the program. Treasury must also publish a quarterly report

---

4(a)(2) of this appendix A; 3 The amount of the allowance for loan and lease losses that may be included in capital is based on a percentage of risk-weighted assets."

[66] U.S. Department of the Treasury, "Small Business Lending Fund Cost Report, Report to Congress submitted pursuant to Section 4106(2) of the Small Business Jobs Act of 2010," July 19, 2011, p. 1, at http://www.treasury.gov/ resource-center/sb-programs/ DocumentsSBLFTransactions/SBLF%204106(2)%20Cost%20Report.pdf.

[67] U.S. Department of the Treasury, "SBLF Investments as of September 27, 2011," at http://www.treasury.gov/resource-center/sb-programs/DocumentsSBLFTransactions/ SBLF_BiWeekly_Transactions_Report_THRU_09272011.pdf.

[68] Ibid.

[69] Ibid.

describing how participating institutions have used the funds they have received.[70]

SBLF participants must submit an initial supplemental report to Treasury no later than five business days before closing. The report provides information from the institution's FDIC call reports or, for holding companies, from their subsidiaries' FDIC call reports, that Treasury uses to establish an initial baseline for measuring the SBLF participants' progress in making loans to small businesses.[71]

The initial baseline is the average amount of qualified small business lending that was outstanding for the four full quarters ending on June 30, 2010.[72] It is derived by first adding the outstanding amount of lending reported for all commercial and industrial loans, owner-occupied nonfarm, nonresidential real estate loans, loans to finance agricultural production and other loans to farmers, and loans secured by farmland. Then, the outstanding amount of lending for large loans (defined as any loan or group of loans greater than $10 million), loans to large businesses (defined as businesses with annual revenues greater than $50 million), and the portion of any loans guaranteed by the U.S. government or for which the risk is assumed by a third party is subtracted from that amount. The lending institution then adds back any cumulative charge-offs with respect to such loans since July 1, 2010. This last adjustment is done to prevent lending institutions from being penalized for appropriately charging off loans.[73]

Each SBLF participant's small business lending baseline is also adjusted to take into account any gains in qualified small business lending during the four baseline quarters resulting from mergers, acquisitions, and loan purchases. This adjustment is designed to ensure that dividend rate reductions provided to any SBLF participant correspond to additional

---

[70] P.L. 111-240, the Small Business Jobs Act of 2010, §4106. Reports.
[71] U.S. Department of the Treasury, "SBLF: Getting Started Guide," June 27, 2011, p. 13, at http://www.treasury.gov/resource-center/sb-programs/Documents/SBLF%20Getting%20Started%20Guide.pdf.
[72] Ibid.
[73] Ibid., p. 15.

lending to small businesses and not to the acquisition of existing loans.[74] In addition, the cumulative baseline for all SBLF participants will decrease over time as SBLF participants repay their SBLF loans and exit the program. For example, the initial small business lending baseline for the 332 SBLF participants as of March 31, 2011, was $35.52 billion ($34.75 billion for 281 banks and $770.48 million for 51 CDFIs).[75] The small business lending baseline for the 50 institutions that continued to participate in the SBLF as of September 30, 2018, was $1.5 billion ($808.8 million for 7 banks and $714.3 million for 43 CDFIs).[76]

Table 3 provides the number and type of SBLF participating institutions, the small business lending baseline, the amount of small business lending by participants, the change in small business lending by participants, and the change in small business lending by both current and former participants from 2011 to 2018. The number of SBLF participating institutions is declining as institutions repay their loans and exit the program. As Treasury anticipated, this decline has accelerated following the first quarter of 2016 because the dividend rates for C corporation banks and savings associations and for S corporation banks and mutual lending institutions were increased at that time (to 9% and 13.8%, respectively).[77]

SBLF institutions are also required to submit quarterly supplemental reports, due in the calendar quarter following submission of the initial supplemental report and in each of the next nine quarters, to determine their dividend rate for the next quarter.[78]

---

[74] U.S. Department of the Treasury, "SBLF Quarterly 4106(3) Report – 4Q 2011," at http://www.treasury.gov/resourcecenter/sb-programs/DocumentsSBLFTransactions/Use%20of%20Funds%204016(3)%20Report%20-%2001-09-12.pdf.
[75] U.S. Department of the Treasury, "SBLF Use of Funds Report: Third Quarter 2011 (excel file)," October 26, 2011, at http://www.treasury.gov/resource-center/sb-programs/Pages/sblf_transactions.aspx.
[76] U.S. Department of the Treasury, "Report on SBLF Participants' Small Business Lending Growth," January 1, 2019, at https://www.treasury.gov/resource-center/sb-programs/DocumentsSBLFTransactions/C1_LGR_01-01-19_LendingGrowthReport_20181218_CRE.xlsx.
[77] U.S. Department of the Treasury, "Small Business Lending Fund, Lending Growth Report," April 8, 2016, p. 1, at https://www.treasury.gov/resource-center/sb-programs/Documents SBLFTransactions/LGR%20April%202016%20FINAL%204-1-2016.pdf.
[78] U.S. Department of the Treasury, "SBLF: Getting Started Guide," June 27, 2011, p. 13, at http://www.treasury.gov/resource-center/sb-programs/Documents/SBLF%20Getting%20Started%20Guide.pdf.

Table 3. SBLF Participants: Baseline, Lending, and Change in Lending, 2011-2018 (billions of dollars)

Date	Banks	CDFIs	#	Lending Baseline (current participants)	Lending (current participants)	Change in Lending (current participants)	Change in Lending (current & former participants)
Sept. 30, 2018	7	43	50	$1.523	$2.871	$1.348	$19.100
June 30, 2018	8	46	54	$1.597	$2.901	$1.304	$19.000
March 31, 2018	10	46	56	$2.075	$4.281	$2.206	$19.100
Dec. 31, 2017	10	46	56	$2.075	$4.168	$2.093	$18.900
Sept. 30, 2017	10	46	56	$2.074	$4.082	$2.007	$18.907
June 30, 2017	13	46	59	$2.655	$4.922	$2.267	$18.697
March 31, 2017	15	46	61	$2.746	$5.157	$2.411	$18.761
Dec. 31, 2016	20	46	66	$3.497	$6.726	$3.229	$18.809
Sept. 30, 2016	23	46	69	$3.683	$7.024	$3.341	$18.711
June 30, 2016	31	46	77	$4.806	$8.561	$3.755	$18.735
March 31, 2016	39	46	85	$5.109	$9.454	$4.344	$18.464
Dec. 31, 2015	115	47	162	$15.824	$24.614	$8.790	$18.410
Sept. 30, 2015	183	47	230	$28.378	$41.815	$13.437	$17.967
June 30, 2015	212	47	259	$31.843	$47.063	$15.220	$17.660
March 31, 2015	219	48	267	$31.292	$46.686	$15.394	$16.364
Dec. 31, 2014	226	48	274	$31.494	$46.613	$15.119	$15.819
Sept. 30, 2014	232	48	280	$31.571	$45.844	$14.273	$14.713
June 30, 2014	241	49	290	$32.975	$46.505	$13.530	$13.790
March 31, 2014	245	50	295	$33.148	$45.541	$12.393	$12.623
Dec. 31, 2013	248	50	298	$32.985	$45.491	$12.506	$12.356
Sept. 30, 2013	257	50	307	$35.056	$46.213	$11.157	$11.387
June 30, 2013	265	50	315	$36.544	$46.937	$10.393	$10.396
March 31, 2013	267	50	317	$36.320	$45.310	$8.990	$8.992

Date	Banks	CDFIs	#	Lending Baseline (current participants)	Lending (current participants)	Change in Lending (current participants)	Change in Lending (current & former participants)
Dec. 31, 2012	270	50	320	$36.886	$45.811	$8.925	$8.934
Sept. 30, 2012	275	51	326	$36.544	$43.982	$7.438	$7.443
June 30, 2012	277	51	328	$35.990	$42.665	$6.675	$6.675
March 31, 2012	281	51	332	$36.124	$41.322	$5.198	$5.198
Dec. 31, 2011	281	51	332	$35.975	$40.794	$4.819	$4.819
Sept. 30, 2011	281	51	332	$35.878	$39.412	$3.534	$3.534
June 30, 2011	281	51	332	$35.597	$38.430	$2.833	$2.833
March 31, 2011	281	51	332	$35.521	$37.134	$1.613	$1.613

Source: U.S. Department of the Treasury, "Report on SBLF Participants' Small Business Lending Growth," January 1, 2019 (.pdf and excel files), pp. 6, 7, at https://www.treasury.gov/resource-center/sb-programs/Pages/sblf_transactions.aspx.

Notes: In the fourth quarter of 2013 redemptions by SBLF participants with negative lending balances outpaced that of institutions with positive lending balances. As a result of these redemptions, cumulative lending growth reported for the period decreased by $150 million when former participants are included.

Using information contained in the quarterly supplemental reports, Treasury announced in its January 2019 quarterly report on *SBLF Participants' Small Business Lending Growth* that, as of September 30, 2018

- The 50 current SBLF participants (7 banks and 43 CDFIs) increased their small business lending by $1.348 billion over a $1.523 billion baseline.[79]
- Since inception, the total increase in small business lending reported by both current and former SBLF participants is more than $19.1 billion over the baseline.
- All seven of the currently participating community banks and 38 of the 43 currently participating CDLFs increased their small business lending over baseline levels.
- Most current participants report that their small business lending increases have been substantial, with 43 of 50 current SBLF participants (86.0%) increasing small business lending by 10% or more.[80]

Treasury officials have praised the SBLF's performance. For example, on October 9, 2012, then-Deputy Secretary of the Treasury Neal Wolin announced that the SBLF quarterly use of funds report released that day "is further indication that the Administration's Small Business Lending Fund is continuing to help create an environment in which entrepreneurial small

---

[79] U.S. Department of the Treasury, "Report on SBLF Participants' Small Business Lending Growth," January 1, 2019, pp. 1, 6, 7, at https://www.treasury.gov/resource-center/sb-programs/DocumentsSBLFTransactions/LGR%20Jan%202019%20Final%2001-01-2019%20Clean.pdf.
As of December 1, 2018, 280 institutions with aggregate investments of $3.8 billion have fully redeemed their SBLF funding and exited the program, and 4 institutions have partially redeemed $11.4 million (or 57% of their SBLF securities) while continuing to participate in the program. Ibid., p. 1.

[80] U.S. Department of the Treasury, "Report on SBLF Participants' Small Business Lending Growth," January 1, 2019, at https://www.treasury.gov/resource-center/sb-programs/DocumentsSBLFTransactions/C1_LGR_01-01-19_LendingGrowthReport_20181218_CRE.xlsx.

businesses can succeed and excel."[81] He added that "banks in the SBLF program continue to show large increases in the lending available for small businesses to grow, create jobs, and support families in communities across the country."[82]

Some financial commentators have expressed a somewhat less sanguine view of the program's performance. For example, one commentator noted, after the release of the quarterly use of funds report in January 2012, that although the report of increased small business lending was positive news "it is difficult to isolate the proportion of new lending that would have occurred anyway" due to improvements in the economy.[83] Another commentator noted that the data may have been skewed by SBLF participants who were entering the small business lending market for the first time, making the increases appear larger and more significant than they actually are; yet another noted that the reported growth in small business lending occurred over six quarters (since June 30, 2010) and that the results, although positive, are "not as impressive as it may seem."[84] A commentator argued in September 2012 that "if the SBLF ends up being a success story, it will have been on a far smaller scale than either Obama or Congress had originally expected. What's more, it's become clear that even boatloads of financing won't change the fact that demand for the loans themselves has also fallen off, as small businesses themselves are reluctant to expand in a stagnant economy."[85]

---

[81] U.S. Department of the Treasury, "Treasury Announces $6.7 Billion Increase in Small Business Lending at Banks Receiving Capital through the Small Business Lending Fund (SBLF)," October 9, 2012, at http://www.treasury.gov/press-center/press-releases/Pages/tg1731.aspx.

[82] Ibid.

[83] Harry Terris, "Former TARP Banks Lag Peers in SBLF Lending," *American Banker*, vol. 177, no. 16, January 25, 2012.

[84] Kate Davidson, "Was the SBLF Program a Success?" *American Banker*, vol. 177, no. 8, January 12, 2012.

[85] Suzy Khimm, "Has Obama Really Helped Small Business?" *The Washington Post*, September 11, 2012, at http://www.washingtonpost.com/blogs/ezra-klein/wp/2012/09/11/has-obama-really-helped-small-businesses/.

In addition, on August 29, 2013, Treasury's Office of Inspector General (OIG) released an audit of Treasury's reporting of small business lending gains relative to small business lending levels prior to the lenders' participation in the program. The OIG found that "small business lending gains reported by Treasury are significantly overstated and cannot be linked directly to SBLF funding."[86] Specifically, the OIG noted that "substantial amounts [$3.4 billion of the then reported $8.9 billion] of the reported gains occurred prior to participants receiving SBLF funding." As the OIG explained,

> the lending gains reported [by Treasury] were measured against the same baseline period that the Small Business Jobs Act of 2010 (the Act) instructs Treasury to use for setting dividend rates for repayment of the SBLF capital, which is the four calendar quarters [which] ended [on] June 30, 2010. However, measuring program performance against a baseline with a midpoint seven quarters prior to when most participants received funding inflates program accomplishments and is not responsive to provisions in the Act that direct Treasury to report on participant use of the SBLF funds received.[87]

The OIG also argued that the reported lending gains cannot be directly linked to the SBLF capital that Treasury invested in the financial institutions because the lending gains reported "represent all small business lending gains that institutions participating in the SBLF achieved, regardless of how the loans were funded."[88] In addition, the OIG noted, among other findings, that "a relatively small number (35 or 11%) of SBLF participants accounted for half of small business lending increases between the baseline figure and December 31, 2012."[89]

---

[86] U.S. Department of the Treasury, Office of the Inspector General, *Small Business Lending Fund: Reported SBLF Program Accomplishments Are Misleading Without Additional Reporting*, August 29, 2013, p. 8, at http://www.treasury.gov/about/organizational-structure/ig/Audit%20Reports%20and%20 Testimonies/OIG-SBLF-13- 012%20fix%209%2010%2013.pdf.

[87] Ibid., pp. 3, 9-11.

[88] Ibid., pp. 3, 11-13.

[89] Ibid., p. 11.

PROPOSED LEGISLATION

During the 112th Congress, several bills were introduced to change the SBLF. None of the bills were enacted. For example, then-Senator Snowe introduced S. 681, the Greater Accountability in the Lending Fund Act of 2011, on March 30, 2011. Senator Snowe argued that

> While I would prefer to terminate this fund altogether, it is unlikely based on the current political environment, which is why we must work to protect taxpayers from some of its most egregious provisions. My goal with this legislation is to ensure that only healthy banks have access to taxpayer money, that they are required to repay loans within a reasonable period of time, and that small businesses find the affordable credit they need.[90]

The bill would have, among other things,

- required recipients to repay SBLF distributions within 10 years of the receipt of the investment;[91]
- terminated the program no later than 15 years after the date of the bill's enactment;[92]
- prohibited the Secretary of the Treasury from making capital investments under the program if the FDIC is appointed receiver of 5% or more of the institutions receiving an investment under the program;

---

[90] U.S. Senator Olympia Snowe, "Snowe Calls for Comprehensive Fixes to Small Business Lending Fund," press release, March 30, 2011, at http://snowe.senate.gov/public/index.cfm/pressreleases?ContentRecord_id=b1507369-8193-44ff-94ae-ceb94d5debe8&ContentType_id=ae7a6475-a01f-4da5-aa94-0a98973de620&Group_id=2643ccf9-0d03-4d09-9082-3807031cb84a&MonthDisplay=3&YearDisplay=2011.

[91] Current law provides the Treasury Secretary the discretion to extend the repayment period beyond 10 years. P.L. 111-240, the Small Business Jobs Act of 2010, §4103(d)(5)(h); 12 U.S.C. §4741.

[92] Current law does not include a termination date for the program, other than terminating the authority to make capital investments in eligible institutions one year after the date of enactment. P.L. 111-240, the Small Business Jobs Act of 2010, §4109. Termination and Continuation of Authorities.

- prohibited participation by any institution that received an investment under TARP (effective on the date of the bill's enactment);
- removed provisions allowing the Secretary of Treasury to make a capital investment in institutions that would otherwise not be recommended to receive the investment based on the institution's financial condition, but are able to provide a matching investment from private, nongovernmental investors;
- required the approval of appropriate financial regulators when determining whether an institution should receive a capital investment;[93] and
- revised the benchmark against which changes in the amount of small business lending is measured from the four full quarters immediately preceding the date of enactment to calendar year 2007.[94]

In addition, H.R. 1387, the Small Business Lending Fund Accountability Act of 2011, would have provided the Special Inspector General for TARP responsibility for providing oversight over the SBLF.

S.Amdt. 279 to S. 493, the Small Business Innovation Research, Small Business Technology Transfer Reauthorization Act of 2011, would have prevented TARP recipients from using funds received in any form under any other federal assistance program, including the SBLF program.

H.R. 2807, the Small Business Leg-Up Act of 2011, would have transferred any unobligated and repaid funds from the SBLF to the Community Development Financial Institutions Fund beginning on the

---

[93] Current law requires the Treasury Secretary to consult with appropriate financial regulators to determine if the eligible institution may receive a capital investment under the program. P.L. 111-240, the Small Business Jobs Act of 2010, §4103(d); 12 U.S.C. §4741.

[94] Senator Snowe indicated that this change "would address concerns that the existing benchmark may be too low, by historical standards, and that an adjustment could result in additional small business lending. See U.S. Senator Olympia Snowe, "Snowe Calls for Comprehensive Fixes to Small Business Lending Fund," Washington, DC, March 30, 2011, at http://snowe.senate.gov/public/index.cfm/pressreleases?ContentRecord_id=b1507369-8193-44ff-94aeceb94d5debe8&ContentType_id=ae7a6475-a01f-4da5-aa94-0a98973de620&Group_id=2643ccf9-0d03-4d09-9082-3807031cb84a&MonthDisplay=3&YearDisplay=2011.

date when the Secretary of the Treasury's authority to make capital investments in eligible institutions expired (on September 27, 2011). The bill's stated intent was "to increase the availability of credit for small businesses."[95]

H.R. 3147, the Small Business Lending Extension Act, would have extended the Department of the Treasury's investment authority from one year following enactment to two years and required the Treasury Secretary to provide any institution not selected for participation in the program the reason for the rejection, ensure that the rejection reason remains confidential, and establish an appeal process that provides the institution an opportunity to contest the reason provided for the rejection of its application.

During the 113th Congress, H.R. 2474, the Community Lending and Small Business Jobs Act of 2013, would have, among other provisions, transferred any unobligated and repaid funds from the SBLF to the Community Development Financial Institutions Fund.[96]

CONCLUSION

The SBLF was enacted as part of a larger effort to enhance the supply of capital to small businesses. Advocates argued that the SBLF would help to address the decline in small business lending and create jobs. Opponents were not convinced that it would enhance small business lending and worried about the program's potential cost to the federal treasury and its similarities to TARP.

Participating institutions are reporting they have increased their small business lending. However, as has been discussed, questions have been raised concerning the validity of these reported amounts. Specifically, as Treasury's OIG argued in its August 2013 audit, more than one-third of the

---

[95] H.R. 2807, the Small Business Leg-Up Act of 2011.
[96] H.R. 2474 was introduced on June 20, 2013, and referred to the Committee on Financial Services, and, in addition, to the Committees on Small Business, and Education and the Workforce, for a period to be subsequently determined by the Speaker, in each case for consideration of such provisions as fall within the jurisdiction of the committee concerned.

reported lending gains at that time occurred prior to September 30, 2011, the quarter in which most SBLF participants received their SBLF funds; the reported small business lending gains reflect all of the small business lending gains that the participants achieved, regardless of how the loans were funded; and previous OIG audits "have shown that a large number of participants misreport their small business lending activity."[97] In those previous audits, "50% or more of the institutions reviewed submitted erroneous lending data to Treasury, either overstating or understating their small business lending gains."[98]

In addition to questions related to the validity of the reported small business lending gains, any analysis of the program's influence on small business lending is likely to be more suggestive than definitive because differentiating the SBLF's effect on small business lending from other factors, such as changes in the lender's local economy, is methodologically challenging, especially given the relatively small amount of financing involved relative to the national market for small business loans. The

---

[97] U.S. Department of the Treasury, Office of the Inspector General, *Small Business Lending Fund: Reported SBLF Program Accomplishments Are Misleading Without Additional Reporting*, August 29, 2013, pp. 3, 4, at http://www.treasury.gov/about/organizational-structure/ig/Audit%20Reports%20and%20Testimonies/OIG-SBLF-13-012%20fix%209%2010%2013.pdf.

[98] Ibid., p. 4. Under the Small Business Jobs Act, the Department of the Treasury's Inspector General is required to conduct audits and investigations of the SBLF and to report its findings to Congress and the Secretary of the Treasury no less than two times a year. To date, Treasury's Inspector General has released 10 SBLF reports (one informal and nine formal). These reports examined and made recommendations for improving Treasury's early investment decision process for evaluating SBLF applicants (informal audit, May 13, 2011); Treasury's SBLF cost and liabilities projections (December 22, 2011); Treasury's investment decisions concerning early-entry SBLF participants (February 17, 2012); Treasury's investment decisions concerning later-entry SBLF participants (July 3, 2012); the accuracy of SBLF participants' reports of their baseline lending amounts (August 21, 2012); the accuracy of third quarter 2012 dividend rate adjustments (January 29, 2013); the accuracy of fourth quarter 2012 dividend rate adjustments (August 9, 2013); the accuracy of reported small business lending gains (August 29,2013); the accuracy of first quarter 2013 dividend rate adjustments (September 27, 2013); and use of capital, plans for repaying SBLF funds, and recipient satisfaction with Treasury's administration of the program (March 27, 2014). To view the OIG's audits see U.S. Department of the Treasury, Office of the Inspector General, "Office of Small Business Lending Fund (SBLF) Oversight," at http://www.treasury.gov/about/organizational-structure/ig/Pages/Office-of-Small-Business-LendingFund-Program-Oversight.aspx. In addition, the Government Accountability Office (GAO) was required to audit the program annually. P.L. 113-188, the Government Reports Elimination Act of 2014, repealed this requirement.

SBLF's $4.0 billion in financing represents less than 0.7% of outstanding small business loans (as defined by the FDIC).[99]

In terms of the concerns expressed about the program's potential cost, Treasury initially estimated in December 2010 that the SBLF could cost taxpayers up to $1.26 billion (excluding administrative costs that were initially estimated at about $26 million annually but actual outlays were $4.54 million in FY2014, $9.05 million in FY2015, $5.01 million in FY2016, and $3.4 million in FY2017).[100] Treasury based that estimate on an expectation that about $17 billion in SBLF financings would be disbursed. In October 2011, Treasury estimated the program's costs based on actual participant data. It estimated that the SBLF would generate a savings of $80 million (excluding administrative costs), with the savings coming primarily from a lower-thanexpected financing level and, to a lesser extent, improvements in projected default rates "due to higher participant quality than expected" and lower market interest rates.[101] Treasury issues a semiannual report on SBLF costs. In its latest semiannual cost report, released on August 16, 2018, Treasury estimated that the SBLF

---

[99] As of September 30, 2018 (the latest available data), the FDIC reports that small business loans (defined by the FDIC as commercial and industrial loans of $1 million or less) for nonagricultural purposes was $620.5 billion ($4 billion/$620.5 billion = 0.644%). See Federal Deposit Insurance Corporation, "Statistics on Depository Institutions: Standard Industry Reports," at https://www.fdic.gov/bank/statistical/.

[100] Program administrative costs (e.g., monitoring the performance and compliance of participants, reporting on the program's performance and costs, and managing the securities purchased through the SBLF program) must be excluded from subsidy cost estimates in accordance with guidelines in the Federal Credit Reform Act of 1990. See OMB Circular A-11, §185.2. Also, see U.S. Department of the Treasury, "Cost report," January 30, 2015, p. 4 at http://www.treasury.gov/resource-center/sb-programs/DocumentsSBLFTransactions/ FY2014%20Midyear%20SBLF%20Cost%20Report.pdf; U.S. Department of the Treasury, "Cost report," July 25, 2016, pp. 2-4, at https://www.treasury.gov/resource-center/sb-programs/DocumentsSBLFTransactions/ FY2015%20SBLF%20Cost%20Report.pdf; U.S. Department of the Treasury, "Cost report," June 5, 2017, pp. 2-4, at https://www.treasury.gov/resource-center/sb-programs/DocumentsSBLFTransactions/ FY2016%20Year%20End%20Cost%20Report.pdf; and U.S. Department of the Treasury, "Cost report," May 2, 2018, p. 4, at https://www.treasury.gov/resource-center/sb-programs/DocumentsSBLFTransactions/ FY2017%20Year%20End%20Cost%20Report_Final.pdf.

[101] U.S. Department of the Treasury, Office of the Inspector General, *Small Business Lending Fund: Treasury Should Consider Concerns Regarding Participants Management and Historical Retained Earnings When Estimating the Cost of the SBLF Program*, December 22, 2011, pp. 1-3, at https://www.treasury.gov/about/organizationalstructure/ig/Documents/ OIG-SBLF-12-001[1].pdf.

will "generate a lifetime positive return of $31 million [excluding administrative costs] for the Treasury General Fund."[102]

One issue that arose relative to the program's projected cost is the noncumulative treatment of dividends. Treasury's OIG reported in May 2011 that

> Under the terms set by legislation, dividend payments are non-cumulative, meaning that institutions are under no obligation to make dividend payments as scheduled or to pay off previously missed payments before exiting the program. This dividend treatment differs from the TARP programs, in which many dividend payments were cumulative. This change in dividend treatment was driven by changes in capital requirements mandated by the Collins Amendment to the Dodd-Frank Act.
>
> The amendment equalizes the consolidated capital requirements for Tier 1 capital of bank holding companies by requiring that, at a minimum, regulators apply the same capital and risk standards for FDIC-insured banks to bank holding companies. Under TARP, the FRB [Federal Reserve Board] and FDIC treated capital differently at the holding company and depository institution levels. The FRB treated cumulative securities issued by holding companies as Tier 1 capital, while FDIC treated non-cumulative securities issued by depository institutions as Tier 1 capital. In order to comply with the Dodd-Frank Act requirement that securities purchased from holding companies receive the same capital treatment as those purchased from depository institutions, Treasury made the dividends under SBLF non-cumulative.
>
> Additionally, given that Tier 1 capital must be perpetual and cannot have a mandatory redemption date, the 10-year repayment period in the Small Business Jobs Act cannot be enforced.[103]

---

[102] U.S. Department of the Treasury, "Cost report," August 16, 2018, p. 3, at https://www.treasury.gov/resourcecenter/sb-programs/DocumentsSBLFTransactions/FY2018_Mid-year_SBLFCost_Report.pdf.

[103] U.S. Department of the Treasury, Office of the Inspector General, *Small Business Lending Fund: Investment Decision Process for the Small Business Lending Fund*, May 13, 2011, p. 19, at https://www.treasury.gov/about/organizational-structure/ig/Audit%20Reports%20and%20Testimonies/OIG-SBLF-11- 001.pdf.

Treasury addressed this issue by placing the following additional requirements and restrictions on participants who miss dividend payments:

- the participant's CEO [Chief Executive Office] and CFO [Chief Financial Officer] must provide written notice regarding the rationale of the board of directors (BOD) for not declaring a dividend;
- no repurchases may be affected and no dividends may be declared on any securities for the applicable quarter and the following three quarters;
- after four missed payments (consecutive or not), the issuer's BOD must certify in writing that the issuer used best efforts to declare and pay dividends appropriately;
- after five missed payments (consecutive or not), Treasury may appoint a representative to serve as an observer on the issuer's BOD; and
- after six missed payments (consecutive or not), Treasury may elect two directors to the issuer's BOD if the liquidation preference is $25 million or more.[104]

Treasury's OIG agreed that Treasury's equity investment policy is consistent with the legislation and that "it has reasonably structured the program to incentivize payment of dividends."[105] However, it recommended that "Congress consider whether an amendment to the Small Business Jobs Act and/or waiver from the Collins Amendment to the Dodd-Frank Act is needed to make the repayment of dividends a requirement for exiting the program."[106]

In conclusion, congressional oversight of the SBLF is currently focused on the program's potential long-term costs and effects on small business lending. Underlying those concerns are fundamental disagreements regarding the best way to assist small businesses. Some

---

[104] Ibid., pp. 19, 20.
[105] Ibid., p. 20.
[106] Ibid., p. 25.

advocate the provision of additional federal resources to assist small businesses in acquiring capital necessary to start, continue, or expand operations and create jobs. Others worry about the long-term adverse economic effects of spending programs that increase the federal deficit. They advocate business tax reduction, reform of financial credit market regulation, and federal fiscal restraint as the best means to assist small businesses and create jobs.

APPENDIX. THE SBLF'S LEGISLATIVE HISTORY

The SBLF's Legislative Origin

On March 16, 2009, President Obama announced the first SBLF-like proposal. Under that proposal, the Department of the Treasury would have used TARP funds to purchase up to $15 billion of SBA-guaranteed loans.[107] The purchases were intended to "immediately unfreeze the secondary market for SBA loans and increase the liquidity of community banks."[108] The plan was dropped after it met resistance from lenders. Some lenders objected to TARP's requirement that participating lenders comply with executive compensation limits and issue warrants to the federal government. Smaller, community banks objected to the program's

---

[107] P.L. 110-343, the Emergency Economic Stabilization Act of 2008, was designed to enhance the supply of loans to businesses of all sizes. The act authorized the Troubled Asset Relief Program (TARP) to "restore liquidity and stability to the financial system of the United States" by purchasing or insuring up to $700 billion in troubled assets from banks and other financial institutions. TARP's purchase authority was later reduced from $700 billion to $475 billion by P.L. 111-203, the Dodd-Frank Wall Street Reform and Consumer Protection Act. The Department of the Treasury has disbursed $389 billion in TARP funds, including $337 million to purchase SBA 7(a) loan guaranty program securities. The authority to make new TARP commitments expired on October 3, 2010. U.S. Department of the Treasury, Troubled Assets Relief Program Monthly 105(a) Report—November 2010, December 10, 2010, pp. 2-4, at http://www.treasury.gov/initiatives/financial-stability/briefing-room/reports/105/Documents105/November%20105(a)%20FINAL.pdf. For further analysis, see CRS Report R41427, *Troubled Asset Relief Program (TARP): Implementation and Status*, by Baird Webel.

[108] The White House, "Remarks by the President to Small Business Owners, Community Leaders, and Members of Congress," March 16, 2009, at https://www.gpo.gov/fdsys/pkg/PPP-2009-book1/pdf/PPP-2009-book1-doc-pg255.pdf.

paperwork requirements, such as the provision of a small-business lending plan and quarterly reports.[109]

In his January 2010 State of the Union address, President Obama proposed the creation of a $30 billion SBLF to enhance access to credit for small businesses:

> When you talk to small business owners in places like Allentown, Pennsylvania, or Elyria, Ohio, you find out that even though banks on Wall Street are lending again, they're mostly lending to bigger companies. Financing remains difficult for small business owners across the country, even those that are making a profit.
>
> Tonight, I'm proposing that we take $30 billion of the money Wall Street banks have repaid and use it to help community banks give small businesses the credit they need to stay afloat.[110]

In response to the opposition community lenders had expressed concerning TARP's restrictions in 2009, the Obama Administration proposed that Congress approve legislation authorizing the transfer of up to $30 billion in TARP spending authority to the SBLF and statutorily establish the new program as distinct and independent from TARP and its restrictions.[111] The Administration's legislative proposal was finalized and sent to Congress on May 7, 2010.[112] Representative Barney Frank, then-chair of the House Committee on Financial Services, introduced H.R. 5297, the Small Business Lending Fund Act of 2010, on May 13, 2010.

The House Committee on Financial Services held a hearing on H.R. 5297 on May 18, 2010, and passed the bill, as amended to include a State Small Business Credit Initiative, the following day. The House passed the

---

[109] Emily Flitter, "Fix for SBA Snagged by Tarp's Exec Comp Limits," *American Banker*, vol. 174, no. 61 (March 31, 2009), p. 1.

[110] The White House, "Remarks by the President in State of the Union Address," January 27, 2010, at https://obamawhitehouse.archives.gov/the-press-office/remarks-president-state-union-address.

[111] The White House, "President Obama Outlines New Small Business Lending Fund," February 2, 2010, at https://obamawhitehouse.archives.gov/the-press-office/president-obama-outlines-new-small-business-lending-fund.

[112] The White House, "Remarks by the President on the Monthly Job Numbers," May 7, 2010, at https://www.cspan.org/video/?293389-2/presidential-remarks-unemployment-numbers.

bill, as amended to include a Small Business Early-Stage Investment Program, a Small Business Borrower Assistance Program, and some small business tax reduction provisions, on June 17, 2010.

The House-Passed Version of the SBLF

Title I of the House-passed version of H.R. 5297 authorized the Secretary of the Treasury to establish a $30 billion SBLF "to address the ongoing effects of the financial crisis on small businesses by providing temporary authority to the Secretary of the Treasury to make capital investments in eligible institutions" with total assets equal to or less than $1 billion or $10 billion (as of the end of the fourth quarter of calendar year 2009) "in order to increase the availability of credit for small businesses."[113] The authority to make capital investments in eligible institutions was limited to one year after enactment.

Eligible financial institutions having total assets equal to or less than $1 billion as of the end of the fourth quarter of calendar year 2009 could apply to receive a capital investment from the SBLF in an amount not exceeding 5% of risk-weighted assets, as reported in the FDIC call report immediately preceding the date of application. During the fourth quarter of 2009, 7,340 FDIC-insured lending institutions reported having assets amounting to less than $1 billion.[114]

Eligible financial institutions having total assets equal to or less than $10 billion as of the end of the fourth quarter of calendar year 2009 could apply to receive a capital investment from the fund in an amount not exceeding 3% of risk-weighted assets, as reported in the FDIC call report

---

[113] H.R. 5297, the Small Business Jobs and Credit Act of 2010, §101. Small Business Lending Fund Purpose. In 2011, there were 7,513 FDIC-insured lending institutions in the United States. Of that number, 6,846 lending institutions had assets amounting to less than $1 billion (totaling $1.42 trillion), 561 lending institutions had assets of $1 billion to $10 billion (totaling $1.43 trillion), and 106 lending institutions had assets greater than $10 billion (totaling $10.76 trillion). See FDIC, "Quarterly Banking Profile: Second Quarter 2011," at https://www.fdic.gov/bank/analytical/quarterly/2011- vol5-3/fdic-quarterly-vol5no3.pdf.

[114] FDIC, "Quarterly Banking Profile: Fourth Quarter 2009," at https://www.fdic.gov/bank/analytical/quarterly/2010-vol4-1/fdic-quarterly-vol4no1-full.pdf.

immediately preceding the date of application. During the fourth quarter of 2009, 565 FDIC-insured lending institutions reported having assets of $1 billion to $10 billion.[115]

Risk-weighted assets are assets such as cash, loans, investments, and other financial institution assets that have different risks associated with them. FDIC regulations (12 C.F.R. §567.6) establish that cash and government bonds have a 0% risk-weighting; residential mortgage loans have a 50% risk-weighting; and other types of assets (such as small business loans) have a higher risk-weighting.[116]

Lending institutions on the FDIC problem bank list or institutions that have been removed from the FDIC problem bank list for less than 90 days were ineligible to participate in the program. Lending institutions could refinance securities issued through the Treasury Capital Purchase Program (CPP) and the Community Development Capital Incentive (CDCI) program under TARP, but only if the institution had not missed more than one dividend payment due under those programs.

Participating banks would be charged a dividend rate of no more than 5% per annum initially, with reduced rates available if the bank increased its small business lending. For example, during any calendar quarter in the initial two years of the capital investments under the program, the bank's rate would be lowered if it had increased its small business lending compared to the average small business lending it made in the four previous quarters immediately preceding the enactment of the bill, minus some allowable adjustments. A 2.5% to less than 5% increase in small business lending would have lowered the rate to 4%, a 5% to less than 7.5% increase would have lowered the rate to 3%, a 7.5% to less than 10% increase would have lowered the rate to 2%, and an increase of 10% or greater would have lowered the rate to 1%.

Table A-1 shows the dividend rates associated with small business lending increases for C corporation banks and savings institutions under H.R. 5297. These rates were subsequently included in the final law.

---

[115] Ibid. In the fourth quarter of 2009, 107 FDIC-insured lending institutions had assets greater than $10 billion.
[116] For further analysis of risk-weighted assets, see CRS Report R44918, *Who Regulates Whom? An Overview of the U.S. Financial Regulatory Framework*, by Marc Labonte.

Table A-1. SBLF Lending Increases and Dividend Rates for C Corporation Banks and Savings Associations under the House-Passed Version of H.R. 5297

Small Business Lending Increase	Dividend Rate Following Investment Date		
	1st 9 Quarters	Quarter 10 to Year 4.5	After Year 4.5
10% or greater	1%	1%	9%
At least 7.5% but less than 10%	2%	2%	9%
At least 5% but less than 7.5%	3%	3%	9%
At least 2.5% but less than 5%	4%	4%	9%
Less than 2.5%	5%	5%	9%
No increase	5%	7%	9%

Source: H.R. 5297, the Small Business Jobs and Credit Act of 2010, Section 103. Small Business Lending Fund.

Notes: The Senate-passed version of H.R. 5297, which became the Small Business Jobs Act of 2010, authorizes the same dividend rates.

The bill also authorized the Secretary of the Treasury to adjust these dividend rates for S corporations "to take into account any differential tax treatment of securities issued by such eligible institution."[117] Also, Community Development Financial Institutions were to be charged a dividend rate of 2% per annum for eight years, and 9% thereafter.[118]

SBLF applicants were also required to submit a small business lending plan to the appropriate federal banking agency and, for applicants that are state-chartered banks, to the appropriate state banking regulator. The plan was to describe how the applicant's business strategy and operating goals will allow it to address the needs of small businesses in the areas it serves, as well as a plan to provide linguistically and culturally appropriate outreach, where appropriate. The plan was to be treated as confidential supervisory information. The Secretary of the Treasury was required to consult with the appropriate federal banking agency or, in the case of an eligible institution that is a nondepository community development financial institution, the Community Development Financial Institution

---

[117] H.R. 5297, the Small Business Jobs and Credit Act of 2010, Section 103. Small Business Lending Fund.
[118] Ibid.

Fund, before determining if the eligible institution was to participate in the program.[119]

The bill specified that the SBLF would be "established as separate and distinct from the Troubled Asset Relief Program established by the Emergency Economic Stabilization Act of 2008. An institution shall not, by virtue of a capital investment under the Small Business Lending Fund Program, be considered a recipient of the Troubled Asset Relief Program."[120]

The bill also directed that all funds received by the Secretary of the Treasury in connection with purchases made by the SBLF, "including interest payments, dividend payments, and proceeds from the sale of any financial instrument, shall be paid into the general fund of the Treasury for reduction of the public debt."[121]

The Senate-Passed Version of the SBLF

Title IV of the Senate-passed version of H.R. 5297, which later became law, authorized the Secretary of the Treasury to establish a $30 billion SBLF to make capital investments in eligible community banks with total assets equal to or less than $1 billion or $10 billion. There were several differences between the Senate-passed version of H.R. 5297's

---

[119] If the appropriate banking agency would not otherwise recommend that the eligible institution receive the capital investment, the Secretary of the Treasury was authorized, in consultation with the appropriate banking agency, to consider allowing the eligible institution to participate in the program if the eligible institution provided matching capital from private, nongovernmental sources that is equal to or greater than 100% of the SBLF investment and that matching capital was subordinate to the capital investment from the SBLF.

[120] H.R. 5297, the Small Business Lending Fund Act of 2010, §111. Assurances.

[121] H.R. 5297, the Small Business Lending Fund Act of 2010, §103. Small Business Lending Fund. Using a cost-based estimate, CBO estimated that the SBLF would result in net outlays of $3.3 billion over 2010-1015, and would reduce outlays by $1.1 billion over the 2010-2020 period. Using an alternative fair-value estimate, CBO estimated that the SBLF would result in net outlays of $6.2 billion over the 2010-2020 period. See CBO, "Cost Estimate: H.R. 5297, Small Business Lending Fund Act of 2010," June 28, 2010, pp. 3, 4, at https://www.cbo.gov/sites/default/files/111thcongress-2009-2010/costestimate/hr5297housepassed0.pdf.

SBLF provisions and the SBLF provisions in the House-passed version of H.R. 5297. Specifically, the

- House-passed version of H.R. 5297 indicated that eligible institutions may be insured depository institutions that are not controlled by a bank holding company or a savings and loan holding company that is also an eligible institution and is not directly or indirectly controlled by any company or other entity that has total consolidated assets of more than $10 billion, bank holding companies, savings and loan holding companies, community development financial institution loan funds, and small business lending companies, all with total assets of $10 billion or less (as of the end of 2009).[122] The Senate-passed version of H.R. 5297 did not provide eligibility to small business lending companies.[123]
- House-passed version of H.R. 5297 defined small business lending "as small business lending as defined by and reported in an eligible institution's quarterly call report, where each loan comprising such lending is made to a small business and is one the following types: (1) commercial and industrial loans; (2) owner-occupied nonfarm, nonresidential real estate loans; (3) loans to finance agricultural production and other loans to farmers; (4) loans secured by farmland; (5) nonowner-occupied commercial real estate loans; and (6) construction, land development and other land loans."[124] The Senate-passed version of H.R. 5297's definition of small business lending did not include nonowner-occupied commercial real estate or construction, land development and other land loans.[125]
- Senate-passed version of H.R. 5297 had an exclusion provision prohibiting recipient lending institutions from using the funds to

---

[122] H.R. 5297, the Small Business Lending Fund Act of 2010, §102. Definitions.
[123] P.L. 111-240, the Small Business Jobs Act of 2010, §4102. Definitions.
[124] H.R. 5297, the Small Business Lending Fund Act of 2010, §102. Definitions.
[125] P.L. 111-240, the Small Business Jobs Act of 2010, §4102. Definitions.

issue loans that have an original amount greater than $10 million or that would be made to a business with more than $50 million in revenues.[126] The House-passed version of H.R. 5297 did not contain this provision.

- House-passed version of H.R. 5297 indicated that the incentives received in the form of reduced dividend rates during the first 4.5-year period following the date on which an eligible institution received a capital investment under the program would be contingent on an increase in the number of loans made.[127] If the number of loans made by the institution did not increase by 2.5% for each 2.5% increase of small business lending, then the rate at which dividends and interest would be payable during the following quarter on preferred stock or other financial instruments issued to the Treasury by the eligible institution would be (i) 5%, if this quarter is within the two-year period following the date on which the eligible institution received the capital investment under the program; or (ii) 7%, if the quarter is after the two-year period. The Senate-passed version of H.R. 5297 did not contain this legislative language.

- House-passed version of H.R. 5297 included an alternative computation provision that would have allowed eligible institutions to compute their small business lending amounts for incentive purposes as if the definition of their small business lending amounts did not require that the loans comprising such lending be made to small business.[128] This alternative computation would have been allowed if the eligible institution certified that all lending included by the institution for purposes of computing the increase in lending was made to small businesses. The Senate-passed version of H.R. 5297 did not contain this provision.

---

[126] H.R. 5297, the Small Business Lending Fund Act of 2010, §103. Small Business Lending Fund.
[127] Ibid.
[128] Ibid.

- House-passed version of H.R. 5297 indicated that an eligible institution that is a community development loan fund may apply to receive a capital investment from the SBLF in an amount not exceeding 10% of total assets, as reported in the audited financial statements for the fiscal year of the eligible institution that ended in calendar year 2009.[129] The Senate-passed version of H.R. 5297 specifies 5%.[130]
- House-passed version of H.R. 5297 would have required the Secretary of the Treasury, in consultation with the Community Development Financial Institutions Fund, to develop eligibility criteria to determine the financial ability of a Community Development Loan Fund to participate in the program and repay the investment. It provided a list of recommended eligibility criteria that the Secretary of the Treasury could use for this purpose.[131] The Senate-passed version of H.R. 5297 provided a similar, but mandatory, list of eligibility criteria that must be used for this purpose.[132]
- House-passed version of H.R. 5297 contained a temporary amortization authority provision which would have allowed an eligible institution to amortize any loss or write-down on a quarterly straight-line basis over a period of time, adjusted to reflect the institution's change in the amount of small business lending relative to the baseline.[133] The Senate-passed version of H.R. 5297 did not contain this provision.

The Senate's version of H.R. 5297 was agreed to in the Senate on September 16, 2010, after considerable debate and amendment to remove the Small Business Early-Stage Investment Program and Small Business

---

[129] Ibid.
[130] P.L. 111-240, the Small Business Jobs Act of 2010, §4103. Small Business Lending Fund.
[131] H.R. 5297, the Small Business Lending Fund Act of 2010, §103. Small Business Lending Fund.
[132] P.L. 111-240, the Small Business Jobs Act of 2010, §4103. Small Business Lending Fund.
[133] H.R. 5297, the Small Business Lending Fund Act of 2010, §113. Temporary Amortization Authority.

Borrower Assistance Program, revise the SBLF, and add numerous other provisions to assist small businesses, including additional small business tax reduction provisions.[134] The House agreed to the Senate amendments on September 23, 2010, and President Obama signed the bill, retitled the Small Business Jobs Act of 2010 (P.L. 111-240), into law on September 27, 2010.

---

[134] For additional information and analysis concerning P.L. 111-240, the Small Business Jobs Act of 2010, see CRS Report R40985, *Small Business: Access to Capital and Job Creation*, by Robert Jay Dilger.

In: Small Business
Editor: Angel Becker

ISBN: 978-1-53615-969-1
© 2019 Nova Science Publishers, Inc.

Chapter 2

SMALL BUSINESS LOANS: ADDITIONAL ACTIONS NEEDED TO IMPROVE COMPLIANCE WITH THE CREDIT ELSEWHERE REQUIREMENT[*]

United States Government Accountability Office

ABBREVIATIONS

NAICS	North American Industry Classification System
SBA	Small Business Administration

WHY GAO DID THIS STUDY

SBA's 7(a) program is required to serve creditworthy small business borrowers who cannot obtain credit through a conventional lender at

---

[*] This is an edited, reformatted and augmented version of United States Government Accountability Office; Report to Congressional Committees, Publication No. GAO-18-421, dated June 2018.

reasonable terms. The Joint Explanatory Statement of the Consolidated Appropriations Act, 2017 includes a provision for GAO to review the 7(a) program.

This chapter discusses, among other things, (1) how SBA monitors lenders' compliance with the credit elsewhere requirement, (2) the extent to which SBA evaluates trends in lender credit elsewhere practices, and (3) lenders' views on the credit elsewhere criteria for 7(a) loans.

GAO analyzed SBA data on 7(a) loans approved for fiscal years 2007–2016, the latest available, and reviewed literature on small business lending; reviewed standard operating procedures, other guidance, and findings from SBA reviews performed in fiscal year 2016; and interviewed lender associations and a nonrepresentative sample of 7(a) lenders selected that concentrated on larger lenders.

WHAT GAO RECOMMENDS

GAO recommends that SBA (1) require its on-site reviewers to document their assessment of lenders' policies and procedures related to the credit elsewhere documentation requirement, (2) collect information on lenders' use of credit elsewhere criteria, and (3) analyze that information to identify trends. SBA generally agreed with the recommendations.

WHAT GAO FOUND

For its 7(a) loan program, the Small Business Administration (SBA) has largely delegated authority to lenders to make 7(a) loan determinations for those borrowers who cannot obtain conventional credit at reasonable terms elsewhere. To monitor lender compliance with the "credit elsewhere" requirement SBA primarily uses on-site reviews conducted by third-party contractors with SBA participation and oversight, and other reviews. According to SBA guidance, lenders making 7(a) loans must take steps to ensure and document that borrowers meet the program's credit elsewhere requirement. However, GAO noted a number of concerns with SBA's monitoring efforts. Specifically, GAO found the following:

- Over 40 percent (17 of 40) of the on-site lender reviews performed in fiscal year 2016 identified lender noncompliance with the requirement.
- On-site reviewers identified several factors, such as weakness in lenders' internal control processes that were the cause for lender noncompliance.
- Most on-site reviewers did not document their assessment of lenders' policies or procedures, because SBA does not require them to do so. As a result SBA does not have information that could help explain the high noncompliance rate.

Federal internal control standards state that management should design control activities, including appropriate documentation, and use quality information to achieve the entity's objectives. Without better information on lenders' procedures for complying with the documentation requirement, SBA may be limited in its ability to promote compliance with requirements designed to help ensure that the 7(a) program reaches its target population.

SBA does not routinely collect or analyze information on the criteria used by lenders for credit elsewhere justifications. SBA recently began collecting some information on lenders' use of the criteria, but this information is limited, and SBA does not analyze the information that it does collect to better understand lenders' practices. Federal internal control standards state that management should use quality information to achieve the entity's objectives. Without more robust information and analysis, SBA may be limited in its ability to understand how lenders are using the credit elsewhere criteria and identify patterns of use by certain lenders that place them at a higher risk of not reaching borrowers who cannot obtain credit from other sources at reasonable terms.

In general, representatives from 8 of 11 lenders that GAO interviewed stated that SBA's credit elsewhere criteria are adequate for determining small business eligibility for the 7(a) program. These criteria help them target their lending to small businesses that would otherwise have difficulty obtaining conventional credit because they are often new businesses or have a shortage of collateral. However, they also said that other factors—such as lender policies and economic conditions—can affect their decisions to offer 7(a) loans. In January 2018, SBA issued revised guidance for the 7(a) program and has provided training on this new guidance to lenders and trade associations. Lenders told GAO they are still in the process of understanding the new requirements.

June 5, 2018
Congressional Committees

In recent years, the Small Business Administration's (SBA) 7(a) program—SBA's largest loan guarantee program for small businesses—has grown considerably.[1] The program is required to serve creditworthy small business borrowers who cannot obtain credit through a conventional lender at reasonable terms—commonly referred to as the "credit elsewhere" requirement.[2] In July 2015, SBA was forced to suspend 7(a) lending after the program hit its $18.75 billion annual loan ceiling with more than 2 months left in the fiscal year. Congress subsequently raised the loan ceiling to $23.5 billion and further to $27.5 billion in fiscal year 2017. In response to this growth, members of Congress have raised concerns about guaranteed loans going to borrowers that are able to obtain conventional credit at reasonable terms and whether the criteria currently used to satisfy the credit elsewhere requirement provide reasonable assurance that guaranteed loans are approved for only qualified borrowers.

---

[1] The loan guarantee covers part of a lender's losses in the event of a borrower default, reducing the risk of lending to small businesses that would otherwise not qualify for loans at reasonable terms from commercial lenders. Section 7(a) of the Small Business Act, now codified at 15 U.S.C. § 636(a), provides the authority for the 7(a) program.

[2] Reasonable terms and conditions take into consideration "the prevailing rates and terms in the community in or near which the concern transacts business, or the homeowner resides, for similar purposes and periods of time." 15 U.S.C. § 632(h). SBA also requires lenders certify that 7(a) borrowers cannot obtain financing from personal resources or the resources of the business or its owners of 10 percent or more.

The Joint Explanatory Statement of the Consolidated Appropriations Act, 2017, includes a provision for us to conduct a study of the credit elsewhere requirement, including the sufficiency of the credit elsewhere criteria. This chapter discusses (1) 7(a) lending to selected categories of small business borrowers from fiscal years 2007 through 2016; (2) how SBA monitors lenders' compliance with the credit elsewhere requirement; (3) the extent to which SBA evaluates trends in lender practices related to the credit elsewhere requirement; and (4) lenders' views on the criteria used to determine eligibility for 7(a) loans and other issues related to the 7(a) program.

To determine 7(a) lending to selected categories of small business borrowers, we identified the characteristics of small business borrowers that receive SBA-guaranteed loans through the 7(a) program. To do so, we analyzed loan-level data from SBA on the characteristics of small businesses that received 7(a) loans from fiscal years 2007 through 2016, the most current information available at the time of our review, including whether businesses were women-owned or minority-owned and their geographic location. To assess the reliability of loan-level data from SBA, we interviewed SBA officials, reviewed related documentation, and tested the data for missing or erroneous values. We determined the data we used were sufficiently reliable for purposes of describing the characteristics of borrowers who received 7(a) loans.

To examine how SBA conducts oversight of 7(a) lenders' compliance with the credit elsewhere requirement, we reviewed SBA's standard operating procedures and other guidance, interviewed SBA officials, and reviewed reports of SBA's on-site reviews, corrective actions, and targeted lender reviews related to the credit elsewhere requirement conducted in fiscal year 2016. To assess the extent to which SBA evaluates trends in lender practices related to the credit elsewhere requirement, we interviewed SBA officials and reviewed documentation for SBA's online portal for loan origination. To obtain lenders' views on the adequacy of the criteria SBA uses to determine eligibility for 7(a) loans and other issues related to the 7(a) program, we interviewed representatives from industry groups and a nonrepresentative, nongeneralizable sample of 11 lenders, of which 9 lenders were selected using a random process that concentrated on larger lenders and two additional lenders we interviewed that represented an industry group. Appendix I describes our objectives, scope, and methodology in greater detail.

We conducted this performance audit from August 2017 to June 2018 in accordance with generally accepted government auditing standards. Those standards require that we plan and perform the audit to obtain sufficient, appropriate evidence to provide a reasonable basis for our findings and conclusions based on our audit objectives. We believe that the evidence obtained provides a reasonable basis for our findings and conclusions based on our audit objectives.

BACKGROUND

Under SBA's 7(a) loan program, SBA guarantees loans made by commercial lenders to small businesses for working capital and other general business purposes.[3] These lenders are mostly banks, but some are non-bank lenders, including small business lending companies— lenders whose lending activities are not subject to regulation by any federal or state regulatory agency, but were previously licensed by SBA and authorized to provide 7(a) loans to qualified small businesses.[4] The guarantee assures the lender that if a borrower defaults on a loan, the lender will receive an agreed-upon portion (generally between 50 percent and 85 percent) of the outstanding balance. For a majority of 7(a) loans, SBA relies on lenders with delegated authority to approve and service 7(a) loans and to ensure that borrowers meet the program's eligibility requirements. To be eligible for the 7(a) program, a business must be an operating for-profit small firm

---

[3] Although SBA has legislative authority to make direct loans to borrowers unable to obtain loans from conventional lenders, SBA has, with the exception of disaster loans and loans to Microloan program intermediaries, not exercised that authority since 1998.

[4] As of the first quarter of fiscal year 2018, small business lending companies accounted for less than 4 percent of SBA's total 7(a) loan portfolio, excluding loans made through SBA's Community Advantage pilot program.

(according to SBA's size standards) located in the United States and must meet the credit elsewhere requirement.[5]

Because the 7(a) program is required to serve borrowers who cannot obtain conventional credit at reasonable terms, lenders making 7(a) loans must take steps to ensure that borrowers meet the program's credit elsewhere requirement. Because SBA relies on lenders with delegated authority to make these determinations, SBA's oversight of these lenders is particularly important. However, we found in a 2009 report that SBA's lack of guidance to lenders on how to document compliance with the credit elsewhere requirement was impeding the agency's ability to oversee compliance with the credit elsewhere requirement. To improve SBA's oversight of lenders' compliance with the credit elsewhere requirement, we recommended in 2009 that SBA issue more detailed guidance to lenders on how to document their compliance with the credit elsewhere requirement.[6] As a result, SBA revised its standard operating procedure to state that each loan file must contain documentation that specifically identifies the factors in the present financing that meet the credit elsewhere test, which we believe met the spirit of our recommendation.

SBA's current credit elsewhere criteria for determining 7(a) loan eligibility include the following factors:

1. the business needs a longer maturity than the lender's policy permits;

---

[5] In establishing size standards, SBA considers economic characteristics of the industry, including degree of competition; average firm size; start-up costs and entry barriers; and distribution of firms by size. It also considers growth trends, competition from other industries, and other factors that may distinguish small firms from other firms. SBA's size standards seek to ensure that a firm that meets a specific size standard is not dominant in its field of operation. The Small Business Jobs Act of 2010 also mandated that SBA establish an alternative size standard for 7(a) applicants using maximum tangible net worth and average net income after federal income taxes. *See* Pub. L. No. 111-240 § 1116 (codified at 15 U.S.C. § 632(a)(5)). Until 2014, borrowers also had to meet the "personal resources test," which required certain owners to inject personal liquid assets into the business to reduce the amount of SBA-guaranteed funds that would otherwise be needed.

[6] GAO, *Small Business Administration: Additional Guidance on Documenting Credit Elsewhere Decisions Could Improve 7(a) Program Oversight*, GAO-09-228 (Washington, D.C.: Feb. 12, 2009).

2. the requested loan exceeds the lender's policy limit regarding the amount that it can lend to one customer;
3. the collateral does not meet the lender's policy requirements;
4. the lender's policy normally does not allow loans to new businesses or businesses in the applicant's industry; or
5. any other factors relating to the credit which, in the lender's opinion, cannot be overcome except for the guarantee.

When the 7(a) program was first implemented, borrowers were generally required to show proof of credit denials from banks that documented, among other things, the reasons for not granting the desired credit. Similar requirements remained in effect until 1985, when SBA amended the rule to permit a lender's certification made in its application for an SBA guarantee to be sufficient documentation.[7] This certification requirement remained when the rule was rewritten in 1996. SBA stated that it believed requiring proof of loan denials was demoralizing to small businesses and unenforceable by SBA.

SBA and lender roles vary among 7(a) program categories—including regular 7(a), the Preferred Lenders Program, and SBA Express.[8] Under the regular (nondelegated) 7(a) program, SBA makes the loan approval decision, including the credit determination. Under the Preferred Lenders Program and SBA Express, SBA delegates to the lender the authority to make loan approval decisions, including credit determinations, without prior review by SBA. For each 7(a) program category, lenders are required to ensure that borrowers meet the credit elsewhere requirement for all 7(a) loans. The maximum loan amount under the SBA Express program is

---

[7] By signing the loan guarantee application, the lender is certifying that "without the participation of SBA, to the extent applied for, [the lender] would not be willing to make this loan, and, in [the lender's] opinion, the financial assistance applied for is not otherwise available on reasonable terms."

[8] According to SBA, other categories include Export Express; which processes delegated loans, International Trade Loans, which can process both nondelegated and delegated loans; and Export Working Capital Program, which can process both nondelegated and delegated loans. Additionally, the Community Advantage is a pilot loan program introduced by SBA to meet the credit, management, and technical assistance needs of small businesses in underserved markets. Community Advantage provides mission-oriented lenders access to 7(a) loan guaranties for loans of $250,000 or less.

$350,000, as opposed to $5 million for other 7(a) loans. The program allows lenders to utilize, to the maximum extent possible, their own credit analyses and loan underwriting procedures. In return for the expanded authority and autonomy provided by the program, SBA Express lenders agree to accept a maximum SBA guarantee of 50 percent. Other 7(a) loans generally have a maximum guarantee of 75 percent or 85 percent, depending on the loan amount. In fiscal year 2016, 1,991 lenders approved 7(a) loans, of which 1,321 approved at least one loan with some form of delegated authority.

SBA's Office of Credit Risk Management is responsible for overseeing 7(a) lenders, including those with delegated authority. SBA created this office in fiscal year 1999 to help ensure consistent and appropriate supervision of SBA's lending partners.[9] The office is responsible for managing all activities regarding lender reviews; preparing written reports; evaluating new programs; and recommending changes to existing programs to assess risk potential. Generally, the office oversees SBA lenders to identify unacceptable risk profiles using its risk rating system and enforce loan program requirements.[10] According to SBA's standard operating procedures, one of the agency's purposes of its monitoring and oversight activities is to promote responsible lending that supports SBA's mission to increase access to capital for small businesses.

In the federal budget, the 7(a) program is generally required to set fees that it charges to lenders and borrowers at a level to cover the estimated cost of the program associated with borrower defaults (in present value terms). To offset some of the costs of the program, such as default costs, SBA assesses lenders two fees on each 7(a) loan. First, depending on the term of the loan, the guarantee fee must be paid by the lender within either 90 days of loan approval or 10 business days of the SBA loan number being assigned.[11] This fee is based on the amount of the loan and the level

---

[9] Prior to a reorganization in May 2007, the office was called the Office of Lender Oversight.
[10] GAO, *Small Business Administration: Actions Needed to Improve the Usefulness of the Agency's Lender Risk Rating System*, GAO-10-53 (Washington, D.C.: Nov. 6, 2009).
[11] Prior to September 2017, lenders were required to submit the guarantee fee at the time of the loan application (instead of within 10 days of loan approval) for loans with maturities of 12 months or less.

of the guarantee, and lenders can pass the fee on to the borrower. Second, the servicing fee must be paid annually by the lender and is based on the outstanding balance of the guaranteed portion of the loan.[12]

The 7(a) program accounts for a small portion of total small business lending. According to a May 2017 report by the Consumer Financial Protection Bureau, the total debt financing available to small businesses was estimated to be $1.4 trillion. Of that amount, the Consumer Financial Protection Bureau estimated that about 7 percent was SBA loans, including 7(a) loans.[13]

SBA and some other researchers have suggested that there may be disparities in credit access among small businesses, based on characteristics of the borrower and firm. SBA lists as a strategic objective to "ensure inclusive entrepreneurship by expanding access and opportunity to small businesses and entrepreneurs in communities where market gaps remain." In 2007, we reported that some studies had noted disparities among some races and genders in the conventional lending market, but the studies did not offer conclusive evidence on the reasons for those differences.[14] Much of the research we reviewed in 2007 relied on the Board of Governors of the Federal Reserve System's Survey of Small Business Finance, which was last implemented in 2003.[15] Although this survey is no longer available, recently the 12 Federal Reserve Banks conducted the Small Business Credit Survey.[16]

---

[12] The servicing fee cannot exceed 0.55 percent of the outstanding balance of the guaranteed portion and is required to be no more than "the rate necessary to reduce to zero the cost to the Administration of making guarantees." See 15 U.S.C. § 636(a)(23)(A). This fee cannot be charged to the borrower.

[13] In addition to the 7(a) loan program, SBA has two other capital loan programs—504 loans and Microloans. 504 loans are long-term, fixed-rate loans of up to $5.5 million to support investment in major assets such as real estate and heavy equipment that are delivered by certified development companies (private, nonprofit corporations). Microloans are loans provided to nonprofit intermediary lenders (community-based organizations) that in turn make loans of up to $50,000 to small businesses needing financing or assistance for start-up or expansion. In fiscal year 2016, SBA approved $4.7 billion and $58 million in 504 loans and Microloans, respectively (by gross loans approved).

[14] GAO, *Small Business Administration: Additional Measures Needed to Assess 7(a) Loan Program's Performance,* GAO-07-769 (Washington, D.C.: July 13, 2007).

[15] The survey gathered data from 4,240 firms selected to be representative of small businesses operating in the United States at the end of 2003.

[16] The Small Business Credit Survey is a national collaboration among the 12 Federal Reserve Banks. In 2016, it yielded 10,303 responses from small businesses with employees, or employer firms, located in 50 states and the District of Columbia.

In a series of reports based on the more recent survey, researchers found disparities in credit availability based on gender, the age of the firm, and minority status.[17]

BUSINESSES THAT WERE NEW, WOMEN-OWNED, OR LOCATED IN DISTRESSED AREAS RECEIVED A MAJORITY OF 7(A) LOAN DOLLARS OVER THE PAST 10 YEARS

From fiscal years 2007 through 2016, a majority of loan dollars guaranteed under the 7(a) program went to small businesses that were new, partially or wholly owned by women, or located in a distressed area.[18] As previously mentioned, recent studies we reviewed by the Federal Reserve Banks and other researchers suggest that certain small business borrowers—including businesses that are new or owned by women—have difficulty obtaining conventional small business loans, which may put them at a disadvantage.[19] As shown in Figure 1, almost two-thirds of loan dollars guaranteed under the 7(a) program for this period went to small businesses that were in these two categories or located in a distressed area.[20] The remaining 37 percent of 7(a) loan dollars went to businesses that were established, solely male-owned, and not located in economically

---

[17] See for example, Federal Reserve Banks of Cleveland and Atlanta, *Small Business Credit Survey: Report on Minority-Owned Firms,* November 2017; Federal Reserve Banks of New York and Kansas City, *Small Business Credit Survey: Report on Women-Owned Firms,*(November 2017; and Federal Reserve Bank of New York, *Small Business Credit Survey: Report on Start-Up Firms,* November 2017.

[18] SBA defines new businesses as businesses in operation 2 years or less at the time the loan is approved or, in some cases, within 2 years of a change of ownership. We determined economically distressed areas using American Community Survey data, discussed in greater detail below.

[19] Other studies reviewed include Sterling A. Bone, Glenn L. Christensen, Jerome D. Williams, Stella Adams, Anneliese Lederer, and Paul C. Lubin, "*Detecting Discrimination in Small Business Lending*" (2017), *Management Faculty Publications,* Paper 366, accessed on April 25, 2018, http://digitalcommons.usu.edu/manage_facpub/366; and Shaoming Cheng, "Potential Lending Discrimination? Insights from Small Business Financing and New Venture Survival,*" Journal of Small Business Management 2015 53(4), pp. 905–923.*

[20] For 7(a) loans over this period, borrowers did not report race and ethnicity for about 11 percent of the loans. We present statistics based on minority status separately to more clearly identify the three categories: minority, nonminority, and undetermined.

distressed areas. See appendixes II and III for additional data on 7(a) loans, such as the total volume, percentage of lending provided by year and by state, and other borrower characteristics, including SBA's loan- and lender-level Small Business Risk Portfolio Solutions score (predictive score) information.[21]

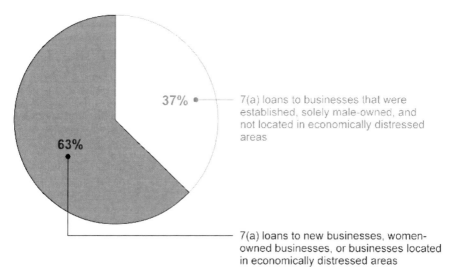

Source: GAO analysis of Small Business Administration and Census Bureau data. | GAO-18-421.

Note: Data for women-owned businesses include businesses that were partially or majority owned by women.

Figure 1. Percentage of 7(a) Loan Dollars That Went to Businesses That Were New, Women-Owned, or Located in Distressed Areas, Fiscal Years 2007–2016.

In the following figures, we present more detailed data on 7(a) loans to small businesses based on their status as a new business; gender of ownership; location relative to economically distressed areas; and minority ownership for fiscal years 2007 through 2016.

---

[21] According to SBA, the Small Business Risk Portfolio Solutions score is a portfolio management credit score that is used by SBA to predict the likelihood of severe delinquency at the loan level. These scores risk rank loans based on their probability of severe delinquency within a range between 70 and 300. As scores increase for a given set of loans, the probability of delinquency decreases.

New Businesses

As shown in Figure 2, the percentage of 7(a) loans that went to new businesses decreased from 36 percent in fiscal year 2007 to 23 percent in fiscal year 2011 before increasing to 35 percent by 2016.

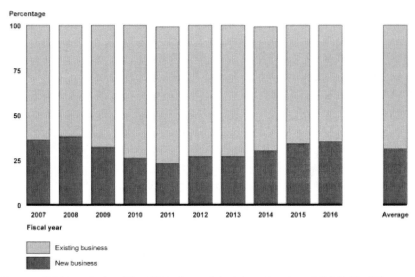

Source: GAO analysis of Small Business Administration data. | GAO-18-421.

Figure 2. Percentage of 7(a) Loans by Status as a New Business, Fiscal Years 2007-2016.

Gender

From fiscal years 2007 through 2016, the share of the total value of approved 7(a) loans by gender of owner remained fairly consistent (see Figure 3). An average of 70 percent of the total loan value went to male-owned businesses, and the remaining 30 percent went to businesses that were majority (more than 50 percent) or partially (50 percent or less) owned by women.[22]

---

[22] An SBA staff member told us that the gender of the owners of small business applicants is collected from the application form submitted by the applicant at the time of origination.

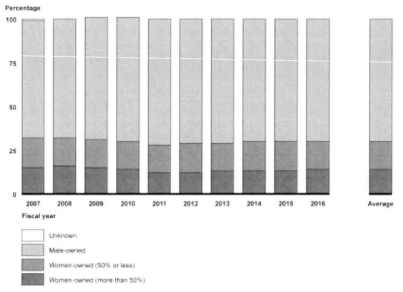

Source: GAO analysis of Small Business Administration data. | GAO-18-421.

Notes: According to SBA, gender is voluntarily provided at the discretion of the borrower and may not be reliable.

Figure 3. Percentage of 7(a) Loans by Gender of Ownership, Fiscal Years 2007-2016.

Economically Distressed Areas

SBA did not provide data on whether 7(a) loans go to businesses located in economically distressed neighborhoods. However, we used data from the American Community Survey for 2011 through 2015, the most recent version available at the time of our analysis, along with zip code information provided by SBA to determine the average poverty rate by zip code (see Figure 4).[23] From fiscal years 2007 through 2016, the proportion

---

The disclosure of this information is voluntary and used for statistical or reporting purposes only; it has no bearing on the credit decision.

[23] The American Community Survey is an ongoing survey conducted by the U.S. Census Bureau on topics such as social; economic; demographic; and housing characteristics of the U.S. population. The 5-year estimates from the survey are "period" estimates that represent data collected over a period of time. We merged the ACS data to the SBA data by zip code. Because in the ACS data poverty rate by zip code is only available for 5-year files, we could

of the total value of 7(a) loans approved that went to borrowers in economically distressed areas remained between 23 percent and 26 percent. We defined distressed areas as zip codes where at least 20 percent of the households had incomes below the national poverty line.

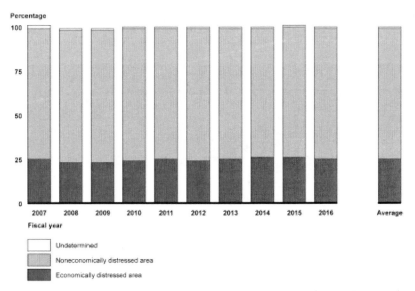

Source: GAO analysis of Small Business Administration and Census Bureau data. | GAO-18-421.

Notes: A borrower was determined to be in an economically distressed area if the zip code associated with that borrower had a poverty rate of 20 percent or higher. In about 1 percent of the cases, we were unable to determine a poverty rate for that zip code, in which case it was undetermined whether the zip code met our criteria.

Figure 4. Percentage of 7(a) Loans to Borrowers in Economically Distressed Areas and Noneconomically Distressed Areas, Fiscal Years 2007–2016.

Minority/Nonminority Status of Borrower

From fiscal years 2007 through 2016, the proportion of the total value of 7(a) loans approved that went to minority borrowers decreased overall—

---

not obtain yearly poverty rates, so we merged in the average poverty rate over the period. Because of this, the analysis does not reflect yearly changes in poverty over the period.

from 43 percent to 30 percent—with the lowest share at 24 percent in fiscal year 2010 (see Figure. 5).[24]

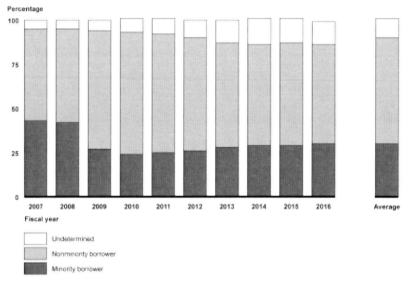

Source: GAO analysis of Small Business Administration data. | GAO-18-421.

Notes: Race and ethnicity are voluntarily provided at the discretion of the borrower. The undetermined category represents borrowers that did not identify their race or ethnicity.

SBA data contained nine categories for race/ethnicity, including one category for undetermined. Figure 5 condenses the nine categories into three groups: nonminority borrowers (borrowers who reported their race/ethnicity as white), minority borrowers (borrowers who reported categories other than white), and undetermined.

Figure 5. Percentage of 7(a) Loans to Minority and Nonminority Borrowers, Fiscal Years 2007–2016.

The share of approved loan dollars that went to nonminority borrowers varied, increasing to 69 percent in fiscal year 2010 before decreasing to 56 percent in fiscal year 2016. Notably, the share of the total value of loans approved that went to borrowers whose race/ethnicity was categorized as

---

[24] We define minority-owned businesses as those whose majority owner or owners are American Indian; Asian or Pacific Islander; Black or African American; Hispanic or Latino; Eskimo or Aleuts; Puerto Rican or Multi-group.

undetermined increased from 5 percent in fiscal year 2007 to 13 percent in fiscal year 2016. This increase does not fully account for the declined share for minority borrowers. However, according to SBA officials, borrowers voluntarily provide self-reported information on race and ethnicity and therefore the associated trend data should be viewed with caution.

SBA HAS PROCESSES IN PLACE TO EVALUATE LENDER COMPLIANCE, BUT ITS LENDER REVIEWS DO NOT DOCUMENT REASONS FOR NONCOMPLIANCE

SBA Conducts On-Site and Targeted Lender Reviews to Evaluate Lender Compliance with the Credit Elsewhere Documentation Requirement

SBA relies on on-site reviews as its primary mechanism for evaluating lenders' compliance with the credit elsewhere requirement. The reviews are performed by third-party contractors with SBA staff participation and additional oversight from SBA. According to SBA's standard operating procedures, these reviews are generally conducted every 12 to 24 months for all 7(a) lenders with outstanding balances on the SBA-guaranteed portions of their loan portfolios of $10 million or more, although SBA may conduct on-site reviews of any SBA lender at any time as it considers necessary. In fiscal year 2016, SBA conducted 40 on-site reviews of 7(a) lenders, representing approximately 35 percent of SBA's total outstanding 7(a) loan portfolio.[25]

As part of SBA's on-site reviews, reviewers judgmentally selected a sample of approximately 30 to 40 loan files using a risk-based approach. These loan files accounted for approximately 6 percent to 19 percent of

---

[25] The 35 percent represents the sum of the 40 lenders' gross balance ($25.7 billion) divided by SBA's total 7(a) loan portfolio as of the fourth quarter of fiscal year 2015 ($73.2 billion).

each lender's total gross SBA dollars in fiscal year 2016.[26] For each lender, approximately 70 percent to 90 percent of the loan files in the sample were reviewed to evaluate compliance with the credit elsewhere requirement.[27] According to SBA's contractors, loans that were selected for other reasons, such as issues related to liquidation, were not required to be reviewed for credit elsewhere compliance.

SBA requires lenders to provide a narrative to support the credit elsewhere determination in the credit memorandum included in each loan file. SBA's standard operating procedures state that lenders must substantiate that credit is not available elsewhere by (1) discussing the criteria that demonstrate an identifiable weakness in a borrower's credit and (2) including the specific reasons why the borrower does not meet the lender's conventional loan policy requirements.

In keeping with SBA's documentation requirement, third-party contractors and SBA staff who conduct on-site reviews are supposed to assess whether lenders have adequately documented the credit elsewhere criteria and provided specific reasons supporting the criteria in the credit memorandum. According to SBA's contractors, adequate documentation of the credit elsewhere determination in the credit memorandum would include not just which of the criteria a borrower met but also a discussion of the basis or justification for the decision. For example, if a lender determined that a borrower needed a longer maturity, the lender should explain in the credit memorandum the reasons why a longer maturity was necessary. SBA's contractors also told us that they carefully review a lender's loan policies in preparation for on-site reviews and refer to a

---

[26] These figures represent the 25th and 75th percentile, respectively, for the 40 on-site reviews conducted in fiscal year 2016. The number of loan files in the sample ranged from 29 to 81 (median = 32). The percentage of total gross SBA dollars ranged from 1 percent to 95 percent (median = 10 percent). The loan selection criteria were mostly based on potential risk to SBA as evidenced from lenders' Lender Profile Assessment metrics and other areas of emerging risk. The Lender Profile Assessment is a data-driven off-site review that computes quantitative factors for the following five components: portfolio performance; asset management; regulatory compliance; risk management; and special items. These quantitative factors are then scored against set risk tolerance levels established by SBA.

[27] These figures represent the 25th and 75th percentile, respectively, for the 40 reviews. The percentage of loan files of the sample that were reviewed for the credit elsewhere requirement ranged from 20 percent to 100 percent (median = 83 percent).

lender's policies throughout the reviews. Reviewers do not attempt to verify the evidence given in support of the credit elsewhere reason beyond the information provided in the credit memorandum.

Based on our review of fiscal year 2016 reports, on-site reviews can result in three levels of noncompliance response:

- Finding: This is the most severe result and is associated with a corrective action for the lender to remedy the issue.
- Observation: This is a deficiency recorded in the review's summary but may not warrant a corrective action for the lender.
- Deficiency Noted: This is the lowest level of response. It is a deficiency noted as part of the review that is not included in the review's summary and also may not warrant a corrective action.

According to SBA officials, SBA's policy has been that any noncompliance with SBA loan program requirements results in a finding. However, according to SBA officials and our review of the fiscal year 2016 on-site review reports, if a single instance of noncompliance was identified in fiscal year 2016, SBA generally would not issue a finding. Instead, SBA's contractors said they would attempt to determine whether that instance was an inadvertent error, such as by examining additional loan files.

Lenders that are subject to corrective actions are generally required to submit a response to SBA within 30 days to document how they have addressed or plan to address the identified issues. SBA subsequently asks for documentation to show that the lender has remedied the issue, and in some cases will conduct another review that usually includes an assessment of 5 to 10 additional loan files to determine whether the credit elsewhere reason has been adequately documented. According to SBA officials, SBA may also review lenders' compliance with corrective actions from recent on-site reviews during targeted reviews (discussed below) and delegated authority renewal reviews (for lenders with delegated authority).[28]

In addition to on-site reviews, SBA also monitors lenders' compliance with the credit elsewhere requirement through targeted reviews (performed on- or off-site). Targeted reviews of a specific process or issue may be conducted for a variety of reasons at SBA's discretion, including assessing a lender's compliance with the credit elsewhere requirement. In fiscal year 2016, SBA conducted 24 targeted reviews that included an examination of lenders' compliance with the credit elsewhere documentation requirement. For these reviews, SBA examined loan files for 5 judgmentally selected loans that were provided to SBA electronically, as well as copies of the credit elsewhere reasoning (among other underwriting documentation) for 10 additional recently-approved loans.[29]

SBA also conducts periodic off-site reviews that use loan- and lender-level portfolio metrics to evaluate the risk level of lenders' 7(a) portfolios. According to agency officials, SBA also began using off-site reviews to evaluate lenders' compliance with the credit elsewhere requirement in fiscal year 2016. In that year, SBA conducted off-site reviews of 250 lenders and required these lenders to report the credit elsewhere justification for a sample of 10 loans per lender that were identified by SBA's selection process.[30] Lenders were not required to provide supporting documentation, and SBA did not follow up with lenders or review loan files to ensure the validity of the self-reported reasons. According to SBA, off-site reviews followed the same procedures in fiscal year 2017 as in 2016 and that the agency planned to use the same procedures for these reviews in the future.

---

[28] Lenders with delegated authority, such as Preferred Lenders Program status, are subject to periodic delegated authority renewal reviews to maintain their authority.

[29] The five judgmentally selected loans were selected based on potential risk to SBA as evidenced by Loan Portfolio Assessment metrics and other areas of emerging risk. Our characterization of the scope of these targeted reviews is based on our review of 7 of the 24 targeted reviews, which SBA identified as those reviews that identified issues with the credit elsewhere requirement.

[30] For each lender, loans were selected among those that were disbursed within 24 months of the lender reporting cut-off date; approved through the Preferred Lenders Program or Certified Lenders Program; had approval amounts greater than $350,000; and were nonacquired. The selection process was further targeted towards loans with larger approval amounts; loans that were more recently disbursed; loans that were disbursed using a loan agent; and loans that were disbursed in the top industry group.

According to the agency, it also routinely evaluates and revises its review processes and procedures.

In addition, SBA's Loan Guaranty Processing Center and National Guaranty Purchase Center conduct Improper Payments Elimination and Recovery Act and quality control reviews at the time of loan approval and at the time of guaranty purchase, respectively.[31] These reviews examine the credit elsewhere requirement, among other issues. Lastly, since 2014 SBA's Office of Inspector General has also examined whether high-dollar or early-defaulted 7(a) loans were made in accordance with rules; regulations; policies; and procedures, including the credit elsewhere requirement.

SBA's Lender Reviews in 2016 Identified a High Rate of Noncompliance with the Credit Elsewhere Documentation Requirement

Our review of the on-site reviews conducted in fiscal year 2016 found that 17 of the 40 reviews—more than 40 percent—identified compliance issues with the credit elsewhere documentation requirement. Of those 17 reviews,

- 10 reviews resulted in a Finding (all with associated corrective actions),
- 3 reviews resulted in an Observation (none with associated corrective actions or requirements), and
- 4 reviews resulted in a Deficiency Noted (one with an associated requirement).

---

[31] The Improper Payments Elimination and Recovery Act, as amended, requires among other things that federal executive branch agencies take actions to reduce improper payments, including a thorough review of available databases before the release of federal funds. See Improper Payments Elimination and Recovery Improvement Act of 2012, Pub. L. No.112-248, 126 Stat. 2390 (Jan. 10, 2013), *codified* at 31 U.S.C. 3321 note, *as amended by* the Bipartisan Budget Act of 2013, Pub. L. No. 113-67, § 204, 127 Stat. 1165, 1181 (Dec. 26, 2013), and the Federal Improper Payments Coordination Act of 2015, Pub. L. No. 114-109, §§ 2-4,129 Stat. 2225, 2225-27 (Dec. 18, 2015).

For all of the 17 on-site reviews that identified an instance of noncompliance, the issue was related to the lender's documentation of the credit elsewhere criteria or justification.[32] For example, one review found that the lender's "regulatory practices demonstrate material noncompliance with SBA Loan Program requirements regarding documentation of the Credit Elsewhere Test." Another review found that the lender "failed to demonstrate with adequate documentation that credit was not available elsewhere on reasonable terms and conditions." For 2 of the 17 reviews, the issue was partly related to a discrepancy between the credit elsewhere justification used for some of the sample loan files and the lender's own loan policy limits.[33]

With regard to SBA's targeted reviews, 7 of 24 reviews (29 percent) conducted in fiscal year 2016 found a compliance issue with the credit elsewhere requirement. Of those 7 reviews, 6 reviews resulted in a Finding (all with associated corrective actions),

- 1 review resulted in an Observation (without an associated corrective action), and
- no reviews resulted in a Deficiency Noted.

For all of the 7 targeted reviews that identified a compliance issue, the issue was wholly related to the lender's documentation of the credit elsewhere reason or justification. For example, 4 reviews found that for at least one loan reviewed, "the Lender failed to document justification that credit was unavailable elsewhere." Another review found that for "three SBA Express loans and one Small Loan Advantage loan [the lender] reported "other factors relating to the credit that in the lender's opinion

---

[32] A given lender can be cited for multiple issues that result in a single finding.
[33] Specifically, one of the reviews found that in three of the loan files reviewed, the credit elsewhere reasons did not appear to be justified. The loan files in question stated that credit was not available elsewhere as the debt service coverage was insufficient based on the lender's policy; however, in all three instances, the debt service coverage was well within the lender's policy limits. The second review found that in five of the loan files reviewed, the reason given was that the loan did not meet the lender's conventional loan guidelines although that lender was only authorized to make SBA loans.

cannot be overcome except for the guaranty' without specific identification of the factors."

Lack of Internal Controls Led to Lender Noncompliance, but Were Not Documented by SBA's Reviews

Based on our review of on-site review reports and an interview with one reviewer, the key factors underlying lenders' high rate of noncompliance with the credit elsewhere documentation requirement were lenders' lack of proper internal controls and procedures and lack of awareness of the credit elsewhere documentation requirement.[34] In fiscal year 2016, SBA's corrective actions related to the credit elsewhere requirement required the lenders to establish or strengthen their policies; procedures; underwriting processes; or internal controls. In addition, contractors conducting the on-site reviews with whom we spoke stated that some lenders appeared to be unfamiliar with SBA's standard operating procedures or were unclear on how to interpret them.

For the 11 on-site reviews conducted in 2016 that included corrective actions, SBA generally required lenders to improve controls or procedures. For example, one lender was required to "correct its policy, modify its procedure, and amend its internal controls to ensure that its consideration and documentation of credit unavailable elsewhere identifies the specific fact(s) which are applicable to the specific loan and the determination is rendered and accurate for each individual SBA loan that it originates." Another lender was required to "improve underwriting processes and controls to ensure that the borrower meets the [credit elsewhere] requirement" and to "document the loan file with the reasons for the determination."

Similarly, for the six targeted reviews in 2016 that included corrective actions, SBA issued a general requirement for the lender to "identify the causes for the Findings and implement corrective actions." Based on our

---

[34] The second contractor we spoke to began conducting reviews for SBA at the beginning of 2017 and thus did not conduct on-site reviews during fiscal year 2016.

review of these targeted reviews, lenders generally remedied or intended to remedy the issue by amending their internal controls or procedures.[35] For example, one lender stated that the "Credit Elsewhere test will be incorporated into the Credit Department process." Another lender stated that it would "centralize all SBA underwriting and has developed an SBA addendum that will be utilized for all SBA-guaranteed loans."

Although some of SBA's on-site reviews for fiscal year 2016 identified factors leading to noncompliance, they generally did not document reviewers' assessment of lenders' policies and practices for complying with the credit elsewhere documentation requirement. SBA's standard operating procedures state that the on-site reviewers should determine whether or not lenders' policies and practices adhere to the requirement, but they do not require them to document their assessment of these policies and practices. Only 4 of the 40 fiscal year 2016 review reports that we examined included such an assessment. As a result, although SBA required corrective actions by the lender to address deficiencies, there usually was no record of the underlying factors that resulted in the lender's noncompliance.

Federal internal control standards state that management should design control activities to achieve objectives and respond to risks, including appropriate documentation of transactions and internal control.[36] Because SBA does not require reviewers to document their assessment of lenders' policies and practices for complying with the credit elsewhere documentation requirement, the agency does not have good information to help explain why so many lenders are not in compliance. This hinders SBA's ability to take informed and effective actions to improve lender compliance with the requirement and ensure that the program is reaching its intended population.

---

[35] SBA did not provide us with documentation of the lenders' response for two of the six lenders.
[36] GAO, *Standards for Internal Control in the Federal Government*, GAO-14-704G (Washington, D.C.: September 2014).

SBA COLLECTS LIMITED DATA ON CRITERIA USED FOR CREDIT ELSEWHERE JUSTIFICATIONS AND DOES NOT ANALYZE PATTERNS IN LENDER PRACTICES

SBA Collects Limited Data on Criteria Used for Credit Elsewhere Justifications

SBA does not routinely collect information on the criteria lenders use in their credit elsewhere justifications. As previously discussed, lenders are required to maintain documentation of borrower eligibility (including the credit elsewhere justification) in each loan file for loans approved through lenders' delegated authority. However, SBA cannot readily aggregate information on lenders' credit elsewhere justifications for both delegated and nondelegated loans:

- For delegated loans, lenders are required to certify the loan's credit elsewhere eligibility on E-Tran, SBA's online portal for origination of delegated and nondelegated loans. However, lenders are only required to check a box to certify that the loan file contains the required credit elsewhere justification and are not required to submit any additional information, including which of the criteria was used to make the determination. According to SBA officials, delegated loans account for loans approved by approximately 70 percent of lenders.
- For nondelegated loans, lenders are required to submit credit elsewhere documentation to be reviewed by SBA's Loan Guaranty Processing Center. For these loans, which comprise loans approved by the remaining 30 percent of lenders, SBA might maintain paper records of data on borrowers' eligibility but does not compile such data electronically and thus cannot readily aggregate the data for analysis.[37]

---

[37] The Loan Guaranty Processing Center has two locations: Citrus Heights, California and Hazard, Kentucky.

Instead, SBA relies on on-site reviews or lender-reported information to review lenders' credit elsewhere justifications and collects limited data from these reviews. For its on-site reviews, SBA does not collect sample data on lenders' use of the credit elsewhere criteria. For its off-site reviews, SBA collected sample data on lenders' use of the credit elsewhere criteria based on 250 such reviews conducted in fiscal year 2016. For these reviews, SBA asked lenders to self-report a short description of the credit elsewhere justifications used for an SBA-selected sample of 10 loans.[38] However, as discussed earlier, SBA did not request or examine loan files as part of these off-site reviews and did not follow up with lenders or review loan files to ensure the validity of the self-reported reasons.

One reason why SBA does not routinely collect complete information on lenders' use of the credit elsewhere criteria is that SBA's loan origination system, E-Tran, is not equipped to record or tabulate this information. In addition, according to an SBA official, on-site reviews do not collect data on the credit elsewhere criteria because the loans reviewed are judgmentally selected and would not accurately represent the larger population.

Federal internal control standards state that management should use quality information to achieve the entity's objectives. To do so, management should identify the information needed to achieve the objectives and address the risks, obtain relevant data from reliable internal and external sources in a timely manner, and process the obtained data into quality information.[39] More robust information on lenders' credit elsewhere justifications, including the credit elsewhere criteria, would allow SBA to evaluate patterns in lender practices related to the credit elsewhere requirement and, in turn, help the agency ensure compliance with the requirement. In this context, generalizable data, which can be collected through random sampling, or complete data through required

---

[38] SBA's loan sample selection process gives more weight to loans with larger approval amounts and more recently disbursed loans (as of the time of the review). Data collected may also give more weight to loans that were disbursed using a loan agent and loans that were disbursed in certain industry groups.

[39] GAO-14-704G.

reporting for every loan would allow SBA to better understand patterns in lender practices across the 7(a) program. Further, nongeneralizable data, which are available through SBA's current off- and on-site review processes, would allow SBA to examine specific groups of lenders and could help SBA determine if it is necessary to collect additional data.

SBA Has Not Conducted Analysis to Determine If There Are Any Patterns of Noncompliance or Identified Lenders That May Be at Risk

SBA does not analyze the limited data it collects to help it monitor lenders' compliance with the credit elsewhere requirement. According to agency officials, SBA has not performed lender-level analyses of the criteria lenders use for their credit elsewhere justifications. Additionally, SBA has not analyzed 7(a) lenders' use of the "other factors" criterion— that is, factors not specified in the other criteria that, in the lender's opinion, cannot be overcome except for the guarantee—for example, by collecting data on the frequency of its use or examining why lenders rely on it. While some 7(a) lenders told us they avoided relying on the "other factors" criterion because it was vague and open to interpretation, some lenders have used it when a borrower's profile did not meet any of the other criteria. For example, one lender stated that this criterion was used for a borrower who was no longer a start-up but had experienced fluctuations in cash flow due to relocation or change in ownership. Another lender stated that the criterion was used more frequently during the 2007-2009 financial recession to extend financing to borrowers whose owners had experienced a home foreclosure but were otherwise sound.

Federal internal control standards state that management should establish and operate monitoring activities to monitor the internal control system and evaluate the results.[40] Analyzing data on lenders' use of the credit elsewhere criteria as part of its monitoring procedures could help

---

[40] GAO-14-704G.

SBA determine whether there are patterns in lender practices related to the criteria that could predict lender noncompliance. For example, SBA could analyze lenders' use of the criteria along with lender review results and other data on loan characteristics and performance to determine whether certain patterns indicate that a lender might be applying the requirement inconsistently. Additionally, such analysis could inform SBA's selection of which lenders to review by improving its ability to identify lenders at risk of noncompliance with the credit elsewhere requirement. Better selection criteria for its lender reviews could, in turn, improve identification and remediation of such noncompliance, helping ensure that the 7(a) program serves its target population.

LENDERS GENERALLY VIEW CREDIT ELSEWHERE CRITERIA AS ADEQUATE, AND SBA HAS IMPLEMENTED NEW PROCEDURES FOR REVIEWING ELIGIBILITY

Lenders Said Credit Elsewhere Criteria are Generally Adequate for Determining Borrower Eligibility

Representatives at 8 of the 11 lenders that we contacted said they believed that SBA's current credit elsewhere criteria are adequate in targeting small business borrowers who cannot obtain credit at reasonable terms.[41] Representatives of these lenders also agreed that the criteria generally serve the types of small businesses that would otherwise have trouble obtaining conventional credit, such as new businesses or those with

---

[41] Two lenders that represented a trade group commented that the criteria did cover many of the common reasons for offering a 7(a) loan, but they did not opine on whether the criteria were adequate. One other lender questioned whether the 7(a) program needed a credit elsewhere test explaining that the 7(a) loan program was slower to process and more expensive than a conventional loan. The lender representative added that borrowers who could get conventional financing would not take a 7(a) loan. Also, the sample of 11 lenders, of which 9 lenders were selected using a random process that concentrated on larger lenders and two additional lenders we interviewed representing an industry group, was nongeneralizable to the total population of 7(a) lenders. See appendix I for more information on lender selection.

a shortage of collateral. One lender representative told us its most commonly used criterion related to the overall time in business because of the higher risk of failure. Another lender representative cited the lack of collateral as the most common criterion used. Additionally, representatives at an industry association told us that one of the most commonly used criteria was the one related to loan maturity and many small businesses seek 7(a) loans because they offer repayment terms of up to 10 years, compared to 1 to 3 years for conventional loans.

Representatives of two other lenders suggested that the credit elsewhere criteria should not be overly prescriptive, which could limit lenders' ability to make 7(a) loans to some businesses. For example, one representative said the credit elsewhere criteria should remain flexible because banks have different lending policies.

In addition, representatives at three lenders indicated that they were hesitant to use the "other factors" criterion. One lender believed the requirement was open to interpretation and could be used inappropriately with lenders determining their own individual conventional loan policies. Another lender commented that the criterion was vague and rarely used by his institution, noting that SBA should provide some additional guidance on its use.

Factors Such as Lender Policies and Economic Conditions Also Affect Lenders' Decisions to Offer a SBA 7(a) Loan

Lenders consider multiple factors in determining whether to offer small businesses a conventional loan or a 7(a) loan, according to stakeholders with whom we spoke. For example, representatives at an industry association stated that a bank goes through several analyses to determine what loan product to offer the borrower. These representatives stated that the credit elsewhere requirement is embedded in the analysis a bank performs, such as whether the borrower qualifies for a loan and has a financial need for an SBA loan and whether the 7(a) program is right for that borrower.

SBA Has Issued New Procedures for Reviewing Liquidity of Small Business Borrowers, and Additional Lender Training Is Underway

Representatives at two other lenders also stated that many small businesses have already been turned down for conventional loans before they seek a 7(a) loan. One representative noted that the "reasonable rates and terms" component of the 7(a) program was important as it allows lenders to look more broadly at a borrower's needs. For instance, the representative explained, lenders can assess whether repayment terms are reasonable given a particular borrower's situation and the resources the borrower will have to repay the loan.

Economic conditions also affect lending policies, including whether borrowers qualify for a conventional loan, according to representatives at seven lenders with whom we spoke. For example, during the recent economic downturn, banks tightened their underwriting standards for small businesses and were less willing to lend without a government guarantee, according to one lender representative.

SBA has issued revised primary operational guidance for the 7(a) program, effective January 1, 2018.[42] As discussed previously, lenders are required to make a determination that the desired credit is not available to the applicant from nonfederal sources. Under the previous guidance, the lender had to determine that some or the entire loan was not available from nonfederal sources or the resources of the applicant business. However under the revised guidance, the scope of nonfederal sources a lender must review was further defined to include sources both related and unrelated to the applicant. The updated guidance states that lenders must consider:

---

[42] SBA, SBA SOP 50 10 5 (J), Lender and Development Company Loan Programs, (Jan. 1, 2018).

- Nonfederal sources related to the applicant, including the liquidity of owners of 20 percent or more of the equity of the applicant, their spouses and minor children, and the applicant itself[43]; or
- Nonfederal sources unrelated to the applicant, including conventional lenders or other sources of credit.

Representatives of five lenders told us they have been determining how to interpret the new procedures with a few stating they would like additional guidance, including what information to retain in the file. Representatives of two lenders stated that there is some ambiguity in how to determine nonfederal resources and how to assess whether small business owners have too many available liquid resources to qualify for a 7(a) loan. One representative said that lenders can have different interpretations of what constitutes "available resources," which is not specified in the new SOP. As a result, he said, there may be some confusion about how to assess family members of the borrower who have high net worths and whether the borrower should decline a family member contribution to qualify for an SBA loan. A representative of one lender stated that lenders will not know what SBA expects until loans are approved under the new procedures, default, and are then reviewed. Another lender's representative suggested additional guidance on documentation, such as whether the bank must obtain a personal financial statement for each owner of the business.

A SBA staff told us SBA has provided multiple training presentations to SBA staff, lenders, and trade associations on the statutory changes to the credit elsewhere requirements and standard operating procedure updates.[44] These have included a presentation at a trade association conference, four

---

[43] SBA Policy Notice 5000-17057, effective April 3, 2018 increased the minimum percentage ownership at which owners are subject to personal liquidity consideration from 10 percent to 20 percent. The liquidity of the owner includes the liquid assets of the owner's spouse and any minor children. See SBA, SBA POLICY NOTICE 5000-17057, REVISED GUIDANCE ON CREDIT ELSEWHERE AND OTHER PROVISIONS IN SOP 50 10 5(J), 1 (Apr. 3, 2018).

[44] According to SBA, these presentations included changes to the credit elsewhere requirement in the Veteran Entrepreneurship Act of 2015 and the subsequent standard operating procedure updates (both versions I and J).

monthly conference calls for SBA staff, and two conference calls for SBA lenders. SBA staff said SBA also plans to hold monthly training sessions with SBA field offices, quarterly training sessions with the industry, and at least four training sessions in 2018 at lender trade conferences. Additionally, a representative from an industry association told us it is providing industry training on SBA's revised procedures, including the credit elsewhere liquidity requirement.

CONCLUSION

SBA's 7(a) loan program is required to serve creditworthy small business borrowers who cannot obtain credit through a conventional lender at reasonable terms, and SBA largely relies on lenders with delegated authority to make credit elsewhere determinations. However, although there is a high rate of lender noncompliance with the credit elsewhere documentation requirement, SBA does not require its reviewers to document their assessment of the policies and procedures lenders use to meet the requirement. Without better information from lender reviews on how lenders are implementing the requirement to document their credit elsewhere decisions, SBA may be limited in its ability to promote compliance with requirements and, in turn, use such information to help ensure that 7(a) loans are reaching their target population.

Furthermore, SBA does not routinely collect or analyze information on the criteria used for credit elsewhere justifications to evaluate patterns in lender practices. SBA recently began collecting some information on lenders' use of the criteria, but this information is limited, and SBA does not analyze the information that it does collect to better understand lenders' practices. Without more robust information and analysis, SBA may be limited in its ability to understand how lenders are using the credit elsewhere criteria and whether 7(a) loans are reaching borrowers who cannot obtain credit from other sources at reasonable terms.

RECOMMENDATIONS FOR EXECUTIVE ACTION

We are making the following three recommendations to SBA.

The Administrator of SBA should require reviewers to consistently document their assessments of a lender's policies and practices. (Recommendation 1)

The Administrator of SBA should use its on-site and off-site reviews to routinely collect information on lenders' use of credit elsewhere criteria as part of its monitoring of lender practices related to the credit elsewhere requirement. (Recommendation 2)

The Administrator of SBA should analyze information on lenders' use of credit elsewhere criteria obtained from its reviews to identify lenders that may be at greater risk of noncompliance and to inform its selection of lenders for further review for credit elsewhere compliance. (Recommendation 3)

AGENCY COMMENTS AND OUR EVALUATION

We provided a draft of this chapter for review and comment. SBA's written comments are reprinted in appendix IV. SBA generally agreed with the recommendations. SBA also provided additional comments on certain statements in the draft report, which are summarized below with our responses.

- SBA noted that the draft Highlights did not discuss how credit elsewhere is determined for nondelegated loans. We have not revised the Highlights in response to this comment because our review focused on delegated lenders. In the body of the report we note that approximately 70 percent of 7(a) loans are approved under delegated authority. We also refer to SBA's nondelegated loans in the report for additional context.

- According to SBA, the statement on our draft Highlights did not fully reflect its monitoring of lender compliance. SBA identified a variety of reviews it uses in addition to on-site reviews by third party contractors, which we discuss in the body of the report. We have modified the Highlights to reflect these other reviews.
- Also in reference to the draft Highlights, SBA stated that it provides oversight on every on-site lender review and that an SBA employee is present as a subject-matter expert on every review. We revised the Highlights by adding that SBA provides oversight to the on-site reviews conducted by third-party contractors.
- In response to a statement in our draft report that SBA guarantees loans to small businesses for working capital and other general business purposes, SBA commented that working capital generally is not the primary purpose for SBA-guaranteed loans. We did not revise the statement because SBA's SOP 50 10 5 (version J) specifies that SBA's 7(a) loan proceeds may be used for permanent working capital and revolving working capital, among other things.
- In relation to a footnote in our report that mentions two lender reviews for which we did not receive documentation, SBA stated that on February 15, 2018, it provided documentation to us related to the reviews and that we had confirmed its receipt. However, the text in the footnote in question refers to two targeted lender reviews from 2016 that included corrective actions. The information SBA provided to us on February 15, 2018, was related to on-site reviews conducted in 2016. As a result, we did not revise the footnote.

SBA's letter also contained technical comments that we incorporated as appropriate.

We are sending copies of this chapter to congressional committees, agencies, and other interested parties.

William B. Shear
Director, Financial Markets and Community Investment

List of Committees

The Honorable James Risch
Chairman

The Honorable Benjamin Cardin
Ranking Member
Committee on Small Business and Entrepreneurship
United States Senate

The Honorable James Lankford
Chairman

The Honorable Christopher Coons
Ranking Member
Subcommittee on Financial Services and General Government
Committee on Appropriations
United States Senate

The Honorable Steve Chabot
Chairman

The Honorable Nydia Velázquez
Ranking Member
Committee on Small Business
House of Representatives

The Honorable Tom Graves
Chairman

The Honorable Mike Quigley
Ranking Member
Subcommittee on Financial Services and General Government
Committee on Appropriations
House of Representatives

APPENDIX I: OBJECTIVES, SCOPE, AND METHODOLOGY

This chapter discusses (1) 7(a) lending to selected categories of small business borrowers from fiscal years 2007 through 2016; (2) how the Small Business Administration (SBA) monitors lenders' compliance with the credit elsewhere requirement; (3) the extent to which SBA evaluates trends in lender practices related to the credit elsewhere requirement; and (4) lenders' views on the criteria used to determine eligibility for 7(a) loans and other issues related to the 7(a) program.

For background on the 7(a) program and the credit elsewhere requirement, we reviewed the legislative history of the 7(a) program and our previous reports.[45] We also interviewed officials from SBA's Office of Credit Risk Management on guidance provided to 7(a) lenders.

For background on constraints in the small business credit market, we reviewed recent academic literature on the characteristics of small businesses that historically have had more difficulty accessing credit. In addition, we reviewed recent studies published by the Federal Reserve Banks of Atlanta; Cleveland; Kansas City; and New York.

To describe the population of borrowers served by the 7(a) program, we selected characteristics (such as gender, minority status, and percentage of new business) that we used in our 2007 report and that were the subject of the recent studies by Federal Reserve Banks.[46] We obtained and analyzed SBA loan-level data to describe 7(a) loans and borrowers. Specifically, SBA provided us with 581,393 records from its administrative data systems, which contained information on all loans approved and disbursed in fiscal years 2007 through 2016. The SBA data included various types of information describing each loan, including the total gross approval amount; the amount guaranteed by SBA; the loan term; and the interest rate; delivery method; and status of the loan. The SBA data also included information on borrower characteristics:

---

[45] GAO, *Small Business Administration: Additional Guidance on Documenting Credit Elsewhere Decisions Could Improve 7(a) Program Oversight*, GAO-09-228 (Washington, D.C.: Feb. 12, 2009) and *Small Business Administration: Additional Measures Needed to Address 7(a) Loan Program's Performance*, GAO-07-769 (Washington, D.C.: July 13, 2007).

[46] GAO-07-769.

- Age of business. Firms were classified as new (less than 2 years in operation) or existing.
- Gender. Firms were classified as 100 percent male-owned; 50 percent or greater women owned; 50 percent or less women-owned; or "unknown." Information on gender was voluntarily provided by borrowers.
- Economically distressed area. We identified borrowers in economically distressed areas by matching borrower zip codes provided by SBA to those in the 2011 through 2015 American Community Survey. We defined distressed areas as zip codes where at least 20 percent of households had incomes below the national poverty line. In about 1 percent of the cases, we were unable to classify a lender because a zip code had changed or had insufficient population to report a poverty rate. We consider 1 percent of unmatched cases to be low by data reliability standards.[47]
- Race/ethnicity. Borrowers were placed in one of nine categories of race/ethnicity, including an "unknown" category. We aggregated these to create minority, nonminority, and undetermined categories. The minority category included all borrowers who reported being a race/ethnicity other than white. The nonminority category included borrowers who reported being white. Information on race was voluntarily provided by borrowers.
- Industry. Firms were assigned a North American Industrial Classification code. These six-digit codes begin with a two-digit sector code that we used to draw more general conclusions about industries.[48]
- Geographic information. The data provided the state where the borrower is located.

---

[47] Our procedure for determining whether a zip code was economically distressed was a similar procedure to that used in our 2007 report; see GAO-07-769.

[48] For example, all industry codes beginning with 72 are part of the sector "Accommodation and Food Services." While North American Industrial Classification codes have been updated every 5 years since their implementation in 1997, these two-digit sector codes have not changed since 1997.

In addition, we obtained information from SBA on loan- and lender-level Small Business Risk Portfolio Solution scores (predictive scores) provided by Dunn & Bradstreet and Fair Isaac Company, for loans approved in fiscal year 2016, the latest available. We were able to obtain predictive scores for approximately 81 percent of the loans for which SBA had provided other information. According to SBA, some loans may not have been disbursed at the time we obtained the predictive scores and, as a result, we do not have scores associated with these loans. We analyzed the information to determine the range of predictive scores and the range of average predictive scores by lender.

To assess the reliability of loan-level data on borrower and loan characteristics and predictive scores we received from SBA, we interviewed agency officials knowledgeable about the data and reviewed related documentation. We also conducted electronic testing, including checks for outliers, missing data, and erroneous values. We determined that the data were sufficiently reliable for the purposes of describing the characteristics of borrowers who received 7(a) loans and the distribution of predictive scores.

To assess how SBA monitors lenders' compliance with the credit elsewhere requirement and criteria, we reviewed SBA's standard operating procedures and other guidance on 7(a) program regulations and lender oversight. Specifically, we reviewed SOP 50 10 5 (versions I and J) on Lender and Development Company Loan Programs, SOP 50 53(A) on Lender Supervision and Enforcement, and SOP 51 00, On-Site Lender Reviews/Examinations, as well as information and policy notices related to the credit elsewhere requirement. Additionally, we interviewed representatives including those at SBA's Office of Capital Access and Office of Credit Risk Management on lender oversight and lender review processes. We reviewed all the on-site lender review reports (40 reviews), including corrective actions or requirements related to the credit elsewhere requirement (documentation for 11 lenders), and targeted review reports that had credit elsewhere findings (7 reviews) that SBA conducted in fiscal year 2016. We also interviewed officials and reviewed recent reports from SBA's Office of Inspector General.

To assess the extent to which SBA evaluates trends in lender practices related to the credit elsewhere requirement, we interviewed SBA officials and reviewed documentation for SBA's online portal for loan origination. We also incorporated information from interviews with a nongeneralizable, nonrepresentative sample of 7(a) lenders, which we discuss below.

To obtain lenders' views on the criteria used to determine eligibility for 7(a) loans and other program-related issues, we interviewed SBA staff including from the Office of Capital Access, and representatives of the National Association of Government Guaranteed Lenders; American Bankers Association; Independent Community Bankers Association; and National Federation of Independent Businesses. We also interviewed 11 banks (one bank provided written responses) in order to obtain the lender perspective of credit elsewhere. Nine of the banks were selected by us using a random process that concentrated on larger lenders. These nine lenders selected by us represent about 13 percent of the loans approved and 16 percent of the dollars approved in 2016. In addition, we interviewed two additional banks that represented an industry group – one larger bank and one small bank. Although we partially selected at random, the lenders we interviewed should not be considered generalizable because of the small number.

We conducted this performance audit from August 2017 to June 2018 in accordance with generally accepted government auditing standards. Those standards require that we plan and perform the audit to obtain sufficient, appropriate evidence to provide a reasonable basis for our findings and conclusions based on our audit objectives. We believe that the evidence obtained provides a reasonable basis for our findings and conclusions based on our audit objectives.

APPENDIX II: SELECTED CHARACTERISTICS OF 7(A) LENDING, FISCAL YEARS 2007–2016

In this appendix, we provide information on the total amount and number of approved 7(a) loans and the top eight industry sectors receiving

7(a) loans. Data are also presented on fiscal year 2016 loan volume by state and per capita. As shown in Figure 6 below, the total amount of approved 7(a) loans decreased during the period associated with the Great Recession (2007 through 2009). From fiscal year 2009 on, the total amount of approved 7(a) loans increased until a decline in fiscal year 2012. During this timeframe, the American Recovery and Reinvestment Act of 2009 and the Small Business Jobs Act of 2010 provided fee relief and higher guaranties. The Small Business Jobs Act of 2010 also provided a temporary increase in Small Business Administration (SBA) Express loan limits to $1 million (instead of $350,000). These programs have since expired.

7(a) Loans by North American Industry Classification System (NAICS) Code

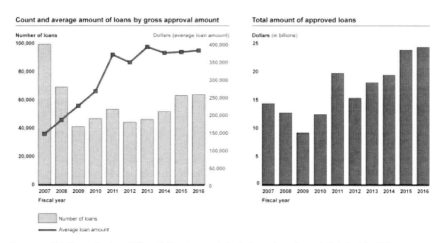

Source: GAO analysis of Small Business Administration data. | GAO-18-421.

Figure 6. Number, Average Amount, and Total Amount of 7(a) Loans Approved, Fiscal Years 2007–2016.

Table A-1. Share of the Total 7(a) Loans for the Top Eight Industrial Sectors by NAICS Code, Fiscal Years 2007–2016

NAICS code		Fiscal year										
		2007	2008	2009	2010	2011	2012	2013	2014	2015	2016	Average
72: Accommodation & Food Services	Percentage	18	18	15	14	16	16	18	18	18	18	17
44-45: Retail Trade	Percentage	20	18	15	16	15	15	15	14	14	14	15
62: Health Care & Social Assistance	Percentage	9	11	12	12	11	11	11	11	11	12	11
32-33: Manufacturing	Percentage	10	9	12	12	13	12	12	11	10	10	11
81: Other Services (except Public Administration)	Percentage	10	9	8	8	7	7	8	8	8	8	8
54: Professional, Scientific, & Technical Service	Percentage	7	9	9	9	8	8	8	7	7	7	8
42: Wholesale Trade	Percentage	6	6	7	7	8	8	7	7	7	6	7
23: Construction	Percentage	7	6	7	6	5	6	5	6	5	6	6
Total NAICS code	Percentage	85	86	85	84	82	82	83	82	80	80	82

Source: GAO analysis of Small Business Administration data. | GAO-18-421.

Notes: North American Industry Classification System (NAICS) codes range from two to six digits and increase in specificity of description as the number of digits increase. We grouped the economic sectors using the first two digits of the NAICS code.

Table A-1 shows the largest eight industrial sectors by proportion of the total amount of 7(a) loans approved, using the NAICS code. The combined share of the top eight sectors declined slightly from 85 percent to 80 percent of the total lending from fiscal years 2007 through 2016, with an average of 82 percent. During this period, the Accommodation and Food Services sector had the largest average share of total loan amount at 17 percent, followed by the Retail Trade sector at 15 percent.

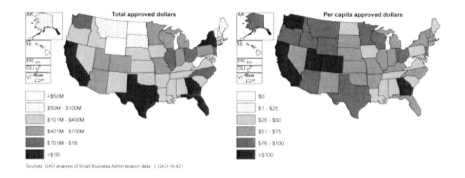

Figure 7. Fiscal Year 2016 Total Approved 7(a) Loan Dollars and Per Capita Approved Loan Dollars by State.

Approved Loan Amount and Per Capita Dollars by State

As shown in Figure 7, California; Texas; Florida; Georgia; and New York received the highest total of approved loan dollars in fiscal year 2016. The average approval amount across all loans was $380,619. Georgia and Arkansas had the largest average approval amount in 2016. Also, during this period, Utah; Colorado; Georgia; California; and Washington received the highest per capita approved loan dollars.

APPENDIX III: INFORMATION ON BORROWER CHARACTERISTICS BASED ON SBA'S PREDICTIVE SCORES

In fiscal-year 2016, creditworthiness varied widely among 7(a) program borrowers. We analyzed creditworthiness using the Small Business Administration's (SBA) Small Business Risk Portfolio Solution score (predictive score), which ranges from 70 to 300, with 300 indicating the least risky loan.[49] According to SBA, loans with scores above 180 are considered "lower risk," scores between 140 and 179 are considered "moderate risk," and scores 139 and lower are considered "higher risk." There did not appear be differences in score based on the gender of the borrower or the age of the business. While SBA relies on the Predictive Score data to identify lenders that may pose excessive risk to the SBA 7(a) portfolio, the data also provide potential insights related to lender implementation of the credit elsewhere requirement.

- Variation. We found that some 7(a) borrowers were much more creditworthy than others. In 2016, the only year for which we obtained data, the predictive score at origination varied widely among borrowers. In 2016, the scores of borrowers ranged from a low of 91 to a high of 246. However, most scores were between 171 and 203, and the median score was 188.
- Race/ethnicity. We found that there were slight differences in creditworthiness by race/ethnicity, with median scores ranging from 180 to 189 depending on the category. Specifically, loans to African Americans in 2016 had a median score of 180, and loans to Hispanics had a median score of 183. In contrast, loans to

---

[49] According to SBA, the Small Business Risk Portfolio Solution score is a portfolio management credit score that is used by SBA to predict the likelihood of severe delinquency at the loan level. These scores rank loans based on their probability of severe delinquency within a range between 70 and 300. As scores increase for a given set of loans, the probability of delinquency decreases. Also, the predictive score data is one of several components used to identify lenders that may pose a risk.

whites had a median score of 188, and loans to Asian and Pacific Islanders had a median score of 189.

- Lender size. We found that lenders with larger numbers of SBA loans tended to have slightly more creditworthy borrowers. The top 5 percent of lenders had a median average score of 187, whereas the bottom 75 percent of lenders had a median average score of 182.5. Among the top 5 percent of lenders (with 374 loans per lender on average, collectively representing about 70 percent of the loans approved), the average score ranged from 171 to 195.[50] Among all lenders, the average score ranged from 116 to 233. However, because many lenders only approved one or two loans in 2016, the average may reflect very few borrowers for that lender, making it difficult to tell whether the scores reflect a real difference between lenders.

APPENDIX IV: COMMENTS FROM THE SMALL BUSINESS ADMINISTRATION

U.S. SMALL BUSINESS ADMINISTRATION
WASHINGTON, DC 20416

May 17, 2018

Mr. William B. Shear, Director
Financial Markets and Community Investment
U.S. Government Accountability Office
Washington, D.C. 20548

---

[50] The top 5 percent represented 96 lenders, which represented approximately 70 percent of the loans approved in fiscal year 2016.

Dear Mr. Shear:

Thank you for providing the U.S. Small Business Administration (SBA) with a copy of the U.S. Government Accountability Office (GAO) draft report titled *"Small Business Loans: Additional Actions Needed to Improve Compliance with the Credit Elsewhere Requirement"* (Draft Report). The Draft Report discusses how SBA monitors lenders' compliance with the credit elsewhere requirement, the extent to which SBA has evaluated trends in lender credit elsewhere practices, and lender views on the credit elsewhere criteria. SBA generally agrees with GAO's recommendations, but has the following comments with respect to the recommendations:

(1) *The Administrator of SBA should require reviewers to consistently document their assessments of a lender's policies and practices.*

SBA has instructed reviewers to document their assessments of a lender's policies and practices. Going forward, SBA will take necessary steps to ensure that reviewers are consistent in documenting their assessments of lenders' policies and practices for complying with the credit elsewhere requirement.

(2) *The Administrator of SBA should use its on-site and off-site reviews to routinely collect information on lenders' use of credit elsewhere criteria as part of its monitoring of lender practices related to the credit elsewhere requirement.*

SBA has been collecting information on lenders' use of the credit elsewhere criteria for the reviews it conducts virtually (formerly referred to as "off-site reviews"). Going forward, SBA will also collect information on lenders' use of the credit elsewhere criteria when conducting reviews that include loan file reviews, whether performed at the lender's location (formerly referred to as "on-site reviews") or virtually.

(3) *The Administrator of SBA should analyze information on lenders' use of credit elsewhere criteria obtained from its reviews to identify lenders that may be at greater risk of noncompliance and to inform its selection for further review for credit elsewhere compliance.*

SBA currently incorporates several data elements and information from prior reviews, including Findings and deficiencies related to credit elsewhere, to inform its selection of lenders for review. SBA will incorporate data on lenders' use of the credit elsewhere

criteria obtained from reviews to determine whether further review of that lender is warranted.

In addition, SBA has the following concerns with some of the language in the Draft Report:

On the GAO Highlights page, in the first paragraph of the Draft Report, GAO states that SBA "has largely delegated authority to lenders to make 7(a) loan determinations for those borrowers who cannot obtain conventional credit at reasonable terms elsewhere." While SBA has delegated the determination of whether the applicant has credit available elsewhere to participating lenders that have been granted delegated authority, this is not the case for applications submitted to SBA on a non-delegated basis. Delegated Lenders are required, when requesting an SBA loan number, to certify to having met the credit elsewhere requirement and to have documentation to substantiate the credit elsewhere determination in the loan file. With respect to applications submitted to SBA under non-delegated processing, SBA makes the final determination as to whether the applicant has credit available elsewhere as part of its overall decision of whether to approve the request to guarantee the loan.

In the same paragraph, GAO also states that "[t]o monitor lender compliance with the 'credit elsewhere' requirement SBA primarily uses on-site reviews conducted by third-party contractors." This statement is not entirely accurate. As SBA explained to GAO in its March 23, 2018 technical comments to GAO's Statement of Facts for this review (SBA's Technical Comments), the Agency reviews lender files in multiple risk-based review approaches, including targeted reviews and ad hoc virtual file reviews. In addition, Improper Payments Elimination and Recovery Act (IPERA) and quality control reviews, which include credit elsewhere among other issues, are performed in SBA's Loan Guaranty Processing Center at time of loan approval and at the National Guaranty Purchase Center at time of guaranty purchase. Thus, SBA does not primarily use on-site reviews to monitor lender compliance with the credit elsewhere requirement. With respect to GAO's statement in the Draft Report that the on-site reviews are "conducted by third-party contractors," SBA also clarified this issue in its comments provided to GAO on March 23, 2018. On page 2 of SBA's Technical Comments, we stated that SBA provides oversight on every on-site review and an SBA employee is present as a subject matter expert on every review, regardless of the type of review. Further, all reviews are overseen by an SBA employee, and primary responsibility for oversight is the Agency's, not the contractors'.

On page 2 of the Draft Report, GAO states that "… SBA guarantees loans made by commercial lenders to small businesses for working capital and other general business purposes." Generally, working capital is not the primary purpose for SBA-guaranteed loans.

On page 15 of the Draft Report, in paragraph 2, GAO states "[a]n SBA official stated that off-site reviews followed the same procedures in fiscal year 2017 and that the agency planned to use the same procedures for these reviews in the future." SBA also clarified this issue for GAO in its March 23, 2018 Technical Comments by stating that the Office of Credit Risk Management is constantly implementing improvements to its review processes and procedures. SBA reiterates

that it routinely evaluates and revises its review processes and procedures to strengthen the effectiveness of SBA's oversight.

On page 18 of the Draft Report, Footnote 34 states that SBA did not provide documentation of lenders' responses for two of six lenders. On February 15, 2018 SBA provided a flash drive to GAO with responses for the two lenders. We received confirmation of receipt of the flash drive by GAO on February 20, 2018. GAO subsequently confirmed receipt of the documentation for the corrective action assessments for the last two lenders on March 20, 2018.

Finally, on page 23 of the Draft Report, GAO states, "[t]he new guidance states that lenders must consider nonfederal sources related to the applicant, including the liquidity of owners of 10 percent or more… ." In SBA's Technical Comments on March 23, 2018, SBA advised GAO that it was in the process of revising this guidance. SBA issued Policy Notice 5000 – 17057, effective on April 3, 2018, which changed this requirement from owners of 10 percent or more to owners of 20 percent or more.

Thank you for giving SBA the opportunity to comment on GAO's draft report, *"Small Business Loans: Additional Actions Needed to Improve Compliance with the Credit Elsewhere Requirement"* and for taking SBA's comments into consideration.

Sincerely,

William M. Manger, Jr.
Associate Administrator
Office of Capital Access

In: Small Business
Editor: Angel Becker

ISBN: 978-1-53615-969-1
© 2019 Nova Science Publishers, Inc.

Chapter 3

STATE SMALL BUSINESS CREDIT INITIATIVE: IMPLEMENTATION AND FUNDING ISSUES (UPDATED)[*]

Robert Jay Dilger

SUMMARY

Congressional interest in small business access to capital has increased in recent years because of concerns that small businesses might be prevented from accessing sufficient capital to enable them to start, continue, or expand operations and create jobs. Some have argued that the federal government should provide additional resources to assist small businesses. Others worry about the long-term adverse economic effects of spending programs that increase the federal deficit. They advocate business tax reduction, reform of financial credit market regulation, and federal fiscal restraint as the best means to assist small businesses and create jobs.

During the 111th Congress, P.L. 111-240, the Small Business Jobs Act of 2010, provided the Small Business Administration (SBA)

---

[*] This is an edited, reformatted and augmented version of Congressional Research Service, Publication No. R42581, dated April 23, 2018.

additional funding and enhanced several SBA lending programs in an effort to assist small businesses access capital. The act also authorized the Secretary of the Treasury to establish and administer a $1.5 billion State Small Business Credit Initiative (SSBCI). Treasury's role in administrating the program ended on September 27, 2017.

The SSBCI provided funding, allocated by formula and distributed in one-third increments, to states, territories, and eligible municipalities (hereinafter referred to as states) to expand existing or create new state small business investment programs, including state capital access programs, collateral support programs, loan participation programs, loan guarantee programs, and venture capital programs. In most instances, the initial round of funding (called a tranche) took place in FY2011. Most states received their second tranche during FY2013. As of December 31, 2016, 98% of total allocated funding had been disbursed to the states and all 57 participants had received their first tranche, 56 had received at least two tranches, and 53 had received their third and final tranche.

SSBCI participants were expected to leverage their SSBCI funds to generate new small business lending that is at least 10 times the amount of their SSBCI funds. As of December 31, 2016, SSBCI participants had leveraged $8.95 in new financing for every $1 in SSBCI funds. Forty-seven states; American Samoa; the District of Columbia; Guam; the Northern Mariana Islands; Puerto Rico; the U.S. Virgin Islands; Anchorage, Alaska; two consortiums of municipalities in North Dakota; and a consortium of municipalities in Wyoming participate in the program.

The Obama Administration recommended in its FY2015, FY2016, and FY2017 budget requests that another $1.5 billion round of funding take place, with $1 billion competitively awarded to states and $500 million awarded "by a need-based formula based on economic factors such as job losses and pace of economic recovery." Legislation with provisions similar to the Obama Administration's proposal was introduced during the 113th Congress (H.R. 4556 and S. 2285), the 114th Congress (S. 1901, H.R. 5144, and H.R. 5672), and the 115th Congress (S. 1897).

This chapter examines the SSBCI and its implementation, including Treasury's response to initial program audits conducted by the U.S. Government Accountability Office (GAO) and Treasury's Office of Inspector General (OIG). These initial audits suggest that SSBCI participants generally met the statute's requirements but that there were some compliance problems. They also indicate that Treasury's program oversight could have been improved and that performance measures are needed to assess the program's efficacy.

OVERVIEW

Congressional interest in small business access to capital has increased in recent years because of concerns that small businesses might be prevented from accessing sufficient capital to enable them to start, continue, or expand operations and create jobs. Some have argued that the federal government should provide additional resources to assist small businesses. They argue that in recent years many financial institutions have tightened their small business lending standards in reaction to higher loan default rates and higher percentages of loans in arrears resulting largely from relatively weak economic conditions in many parts of the nation. They also assert that the federal government should intervene because it is relatively difficult for many small businesses, including some with excellent credit histories, to access the capital they need to expand their operations.[1]

Others worry about the long-term adverse economic effects of spending programs that increase the federal deficit. They advocate business tax reduction, reform of financial credit market regulation, and federal fiscal restraint as the best means to assist small businesses and create jobs.[2]

During the 111th Congress, P.L. 111-240, the Small Business Jobs Act of 2010, provided the Small Business Administration (SBA) additional funding, authorized several SBA pilot programs, and enhanced several of the SBA's lending programs in an effort to assist small businesses access capital.[3] The act also authorized the Secretary of the Treasury to establish and administer a $30 billion Small Business Lending Fund (SBLF), in

---

[1] The Obama White House, "American Jobs Act," at https://obamawhitehouse.archives. gov/sites/default/files/jobs_act.pdf; and The Obama White House, "Startup America Initiative," at https://obamawhitehouse.archives.gov/ economy/business/startup-america.

[2] U.S. Congress, House Committee on Financial Services, *To Create the Small Business Lending Fund Program to Direct the Secretary of the Treasury to make Capital Investments in Eligible Institutions in order to Increase the Availability of Credit for Small Businesses, and for other Purposes*, report to accompany H.R. 5297, 111th Cong., 2nd sess., May 27, 2010, H.Rept. 111-499 (Washington: GPO, 2010), pp. 37, 38; and National Federation of Independent Businesses, "Issues: The Economy," Washington, DC, at http://www.nfib.com/advocacy/economy.

[3] For further information and analysis concerning the Small Business Jobs Act of 2010, see CRS Report R40985, *Small Business: Access to Capital and Job Creation*, by Robert Jay Dilger.

which $4.0 billion was issued to encourage community banks with less than $10 billion in assets to increase their lending to small businesses, and a $1.5 billion State Small Business Credit Initiative (SSBCI).[4] The act limited Treasury's role in administrating the SSBCI program to seven years from enactment (September 27, 2010). As a result, Treasury role in administering the program sunset on September 27, 2017.

The SSBCI provided funding, allocated through a statutorily created formula and distributed in one-third increments (called tranches), to states, the District of Columbia, eligible territories, and eligible municipalities (hereinafter states) to expand existing or create new state small business investment programs, including capital access programs, collateral support programs, loan participation programs, loan guarantee programs, and venture capital programs. In most instances, states received their initial tranche in FY2011, with more than $366 million in SSBCI funds transferred to states.[5] At that time, Treasury anticipated providing another $859 million in SSBCI funds to states in FY2012.[6] However, because it took states longer than anticipated to expend, transfer, or obligate their first tranche of SSBCI funds, Treasury transferred less SSBCI funding to states in FY2012 than in FY2011 ($187 million, for a total of $553 million).[7] Treasury transferred $364 million in SSBCI funds to states (totaling $917 million) in FY2013, $229 million in FY2014 (totaling $1.146 billion), $216 million in FY2015 (totaling $1.362 billion), and $50 million in FY2016 (totaling $1.412 billion).[8]

---

[4] For further information and analysis concerning the Small Business Lending Fund, see CRS Report R42045, *The Small Business Lending Fund*, by Robert Jay Dilger.

[5] U.S. Office of Management and Budget, *Appendix, Budget of the U.S. Government, FY2013: Department of the Treasury*, p. 1061, at http://www.gpo.gov/fdsys/pkg/BUDGET-2013-APP/pdf/BUDGET-2013-APP.pdf.

[6] Ibid.

[7] U.S. Office of Management and Budget, *Appendix, Budget of the U.S. Government, FY2014: Department of the Treasury*, p. 991, at https://www.gpo.gov/fdsys/pkg/BUDGET-2014-APP/pdf/BUDGET-2014-APP.pdf.

[8] U.S. Department of the Treasury, *State Small Business Credit Initiative, FY 2016: President's Budget*, p. 6, at http://www.treasury.gov/about/budget-performance/CJ16/18.%20SSBCI%20FY%202016%20CJ.pdf; U.S. Department of the Treasury, *State Small Business Credit Initiative: A Summary of States' Quarterly Reports as of September 30, 2015*, p. 1, at https://www.treasury.gov/resource-center/sb-programs/DocumentsSBLFTransactions/SSBCI%20Quarterly%20Report%20Summary%20September%202015_FINAL.pdf; and U.S. Department of the Treasury, *State Small Business Credit Initiative: A Summary of*

As of December 31, 2016, Treasury had disbursed $1.43 billion, or about 98%, of the $1.45 billion available to states ($1.5 billion minus Treasury's administrative costs).[9] As of December 31, 2016, all 57 participants had received their first tranche, 56 had received their second tranche, and 53 had received their third tranche.[10]

States were expected to leverage their SSBCI funds to generate new small business lending that is at least 10 times the amount of their SSBCI funds (a leverage ratio of 10:1). As of December 31, 2016, SSBCI participants had leveraged $8.95 in new financing for every $1 in SSBCI funds.[11] There are 57 participants: 47 states; American Samoa; the District of Columbia; Guam; the Northern Mariana Islands; Puerto Rico; the U.S. Virgin Islands; Anchorage, Alaska; two consortiums of municipalities in North Dakota; and a consortium of municipalities in Wyoming.

During congressional consideration, advocates argued that the SBLF and SSBCI will promote economic growth and job creation by enhancing small business access to capital. Opponents argued that the SBLF and SSBCI did not address the need to stimulate demand for credit by small businesses, which, in the opponents' view, is the core issue affecting the role of small business in job creation. They argued that "the solutions to America's economic problems do not lie in more taxpayer-funded bailouts" and advocated small business tax reductions as a more effective means to stimulate job creation and economic growth.[12]

States' Quarterly Reports as of September 30, 2016, p. 1, at https://www.treasury.gov/resource-center/sb-programs/Documents/SSBCI%20Quarterly%20Report%20Summary%20September%202016_Final.pdf.

[9] U.S. Department of the Treasury, *State Small Business Credit Initiative: A Summary of States' Quarterly Reports as of December 31, 2016*, p. 1, at https://www.treasury.gov/resource-center/sb-programs/Documents/ SSBCI_Quarterly_Report_Summary_December_2016.pdf.

[10] Ibid.

[11] U.S. Department of the Treasury, *State Small Business Credit Initiative: A Summary of States' 2016 Annual Reports*, p. 2, at https://www.treasury.gov/resource-center/sb-programs/Documents/SSBCI%20Summary%20of%20States%20Annual%20Report%202016_508%20Compliant.pdf.

[12] U.S. Congress, House Committee on Financial Services, *To Create the Small Business Lending Fund Program to Direct the Secretary of the Treasury to make Capital Investments in Eligible Institutions in order to Increase the Availability of Credit for Small Businesses, and for other Purposes*, report to accompany H.R. 5297, 111th Cong., 2nd sess., May 27, 2010, H.Rept. 111-499 (Washington: GPO, 2010), pp. 37, 38.

It is difficult to determine the full extent of the SSBCI's effect on small business lending. As of December 31, 2016, states had spent or obligated about 88% of the $1.45 billion available ($1.27 billion of $1.45 billion), which is sufficient to provide an indication of the program's impact on small business lending.[13] However, determining the program's influence on small business lending is likely to be more suggestive than definitive because differentiating the SSBCI's effect on small business lending from other factors, such as changes in the lender's local economy, is methodologically challenging, especially given the relatively small amount of financing involved relative to the national market for small business loans. The SSBCI's $1.5 billion in financing represents about 0.24% of outstanding non-agricultural small business loans.[14]

Treasury has reported that SSBCI funds supported more than 21,000 loans and investments in small business amounting to over $10.7 billion, with more than 80% of the funds and investments made to small businesses with 10 or fewer full-time employees. Treasury has also reported that small business owners indicated that the funds helped them to create or retain 240,669 jobs (79,193 new jobs and 161,476 retained jobs).[15]

The Obama Administration recommended in its FY2015, FY2016, and FY2017 budget requests that another $1.5 billion round of funding take place. Under their proposal, $1 billion would have been competitively awarded to states "best able to target local market needs, promote inclusion, attract private capital for start-up and scale-up businesses,

---

[13] U.S. Department of the Treasury, *State Small Business Credit Initiative: A Summary of States' Quarterly Reports as of December 31, 2016*, p. 1, at https://www.treasury.gov/resource-center/sb-programs/Documents/ SSBCI_Quarterly_Report_Summary_December_2016.pdf. In addition, as of December 31, 2016, 34 states reported that they had spent about $279.9 million for new State Small Business Credit Initiative (SSBCI) supported loans and investments using recycled SSBCI funds generated from SSBCI loan repayments and returns on SSBCI investments.

[14] Federal Deposit Insurance Corporation, "Statistics on Depository Institutions," at https://www5.fdic.gov/sdi/main.asp?formname=compare. As of December 31, 2017, there was $627.8 billion in outstanding non-agricultural small business loans (defined as the sum of "total loans secured by nonfarm nonresidential properties of $1,000,000 or less" and "total commercial and industrial loans to U.S. addressees of $1,000,000 or less").

[15] U.S. Department of the Treasury, *State Small Business Credit Initiative: A Summary of States' 2016 Annual Reports*, pp. 2, 3, 15, at https://www.treasury.gov/resource-center/sb-programs/Documents/SSBCI%20Summary%20of%20States%20Annual%20Report%202016_508%20Compliant.pdf.

strengthen regional entrepreneurial ecosystems, and evaluate results," and $500 million awarded "by formula based on economic factors such as job losses and pace of economic recovery."[16]

Legislation containing provisions similar to the Obama Administration's proposal was introduced during the 113th Congress (H.R. 4556, the Small Business Access to Capital Act of 2014, and S. 2285, its companion bill in the Senate), the 114th Congress (S. 1901, the Small Business Access to Capital Act of 2015, H.R. 5144, the Jumpstart Housing Opportunities Utilizing Small Enterprises Act of 2016, and H.R. 5672, the Small Business Access to Capital Act of 2016), and the 115th Congress (S. 1897, the Small Business Access to Capital Act of 2017).[17]

This chapter examines the SSBCI and its implementation, including Treasury's response to initial program audits conducted by the U.S. Government Accountability Office (GAO) and Treasury's Office of Inspector General (OIG). These audits suggested that states generally met the statute's requirements but that there were some compliance problems. They also indicated that Treasury's oversight of the program could have been improved and that performance measures are needed to assess the program's efficacy.

---

[16] U.S. Office of Management and Budget, *The Appendix, Budget of the United States Government, Fiscal Year 2017: Department of the Treasury*, pp. 1034, 1035, at https://www.gpo.gov/fdsys/pkg/BUDGET-2017-APP/pdf/BUDGET2017-APP.pdf.

[17] H.R. 5144, the Jumpstart HOUSE Act of 2016, added a provision (SEC. 3. Support for affordable housing projects) designed to facilitate the financing of affordable housing projects: " ... to develop, acquire, construct, rehabilitate, maintain, operate, or manage housing projects that provide housing that is affordable for low- or moderate-income households, as determined by the Secretary, in consultation with the Secretary of Housing and Urban Development."

H.R. 5672, the Small Business Access to Capital Act of 2016, added a provision (SEC. 2. New tranches of capital for successful State programs) that would have included competitive award factors designed to provide preference to participants based on their plans to (I) leverage private sector capital; (II) create and retain jobs during the 2-year period beginning on the date of the award; (III) serve small businesses that have been incorporated or in operation for not more than 5 years; (IV) serve low- or moderate-income communities; (V) serve minority- and women-owned small businesses; and establish or continue a robust self-evaluation of their use of awarded funds; provide non-federal funds in excess of the amount required; and the extent to which the participant expended, obligated, or transferred their 2010 allocation.

LEGISLATIVE ORIGINS

On January 27, 2010, President Obama announced in his State of the Union Address that because "financing remains difficult for small business owners across the country, even those that are making a profit," he would send Congress several legislative proposals designed to enhance small business access to capital, including a proposal to establish a $30 billion SBLF.[18] On May 7, 2010, the Obama Administration sent Congress draft legislation to establish the SBLF and the SSBCI.[19]

On May 13, 2010, Representative (now Senator) Gary Peters introduced H.R. 5302, the State Small Business Credit Initiative Act of 2010. The bill would have authorized a $2 billion SSBCI modeled on the President's SSBCI proposal. That same day, then-Representative Barney Frank, then-chair of the House Committee on Financial Services, introduced H.R. 5297, initially titled the Small Business Lending Fund Act of 2010. Based on the President's SBLF proposal, the bill was designed to encourage lending to small businesses by creating a $30 billion SBLF to make capital investments in eligible community banks with total assets of less than $10 billion.[20] On May 18, 2010, the Committee on Financial Services held a hearing on H.R. 5297 and, the following day, approved the bill, 42-23, as amended.[21] Perhaps the most significant amendment approved was an amended version of the $2 billion State Small Business Credit Initiative Act of 2010. It was approved by a vote of 39-23.[22]

---

[18] The Obama White House, "Remarks by the President in State of the Union Address," at https://obamawhitehouse.archives.gov/the-press-office/remarks-president-state-union-address.

[19] U.S. Congress, House Committee on Financial Services, *To Create the Small Business Lending Fund Program to Direct the Secretary of the Treasury to make Capital Investments in Eligible Institutions in order to Increase the Availability of Credit for Small Businesses, and for other Purposes*, report to accompany H.R. 5297, 111th Cong., 2nd sess., May 27, 2010, H.Rept. 111-499 (Washington: GPO, 2010), p. 17.

[20] Ibid., p. 18.

[21] U.S. Congress, House Committee on Financial Services, *Incentives to Promote Small Business Lending, Jobs, and Economic Growth*, 111th Cong., 2nd sess., May 18, 2010, Serial No. 111-137 (Washington: GPO, 2010).

[22] U.S. Congress, House Committee on Financial Services, *To Create the Small Business Lending Fund Program to Direct the Secretary of the Treasury to make Capital Investments in Eligible Institutions in order to Increase the Availability of Credit for Small Businesses, and*

SBLF and SSBCI advocates argued that the programs were necessary because "many companies, particularly small businesses, claim that it is becoming harder to get new loans to keep their business operating and that banks are tightening requirements or cutting off existing lines of even when the businesses are up to date on their loan repayments."[23] In their view, the SBLF and SSBCI would promote economic growth and job creation by enhancing small business access to capital.

The House Committee on Financial Services' Republicans indicated in the report accompanying H.R. 5297 that they "were unanimous in our opposition to this misguided legislation."[24] They argued that the SBLF and SSBCI did not address what they considered to be the core issue affecting small business job creation during the economic recovery—the need to stimulate demand for credit by small businesses.[25] They argued that the bill would fail to help small businesses or create jobs, would succeed only in adding billions of dollars to the national debt, and concluded that "the solutions to America's economic problems do not lie in more taxpayer-funded bailouts."[26] Instead of supporting federal spending programs to enhance small business access to capital, they advocated an extension of a series of small business tax credits as a more effective means to stimulate small business job creation and economic growth.[27]

On June 14, 2010, the House Committee on Rules issued a rule for H.R. 5297 (H.Res. 1436) that provided that "in the engrossment of H.R. 5297, the Clerk shall add the text of H.R. 5486, as passed by the House, at the end of H.R. 5297 and that H.R. 5486 shall be laid on the table."[28] H.R. 5486, To Amend the Internal Revenue Code of 1986 to Provide Tax Incentives for Small Business Job Creation, and for Other Purposes, included several tax incentives for small businesses and several revenue-

---

for other Purposes, report to accompany H.R. 5297, 111th Cong., 2nd sess., May 27, 2010, H.Rept. 111-499 (Washington: GPO, 2010), pp. 21, 22.
[23] Ibid., p. 16.
[24] Ibid., p. 18.
[25] Ibid., p. 37.
[26] Ibid., p. 38.
[27] Ibid.
[28] H.Res. 1436. A second rule (H.Res. 1448) was issued on June 16, 2010, to allow consideration of two amendments that were revised to comply with House "pay-go" rules.

raising provisions designed to offset the costs of the tax incentives. Also, at that time, the House Committee on Rules posted on its website legislative language for a proposed amendment in the nature of a substitute to H.R. 5297, as reported, which included a proposed $1 billion Small Business Early-Stage Investment Program.

On June 17, 2010, the House passed H.R. 5297, by a vote of 241-182. The engrossed bill, retitled the Small Business Jobs and Credit Act of 2010, also included the language in H.R. 5486 and the Small Business Early-Stage Investment Program, as well as the $30 billion SBLF and $2 billion SSBCI.

The arguments presented in the House report accompanying the bill, both for and against the bill's passage, were also presented during House floor debate. For example, advocates argued that the SSBCI would "increase small business lending which will retain and create jobs."[29] Opponents argued that the bill "is repeating the same failed initiatives that have helped our national debt grow to $13 billion in the past two years" and did not address what they viewed as the top problem facing small businesses—"the lack of sales and demand."[30]

The House-passed version of H.R. 5297 was placed on the Senate Legislative Calendar on June 18, 2010. Following a series of votes on motions to invoke cloture on several amendments in the nature of a substitute to H.R. 5297 and the August recess, the Senate passed an amended version of the bill (S.Amdt. 4594, an amendment in the nature of a substitute for H.R. 5297) on September 16, 2010, by a vote of 61-38.[31]

---

[29] Rep. Melissa Bean, "The Small Business Jobs and Credit Act of 2010," House debate, *Congressional Record*, vol. 156, no. 90 (June 16, 2010), p. H4514.

[30] Rep. Randy Neugebauer, "The Small Business Jobs and Credit Act of 2010," House debate, *Congressional Record*, vol. 156, no. 90 (June 16, 2010), p. H4514, H4515.

[31] On June 29, 2010, cloture on a motion to proceed to H.R. 5297 was invoked in the Senate, by a vote of 66-33. That same day, Sen. Harry Reid proposed a motion to commit H.R. 5297 to the Senate Committee on Finance with instructions to report back forthwith S.Amdt. 4407, an amendment in the nature of a substitute, which included the Small Business Lending Fund (SBLF) and most of the provisions later included in S.Amdt. 4594. In response to perceived opposition to the SBLF, S.Amdt. 4407 was withdrawn on July 21, 2010. In its place, Sen. Harry Reid proposed for Sen. George LeMieux S.Amdt. 4500, to establish the Small Business Lending Fund Program. He also proposed for Sen. Max Baucus S.Amdt. 4499, an amendment in the nature of a substitute, which contained S.Amdt. 4407, with modifications, minus the SBLF. On July 22, 2010, cloture on S.Amdt. 4500 was invoked in

and the borrower, although in some cases loan terms are subject to state approval and, in many cases, the state and lender will discuss and negotiate loan terms and guarantee options prior to reaching agreement to approve the loan and issue a guarantee.[43]

Subject to some restrictions, loans in SSBCI state loan guarantee programs may be used for most business purposes. In addition, SSBCI state loan guarantee programs must target an average borrower size of 500 employees or fewer and may not guarantee credit to borrowers with more than 750 employees. They must also target an average loan amount of $5 million or less and may not guarantee credit for any single loan exceeding $20 million.[44]

State Collateral Support Programs

State collateral support programs are "designed to enable financing that might otherwise be unavailable due to a collateral shortfall."[45] They provide pledged collateral accounts to lenders to enhance the collateral coverage of individual loans. Lenders are required to have at least 20% of their own capital at risk in each loan. Interest rates, maturity, collateral, and other loan terms are negotiated between the lender and the borrower. The state and lender negotiate the amount of cash collateral to be pledged by the state. In practice, state collateral support is rarely provided for more than 50% of the loan value.[46]

Subject to some restrictions, SSBCI state collateral support program loans may be used for most business purposes. In addition, SSBCI state collateral support programs must target an average borrower size of 500 employees or fewer and may not support credit to borrowers with more than 750 employees. They must also target an average loan amount of $5

---

[43] Ibid.
[44] Ibid.
[45] U.S. Department of the Treasury, "SSBCI Program Profile: Collateral Support Program," at http://www.treasury.gov/resource-center/sb-programs/Documents/SSBCI_Program_Profile_Collateral_Support_FINAL_May_17.pdf.
[46] Ibid.

million or less and may not support credit for any single loan exceeding $20 million.[47]

State Venture Capital Programs

State venture capital programs provide "investment capital to create and grow start-up and early-stage businesses."[48] They come in two forms: a state-run fund, which may include private investors, that invests directly in businesses and a fund of funds that invests in other venture capital funds that, in turn, invest in individual businesses.[49] In both cases, the day-to-day management of the fund is typically outsourced to a professional firm. Investments are typically equity (stock) and hybrid investments, such as preferred equity and subordinated debt. Terms are negotiated between the business owner and the venture capital fund. The standard life of most state venture capital funds is 12 years, and individual fund investments are typically for 3 years to 7 years.[50]

Subject to some restrictions, SSBCI state venture capital program investments may be used for most business purposes. In addition, SSBCI state venture capital programs must target their investments to businesses that have 500 employees or fewer and may not invest in businesses with more than 750 employees. They must also target an average investment of $5 million or less and may not make a single investment exceeding $20 million.[51]

---

[47] Ibid.
[48] U.S. Department of the Treasury, "SSBCI Program Profile: Venture Capital Program," at http://www.treasury.gov/resource-center/sb-programs/Documents/SSBCI_Program Profile Venture Capital FINAL May_17.pdf.
[49] Ibid.
[50] Ibid.
[51] Ibid.

SSBCI FUNDING

P.L. 111-240 appropriated $1.5 billion to the Department of the Treasury for the SSBCI program, including the "reasonable costs of administering the program."[52] The 50 states, American Samoa, the District of Columbia, Guam, Puerto Rico, the Northern Mariana Islands, the U.S. Virgin Islands, and, in some instances, municipalities were eligible for funding, with the amount available to each state, territory, and municipality determined by a formula contained in the act (described later in this section).

Application Process

To receive SSBCI funding, states, American Samoa, the District of Columbia, Guam, Puerto Rico, the Northern Mariana Islands, and the U.S. Virgin Islands were required to file a notice of intent to apply for funding with Treasury by November 26, 2010. After filing a notice of intent to apply for funding, they were required to submit to Treasury an application for funding by June 27, 2011.

Municipalities were allowed to apply for funding only in the event their state did not participate in the program. Municipalities were eligible to apply for funding up to the total amount of their state's SSBCI allotment, with the final approved amounts apportioned based on their proportionate share of the population of all approved municipal applicants

---

[52] 12 U.S.C. §5708(b). Treasury reports that SSBCI administrative expenses, which include the cost of government employee salaries, contract support, and reimbursement to the Treasury OIG for program audits, were $5.393 million in FY2011, $4.746 million in FY2012, and $6.431 million in FY2013; and is estimated to be $8,299,000 in FY2014. See U.S. Department of the Treasury, *State Small Business Credit Initiative: FY2013 President's Budget Submission*, pp. 3, 8, at http://www.treasury.gov/about/budget-performance/Documents/16%20-%20FY%202013%20SSBCI%20CJ.pdf; U.S. Department of the Treasury, *State Small Business Credit Initiative: FY2014 President's Budget*, pp. 3, 8, at http://www.treasury.gov/about/budget-performance/CJ14/16.%20SSBCI%20CJ%20FINAL%20ok.pdf; and U.S. Department of the Treasury, *State Small Business Credit Initiative: FY2015 President's Budget*, pp. 3, 9, at http://www.treasury.gov/about/budget-performance/CJ15/21.%20SSBCI.pdf.

in that state, based on the most recent available decennial census.[53] Eligible municipalities were required to submit to Treasury an application for funding by September 27, 2011.

The application for funding requested information concerning such items as

- the amount requested;
- how the funds are to be used (state capital access program, collateral support program, loan participation program, loan guarantee program, venture capital program, or other small business support program);
- confirmation that, at a minimum, $1 of public investment will result in at least $1 of new private credit; that there is a reasonable expectation the funding will result in new small business lending of at least 10 times the amount of the SSBCI federal contribution; that the funding targets small businesses with 500 employees or fewer, does not support borrowers that have more than 750 employees, targets loans with an average principal of $5 million or less, and does not extend credit support to loans that exceed $20 million;
- documentation describing the operational capacity, skills, and experience of the applicant's management team in operating capital access and other small business capital support programs;
- documentation describing the internal accounting and administrative control systems used to safeguard against waste, loss, unauthorized use, and misappropriation; and
- documentation describing how the participant planned to use the funds "to provide access to capital for small businesses (1) in low- and moderate-income communities, (2) in minority communities,

---

[53] 12 U.S.C. §5703(d)(6). If more than three municipalities or combinations of municipalities from the same state are approved, Treasury is required to allocate federal funds to the three municipalities (or combination of municipalities) with the largest populations. See 12 U.S.C. §5703(d)(5).

(3) in other underserved communities, and to (4) women- and minority-owned small businesses."[54]

The Funding Formula

The SSBCI funding formula took into account the number of jobs and job losses for each state in proportion to the aggregate number of jobs and job losses nationally. Specifically, it was based on the average of (1) the number of individuals employed in each state in December 2007 compared with the number of individuals employed in each state in December 2008 and (2) the number of individuals unemployed in each state in December 2009 compared with the number of individuals unemployed nationally in December 2009. After accounting for Treasury's anticipated administrative costs, each participating state was guaranteed a minimum allotment of 0.9% of available funding ($13.168 million).[55]

Funding was provided in three installments (called tranches), each approximately one-third of the participant's approved allotment. The first tranche was provided "immediately following the receipt of the fully signed Allocation Agreement."[56] Allotment agreements described how states were to comply with program requirements and were signed after the state's application was approved.

Prior to the receipt of the second and third tranches, each state was required to certify that it had expended, transferred, or obligated at least 80% of the previous disbursement to, or for the account of, one or more approved state programs.[57] Treasury was authorized to recoup misused funds should the state be found in default of the allocation agreement and

---

[54] U.S. Department of the Treasury, "State Small Business Credit Initiative: Application," at http://www.treasury.gov/resource-center/sb-programs/Documents/SSBCI%20Application.pdf.
[55] Treasury anticipates that its total administrative costs over the lifetime of the SSBCI program will be about $36.85 million.
[56] U.S. Department of the Treasury, "State Small Business Credit Initiative: Frequently Asked Questions," at http://www.treasury.gov/resource-center/sb-programs/Pages/ssbci-faqs.aspx#gen3.
[57] Ibid.

could terminate any portion of an allotment that Treasury had not disbursed within two years of the date on which the allocation agreement with the state was signed. By statute, all SSBCI allocation agreements expired on March 31, 2017.

State-by-State Allotments

By the June 27, 2011, deadline, 48 states, American Samoa, the District of Columbia, Guam, Puerto Rico, the Northern Mariana Islands, and the U.S. Virgin Islands had submitted an application to participate in the program. Collectively, they requested approximately $1.4 billion in funding.[58] North Dakota and Wyoming did not apply. Alaska later withdrew its application. Five municipalities (one in Alaska, two in North Dakota, and two in Wyoming) subsequently requested $39.5 million in SSBCI funding.[59] Funding was allotted to Anchorage, Alaska ($13.168 million); a Laramie, Wyoming, led consortium of 17 municipalities ($13.168 million); a Mandan, North Dakota, led consortium of 37 municipalities and an Indian tribe ($9.711 million); and a Carrington, North Dakota, led consortium of 36 municipalities ($3.458 million).

Table 1 shows the amount of SSBCI funding awarded to each state and territory (hereinafter referred to as states unless otherwise noted) and the types of small business investment programs supported. As shown on Table 1, California received the largest allotment ($167.75 million) and American Samoa, which requested less than the minimum guaranteed allotment, received the smallest allotment ($10.5 million).

---

[58] Applicants were entitled to the funding provided by the SSBCI formula. American Samoa requested $10,418,500. The minimum SSBCI allotment is $13,168,350. All other applicants requested the amount provided by the SSBCI formula. See U.S. Government Accountability Office (GAO), *State Small Business Credit Initiative*, GAO-12-173, December 7, 2011, p. 9, at http://www.gao.gov/assets/590/586727.pdf.

[59] Ibid.

Table 1. SSBCI Programs

Participant	Allotment ($ millions)	Capital Access Program	Loan Participation	Loan Guarantee	Collateral Support	Venture Capital
Alabama	$31.301	X	X	X		
Alaska, Anchorage	$13.168					X
American Samoa	$10.500					X
Arizona	$18.204		X			
Arkansas	$13.168	X	X	X		X
California	$167.755	X	X	X	X	
Colorado	$17.233	X			X	
Connecticut	$13.301					X
Delaware	$13.168	X	X			
District of Columbia	$13.168		X		X	X
Florida	$97.622	X	X	X		X
Georgia	$47.808	X	X	X		
Guam	$13.168	X	X	X		
Hawaii	$13.168					X
Idaho	$13.168				X	
Illinois	$78.365	X	X		X	X
Indiana	$34.339	X				X
Iowa	$13.168	X	X			X
Kansas	$13.168		X			X
Kentucky	$15.487	X	X		X	
Louisiana	$13.168			X		X
Maine	$13.168		X			X
Maryland	$23.025		X	X		X
Massachusetts	$22.023	X	X			
Michigan	$79.157	X	X	X	X	X
Minnesota	$15.463	X	X	X		X
Mississippi	$13.168			X		
Missouri	$26.930		X			X
Montana	$13.168		X			
Nebraska	$13.168		X			X
Nevada	$13.803		X		X	X
New Hampshire	$13.168	X	X	X	X	X
New Jersey	$33.760		X	X		X
New Mexico	$13.168		X			X
New York	$55.351	X		X		X

Table 1. (Continued)

Participant	Allotment ($ millions)	Capital Access Program	Loan Participation	Loan Guarantee	Collateral Support	Venture Capital
North Carolina	$46.061	X	X			X
North Dakota, Mandan & Carrington Consortiums	$13.168		X[a]		X	X
Northern Mariana Islands	$13.168		X		X	
Ohio	$55.138	X			X	X
Oklahoma	$13.168					X
Oregon	$16.516	X	X	X		
Pennsylvania	$29.241		X			X
Puerto Rico	$14.540		X			X
Rhode Island	$13.168		X			X
South Carolina	$17.990	X	X			
South Dakota	$13.168		X			
Tennessee	$29.672					X
Texas	$46.553		X			X
Utah	$13.168		X	X		X
Vermont	$13.168		X			
Virgin Islands	$13.168			X	X	
Virginia	$17.953	X	X		X	X
Washington	$19.722	X	X		X	X
West Virginia	$13.168		X	X	X	X
Wisconsin	$22.363			X		X
Wyoming, Laramie Consortium[b]	$13.168			X		X

Sources: U.S. Department of Treasury, "State Programs Funded by SSBCI," at https://www.treasury.gov/resource-center/sb-programs/Documents/SSBCI%20State%20Programs%20and%20Contacts.pdf; and U.S. Government Accountability Office, *State Small Business Credit Initiative*, GAO-12-173, December 7, 2011.

[a] The Mandan, North Dakota, led consortium of 37 municipalities and an Indian tribe was allotted $9.711 million to administer a loan participation program. The Carrington, North Dakota, led consortium of 36 municipalities was allotted $3.458 million to administer a collateral support program and a venture capital program.

[b] The Laramie, Wyoming, led consortium includes 17 municipalities.

States use SSBCI funding to support small business investment programs: 23 support a capital access program, 40 support a loan participation program, 20 support a loan guarantee program, 16 support a collateral support program, and 38 support a venture capital program.

Approximately 32.5% of SSBCI funds have been allocated to loan participation programs, 29.5% to venture capital programs, 18.4% to collateral support programs, 16.9% to loan guarantee programs, and 2.7% to capital access programs.[60] As mentioned previously, most states received their initial tranche in FY2011 and, as of December 31, 2016, all 57 participants had received their first tranche, 56 had received their second tranche, and 53 had received their third tranche.[61]

States were allowed to use up to 5% of their initial tranche, and up to 3% of their second and third tranches, for administrative expenses related to implementing an approved small business investment program. They were also subject to several reporting requirements. For example, states had to submit quarterly reports to Treasury describing the use of allocated funds for each approved program, including the total amount of allocated funds used for direct and indirect administrative costs, the total amount of allocated funds used, the amount of program income generated, and the amount of charge-offs against the federal contributions to the reserve funds set aside for any approved CAP. States were also required to submit annual reports to Treasury, by March 31 of each year, containing, among other things, transaction-level data for each loan or investment made with SSBCI funds for that year.

AUDITS, EVALUATION REPORTS, AND PROGRAM ADJUSTMENTS

P.L. 111-240 required Treasury's OIG to conduct, supervise, and coordinate audits and investigations into the use of SSBCI funds. The act

---

[60] U.S. Department of the Treasury, *State Small Business Credit Initiative: A Summary of States' Quarterly Reports as of December 31, 2016*, p. 10, at https://www.treasury.gov/resource-center/sb-programs/Documents/SSBCI_Quarterly_Report_Summary_December_2016.pdf.
[61] Ibid., p. 1.

also required GAO to perform an annual audit of the SSBCI program. P.L. 113-188, the Government Reports Elimination Act of 2014, eliminated this requirement.

Treasury's OIG released its first evaluation report of Treasury's implementation of the SSBCI on August 5, 2011, and its first audit of a state's use of SSBCI funds (California) on May 24, 2012. It has completed audits of 24 participants' use of SSBCI funds (California, Montana, Vermont, Michigan, Texas, Massachusetts, Delaware, New Jersey, Alabama, Missouri, Washington, Kansas, Florida, West Virginia, Illinois, South Carolina, American Samoa, North Carolina, Idaho, Indiana, Tennessee, the North Dakota Mandan consortium, Rhode Island, and New York).[62]

GAO released annual audits of the SSBCI program on December 7, 2011, December 5, 2012, December 18, 2013, and December 11, 2014.

GAO's 2011 Audit

GAO noted in its 2011 SSBCI audit that Treasury's early implementation efforts were appropriately focused on establishing the application process and the process for distributing initial installments of funds to recipients as quickly as possible.[63] Left unstated was that Treasury established the program's policy guidelines and paperwork requirements essentially from scratch. Also, participants reported that nearly one-half of their SSBCI investment programs were new.[64] This suggests that at least

---

[62] U.S. Department of the Treasury, Office of Inspector General (OIG), Small Business Lending Fund Program Oversight Office, *Small Business Lending Fund Oversight Reports*, at http://www.treasury.gov/about/organizationalstructure/ig/Pages/Office-of-Small-Business-Lending-Fund-Program-Oversight.aspx. An audit of Louisiana's use of SSBCI funds was issued on January 9, 2014, and removed from the Treasury OIG's website on February 19, 2015, pending further review. The OIG later determined that the work performed was not sufficient to support the findings and conclusions in the report under generally accepted government auditing standards. The audit report will not be reissued.

[63] U.S. Government Accountability Office (GAO), *State Small Business Credit Initiative*, GAO-12-173, December 7, 2011, p. 21, at http://www.gao.gov/assets/590/586727.pdf.

[64] Ibid., p. 11.

some states had limited prior experience operating and overseeing many of their small business investment programs.[65]

GAO found that Treasury issued an initial set of policy guidelines and application materials via its website on December 21, 2010, and "was able to review, approve and obtain signed allocation agreements with and distribute first installments of funds to two states in January 2011."[66] In response to feedback from states, the SBA, and other federal agencies, Treasury revised its policy guidelines and application paperwork in April 2011 "to better articulate what documentation was required for both the application and review processes."[67] The two previously approved states were asked to sign an amended allocation agreement that incorporated the revisions.

GAO reported that several states indicated they had delayed submitting their SSBCI applications until Treasury issued its final application guidance and 37 states submitted their applications in June 2011, the final month that applications were allowed. Although some states had postponed the submission of their applications, GAO found that "despite the delay in providing application guidance, applicants generally viewed Treasury officials as helpful throughout the application process—providing answers to most questions immediately and determining answers as soon as possible when not readily available."[688]

GAO also found that Treasury finalized its disbursement procedures for second and third installments of SSBCI funds at the beginning of November 2011. Treasury officials reported that despite this delay, no state, at that time, had expended 80% of its initial disbursement to support

---

[65] An independent analysis of the SSBCI program funded by Treasury recommended that "future federal venture capital initiatives should require relevant program-specific training for VC [venture capital] program managers. VC program managers empowered by state government leaders range from novice to expert with respect to their preparedness to manage VC programs, and therefor need a common baseline of knowledge about options for design and operation of a state venture capital program." See Cromwell Schmisseur LLC, *Information and Observations on State Venture Capital Programs: Report for the U.S. Department of the Treasury and Interested Parties in the State Small Business Credit Initiative (SSBCI)*, February 2013, p. 6, at http://www.treasury.gov/resource-center/sb-programs/Documents/VC%20Repor.tpdf.
[66] Ibid., p. 14.
[67] Ibid.
[68] Ibid., pp. 14, 15.

loans or investments to small businesses. However, GAO noted that while Treasury was finalizing the disbursement procedures "states were potentially delayed in receiving their remaining SSBCI funding."[69] GAO noted that one state reported it was ready for its second installment before Treasury had finalized the disbursement procedures but told by Treasury officials that it would have to wait until the disbursement procedures were finalized.[70]

GAO concluded its audit by noting that Treasury had not yet developed performance measures for the SSBCI program. According to GAO, "measuring performance allows organizations to track progress toward their goals and gives managers crucial information on which to base decisions" and "until such measures are developed and implemented Treasury will not be in a position to determine whether the SSBCI program is effective in achieving its goals."[71]

Treasury's Response to GAO's 2011 Audit: Performance Measures

In response to GAO's audit, in January 2012, Treasury adopted three performance goals to measure its administration of the program and four performance indicators to measure SSBCI outcomes.

The three administrative performance goals were

- 90% of requests for modifications to allocation agreements are approved or rejected within 90 days of receiving a final submission;
- 90% of requests for subsequent disbursements under existing allocation agreements are approved or rejected within 90 days of receipt of a formal submission; and
- 90% of quarterly reports are received within 5 days of the deadline.[72]

---

[69] Ibid., p. 16.
[70] Ibid.
[71] Ibid., p. 21.
[72] U.S. Treasury, "Correspondence with the author," June 22, 2012. For the first two goals, the measurement period starts once all required documentation from the requesting participating state is received.

Treasury tracked these performance goals continuously and reported 12-month data to the Office of Management and Budget as part of its annual budget submission.

The four performance indicators were

- the amount of SSBCI funds used over time, as reported on SSBCI quarterly reports;
- the volume and dollar amounts of loans or investments supported by SSBCI funds, as reported on SSBCI annual reports;
- the amount of private sector leverage, as reported on SSBCI annual reports; and
- the estimated number of jobs created or retained, as reported on SSBCI annual reports.

Treasury reported performance data internally to the Assistant Secretary of Financial Institutions on an annual basis. Treasury also noted that these outcomes were not directly within its control, given that it approves and provides funding for state loan and investment programs, but the participating states are responsible for designing, establishing, and implementing the state programs. In addition, Treasury noted that

> the results of these outcomes are highly dependent on exogenous factors such as the demand for credit in a given locality and the quality of the small business borrowers' requests for such funds. Establishing these indicators for lending and investing activity as performance goals would imply that Treasury has direct control where none exists.
>
> Nonetheless, measuring these outcomes will be integral to assessing the relative utility of federal support for these state programs and informing future policy di recti on.[73]

---

[73] Ibid.

GAO's 2012 Audit

GAO's second annual SSBCI audit, issued on December 5, 2012, found that as of June 30, 2012, Treasury had transferred $468 million in SSBCI funds to states (about one-third of total SSBCI funds) and states had disbursed about $150 million of that amount (about 10% of total SSBCI funds). GAO reported that the states interviewed said that "disbursing funds was much faster for state programs that were in existence before SSBCI because the infrastructure was already in place and lenders were already familiar with the programs" but that "some states implementing new programs told [GAO] that it could take time to use the funds because they had to conduct extensive outreach to lenders to make them aware of the programs and encourage them to commit to small business lending."[74]

GAO noted that Treasury was authorized to revoke any portion of a participating state's allocated SSBCI funds that had not been transferred to the state by the end of the two-year anniversary of the state's approval to participate in the SSBCI. GAO noted that Treasury had not developed a written policy on how it will use this authority, that most of the participating states' two-year period will end sometime in 2013, and that "it is still unknown if they all will be able to use their funds in the time to obtain the third and final disbursement within this time frame."[75] GAO also stated that although Treasury officials had indicated at an October 2012 conference attended by many SSBCI participants that "Treasury did not currently plan to exercise this authority in the near future," GAO argued that "when states are required to spend federal funds to meet a statutory deadline or specific program requirements, agencies should provide guidance to the states on what they should expect if they are unable to meet the deadline."[76] In the absence of a formal written policy on this matter,

---

[74] GAO, *Small Business Lending: Opportunities Exist to Improve Performance Reporting of Treasury's Programs*, GAO-13-76, December 5, 2012, p. 22, at http://www.gao.gov/assets/660/650555.pdf.
[75] Ibid., p. 24.
[76] Ibid., p. 25.

GAO asserted that it was unclear how Treasury would use this authority in a consistent manner.

GAO also acknowledged that, in response to its first annual audit of the SSBCI, Treasury had created performance measures "to help monitor and measure the effectiveness of SSBCI."[77] However, GAO noted that Treasury "has not yet determined how and when it will make this information public."[78] GAO argued that although "it is still early in the program and results vary greatly across the program participants for a variety of reasons," but "Treasury should make information publicly available concerning its performance indicators" because "performance information is an important tool for policymakers, particularly as Congress reviews and considers programs to assist small businesses going forward."[79]

Treasury's Response to GAO's 2012 Audit: Written Policy Guidance and Publishing Performance Measures

In June 2013, Treasury responded to GAO's recommendation for written policy guidance concerning the Treasury's discretionary authority to revoke a participating state's allocated SSBCI funds that had not been transferred to the state by the end of the two-year anniversary of the state's approval to participate in the SSBCI by disseminating, by email, a "Frequently Asked Question" (FAQ) narrative on the topic to all participating states. Treasury also discussed its policy guidance on this subject at the national SSBCI conference held on June 3 and 4, 2013.[80]

Treasury issued the following policy guidance on this subject:

> Treasury will deem any Participating State that submits its second disbursement request by June 30, 2015 and qualifies to receive that disbursement to have made sufficient progress in implementing its Approved State Programs. For such a Participating State, Treasury will

---

[77] Ibid., p. 40.
[78] Ibid.
[79] Ibid, pp. 40-41.
[80] U.S. Department of the Treasury, State Small Business Credit Initiative Office, "Email correspondence with the author," July 9, 2013.

not terminate the availability of any Allocated Funds that remain untransferred as of that date, and the Participating State will retain access to the full amount of its Allocated Funds for the duration of the Allocation Time Period, which is March 31, 2017. For any Participating State that Treasury determines has not qualified for its second disbursement of Allocated Funds through a submission made by June 30, 2015, Treasury expects to conduct an analysis of the Participating State's progress in implementing its SSBCI programs at that time to determine whether Treasury should exercise its authority to terminate the availability of untransferred funds.[81]

In response to GAO's recommendation that Treasury officials make SSBCI performance information publicly available, on September 25, 2013, Treasury released the first of what would become an annual summary report of performance information drawn from SSBCI participants' annual reports[82]. The summary report contained information drawn from SSBCI participants' 2012 annual reports and included data related to each of the Treasury's four performance measures (amount of SSBCI funds used over time; volume and dollar amounts or investments supported by SSBCI funds; amount, in dollars, of private-sector leverage; and estimated number of jobs created or retained) as of December 31, 2012.

GAO's 2013 Audit

GAO's third annual SSBCI audit, issued on December 18, 2013, found that although the pace of participant SSBCI spending had increased since the second annual audit, participants were still facing several challenges in using their SSBCI funds. For example, as of June 30, 2013, Treasury had disbursed about $811 million in SSBCI funds to participants (about 54% of

---

[81] Ibid.
[82] U.S. Department of the Treasury, *State Small Business Credit Initiative: A Summary of States' 2012 Annual Reports*, September 25, 2013, at http://www.treasury.gov/resource-center/sb-programs/Documents/SSBCI%20Summary%20of%20States%202012%20Annual%20Reports%20FINAL.pdf.

total SSBCI funds). Eight participants had received their third and final tranche, 19 participants had received their second tranche, and 30 participants were "still working to use their first disbursement of SSBCI funding."[83]

Participants told GAO that Treasury's delay in finalizing the program's guidelines and the learning associated with implementing a relatively large number of new small business programs had slowed spending. However, they also reported that those issues were now largely resolved and "were issues that they would expect to occur with the implementation of any new program."[84] Participants also told GAO the unexpected low demand for some SSBCI capital access programs (CAP) further slowed their SSBCI spending. They explained that it took some time for them to reallocate funds from SSBCI programs experiencing low demand to those experiencing higher demand.[85]

Participants indicated they were now facing several new challenges in spending their SSBCI allotment, including (1) the reluctance of large banks to participate in the program, (2) the Small Business Jobs Act of 2010's requirement that participants obtain certifications from lenders and borrowers that they have not been convicted of a sex offense against a minor, and (3) concerns expressed by some lenders that they could be subject to additional regulatory scrutiny for using SSBCI programs to underwrite loans.[86]

Treasury officials and representatives of a trade association told GAO the reluctance of large banks to participate in the SSBCI was due to the variation of SSBCI programs across the nation. They explained that "national banks typically design programs that can be implemented consistently throughout the country and that they are reluctant to tailor different processes to each SSBCI participant's program."[87]

---

[83] GAO, *State Small Business Credit Initiative: Opportunities Exist to Enhance Performance Measurement and Evaluation*, GAO-14-97, December 18, 2013, p. 9, at http://www.gao.gov/products/gao-14-97.
[84] Ibid., 13.
[85] Ibid., p. 16.
[86] Ibid., p. 18.
[87] Ibid.

Two SSBCI participants told GAO there were banks that refused to participate in their SSBCI programs because of the sex offender certification requirement.[88] Several SSBCI participants also told GAO that "some banks have determined that, for legal reasons, they are not able to sign the certification, while other banks do not understand the need for the requirement."[89]

To help address lenders' concerns about being subject to additional regulatory scrutiny for using SSBCI programs to underwrite loans, Treasury officials briefed officials from the Federal Deposit Insurance Corporation (FDIC), the Federal Reserve, and the Office of the Comptroller of the Currency (OCC) concerning the SSBCI program and provided them periodic program updates. The FDIC and OCC also published guidance assuring their regulated entities that solely participating in the SSBCI does not subject them to increased regulatory scrutiny.[90]

GAO concluded its audit by noting that Treasury had developed targets for its three measures relating to administrative performance but had not developed targets for its four measures related to program performance. It recommended that Treasury establish targets for selected performance measures related to monitoring program performance and seek input from program stakeholders, including other agencies involved in promoting small businesses and Congress, as it designs its SSBCI program evaluation.

Treasury's Response to GAO's 2013 Audit: Targets for Program Performance Measures and Outreach

On December 4, 2013, Treasury officials informed GAO that Treasury agrees with both of GAO's recommendations and had begun the process of establishing targets for program performance measures and for gathering input from program stakeholders in designing SSBCI program evaluations.[91]

---

[88] Ibid.
[89] Ibid.
[90] Ibid.
[91] Ibid., p. 44.

GAO's 2014 Audit

GAO's fourth annual SSBCI audit, issued on December 11, 2014, found that although the pace of participant SSBCI spending had increased since its third audit, officials from three of the 10 SSBCI participants it interviewed reported that some banks were still reluctant to participate in the program because they were unfamiliar with it or perceived that it would increase scrutiny from regulators.[92] Officials from three of the 10 SSBCI participants interviewed also indicated that "there continues to be a lack of clarity in Treasury's guidance regarding the use of SSBCI funds for certain transactions."[93]

GAO noted that, consistent with its recommendation in its third annual audit to develop targets for its four performance indicators, Treasury had established targets in October 2014 related to the amount of private-sector leverage raised (to have a cumulative private-sector leverage ratio of 10 to 1 by December 31, 2016); the amount of funds available to states (to disburse 98% of the funds available to states by December 31, 2016); the number of other credit support programs (OCSPs) that target borrowers with 500 or fewer employees (to have 98% of OCSPs expend SSBCI funds to support an average borrower or investee size of 500 employees or fewer by December 31, 2016); and the number of OCSPs that seek to make loans with an average principal amount of $5 million or less (to have 98% of OCSPs expend SSBCI funds to support loans of investments with an average principal amount of $5 million or less by December 31, 2016)[94].

In addition, GAO noted that, consistent with its recommendation in its third annual audit, Treasury had sought input from program stakeholders, including other agencies involved in promoting small businesses and Congress when it designed its SSBCI program evaluation metrics.[95]

---

[92] GAO, Small Business Credit Programs: Treasury Continues to Enhance Performance Measurement and Evaluation but Could Better Communicate and Update Results, GAO-15-105, December 11, 2014, p. 19, at http://www.gao.gov/ assets/670/667450.pdf.
[93] Ibid.
[94] Ibid., p. 31. The SSBCI supports Capital Access Programs and other credit support (OCSP) programs, including collateral support programs, loan participation programs, state-sponsored venture capital programs, loan guarantee programs, and similar programs.
[95] Ibid.

These four performance measures and targets were designed to augment the information provided by Treasury's continued monitoring of the amount of SSBCI funds used over time, the volume and dollar amount of loans or investments supported by SSBCI funds, and the estimated number of jobs created or retained. GAO found that Treasury's efforts to provide additional performance information concerning the SSBCI was a "positive development that could help ensure that the agency decision makers and Congress have information to assist them in making programs more efficient and effective."[96] GAO did not make any recommendations regarding Treasury's administration of the SSBCI.

Treasury's Response to GAO's 2014 Audit

Treasury reported that it appreciated GAO's guidance on developing program evaluation metrics and noted that its final assessment of the SSBCI's performance in 2017 would include three sections:

1) a review of national program-wide outcomes;
2) review of state-by-state variation in program outcomes; and
3) feedback from private sector lenders and investors.[97]

Treasury's Inspector General Evaluation Reports

On August 5, 2011, Treasury's OIG issued its first evaluation report examining the SSBCI program.[98] The OIG praised Treasury officials for "seeking [the OIG's] assistance during the developmental stage of the program."[99] The OIG also noted that Treasury officials had previously made several revisions to the SSBCI's initial policy guidelines, allocation agreement, and application materials following consultation with the OIG, including modifying "the SSBCI application to require that applicants

---

[96] Ibid., p. 34.
[97] Ibid., p. 35.
[98] U.S. Department of the Treasury, OIG, "State Small Business Credit Initiative: Treasury Needs to Strengthen State Accountability for Use of Funds," August 5, 2011, at http://www.treasury.gov/about/organizational-structure/ig/Pages/ by-date-2011.aspx.
[99] Ibid., p. 1.

detail their oversight and compliance regimes prior to receiving program approval."[100]

After examining Treasury's policy guidelines and the allocation agreement between Treasury and participating states, the OIG made nine recommendations for improvements. For example, the OIG recommended that Treasury improve the understanding of state oversight responsibilities by more clearly defining what is meant by the terms "supervision and oversight and accountability" and by setting "minimum standards for participating state oversight of SSBCI recipients, including defining a participating state's role in overseeing compliance with loan use requirements and restrictions."[101] The OIG also recommended that Treasury "either modify the allocation agreement or amend the policy guidelines to require participating states to make a representation that it is aware of, monitoring, and enforcing compliance with the policy guidelines and other restrictions applicable to the other participants [lenders and borrowers] in the program."[102]

Treasury took several immediate actions to address the OIG's recommendations. For example, in response to the recommendation that Treasury more clearly define the terms "supervision and oversight and accountability" and establish minimum standards for participating state oversight of SSBCI recipients, Treasury revised the SSBCI FAQ document on its website "to combine all applicable oversight requirements in one place" and "elaborate on the specific duty that each provision imposes upon the participating state."[103] In addition, Treasury took into consideration the OIG's recommendations as it developed its "SSBCI National Standards for Compliance and Oversight" document, which was released on May 15, 2012.[104]

---

[100] Ibid., p. 14.
[101] Ibid., p. 19.
[102] Ibid., p. 20.
[103] Ibid. p. 10.
[104] U.S. Department of the Treasury, "SSBCI National Standards for Compliance and Oversight," May 15, 2012, at http://www.treasury.gov/resource-center/sb-programs/Pages/ssbci.aspx.

Treasury's Inspector General Use of SSBCI Funds Audit Reports

On May 24, 2012, Treasury's OIG released the first of a planned series of audits of state use of SSBCI funds, starting with California.[105] Treasury's OIG has completed audits of 24 participants' use of SSBCI funds (California, Montana, Vermont, Michigan, Texas, Massachusetts, Delaware, New Jersey, Alabama, Missouri, Washington, Kansas, Florida, West Virginia, Illinois, South Carolina, American Samoa, North Carolina, Idaho, Indiana, Tennessee, the North Dakota Mandan consortium, Rhode Island, and New York).[106] A summary of the OIG's findings for each state follows, starting with California.

In each audit, the OIG reviewed a judgmental sample of small business loans or investments to "determine whether [the loans or investments] complied with program requirements for loan use, capital at risk, and other restrictions."[107] The OIG then determined if there were "any instances of reckless or intentional misuse."[108] Treasury was required to recoup any funds the OIG identifies as intentionally or recklessly misused[109]. To date, only Texas, New Jersey, West Virginia, and the North Dakota Mandan consortium were found to be in full compliance with all SSBCI requirements.

---

[105] U.S. Department of the Treasury, OIG, *Small Business Lending Fund: California Needs to Improve Its Oversight of Programs Participating in the State Small Business Credit Initiative*, May 24, 2012, at http://www.treasury.gov/about/ organizational-structure/ig/Agency%20Documents/OIG-SBLF-12-003.pdf.

[106] U.S. Department of the Treasury, OIG, Small Business Lending Fund Program Oversight Office, *Small Business Lending Fund Oversight Reports*, at http://www. treasury.gov/about/organizational-structure/ig/Pages/Office-of-SmallBusiness-Lending-Fund-Program-Oversight.aspx.

[107] U.S. Department of the Treasury, OIG, *Small Business Lending Fund: California Needs to Improve Its Oversight of Programs Participating in the State Small Business Credit Initiative*, May 24, 2012, p. 2, at http://www.treasury.gov/ about/organizational-structure/ig/Agency%20Documents/OIG-SBLF-12-003.pdf.

[108] U.S. Department of the Treasury, OIG, Small Business Lending Fund Program Oversight Office, *Fiscal Year 2013 Audit Work Plan*, pp. 12-29, at http://www.treasury. gov/about/organizational-structure/ig/Agency%20Documents/ 2013%20SBLF%20Audit%20Work%20Plan.pdf.

[109] Ibid.

California

Treasury's OIG determined that California had properly used the majority of the $3.6 million in SSBCI loans it examined, but it identified $133,250 in loan loss reserves funded under California's Small Business Loan Guarantee Program that did not comply with SSBCI program requirements.[110] The OIG indicated that these noncompliant expenditures "constitute a 'reckless' misuse of funds as defined by Treasury guidance, which under the provisions of the Small Business Jobs Act must be recouped."[111] The OIG also identified $160,988 in administrative expenses charged to the SSBCI program that were "not adequately supported by actual expenses incurred or with proper documentation to validate the costs claimed."[112] In addition, the OIG reported that "42 or approximately 58 percent, of the 73 loans [OIG] tested lacked all of the required borrower and lender assurances."[113]

Treasury agreed to recoup from California the $133,250 in loan loss reserves identified by the OIG as a reckless misuse of funds; required California to provide additional supporting documentation for its SSBCI administrative expenses; and instructed California program officials to address missing borrower and lender certifications and assurances. Treasury subsequently noted that any loans still missing required assurances and certifications had been unenrolled and that all other certification issues had been resolved.[114]

Montana

Treasury's OIG found that Montana had misused $2.73 million of the $4.9 million in SSBCI funds it examined because the funds were used for passive real estate investments and the refinancing of prior debt, which "are prohibited under the Small Business Jobs Act or SSBCI Policy

---

[110] U.S. Department of the Treasury, OIG, *Small Business Lending Fund: California Needs to Improve Its Oversight of Programs Participating in the State Small Business Credit Initiative*, May 24, 2012, p. 3, at http://www.treasury.gov/about/organizational-structure/ig/Agency%20Documents/OIG-SBLF-12-003.pdf.
[111] Ibid.
[112] Ibid.
[113] Ibid.
[114] Ibid., pp. 13-14.

Guidelines."[115] The OIG also found that $3,426 in personnel costs incurred for administering SSBCI funds were not allowable or allocable because the costs were not properly supported as required by OMB Circular A-87.[116]

The OIG "did not find the misuse of funds to be intentional or reckless as Montana sought guidance from Treasury before enrolling the loans."[117] The OIG reported that Treasury officials did not provide definitive guidance on the permissibility of passive real estate loans and informed Montana that refinancing prior debt to the same lender was allowable if the prior debt had matured and new underwriting had occurred. The OIG noted that Treasury attempted to clarify the Small Business Job Act's prohibition on the refinancing of prior debt by defining *refinancing*, which is not defined in the act. The OIG challenged Treasury's conclusion "that the statutory prohibition on refinancing the same lenders' loans pertained only to existing debt that had not yet matured and that refinancing debt after it matures constitutes 'refunding,' a permitted use."[118] The OIG noted that there were no references in the Small Business Jobs Act or in Treasury's SSBCI policy guidelines concerning "re-funding."[119]

Treasury agreed to notify participating states that loans for passive real estate are considered a misuse of funds and encourage them to review their loan enrollments to ensure compliance with guidance that was in place at the time the loans were made.[120] Treasury also agreed to "provide a clear and rigorous analysis documenting how Treasury concluded that some refinancing of existing debt from the same lender, or 're-funding,' is consistent with the statutory language, or amend the program procedural guidance to remove that possibility."[121] Treasury also found that Montana was unable to provide the necessary documentation for the $3,426 in personnel

---

[115] U.S. Department of the Treasury, OIG, *State Small Business Credit Initiative: Montana's Use of Funds Received from the State Small Business Credit Initiative*, September 27, 2012, at http://www.treasury.gov/about/organizationalstructure/ig/Audit%20Reports%20and%20Testimonies/OIGSBLF12006.pdf.

[116] Ibid.

[117] Ibid., pp. 2, 9.

[118] Ibid., p. 3.

[119] Ibid., p. 12.

[120] Ibid., p. 16.

[121] Ibid.

costs cited by the OIG in its review of the state's SSBCI administrative expenses and that those costs would be disallowed.[122]

Vermont

Treasury's OIG examined 26 loans issued under Vermont's four SSBCI programs and found that Vermont's interest rate subsidy program ($931,000 in SSBCI funding) did not comply with the requirements established by its allocation agreement with Treasury.[123] Because the state estimated its interest rate subsidies, the OIG found that Vermont's quarterly reports to Treasury "do not reflect the State's actual use of funds for the program" and, therefore, "the State cannot provide Treasury with accurate information for measuring the leverage achieved with SSBCI funds."[124] The OIG recommended that Treasury require Vermont to provide a subaccounting of all funds transferred in connection with the interest rate subsidy program as well as program income generated from the use of such funds. In addition, the OIG recommended that Treasury determine whether Vermont "is in general default of its Allocation Agreement due to its non-compliance with accounting and lender/borrower assurance requirements, and whether future funding to the State should be reduced, suspended, or terminated."[125] The OIG also found that $216,820 in administrative expenses charged to the SSBCI program did not comply with program guidance.[126]

Treasury agreed to require Vermont to provide a subaccounting of all the funds transferred in connection with the interest rate subsidy program as well as all program income generated from the use of such funds.[127] Treasury also agreed to determine whether "there has been a general event of default under Vermont's Allocation Agreement resulting from the

---

[122] Ibid., p. 18.
[123] U.S. Department of the Treasury, OIG, *State Small Business Credit Initiative: Vermont's Use of Federal Funds for Capital Access and Credit Support Programs*, November 30, 2012, p. 2, at https://www.treasury.gov/about/organizational-structure/ig/Audit%20Reports%20 and%20Testimonies/OIGSBLF13001.pdf.
[124] Ibid, pp. 2-3.
[125] Ibid., pp. 3-4.
[126] Ibid., p. 3.
[127] Ibid., p. 15.

State's noncompliance with the grants management common rule or lender/borrower assurance requirements [and], if such an event has occurred and has not been adequately cured, determine whether it warrants a reduction, suspension, or termination of future funding to the State."[128] In addition, Treasury agreed to disallow the $216,820 in administrative expenses charged to the SSBCI program by Vermont unless the state provides supporting documentation in accordance with OMB Circular A-87.[129]

Michigan

Treasury's OIG found that Michigan had used the majority of the $38.5 million in SSBCI loans it examined properly, but it identified "approximately $2.524 million in misuse, of which $2.5 million was used to finance lender purchase transactions that did not involve extensions of additional credit to borrowers; $3,000 supported a partner buy-out, a prohibited use; and $21,000 was used to pay the CAP insurance premium on a loan closed and funded prior to Michigan's acceptance into the SSBCI program and Treasury's allocation of funds to the State."[130] The OIG determined that the $21,000 used to pay the CAP insurance premium was a "reckless" misuse of funds that must be recouped. Although the OIG did not find the $2.5 million used to finance lender purchase transactions that did not involve extensions of additional credit to borrowers to be a similarly reckless misuse of funds, it did question whether the purchase transactions were "consistent with the intent of the [Small Business Jobs] Act to help small businesses expand, grow, and create jobs."[131] It recommended that Treasury develop guidance for such transactions. In addition, the OIG found $8,506 in administrative expenses charged to the SSBCI program that were incurred prior to the date Michigan was

---

[128] Ibid.
[129] Ibid., p. 14.
[130] U.S. Department of the Treasury, OIG, *State Small Business Credit Initiative: Michigan's Use of Federal Funds for Capital Access and Other Credit Support Programs*, December 13, 2012, pp. 2-3, at http://www.treasury.gov/about/organizational-structure/ig/Audit%20 Reports%20and%20Testimonies/OIG-SBLF-13-002.pdf.
[131] Ibid., p. 3.

approved to participate in the program and notified of its SSBCI allocation. The OIG recommended that those expenses be disallowed.[132]

Treasury agreed to issue guidance to address the conditions under which loan purchase transactions would be permitted.[133] Treasury also agreed to recoup the $21,000 used to pay the CAP insurance premium on a loan closed and funded prior to Michigan's acceptance into the SSBCI program and Treasury's allocation of funds to the state and to disallow the $8,506 in administrative expenses that were incurred prior to the date Michigan was approved to participate in the program and notified of its SSBCI allocation.[134]

Texas

Treasury's OIG examined five investments, totaling $6.3 million, financed by the Texas Small Business Venture Capital Program and $105,000 of administrative costs that the state charged against SSBCI funds. The OIG found the program in full compliance with all SSBCI requirements. The OIG credited the state's "success in ensuring full compliance with SSBCI requirements" to Texas's "use of a checklist to evaluate compliance with program requirements prior to the completion of each transaction."[135]

Massachusetts

Treasury's OIG contracted with an independent certified public accounting firm to audit Massachusetts's use of SSBCI funds. As of June 30, 2012, Massachusetts had obligated or spent approximately $6.6 million of the SSBCI funds disbursed, including $4 million for the Massachusetts Growth Capital Corporation (MGCC) loan participation program, $2.1 million for the Massachusetts Business Development Corporation (MBDC) loan participation program, and $211,000 for the Massachusetts Capital

---
[132] Ibid.
[133] Ibid., p. 13.
[134] Ibid., pp. 15-16.
[135] U.S. Department of the Treasury, OIG, *State Small Business Credit Initiative: Texas' Use of Federal Funds for Other Credit Support Programs*, January 29, 2013, p. 2, at http://www.treasury.gov/about/organizational-structure/ig/Audit%20Reports%20and%20Testimonies/OIG-SBLF-13-003.pdf.

Access Program (MCAP). Massachusetts also incurred approximately $321,000 in administrative costs.

The accounting firm reviewed the state's administrative costs and a randomly selected sample of 35 state SSBCI transactions (3 loan participation loans and 32 capital access loans) to determine their compliance with SSBCI requirements. The audit found that Massachusetts charged $200,000 in administrative costs to the SSBCI program that did not comply with program guidance and that the state did not include in its quarterly reports to Treasury $51,248 of program income. The audit also found that 34 of the 35 transactions were in compliance with program requirements. The accounting firm noted that a transaction for $237,000 made by the MBDC loan participation program appeared to be prohibited by SSBCI policy guidelines because it involved an SBA-guaranteed loan. Massachusetts officials reportedly "believed that the loan in question was compliant with program requirements because Treasury's SSBCI Policy Guidelines prohibit the enrollment of only the unguaranteed portions of federally-guaranteed loans. Therefore, they reasonably believed the prohibition on credit enhancement did not pertain to the *guaranteed* portion of federally-guaranteed loans."[136] In addition, the audit found that Massachusetts did not obtain complete borrower and lender assurances for 89% of the loans reviewed by the time of loan closing.[137]

The OIG recommended that Treasury "revise its program guidance to make the enrollment of federally-guaranteed loans a clear prohibition, disallow $200,000 in administrative expenses unless the Commonwealth can provide adequate support for such costs, and require the Commonwealth to demonstrate that it has a compliant system for allocating administrative costs."[138] The OIG also recommended that Treasury "determine whether there has been a general event of default of the Allocation Agreement resulting from Massachusetts's non-compliance

---

[136] U.S. Department of the Treasury, OIG, *State Small Business Credit Initiative: Massachusetts' Use of Federal Funds for Capital Access and Other Credit Support Programs*, May 14, 2013, p. 7, at http://www.treasury.gov/about/organizational-structure/ig/Audit%20Reports%20and%20Testimonies/OIGSBLF13007.pdf.
[137] Ibid., pp. 1-3.
[138] Ibid., p. 3.

with lender/borrower assurance requirements, materially inaccurate certifications, and failure to report program income."[139]

In response to the OIG's recommendations, Treasury indicated it was in the process of revising its program guidance on the enrollment of federally guaranteed loans. It also stated that it will determine whether Massachusetts has adequately cured its noncompliance with program requirements and whether additional action is warranted. Massachusetts clarified that although it reported $200,000 in administrative expenses; it did not charge the SSBCI fund for these expenses and does not intend to seek reimbursement from SSBCI for them. Massachusetts also reported that many of the transactions examined during the audit "were made in the early stage of the SSBCI program, before suggested reporting forms were promulgated by Treasury."[140]

Delaware

Treasury's OIG found that as of September 30, 2012, Delaware had obligated or spent approximately $4.1 million of its first SSBCI disbursement of $4.3 million—$80,883 for 36 loans enrolled in the Delaware Access Program and approximately $4 million for 14 loans enrolled in the Delaware Strategic Fund (DSF) Loan Program. The OIG reviewed a random sample of 26 loans (19 from the Delaware Access Program and 7 from the DSF Loan Program) that were enrolled as of September 30, 2012, to determine if they were in compliance with program requirements.[141]

The OIG did not identify any instances of intentional or reckless misuse of funds. However, it did find that although Delaware obtained most borrower and lender assurances at loan closing, these assurances did not contain all required affirmations.[142] Several assurances were also

---

[139] Ibid.
[140] Ibid., p. 19.
[141] U.S. Department of the Treasury, OIG, *State Small Business Credit Initiative: Delaware's Use of Federal Funds for Capital Access and Other Credit Support Programs*, March 29, 2013, p. 11, at http://www.treasury.gov/about/organizational-structure/ig/Audit%20Reports%20and%20Testimonies/OIGSBLF13006.pdf.
[142] Participating states must require the financial institution lender to obtain an assurance from each borrower stating that the loan proceeds will not be used for an impermissible purpose

missing signatures or dates. In addition, the OIG found that Treasury became aware of Delaware's noncompliance with the assurance requirements in May 2012, but it was not until October 2012 that Treasury directed Delaware's officials to obtain the missing assurances for each loan. By November 2012, Delaware had retroactively obtained these assurances.

The OIG recommended that Treasury "examine the reasons why appropriate and timely actions were not taken to address Delaware's compliance and certification issues, and take appropriate actions to strengthen its compliance monitoring and enforcement of program requirements."[143] In response to this recommendation, Treasury reported that it "is in the process of adjusting the quarterly certification process to cover circumstances where a participating state has a known unresolved item of noncompliance."[144] Also, Delaware officials reported that they had implemented "additional precautions, including random audits of SSBCI loans, to ensure compliance with use of proceeds, capital-at-risk, and assurance requirements."[145]

New Jersey

Treasury's OIG contracted with an independent certified public accounting firm to audit New Jersey's use of SSBCI funds.[146] The accounting firm found that as of June 30, 2012, New Jersey had spent about $2.9 million of its first SSBCI disbursement of $11.1 million—$1.76

---

under the SSBCI program. For example, the loan proceeds must be used for an approved "business purpose" and they cannot be used to repay delinquent federal or state income taxes, unless the borrower has a payment plan in place with the relevant taxing authority; repay taxes held in trust or escrow; reimburse funds owed to any owner, including any equity injection or injection of capital for the business's continuance; or purchase any portion of the ownership interest of any owner of the business.

[143] Ibid., p. 3.
[144] Ibid., p. 4.
[145] Ibid., pp. 3-4.
[146] U.S. Department of the Treasury, OIG, *State Small Business Credit Initiative: New Jersey's Use of Federal Funds for Other Credit Support Programs*, February 27, 2013, p. 2, at http://www.treasury.gov/about/organizational-structure/ig/Audit%20Reports%20and%20 Testimonies/OIGSBLF13005.pdf.

million for two loan participations, $675,000 for a credit guarantee, and $500,000 for a direct loan.[147]

The accounting firm reviewed all four transactions and determined that New Jersey complied with all program requirements in administering the $2.9 million in SSBCI funds. The OIG concluded that New Jersey's "success in ensuring full compliance was attributable to several best practices that the New Jersey Economic Development Authority [which administers New Jersey's SSBCI program] employed to enhance its program oversight," including the use of an "SSBCI Application Eligibility Criteria Checklist that listed each of the required SSBCI assurances and specific SSBCI program requirements" and that had to be completed and signed prior to each transaction.[148]

Alabama

Treasury's OIG contracted with an independent certified public accounting firm to audit Alabama's use of SSBCI funds. The accounting firm reviewed all 14 loans enrolled in Alabama's loan guarantee program, totaling approximately $3.8 million, made between the signing of the SSBCI allocation agreement on August 24, 2011, and June 30, 2012. The accounting firm also reviewed the $45,172 in administrative expenses Alabama charged against SSBCI funds during that time period to ensure these expenses were allowable, reasonable, and allocable.

The audit found that Alabama complied with all program requirements in administering the $3.8 million of SSBCI funds used as of June 30, 2012. The OIG attributed "the state's success in ensuring full compliance" to the Alabama Department of Economic and Community Affairs' requirement that a checklist containing SSBCI requirements be completed prior to each loan enrollment to ensure the loan was in full compliance with SSBCI requirements.[149] The audit also found that Alabama had overstated the

---

[147] Ibid., p. 4.
[148] Ibid., p. 8.
[149] U.S. Department of the Treasury, OIG, *State Small Business Credit Initiative: Alabama's Use of Federal Funds for Capital Access and Other Credit Support Programs*, June 4, 2013, p. 2, at http://www.treasury.gov/about/organizational-structure/ig/Audit%20Reports%20and %20Testimonies/OIGSBLF13008.pdf.

amount of SSBCI funds used by approximately $1 million in its March 31, 2012, quarterly report and by approximately $4 million in its June 30, 2012, quarterly report. The OIG indicated that the errors occurred because Alabama incorrectly included private-lender contributions to loan loss reserves for loans guaranteed with SSBCI funds. However, because Treasury identified and corrected the inaccuracies prior to the audit, the OIG made no recommendations concerning the errors.[150]

Missouri

Treasury's OIG contracted with an independent certified public accounting firm to audit Missouri's use of SSBCI funds. The accounting firm reviewed all 17 SSBCI transactions between the signing of the SSBCI allocation agreement on May 23, 2011, and March 31, 2012. These transactions included 16 investments, totaling $6.6 million, by the Missouri Innovation, Development, and Entrepreneurship Advancement (IDEA) Fund and one loan, totaling $511,135, by the Grow Missouri Loan Fund. The accounting firm also reviewed the $151,568 in administrative expenses Missouri charged against SSBCI funds during that time period to ensure these expenses were allowable, reasonable, and allocable. Because the audit of the IDEA Fund revealed a prohibited party relationship, the audit's scope was expanded to include seven additional IDEA Fund transactions made between April 1, 2012, and September 30, 2012, "to determine whether additional prohibited party relationships existed."[151]

The OIG found that Missouri "properly used over 96% of the $7.3 million in SSBCI funds expended, and that all related administrative costs were compliant with program requirements."[152] However, the audit revealed that a $240,000 venture capital investment made by the IDEA Fund "constituted a reckless misuse of funds, as defined by Treasury" because a director of the board that approved the investment "had a

---

[150] Ibid., pp. 1-2.
[151] U.S. Department of the Treasury, OIG, *State Small Business Credit Initiative: Missouri's Use of Federal Funds for Other Credit Support Programs*, July 24, 2013, p. 2, at http://www.treasury.gov/about/organizational-structure/ig/Audit%20Reports%20and%20 Testimonies/OIGSBLF13009.pdf.
[152] Ibid., p. 3.

prohibited party relationship with the company that received the investment based on the director's controlling interest in the investee."[153] The director had recused herself from the vote approving the investment. The OIG noted that the board should have known that prohibited party relationships are not allowed because the SSBCI policy guidelines "require every borrower and investee receiving funds to certify that such a relationship did not exist."[154] The OIG recommended that Treasury recoup the $240,000 investment. Missouri disagreed with the OIG's finding that it "recklessly misused funds," arguing that the board was in compliance with its own conflict-of-interest policy and that the relationship with the "potentially interested director" was "disclosed repeatedly in the application materials which were provided to the Board" and that the investment "was made on the merits through a rigorous and independent process."[155] Nonetheless, Missouri took measures "to remedy the situation and prevent similar issues in the future."[156] For example, the board administering the IDEA Fund "replenished the SSBCI program account in the amount of the misused funds and unenrolled the transaction," amended its conflict-of-interest policy to comply with the SSBCI guidelines on conflicts of interest, and created a checklist to ensure that each transaction supported by SSBCI funds is in compliance with the SSBCI guidelines on conflicts of interest.[157]

Treasury agreed to recoup the $240,000 from Missouri. Treasury also agreed to "determine whether Missouri has adequately cured its non-compliance with the related party prohibition, requirements for assurances, and certification filings" and if further action is warranted.[158]

Washington

Treasury's OIG contracted with an independent certified public accounting firm to audit Washington's use of SSBCI funds. The

---

[153] Ibid.
[154] Ibid.
[155] Ibid., p. 26.
[156] Ibid., p. 22.
[157] Ibid.
[158] Ibid.

accounting firm reviewed all of the state's $5.3 million in SSBCI loans issued by Washington's Enterprise Cascadia Loan Participation Program and all of the $1.7 million in investments issued by the state's W Fund Venture Capital Program between the signing of the SSBCI allocation agreement on October 31, 2011, and June 30, 2012. The accounting firm also reviewed the $92,291 in administrative expenses Washington charged against SSBCI funds during that time period to ensure these expenses were allowable, reasonable, and allocable.[159]

The audit determined that all $7.1 million in loans and venture capital investments "complied with SSBCI program requirements and restrictions, and that borrower and lender assurances were complete and timely."[160] However, the audit found that the $92,291 in administrative expenses reported to Treasury "was overstated by $5,779 as a result of an accounting change [comprised of payroll costs for administration of the SSBCI program that were incurred during the reporting period, but subsequently transferred to an alternative funding source] that was not reflected in the state's SSBCI Quarterly Report."[161] When the auditors brought the overstatement to their attention, Washington officials notified Treasury of the need to adjust their SSBCI Quarterly Report to reflect the cost transfer. Treasury "advised Washington that it would authorize the adjustment upon completion of the OIG's audit."[162]

Kansas

Treasury's OIG contracted with an independent certified public accounting firm to audit Kansas's use of SSBCI funds. The accounting firm reviewed all of the state's $1.53 million in SSBCI loans issued by the Kansas Capital Multiplier Loan Fund and the $696,950 in investments issued by the Kansas Capital Multiplier Venture Fund between the signing of the SSBCI allocation agreement on June 28, 2011, and March 31, 2012.

---

[159] U.S. Department of the Treasury, OIG, *State Small Business Credit Initiative: Washington's Use of Federal Funds for Capital Access and Other Credit Support Programs*, August 15, 2013, pp. 1, 2, at http://www.treasury.gov/about/organizational-structure/ig/Audit%20Reports%20and%20Testimonies/OIG-SBLF-13-011.pdf.
[160] Ibid., p. 2.
[161] Ibid.
[162] Ibid., p. 7.

The accounting firm also reviewed the $14,585 in administrative expenses Kansas charged against SSBCI funds during that time period to ensure these expenses were allowable, reasonable, and allocable.

The audit found that Kansas "appropriately used most of the SSBCI funds it had expended" but questioned three $250,000 loans that were issued to affiliated entities as part of a $31 million aggregate financial arrangement.[163] The OIG noted that there is a $20 million cap on SSBCI loans made under other credit support programs (OCSPs) and that Treasury's guidance "does not address how the cap should be applied when funds are used to make companion loans comprising a larger financial package or where multiple loans are made to affiliated entities."[164] The OIG recommended that Treasury clarify the requirement that SSBCI funds not be used to support loans that exceed a principal amount of $20 million. Treasury agreed to revise the SSBCI policy guidelines to clarify the requirement.[165]

The audit also found that Kansas inaccurately reported in its March 31, 2012, SSBCI quarterly report a $173,822 advance for administrative costs issued to NetWork Kansas (a nonprofit entity that, among other activities, administers the Kansas Capital Multiplier Loan Fund and the Kansas Capital Multiplier Venture Fund) as a loan and that $29,247 of that advance was not subsequently reported as administrative expenses in the state's June 30, 2012, SSBCI quarterly report because those spent funds were previously incorrectly reported as a loan.[166] In addition, the audit found that $13,181 of the $29,247 should be disallowed by Treasury because the funds were used to pay audit and tax consulting costs that were

---

[163] U.S. Department of the Treasury, OIG, *State Small Business Credit Initiative: Kansas' Use of Federal Funds for Other Credit Support Programs*, September 5, 2013, p. 2, at http://www.treasury.gov/about/organizational-structure/ig/Audit%20Reports%20and%20Testimonies/OIG-SBLF-13-013.pdf.

[164] Ibid.

[165] Ibid., p. 18. Kansas officials explained that the three loans in question were "made to separate legal entities which were operated as separate businesses at separate locations, but who sold product to a common buyer [and] not contrived to avoid the $20 million cap on loans." Officials also explained that "while the similarity in names and inadvertent language in the applications make the independence of the loans more difficult to ascertain, review of the facts shows SSBCI loan support was not to a single loan in excess of $20 million. Rather, SSBCI funds were used to support separate loans to separate businesses." See ibid., p. 20.

[166] Ibid., pp. 3, 12, 13.

not properly allocated through a cost allocation plan or an indirect cost proposal as required by OMB Circular A-87.[167] Treasury agreed to work with Kansas "to correct its quarterly statements, remove the $13,181 in disallowed audit and tax consulting costs from the State's quarterly reports, and review Kansas' cost allocation plan for administrative costs."[168]

Florida

Treasury's OIG reviewed all 7 SSBCI venture capital investments, totaling $37 million, issued by the Florida Venture Capital Program and all 17 SSBCI loans, totaling approximately $14.6 million, issued by the Florida Loan Participation Program (11 loans, totaling $9.75 million); Florida Direct Loans Program (1 loan, totaling $3.5 million); Florida Loan Guarantee Program (3 loans, totaling $1.37 million); and Florida Capital Access Program (2 loans, totaling $780 for portfolio insurance) between the signing of the SSBCI allocation agreement on August 24, 2011, and December 31, 2012.[169] The OIG also reviewed the $378,634 in administrative expenses Florida charged against SSBCI funds during that time period to ensure these expenses were allowable, reasonable, and allocable.

The OIG found that Florida "properly used the majority (92%) of the SSBCI funds it expended" and that "23 of the 24 transactions ... sampled were compliant with program guidelines related to prohibited relationships, maximum transaction amounts, use-of-proceeds, capital-at-risk, and other restrictions noted in the [Small Business Jobs] Act and SSBCI Guidelines."[170] The questionable transaction involved the use of $4 million

---

[167] Ibid., p. 13.
[168] Ibid., p. 19. Treasury also agreed to inform Kansas "that the State is required to obtain lender assurances from relevant companion lenders in future transactions, but agrees with Kansas that retroactively collecting companion lender assurances [as was recommended by the OIG] is impractical and unnecessary." See ibid., p. 18. Treasury agreed to clarify the "SSBCI National Standards for Compliance and Oversight" document to specify which companion lenders must submit assurances.
[169] U.S. Department of the Treasury, OIG, *State Small Business Credit Initiative: Florida's Use of Federal Funds for Capital Access and Other Credit Support Programs*, November 15, 2013, pp. 1, 13, at https://www.treasury.gov/about/organizational-structure/ig/Audit%20Reports%20and%20Testimonies/OIGSBLF14002R.pdf.
[170] Ibid., p. 7.

in SSBCI funds in a $34.7 million investment "that involved multiple equity instruments, which ... exceeded the $20 million restriction in the [Small Business Jobs] Act intended [to] be placed on the amount of credit support that may be extended to a recipient."[171] The OIG concluded that "although two equity instruments were involved [$4 million from the SSBCI and $30.7 million from private capital], the transaction constituted one investment package because if the business were to fail, both equity instruments would be affected."[172] The OIG recommended that Treasury "revise the SSBCI Policy Guidelines to clarify how the $20 million restriction on credit support should be applied when an investment involves multiple equity instruments."[173] Treasury agreed to revise the program's guidance concerning the $20 million credit support restriction.[174]

The OIG also found that Florida had overstated its administrative expenses by approximately $55,000. Florida officials indicated that the overstatement "occurred because of incorrect selection criteria used to pull administrative cost information from the state accounting system" following the merger of several state agencies. Florida officials informed Treasury of the error and made adjustments to the state's administrative expenses to account for the error in their March 31, 2013, SSBCI quarterly report.[175]

In addition, the OIG found that Florida had "overstated by approximately $23 million the amount of SSBCI funds that had been obligated because it included FLVCP [Florida Venture Capital Program] reserves that were set aside for future follow-on investments to existing investees."[176]

Florida officials asserted that their reporting of these funds was in compliance with the definitions provided in the SSBCI policy guidelines

---

[171] Ibid.
[172] Ibid., pp. 7, 8.
[173] Ibid., p. 11.
[174] Ibid., pp. 12, 15.
[175] Ibid., p. 9.
[176] Ibid., p. 4.

and FAQ documents at the time that the funds were reported.[177] However, state officials also noted that Treasury had informed them in February 2013 that Florida's "reserve commitment letters did not meet Treasury's criteria for designation as obligated funds" and that the state had submitted an updated disbursement request with its second tranche of funding, which was received in June 2013.[178] Subsequently, "Florida adjusted its quarterly statements for June 30, 2012, September 30, 2012, and December 31, 2012, to exclude amounts shown as obligated pursuit to the FLVCP reserve commitment letters."[179] Treasury also agreed to determine whether Florida has adequately addressed its reporting of obligated funds and whether additional action is warranted.[180]

West Virginia

Treasury's OIG reviewed a random sample of 28 SSBCI loans and investments, totaling approximately $9.5 million, made by West Virginia's four SSBCI programs (13 from the Seed Capital Co-Investment Fund, 11 from the West Virginia Collateral Support Program, 3 from the Subordinated Debt Program, and 1 from the West Virginia Loan Guarantee Program) issued between the signing of the allocation agreement on November 18, 2011, and June 30, 2013. The OIG also examined a sample ($170,533) of West Virginia's $181,784 in SSBCI administrative costs. The program was found to be in full compliance with all SSBCI requirements.[181]

Illinois

Treasury's OIG examined a random sample of 48 SSBCI loans and investments, totaling $34.5 million, issued by five SSBCI programs in Illinois (35 from the Illinois Participation Loan Program, 8 from the Invest

---

[177] Ibid., p. 19.
[178] Ibid.
[179] Ibid., p. 20.
[180] Ibid., p. 15.
[181] U.S. Department of the Treasury, OIG, *State Small Business Credit Initiative: West Virginia's Use of Federal Funds for Other Credit Support Programs*, March 19, 2014, pp. 1-2, at https://www.treasury.gov/about/organizationalstructure/ig/Audit%20Reports%20and%20 Testimonies/OIGSBLF14004R.pdf.

Illinois Venture Fund, 3 from the Illinois Capital Access Program, 1 from the Collateral Support Program, and 1 from the Conditional Direct Loan Program) between the signing of the allocation agreement on July 26, 2011, and March 31, 2013. The OIG also examined a sample ($589,882) of the state's $1.03 million in SSBCI administrative costs and found the sampled administrative expenses to be in full compliance with SSBCI requirements.[182]

The OIG found that "Illinois appropriately used most of the $34.5 million in SSBCI funds it had expended as of March 31, 2013, but spent $105,000 to participate in a loan that was used to purchase the stock of a company representing its entire ownership interest, which is prohibited by the SSBCI Policy Guidelines."[183] The OIG also identified 22 other transactions "that did not fully comply with lender sex offender certification requirements" and found that "Illinois neglected to execute lender certifications on the State's behalf as prescribed in the National Standards" for direct loans and state-run venture capital investments.[184] Also, the OIG determined that Illinois unintentionally overstated, in the state's 2012 annual report, the amount of private financing associated with a loan in which the state participated by $4.7 million. This occurred because the financing structure of the transaction was changed without the state's knowledge.[185]

Treasury informed the OIG that it will recoup from Illinois the $105,000 expenditure identified by the OIG as being prohibited, require Illinois to modify any master agreements with lenders that do not include required language mandating that lenders notify the state of changes in the sex-offender status of their principals, and require Illinois to provide lender certifications when it is acting as a direct lender under the SSBCI program. Treasury also indicated that it will work with Illinois to adjust the $4.7

---

[182] U.S. Department of the Treasury, OIG, *State Small Business Credit Initiative: Illinois' Use of Federal Funds for Capital Access and Other Credit Support Programs*, March 26, 2014, p. 17, at https://www.treasury.gov/about/organizational-structure/ig/Audit%20Reports%20and%20Testimonies/OIG-SBLF-14-005R%20(for%20web).pdf.
[183] Ibid., pp. 2-3.
[184] Ibid., p. 3.
[185] Ibid., pp. 12-13.

million overstatement in the state's 2012 annual report and determine whether a general default has occurred as a result of the OIG findings.[186]

South Carolina

Treasury's OIG examined a random sample of 38 SSBCI loans issued by South Carolina's two SSBCI programs (10 from the South Carolina Capital Access Program and 28 from the South Carolina Loan Participation Program), totaling $11.4 million, between the signing of the allocation agreement on July 6, 2011, and June 30, 2013. The OIG also examined South Carolina's $136,449 in SSBCI administrative costs.[187]

The OIG found that South Carolina appropriately used most of its SSBCI funds "but misused $427,500 to participate in a loan that was used to finance the building of a new church sanctuary and make renovations to the existing sanctuary, which is prohibited by the SSBCI Policy Guidelines."[188] The OIG noted, however, that although South Carolina misused those funds, the misuse was "not reckless or intentional because SSBCI Policy Guidelines do not explicitly prohibit the use of SSBCI funds for non-secular purposes."[189] The OIG also identified eight other transactions "that did not comply with the National Standards because the State did not verify that the borrower and lender assurances were complete and duly executed prior to the transfer of SSBCI funds."[190] South Carolina's administrative charges were found to be in full compliance with all SSBCI requirements.

Treasury informed the OIG that it will publish guidance to clarify that using SSBCI funds to support transactions with a non-secular identity is not a permitted business purpose and determine whether a general event of default has occurred as a result of South Carolina's not fully complying

---

[186] Ibid., pp. 19-20.
[187] U.S. Department of the Treasury, OIG, *State Small Business Credit Initiative: South Carolina's Use of Federal Funds for Capital Access and Other Credit Support Programs*, March 26, 2014, p. 12, at http://www.treasury.gov/about/organizational-structure/ig/Audit%20Reports%20and%20Testimonies/OIG-SBLF-14-006.pdf.
[188] Ibid., pp. 2-3.
[189] Ibid., p. 3.
[190] Ibid.

with borrower and lender assurance requirements.[191] South Carolina informed Treasury that it had added an additional line item to its internal control compliance checklist to ensure that all borrower and lender assurance requirements are signed and dated prior to the transfer of SSBCI funds.[192]

American Samoa

American Samoa was awarded $10.5 million in SSBCI funds on January 12, 2012, and received its first disbursement of $3.465 million later that month. Treasury's OIG found that American Samoa had not obligated or spent any SSBCI funds for credit support as of September 30, 2013. As a result, the OIG's audit focused on whether American Samoa's $50,307 in SSBCI administrative costs was "reasonable, whether the territory was fully positioned to extend credit, and whether the territory was in compliance with the program's reporting and certification requirements."[193]

The OIG "identified $49,155 in unsupported personnel and travel expenses that should be disallowed," and found that "American Samoa has not provided Treasury with records that would allow the Department to determine whether the Territory is 'fully positioned' to provide credit support to small businesses, as required by its Allocation Agreement."[194] The OIG also found that American Samoa "did not obtain Treasury's prior approval for three changes to the entity designated to administer the SSBCI funds; did not submit two of its quarterly reports or its 2012 annual report to Treasury on time, causing Treasury to declare a general event of default of American Samoa's Allocation Agreement; and incorrectly certified the accuracy of two quarterly reports to Treasury and did not certify the accuracy of three other quarterly reports."[195] Based on its findings, the OIG

---

[191] Ibid., pp. 13-14.
[192] Ibid., p. 16.
[193] U.S. Department of the Treasury, OIG, *State Small Business Credit Initiative: American Samoa's Administrative Expenses and Reporting*, March 26, 2014, p. 1, at http://www.treasury.gov/about/organizational-structure/ig/Audit%20Reports%20and%20Testimonies/OIG-SBLF-14-007.pdf.
[194] Ibid., p. 2.
[195] Ibid., pp. 2-3.

recommended that Treasury disallow the $49,155 in unsupported administrative expenses, "determine whether a reduction, suspension, or termination of future funding to the Territory is warranted," and, if funding is not terminated, "require that the Territory first comply with the terms of its Allocation Agreement, and approve the agreement modifications, before disbursing additional funds."[196]

Treasury informed the OIG that it will disallow the $49,155 in unsupported administrative costs, determine whether American Samoa has again defaulted on its allocation agreement, and determine what form of remedy may be appropriate.[197] Treasury also indicated that if American Samoa's funding is not terminated, Treasury "will not disburse additional funds before requiring that the Territory first comply with the terms of the Allocation Agreement."[198]

Officials with American Samoa's Department of Commerce agreed with the recommendation to disallow the questioned SSBCI administrative expenses, which, they noted, were made by a previous American Samoa administration. However, they also noted that they were "somewhat taken aback with the harshness and severity of the positions taken" in the OIG's audit.[199] They pointed out that the OIG report did not reflect the "significant organizational issues facing the Governor which necessitated his decision with respect to the location and management of this vital program" and that "to the best of [their] knowledge Treasury SSBCI supported the decision made by the Governor."[200] They also noted that since the audit they had filed with Treasury all missing quarterly and annual reports, hired consultants to design and implement a compliance program for American Samoa's SSBCI program, and sent, in February 2014, a modified allocation agreement for Treasury's review. They requested that Treasury approve the program modification changes this modified agreement requested and maintained that American Samoa's SSBCI program now "complies with all Treasury regulations and guidance

---

[196] Ibid., p. 13.
[197] Ibid., p. 17.
[198] Ibid.
[199] Ibid., p. 19.
[200] Ibid.

and is fully positioned to provide small businesses with credit assistance."[201]

North Carolina

Treasury's OIG examined a random sample of 45 SSBCI loans issued by North Carolina's three SSBCI programs (31 were from the North Carolina Capital Access Program, 9 were from the North Carolina Loan Participation Program, and 5 were from the North Carolina Venture Capital Fund-of-Funds Program), totaling $4.9 million, between the signing of the allocation agreement on May 23, 2011, and December 31, 2012. The OIG also reviewed 46 of the state's SSBCI administrative cost transactions, totaling $720,257.[202]

The OIG found that North Carolina appropriately used most of its SSBCI funds "but [due to misrepresentations by a lender] contributed $6,690 to a reserve fund under the Capital Access Program for a loan that refinanced one previously made to the borrower by the same lender."[203] The OIG noted that "such refinancings are prohibited by the [Small Business Jobs] Act and constitute a misuse of funds" but not an intentional or reckless misuse of funds due to the lender's misrepresentations.[204]

The OIG also found that North Carolina did not obtain fully compliant lender sex-offender assurances for 19 (or 42%) of the 45 transactions tested, as required.[205] The OIG noted that North Carolina chose to rely on annual lender certifications of compliance with this requirement, which is permitted, but it neglected to require lenders to notify the state should an event occur that rendered the certifications obsolete.

In addition, North Carolina "inaccurately reported to Treasury the total amount of an enrolled investment on three separate occasions because it misreported the private investor's contribution to the investment" and

---

[201] Ibid., pp. 14, 19-24.
[202] U.S. Department of the Treasury, OIG, *State Small Business Credit Initiative: North Carolina's Use of Federal Funds for Capital Access and Other Credit Support Programs*, March 27, 2014, pp. 1-2, 16, at https://www.treasury.gov/about/organizational-structure/ig/Audit%20Reports%20and%20Testimonies/ OIGSBLF14009.pdf.
[203] Ibid., pp. 3, 8-9.
[204] Ibid.
[205] Ibid. pp. 10-11.

"reported $10.3 million in capital commitments with SSBCI funds to four angel investment funds as obligated funds even though only $2.9 million had been pledged to investees."[206] The OIG expressed concern that "while obligating funds on a multi-year basis generally is an accepted practice," using capital commitments to angel investment funds with multiyear investment horizons "to measure performance and qualifying a state for additional transfers of SSBCI funds is inappropriate and does not meet the intent of the Small Business Jobs Act."[207] The OIG found that all 46 administrative cost transactions it reviewed were in full compliance with SSBCI guidelines.[208]

The OIG recommended that Treasury (1) verify, as North Carolina had reported, that $6,690 in SSBCI funds has been withdrawn from the prohibited loan and that the SSBCI account has been reimbursed for the same amount; (2) determine whether there has been a general event of default under North Carolina's allocation agreement resulting from the state's failure to fully comply with the lender assurance requirements and for inaccurate reporting of venture capital investment amounts; (3) revise the definition of funds obligated for venture capital programs to include only funds that have been designated for specific investees; (4) require participants to distinguish in their quarterly reports the venture capital funds previously reported as obligated to specific investees from that obligated to angel funds but not yet disbursed to investees; and (5) adopt a standard definition of *funds used* for all program-reporting purposes instead of defining *funds used* differently for different purposes.[209]

Treasury informed the OIG that it will (1) verify that North Carolina has withdrawn SSBCI funds from the prohibited loan and replenished the SSBCI account; (2) determine whether a general event of default has occurred; (3) change its disbursement procedures to confirm prior to making a disbursement that states are not holding excess idle cash that is not likely to be expended, obligated, or transferred to small businesses within a reasonable time period; (4) explain in the summary quarterly

---

[206] Ibid., pp. 3-4.
[207] Ibid., p. 14.
[208] Ibid., p. 16.
[209] Ibid., p. 17.

reports that funds "expended, obligated, or transferred" include obligations to venture capital funds not yet linked to specific small business investments; and (5) make every effort to follow the definition of *funds used* in the SSBCI policy guidelines.[210]

Idaho

Treasury's OIG examined a random sample of 30 SSBCI loans enrolled in the Idaho Collateral Support Program (ICSP), totaling $50.3 million, for which Idaho provided $7.6 million in collateral and 12 loans committed for enrollment into the ICSP, totaling $10.8 million, for which Idaho had reserved $2 million in collateral as of September 30, 2013. Treasury had previously reviewed Idaho's administrative expenses from January 2012 to September 2012 and had reduced Idaho's final allotment by $31,806 for expenses that were not adequately supported in accordance with OMB Circular A-87. Subsequent to that review, Idaho had reported an additional $272,744 in administrative expenses as of September 30, 2013. The OIG reviewed these additional administrative expenses for compliance with SSBCI guidelines.[211]

The OIG found that Idaho appropriately used the $9.6 million in collateral support that was reviewed but "mistakenly overstated by $111,923 the total principal for 3 of [the] 42 loans ... reviewed because the amounts reported were not based on the final loan documents."[212] The OIG also noted that Idaho "inaccurately reported $781,000 as Treasury-approved subsequent private financing," but Treasury acknowledged the mistake "was due to inconsistent guidance to the State."[213]

Idaho was provided a copy of the OIG's audit prior to its deadline for submitting its 2013 SSBCI annual report to Treasury. As a result, the state was able to correct its report prior to submitting it to Treasury to account for two of the three loan principal amounts that were overstated. The state

---

[210] Ibid., pp. 18, 22-23.
[211] U.S. Department of the Treasury, OIG, *State Small Business Credit Initiative: Idaho's Use of Federal Funds for its Collateral Support Program*, May 19, 2014, pp. 2, 10, at https://www.treasury.gov/about/organizational-structure/ig/Audit%20Reports%20and%20Testimonies/OIGSBLF14010R.pdf.
[212] Ibid., p. 3.
[213] Ibid.

also indicated that it had implemented new controls in February 2014 that "require a copy of the Bank's promissory note to verify the actual/final loan origination amount prior to funding the collateral support account on the enrolled loan" to ensure the amount reported is the actual amount of the executed loan.[214] In addition, Idaho noted that it "will work with Treasury to rectify the erroneous inclusion of subsequent private financing and incorrect loan origination amounts in their 2012 report."[215] Treasury informed the OIG that it would work with Idaho to resolve the issues identified in the audit.[216]

Idaho's $272,744 in administrative expenses reported since Treasury's earlier audit were found to be in full compliance with SSBCI guidelines.[217]

Indiana

At the request of Treasury SSBCI program officials, Treasury's OIG was asked to determine whether two investments made by the Indiana Angel Network Fund (IANF) under Indiana's Venture Capital Program complied with SSBCI policy guidelines. The OIG found that the two IANF investments, one totaling $499,986 and the other totaling $300,000, involved transactions between the board chairman of Elevate Ventures and the investees.[218] Elevate Ventures manages the IANF's investments on behalf of the Indiana Economic Development Corporation (IEDC), and it approved and executed the two investments in question.

---

[214] Ibid., pp. 16-17.
[215] Ibid., p. 14.
[216] Ibid.
[217] The OIG also identified five loans, totaling approximately $9.8 million and supported by $1.3 million in SSBCI collateral, that provided interim financing of real estate acquisitions, construction projects, or equipment purchases that had been approved for the SBA's 504/Certified Development Company (CDC) loan guaranty program. The OIG expressed concern that Treasury's reporting of jobs created or retained by recipients of SSBCI supported loans may potentially duplicate the SBA's reporting of jobs created or retained by 504/CDC loan program recipients. Treasury agreed to explain clearly in the summary of states' annual reports that there is a possibility for duplicate reporting of job creation and retention figures in such circumstances. See ibid., pp. 5-7, 11, 15.
[218] U.S. Department of the Treasury, OIG, *State Small Business Credit Initiative: Indiana's Use of Federal Funds for Other Credit Support Programs*, June 18, 2014, pp. 2, 6-10, at http://www.treasury.gov/about/organizational-structure/ig/Audit%20Reports%20and%20 Testimonies/OIGSBLF14011.pdf.

The OIG found that the $499,986 investment constituted an "intentional" misuse of funds because the board chairman of Elevate Ventures had a controlling interest and voting stock ownership of more than 10% in the investee, which created a "prohibited related party interest."[219] The OIG noted that "SSBCI Policy Guidelines prohibit an investee receiving SSBCI funds from a related interest of any such executive officer, director, principal shareholder or immediate family."[220]

Intentional misuse of funds "is defined as a use of allocated funds that the participating state or its administering entity knew was unauthorized or prohibited."[221]

The $300,000 investment was found to be in compliance with SSBCI guidelines. However, the OIG noted that the closeness of the relationship between the Elevate board chairman and the applicant (the board chairman's adult son was the company's chief executive officer), although not prohibited, "may raise the appearance of partiality and should be addressed by SSBCI Policy Guidelines."[222]

The OIG recommended that (1) Treasury recoup the $499,986 of federal funds "intentionally" misused and declare a specific event of default of its allocation agreement with Indiana; (2) determine whether the state's funding should be reduced, suspended or terminated as a result of the specific event of default; and (3) require the state to ensure that IEDC reviews each IANF investment decision going forward.[223]

Treasury agreed with all three recommendations but indicated that it "would not characterize [the $499,986] investment as an 'intentional' misuse of funds based on the facts set forth in the report" because "intentional misuse requires knowledge that the use of the funds is contrary

---

[219] Ibid., p. 6.
[220] Ibid.
[221] Ibid., p. 1.
[222] Ibid., p. 10. The OIG noted that "the son is not considered an immediate family member because he does not reside with his father nor is he a minor. Therefore, while the investment constituted a related party transaction, it did not meet the criteria needed to establish it as a prohibited related party interest. The conflict of interest existing for [the $300,000 investment] ... was disclosed to the Board of Elevate Ventures in accordance with Elevate Venture's conflict-of-interest policy, and the Board approved the investment without any review by the State." See ibid., p. 9.
[223] Ibid., p. 10.

to the program rules, and action taken must be in a knowing effort to violate those rules."[224]

Indiana reported that it had completed an independent audit of the remainder of its SSBCI investments and did not find any other prohibited party transactions or other violations. The state also noted that the board chairman of Elevate Ventures had resigned, effective December 31, 2013; that the $499,986 investment had been repaid with a 15% return on February 6, 2014; and that the investment "had led to the creation of numerous new jobs for the people of Indiana."[225] In addition, Indiana reported that it "will independently review any future potential investment conflict."[226]

Tennessee

Treasury's OIG examined a random sample of 20 SSBCI investments made by Tennessee's INCITE Co-Investment Fund, a venture capital program, totaling $13.5 million. The sample was drawn from the 43 investments made by the fund between October 4, 2011 (the signing of the state's SSBCI allocation agreement), and September 30, 2013. The OIG also reviewed a sample of the state's SSBCI administrative expenses ($483,254 out of $685,880) that had been incurred as of September 30, 2013.[227]

The OIG found that Tennessee had appropriately used all $13.5 million in SSBCI funds that were reviewed but that "investor use-of-proceeds assurances were missing for all 20 transactions reviewed, and investor sex offender assurances had not been executed prior to the transfer of SSBCI funds for 12 of the transactions."[228] As a result, the OIG determined that the state had inaccurately certified that it was in compliance with all SSBCI requirements in several quarterly reports.

---

[224] Ibid., pp. 10-11, 14.
[225] Ibid., pp. 16-17.
[226] Ibid.
[227] U.S. Department of the Treasury, OIG, *State Small Business Credit Initiative: Tennessee's Use of Federal Funds for its Venture Capital Program*, August 20, 2014, pp. 1-2, at http://www.treasury.gov/about/organizational-structure/ig/Audit%20Reports%20and%20Testimonies/OIGSBLF14012.pdf.
[228] Ibid., pp. 3, 5-7.

With the OIG's consent, Treasury provided Tennessee a draft copy of the OIG's findings. Tennessee indicated that it "was made aware of possible inadequacies in their assurances after attending the SSBCI annual training conference in 2012, and has since corrected their process to ensure that assurances meet program guidelines." The state claimed that "its assurances are now 100% complete."[229]

The OIG found that all of Tennessee's sampled administrative expenses were reasonable, allowable, and allocable to the program.[230]

North Dakota Mandan Consortium

Treasury's OIG examined a sample of 15 SSBCI loans made by the Mandan consortium's Loan Participation Program, totaling $8.6 million of the $8.9 million obligated or spent as of March 31, 2014. The sampled loans were made between August 31, 2012 (the signing of the consortium's SSBCI allocation agreement), and March 31, 2014. The OIG also reviewed the consortium's $194,101 in SSBCI administrative expenses.[231]

The OIG found that the Mandan consortium used all of the loan funds it reviewed appropriately. The OIG also determined that the consortium's administrative expenses were reasonable, allowable, and allocable to the program.[232]

Rhode Island (Slater Technology Fund)

At the request of Treasury SSBCI program officials, the OIG audited Rhode Island's Slater Technology Fund. Treasury had informed the OIG that the Slater Technology Fund was potentially in noncompliance with SSBCI program rules. A separate audit of Rhode Island's second capital

---

[229] Ibid., p. 10.
[230] Ibid., p. 8.
[231] U.S. Department of the Treasury, OIG, *State Small Business Credit Initiative: North Dakota Mandan Consortium's Use of Federal Funds for its Loan Participation Program*, August 29, 2014, pp. 1-2, at https://www.treasury.gov/about/organizational-structure/ig/Audit%20 Reports%20and%20Testimonies/OIGSBLF14013R.pdf.
[232] Ibid., p. 7.

venture program (Betaspring) is underway and will be reported at a later date.[233]

The OIG examined all six investments made by the Slater Technology Fund, totaling $1.5 million in SSBCI funds, made between the signing of the allocation agreement on September 6, 2011, and December 31, 2012. The OIG found that the Slater Technology Fund "properly used most of the $1.5 million in SSBCI funds it had expended as of December 31, 2012, but misused $350,000 on two investments by failing to comply with the investor capital-at-risk requirement."[234] As the OIG explained, SSBCI's guidelines require venture capital funds and angel investor networks receiving SSBCI funds to have a "meaningful amount" of their own capital resources at risk. Treasury has determined that this requirement is met when "private lenders or investors bear 20% or more of the risk of loss in any transaction."[235] As the sole investor on the two investments, Rhode Island's Slater Technology Fund, which funded the investments in stages, failed to invest any private capital over the course of the entire funding-commitment period for the first investment and did not inject private capital until the date of final payment for the second investment.[236] The OIG also found that the Slater Technology Fund did not obtain required investee and investor assurances for five of the six investments before the transfer of SSCBI funds.[237]

Treasury indicated that it would, as the OIG recommended in its audit, provide guidance to SSBCI participants that staged funding of a single investment requires that 20% of the capital-at-risk must be from a private source when SSBCI funds are invested. Rhode Island acknowledged that the private capital was not initially invested as required by Treasury guidelines but indicated that the state "has implemented measures to ensure

---

[233] U.S. Department of the Treasury, OIG, *State Small Business Credit Initiative: Rhode Island's Use of Federal Funds for the Slater Technology Fund*, October 31, 2014, pp. 1-2, at http://www.treasury.gov/about/organizational-structure/ig/Audit%20Reports%20and%20Testimonies/OIGSBLF15001.pdf.
[234] Ibid., p. 2.
[235] Ibid.
[236] Ibid.
[237] Ibid., p. 3.

future compliance."[238] Rhode Island also acknowledged that "certain investor and investee assurances were not timely obtained by Slater and will now require that such assurances be obtained prior to the release of funds."[239]

New York (Canrock Innovate NY Fund, LP)

The OIG audited Canrock Innovate NY Fund, LP, one of eight venture capital firms participating in New York's SSBCI venture capital program, called the Innovate Fund. The OIG found that the firm's SSBCI "investments in four of five beneficiary companies constituted a reckless misuse of approximately $1.63 million of SSBCI funds because the investments were prohibited related party interests of its general partner, Canrock Innovate Advisors, LLC."[240] The OIG noted that "through a related entity, the three managing members of Canrock Innovate Advisors, LLC had a controlling interest in each of the four beneficiary companies' voting shares, which violated the SSBCI Policy Guidelines, regarding conflicts of interest."[241]

The OIG recommended that Treasury recoup the $1.63 million. Treasury indicated that in lieu of recoupment, it would not disburse the remainder of New York's SSBCI allocation. Treasury had withheld the amount in question from New York's final disbursement pending the results of the OIG's audit. The OIG responded to Treasury's action by indicating that the withholding of the funds met the intent of its recommendation.[242]

---

[238] Ibid., p. 4.
[239] Ibid.
[240] U.S. Department of the Treasury, OIG, *State Small Business Credit Initiative: New York's Use of Federal Funds for Other Credit Support Programs*, January 24, 2017, p. 2, at https://www.treasury.gov/about/organizational-structure/ig/Audit%20Reports%20and%20Testimonies/OIG-17-035.pdf.
[241] Ibid.
[242] Ibid., pp. 6, 7.

CONCLUSION

The SSBCI was enacted as part of a larger effort to enhance the supply of capital to small businesses. Advocates argued that the SSBCI would help to address the recent decline in small business lending and create jobs. Opponents were not convinced it would enhance small business lending and worried about the program's potential cost to the federal treasury.

It is difficult to determine the full extent of the program's effect on small business lending. As mentioned earlier, as of December 31, 2016, states had spent or obligated about 88% of the $1.45 billion available ($1.27 billion of $1.45 billion), which is sufficient to provide some insight. For example, as mentioned earlier, Treasury has reported that SSBCI funds supported more than 21,000 loans and investments in small business amounting to over $10.7 billion, with more than 80% of the funds and investments made to small businesses with 10 or fewer full-time employees. Treasury has also reported that small businesses indicated that SSBCI funds helped them to create or retain 240,669 jobs (79,193 new jobs and 161,476 retained jobs).[243] But, as Treasury has also noted, determining the SSBCI's influence on small business lending is likely to be more suggestive than definitive because differentiating the SSBCI's effect on small business lending from other, exogenous factors, such as changes in the lender's local economy and changes in the demand for small business loans, is methodologically challenging, especially given the relatively small amount of financing involved relative to the national market for small business loans. As mentioned previously, the SSBCI's $1.5 billion in financing represents about 0.24% of outstanding non-agricultural small business loans.

Treasury's OIG's audits of 24 states' implementation of their SSBCI programs suggest that many states experienced difficulty reaching full compliance with the program's administrative requirements, which were

---

[243] U.S. Department of the Treasury, *State Small Business Credit Initiative: A Summary of States' 2016 Annual Reports*, pp. 3, 15, at https://www.treasury.gov/resource-center/sb-programs/Documents/SSBCI%20Summary%20of%20States%20Annual%20Report%202016_508%20Compliant.pdf.

designed to reduce the likelihood of loan defaults, investment losses, and fraudulent use of funds. The release of Treasury's "SSBCI National Standards for Compliance and Oversight" document on May 15, 2012, proved useful because it helped states become more familiar with, and accustomed to, the SSBCI's rules and regulations.[244] However, given the relatively large number of new small business investment programs receiving SSBCI funding, the relatively large number of entities involved in the program (state officials, hundreds of lenders and investment companies, and thousands of small businesses), and the termination of Treasury's role in SSBCI administration, SSBCI program oversight is likely to remain a congressional interest.

---

[244] U.S. Department of the Treasury, "SSBCI National Standards for Compliance and Oversight," May 15, 2012, at http://www.treasury.gov/resource-center/sb-programs/Pages/ssbci.aspx.

In: Small Business
Editor: Angel Becker

ISBN: 978-1-53615-969-1
© 2019 Nova Science Publishers, Inc.

Chapter 4

SBA ASSISTANCE TO SMALL BUSINESS STARTUPS: CLIENT EXPERIENCES AND PROGRAM IMPACT (UPDATED)[*]

Robert Jay Dilger

SUMMARY

The Small Business Administration (SBA) administers several programs to support small businesses, including loan guaranty and venture capital programs to enhance small business access to capital; contracting programs to increase small business opportunities in federal contracting; direct loan programs for businesses, homeowners, and renters to assist their recovery from natural disasters; and small business management and technical assistance training programs to assist business formation and expansion.

Congressional interest in these programs, and the SBA's assistance provided to small business startups in particular (defined as new businesses that meet the SBA's criteria as small), has increased in recent

---

[*] This is an edited, reformatted and augmented version of Congressional Research Service, Publication No. R43083, dated December 27, 2018.

years, primarily because these programs are viewed by many as a means to stimulate economic activity and create jobs.

Economists generally do not view job creation as a justification for providing federal assistance to small businesses. They argue that in the long term such assistance will likely reallocate jobs within the economy, not increase them. In their view, jobs arise primarily from the size of the labor force, which depends largely on population, demographics, and factors that affect the choice of home versus market production (e.g., the entry of women in the workforce). However, economic theory does suggest that increased federal spending on small business assistance programs may result in additional jobs in the short term.

Congressional interest in assistance to business startups is derived primarily from economic research suggesting that startups play a very important role in job creation. That research suggests that business startups create many new jobs, but have a more limited effect on net job creation over time because fewer than half of all startups remain in business after five years. However, that research also suggests that the influence of small business startups on net job creation varies by firm size. Startups with fewer than 20 employees tend to have a negligible effect on net job creation over time whereas startups with 20-499 employees tend to have a positive employment effect, as do surviving younger businesses of all sizes (in operation for one year to five years).

This chapter examines small business startups' experiences with the SBA's management and technical assistance training programs, focusing on Small Business Development Centers (SBDCs), Women Business Centers (WBCs), and SCORE (formerly the Service Corps of Retired Executives); the SBA's 7(a), 504/CDC, and Microloan lending programs; and the SBA's Small Business Investment Company (SBIC) venture capital program. Although data collected by the SBA concerning these programs' impact on economic activity and job creation are somewhat limited and subject to methodological challenges concerning their validity as reliable performance measures, most small business owners who have participated in these programs report in surveys sponsored by the SBA that the programs were useful. Given the data limitations, however, it is difficult to determine the cost effectiveness of these programs.

The report also discusses the SBA's growth accelerators initiative, which targets entrepreneurs looking to "start and scale their business" by helping them access "seed capital, mentors, and networking opportunities for customers and partners," and the recently sunset SBIC early stage debenture program, which focused on providing venture capital to startups.

THE SBA'S MISSIONS

The Small Business Administration (SBA) administers several programs to support small businesses, including the 7(a), 504/CDC, and Microloan lending programs to enhance small business access to capital; the Small Business Investment Company (SBIC) program to enhance small business access to venture capital; contracting programs to increase small business opportunities in federal contracting; direct loan programs for businesses, homeowners, and renters to assist their recovery from natural disasters; and small business management and technical assistance training programs to assist business formation and expansion.[1] Congressional interest in these programs, and the SBA's assistance to small business startups in particular (defined as new businesses that meet the SBA's criteria as small), has increased in recent years, primarily because these programs are viewed by many as a means to stimulate economic activity and create jobs.

The Small Business Act specifies four missions for the SBA:

> It is the declared policy of the Congress that the Government should aid, counsel, assist, and protect, insofar as is possible, the interests of small-business concerns in order to preserve free competitive enterprise, to insure that a fair proportion of the total purchases and contracts or subcontracts for property and services for the Government (including but not limited to contracts or subcontracts for maintenance, repair, and

---

[1] U.S. Small Business Administration (SBA), *Fiscal Year 2019 Congressional Budget Justification and FY2017 Annual Performance Report*, pp. 1-4, at https://www.sba.gov/sites/default/files/aboutsbaarticle/SBA_FY_19_508-FinalFINAL.PDF. For further analysis of the SBA's loan guaranty programs, see CRS Report R41146, *Small Business Administration 7(a) Loan Guaranty Program*, by Robert Jay Dilger; and CRS Report R41184, *Small Business Administration 504/CDC Loan Guaranty Program*, by Robert Jay Dilger. For further analysis of the SBA's Small Business Investment Company program, see CRS Report R41456, *SBA Small Business Investment Company Program*, by Robert Jay Dilger. For further analysis of the New Markets Venture Capital program, see CRS Report R42565, *SBA New Markets Venture Capital Program*, by Robert Jay Dilger. For further analysis of the SBA's disaster loan programs, see CRS Report R41309, *The SBA Disaster Loan Program: Overview and Possible Issues for Congress*, by Bruce R. Lindsay. For further analysis of the SBA's contracting programs, see CRS Report R41268, *Small Business Administration HUBZone Program*, by Robert Jay Dilger.

construction) be placed with small-business enterprises, to insure that a fair proportion of the total sales of Government property be made to such enterprises, and to maintain and strengthen the overall economy of the Nation.[2]

As part of its mission to maintain and strengthen the overall economy of the nation, the SBA has always been interested in promoting job creation and job retention.[3] For example, the SBA currently gathers data from its clients concerning the number of jobs either created or retained as a result of the assistance they receive from the SBA. The SBA refers to these self-reported data as the number of "jobs supported."[4] The SBA also regularly sponsors research on the role of small businesses in job creation and retention, and considers that research when designing its programs.

Economists generally do not view job creation as a justification for providing federal assistance to small businesses. They argue that in the long term such assistance will likely reallocate jobs within the economy, not increase them. In their view, jobs arise primarily from the size of the labor force, which depends largely on population, demographics, and factors that affect the choice of home versus market production (e.g., the entry of women in the workforce). However, economic research does suggest that increased federal spending on small business assistance programs may result in additional jobs in the short term.[5]

---

[2] 15 U.S.C. §631; and P.L. 83-163, the Small Business Act of 1953 (as amended).

[3] U.S. Senate, Select Committee on Small Business, Citation of Statement by Wendell B. Barnes, SBA Administrator, *Annual Report*, 83rd Cong., 2nd sess., March 25, 1954, H.Rept. 83-1092 (Washington: GPO, 1954), p. 60.

[4] The SBA reports that in FY2018 the 7(a) loan guarantee program supported 543,171 jobs, the 504/CDC loan guarantee program supported 55,729 jobs, the Microloan lending program supported 20,259 jobs, and the Small Business Investment Company venture-capital program supported 106,021 jobs. SBA, Office of Congressional and Legislative Affairs, "Correspondence with the author," October 25, 2018.

[5] For further information concerning economic research and small business assistance, see CRS Report RL32254, *Small Business Tax Benefits: Current Law and Arguments For and Against Them*, by Gary Guenther and CRS Report R41523, *Small Business Administration and Job Creation*, by Robert Jay Dilger. For an economic argument to repeal the SBA, see Veronique de Rugy, *Why the Small Business Administration's Loan Programs Should Be Abolished*, American Enterprise Institute for Public Policy Research, AEI Working Paper #126, April 13, 2006, at http://www.aei.org/wp-content/uploads/2011/10/20060414_wp126.pdf.

SMALL BUSINESS STARTUPS AND JOB CREATION

The SBA's interest, and congressional interest, in providing assistance to small business startups is derived primarily from economic research indicating that startups play an important role in job creation.[6] That research suggests that startups create many, and in some years almost all, net jobs in the national economy.

Although there is a consensus that startups have an important role in job creation and retention, economic research suggests that startups have a more limited effect on net job creation over time because fewer than half of all startups are still in business after five years. That research also suggests that the influence of startups on net job creation varies by firm size. Startups with fewer than 20 employees tend to have a negligible effect on net job creation over time whereas startups with 20-499 employees tend to have a positive employment effect, as do surviving younger businesses of all sizes (in operation for one year to five years).[7]

Given the relatively high rate of firm deaths among startups, providing SBA assistance to startups, especially in the form of a SBA guaranteed loan or venture capital investment, is generally viewed as a relatively "high

---

[6] Charles Brown, James Hamilton, and James Medoff, *Employers Large and Small* (Cambridge: Harvard University Press, 1990); Zoltan Acs, William Parsons, and Spencer Tracy, "High-Impact Firms: Gazelles Revisited," SBA, Office of Advocacy, June 2008, at http://www.massmac.org/newsline/0902/high_impact_firms.pdf; Dane Stangler and Robert E. Litan, "Where Will The Jobs Come From?" Kaufman Foundation Research Series: Firm Formation and Economic Growth, November 2009, at https://www.kauffman.org/-/media/kauffman_org/research-reports-and-covers/2009/11/where_will_the_jobs_come_from.pdf; and Dane Stangler and Paul Kedrosky, "Neutralism and Entrepreneurship: The Structural Dynamics of Startups, Young Firms, and Job Creation," Kaufman Foundation Research Series: Firm Formation and Economic Growth, September 2010, at https://www.kauffman.org/-/media/kauffman_org/researchreports-and-covers/2010/09/firmformationneutralism.pdf.

[7] Zoltan Acs, William Parsons, and Spencer Tracy, "High-Impact Firms: Gazelles Revisited," SBA, Office of Advocacy, June 2008, at http://www.massmac.org/newsline/0902/high_impact_firms.pdf; Dane Stangler and Robert E. Litan, "Where Will The Jobs Come From?" Kaufman Foundation Research Series: Firm Formation and Economic Growth, November 2009, at https://www.kauffman.org/-/media/ kauffman_org/research-reports-and-covers/2009/11/ where_will_the_jobs_come_from.pdf; John Haltiwanger, Ron S. Jarmin, and Javier Miranda, "Who Creates Jobs? Small vs. Large vs. Young," Cambridge, MA: National Bureau of Economic Research, Working Paper 16300, August 2010, at http://www.nber.org/papers/w16300; and Ian Hathaway, "Small Business and Job Creation: The Unconventional Wisdom," *Bloomberg Government*, October 31, 2011.

risk-high reward" endeavor, with advocates focusing on the possibility of job creation and opponents focusing on the risk of default. For example, opponents point to the SBA's experiences with its SBIC Participating Securities program as an example of the risk in providing venture capital to startups. The SBIC Participating Securities program was established in 1994, with congressional authorization, to encourage the formation of participating securities SBICs that would make equity investments in startup and early stage small businesses.[8]

The SBA created the program to fill a perceived investment gap created by the SBIC debenture program's focus on investments in mid- and later-stage small businesses.[9] The SBA stopped issuing new commitments for participation securities on October 1, 2004, following relatively major losses (exceeding $2.7 billion in losses on investments of just over $6.0 billion) in the program following the burst of the "technology stock market bubble" from 2000 to 2002.[10] The SBA's action began a process to end the program, which continues today.

REPORT OVERVIEW

This chapter examines startups' experiences with the SBA's management and technical assistance training programs, focusing on Small Business Development Centers (SBDCs); Women Business Centers

---

[8] P.L. 102-366, the Small Business Credit and Business Opportunity Enhancement Act of 1992 (Title IV, the Small Business Equity Enhancement Act of 1992). For further information and analysis of the SBIC program, see CRS Report R41456, *SBA Small Business Investment Company Program*, by Robert Jay Dilger.

[9] Debenture SBICs are required to pay interest and SBA annual charges semiannually on their debentures through maturity. As a result, although debenture SBICs make a broad range of equity investments, they generally invest in later-stage and mezzanine companies which demonstrate an ability to make early and regular payments on the investment. Participating securities SBICs were not required to make these semiannual payments to encourage investments in firms, such as startups, which had not yet established an ability to make early and regular payments on the investment.

[10] U.S. Congress, House Committee on Small Business, *Proposed Legislative Remedy for the Participating Securities Program*, 109th Cong., 1st sess., July 27, 2005, Serial No. 109-27 (Washington: GPO, 2005), p. 3; and SBA, Office of Inspector General, "The SBIC Program: At Significant Risk For Losses," May 24, 2004, at https://www.sba.gov/sites/default/files/oig/oig_4-21.pdf.

(WBCs); SCORE (formerly the Service Corps of Retired Executives); the SBA's 7(a), 504/CDC, and Microloan lending programs; and the SBA's SBIC venture capital program. The SBA's growth accelerators initiative, which targets entrepreneurs looking to "start and scale their business" by helping them access "seed capital, mentors, and networking opportunities for customers and partners," and the recently sunset SBIC early stage debenture program, which focused on providing venture capital to startups, are also discussed.[11]

With some notable exceptions, such as the Microloan lending program and SBA's growth accelerators initiative, these programs are designed to assist small businesses at all developmental stages, as opposed to targeting startups for special attention. Nonetheless, all of these programs provide assistance to startups, and report both outcome data (e.g., the number of small businesses receiving training and the number and amount of loans and venture capital provided) and performance data (e.g., the usefulness of the training and the number of jobs supported by the loan) based on the age of the business. As a result, the experiences of startups can be compared with the experiences of older firms both within and across the SBA's programs. For example, as will be shown, the SBA programs that specifically target startups for special attention provide a relatively larger share of its assistance to startups than other SBA programs.

Although the data collected by the SBA concerning these programs' impact on economic activity and job creation are somewhat limited and subject to methodological challenges concerning their validity as reliable performance measures, most small business owners who have participated in these programs report in surveys sponsored by the SBA that the programs were useful. Given the data limitations, however, it is difficult to determine the cost effectiveness of these programs.

---

[11] SBA, *Fiscal Year 2018 Congressional Budget Justification and FY2016 Annual Performance Report*, p. 75, at https://www.sba.gov/sites/default/files/aboutsbaarticle/FINAL_SBA_FY_2018_CBJ_May_22_2017c.pdf.

SBA MANAGEMENT AND TECHNICAL ASSISTANCE TRAINING PROGRAMS

The SBA has provided management and technical assistance training "to small-business concerns, by advising and counseling on matters in connection with government procurement and on policies, principles and practices of good management" since it began operations in 1953.[12] Initially, the SBA provided its own management and technical assistance training programs. Over time, the SBA has relied increasingly on third parties to provide that training. The SBA reports that more than 1.5 million aspiring entrepreneurs and small business owners receive training from an SBA-supported resource partner each year.[13]

The SBA has argued that its support of management and technical assistance training for small businesses has contributed "to the long-term success of these businesses and their ability to grow and create jobs."[14] It currently provides financial support to about "14,000 resource partners," including 63 lead SBDCs and nearly 1,000 SBDC local outreach locations, 116 WBCs, and over 300 chapters of the mentoring program, SCORE.[15]

The SBDC, WBC, and SCORE programs are the SBA's three largest management and technical assistance training programs.[16] These programs provide training assistance to small businesses at all stages of development, and do not target their assistance exclusively at startups.

---

[12] U.S. Congress, Senate Committee on Banking and Currency, *Extension of the Small Business Act of 1953*, report to accompany S. 2127, 84th Cong., 1st sess., July 22, 1955, S.Rept. 84-1350 (Washington: GPO, 1955), p. 17.

[13] SBA, *Fiscal Year 2019 Congressional Budget Justification and FY2017 Annual Performance Report*, pp. 80, 81, at https://www.sba.gov/sites/default/files/aboutsbaarticle/SBA_FY_19_508-Final-FINAL.PDF.

[14] SBA, *Fiscal Year 2011 Congressional Budget Justification and FY2009 Annual Performance Report*, p. 4, at https://www.sba.gov/sites/default/files/aboutsbaarticle/Congressional_Budget_Justification.pdf.

[15] SBA, *Fiscal Year 2018 Congressional Budget Justification and FY2016 Annual Performance Report*, p. 48, at https://www.sba.gov/about-sba/sba-newsroom/press-releases-media-advisories/sba-and-naggl-launch-business-smarttoolkit; SBA, "Women's Business Centers Directory," at https://www.sba.gov/tools/local-assistance/wbc; and SCORE, "About SCORE," at https://www.score.org/about-score.

[16] For further information and analysis concerning the SBA's management and technical assistance training programs, see CRS Report R41352, *Small Business Management and Technical Assistance Training Programs*, by Robert Jay Dilger.

All three of these programs provide assistance to small businesses, as defined by the SBA's size standards and regulations.[17] However, there are some differences in the small businesses that tend to seek their services. For example, businesses owned by SBDC clients tend to be somewhat larger, both in terms of annual revenue and employment, than those owned by SCORE and WBC clients.[18] Also, as expected given their mission, WBCs' clients are more likely to be female than SBDC and SCORE clients.[19]

SBDCs, WBCs, and SCORE

SBDCs are "hosted by leading universities, colleges, and state economic development agencies" to deliver management and technical assistance training "to small businesses and nascent entrepreneurs (pre-venture) in order to promote growth, expansion, innovation, increased productivity and management improvement."[20] These services are delivered, in most instances, on a nonfee, one-on-one confidential counseling basis and are administered by 63 lead service centers, with at least one located in each state (four in Texas and six in California), the District of Columbia, Puerto Rico, the U.S. Virgin Islands, Guam, and

---

[17] For further information and analysis concerning the SBA's size standards, see CRS Report R40860, *Small Business Size Standards: A Historical Analysis of Contemporary Issues*, by Robert Jay Dilger.

[18] In 2012, SBDC clients had average revenue of $762,962 and, on average, 10.05 employees; SCORE clients had average revenue of $465,828 and, on average, 5.56 employees; and WBC clients had average revenue of $192,734 and, on average, 4.67 employees. See SBA, Office of Entrepreneurial Development, "Impact Study of Entrepreneurial Dynamics: Office of Entrepreneurial Development Resource Partners' Face-to-Face Counseling," September 2013, p. 26, at https://www.sba.gov/sites/default/files/files/OED_ImpactReport_09302013_Final.pdf.

[19] In 2012, 82% of the businesses served by WBCs were owned by a female compared to 47% of the businesses served by SBDCs and 47% of the businesses served by SCORE. See SBA, Office of Entrepreneurial Development, "Impact Study of Entrepreneurial Dynamics: Office of Entrepreneurial Development Resource Partners' Face-to-Face Counseling," September 2013, p. 17, at https://www.sba.gov/sites/default/files/files/ OED_ImpactReport_09302013_Final.pdf.

[20] SBA, "Small Business Development Center FY/CY 2011 Program Announcement for Renewal of the Cooperative Agreement for Current Recipient Organizations," p. 3, at https://www.sba.gov/sites/default/files/files/ 2011%20Program%20Announcement.pdf.

American Samoa.[21] These lead centers manage nearly 1,000 service centers located throughout the United States and the territories.[22] In FY2017, SBDCs provided technical assistance training services to 245,329 clients and counseling services to 188,225 clients.[23] In addition, 14,491 new businesses were formed with assistance from SBDC counselors in FY2017.[24]

WBCs are private, nonprofit organizations that provide financial, management, and marketing assistance to small businesses, including startup businesses, owned and controlled by women. Since its inception, the program has targeted the needs of socially and economically disadvantaged women.[25] In FY2017, WBCs provided technical assistance training services to 114,310 clients and counseling services to 26,318 clients.[26] They also assisted in the formation of 17,438 new businesses in FY2017.[27]

SCORE is a national volunteer organization which provides management and technical assistance training to small business owners and prospective owners.[28] In FY2017, SCORE's volunteer network of business professionals provided technical assistance training services to 519,368

---

[21] SBA, "OSBDC Program Announcement FY/CY 2016 Program Announcement No. OSBDC-2016-01 & OSBDC2016-02," p. 5, at https://www.sba.gov/sites/default/files/files/2016_Program_Announcement.pdf.

[22] Association of Small Business Development Centers, "About Us," Burke, Virginia, at http://americassbdc.org/aboutus/.

[23] SBA, *Fiscal Year 2019 Congressional Budget Justification and FY2017 Annual Performance Report*, p. 162, at https://www.sba.gov/sites/default/files/aboutsbaarticle/SBA_FY_19_508-Final-FINAL.PDF.

[24] Ibid.

[25] U.S. Congress, House Committee on Small Business, *Review of Women's Business Center Program*, 106th Cong., February 11, 1999, Serial No. 106-2 (Washington: GPO, 1999), p. 4.

[26] SBA, *Fiscal Year 2019 Congressional Budget Justification and FY2017 Annual Performance Report*, p. 163, at https://www.sba.gov/sites/default/files/aboutsbaarticle/SBA_FY_19_508-Final-FINAL.PDF.

[27] Ibid.

[28] U.S. Congress, Senate Select Committee on Small Business and House Select Committee on Small Business, *1966 Federal Handbook for Small Business: A Survey of Small Business Programs in the Federal Government Agencies*, committee print, 89th Cong., 3rd sess., January 31, 1966 (Washington: GPO, 1966), p. 5; and U.S. Congress, House Committee on Small Business, Subcommittee on Rural Development, Entrepreneurship, and Trade, *Subcommittee Hearing on Legislative Initiatives to Modernize SBA's Entrepreneurial Development Programs*, 111th Cong., 1st sess., April 2, 2009 (Washington: GPO, 2009), p. 6.

clients and counseling services to 126,892 clients.[29] They also assisted in the formation of 54,027 new businesses in FY2016 (FY2017 data are not yet available).[30]

Program Performance

In addition to compiling program output data, such as the number of clients served, since 2003 the SBA's Office of Entrepreneurial Development has commissioned an annual "multi-year time series study to assess the impact of the programs it offers to small businesses."[31] The survey asks questions about several aspects of the client's experiences with these programs, including the impact of the programs on their staffing decisions and management practices. The survey is sent each year to a stratified random sample of clients participating in the SBDC, WBC, and SCORE programs. The SBA's 2012 survey included responses from nascent clients (individuals who have taken one or more steps to start a business), startup clients (individuals who have been in business one year or less), and in-business clients (individuals who have been in business more than one year and their business was classified as small by the SBA).

The 2012 survey was released in February 2013. There were 8,263 SBDC client respondents (19% response rate), 7,217 SCORE client respondents (16% response rate), and 340 WBC client respondents (15% response rate).

The survey data reported in Table 1 through Table 6 indicate that (1) these programs assisted small businesses at all stages of development, (2) most of the respondents reported that the assistance they received was useful, and (3) most of the respondents reported that the assistance they received resulted in them changing their management practices or

---

[29] . SBA, *Fiscal Year 2019 Congressional Budget Justification and FY2017 Annual Performance Report*, p. 164, at https://www.sba.gov/sites/default/files/aboutsbaarticle/SBA_FY_19_508-Final-FINAL.PDF.

[30] Ibid.

[31] SBA, Office of Entrepreneurial Development, "Impact Study of Entrepreneurial Development Resources," September 10, 2009, p. 2, at https://www.sba.gov/sites/default/files/2009%20ED%20Impact%20Report.pdf.

strategies. However, relatively few of the respondents reported that the assistance they received resulted in them hiring new staff, retaining staff, or increasing their profit margin.

A statistical analysis of the survey data conducted by the survey's authors suggested that clients receiving three or more hours of counseling, female clients, startups, and clients owning relatively large small businesses were more likely, at a statistically significant level, than clients receiving less than three hours of counseling, male clients, non-startups, and clients owning relatively smaller businesses to report positive results concerning the financial impact of the assistance they received.[32]

Extent of SBA Management and Technical Training Assistance, By Developmental Stage

Table 1. SBA Management and Technical Assistance Training Programs' Clients, Percentage by Client Business Development Stage, 2011

SBA Resource Partner	Nascent	Startup	In-Business	Total
Small Business Development Centers	25%	19%	56%	100%
SCORE	33%	22%	45%	100%
Women Business Centers	32%	15%	53%	100%

Source: U.S. Small Business Administration, Office of Entrepreneurial Development, "Impact Study of Entrepreneurial Dynamics: Office of Entrepreneurial Development Resource Partners' Face-to-Face Counseling," September 2012, pp. 5, 9, at https://www.sba.gov/sites/default/files/files/SBA_Converted_2012_d.pdf.

Notes: The survey's authors defined nascent clients as individuals who have taken one or more steps to start a business; startup clients as individuals who have been in business one year or less; and in-business clients as individuals who have been in business more than one year and their business was classified as small by the SBA.

---

[32] SBA, Office of Entrepreneurial Development, "Impact Study of Entrepreneurial Dynamics: Office of Entrepreneurial Development Resource Partners' Face-to-Face Counseling," September 2012, p. 70, at https://www.sba.gov/sites/ default/files/files/SBA_Converted_ 2012_d.pdf.

As shown in Table 1, the survey indicated that SBDCs, WBCs, and SCORE served businesses at all three stages of development, with 44% of SBDC clients being either a nascent (25%) or startup (19%) client; 55% of SCORE clients being either a nascent (33%) or startup (22%) client; and 47% of WBC clients being either a nascent (32%) or startup (15%) client.

Impact of the SBA's Management and Technical Training Assistance, by Developmental Stage

The survey asked SBA management and training assistance participants if they thought that the information they received from counselors was extremely useful, useful, no opinion, somewhat useful, or not useful. As shown in Table 2, most of the SBDC, WBC, and SCORE clients that responded to the survey, including both nascent and startup clients, rated the usefulness of the information provided during their face-to-face management and technical assistance training as either extremely useful or useful.

Table 2. Usefulness of SBA Management and Technical Assistance Training Programs, Percentage by Client Business Development Stage, 2011 (percentage responding extremely useful or useful)

SBA Resource Partner	Nascent	Startup	In-Business	Overall
Small Business Development Centers	81%	81%	76%	79%
SCORE	76%	72%	71%	73%
Women Business Centers	75%	84%	78%	79%

Source: U.S. Small Business Administration, Office of Entrepreneurial Development, "Impact Study of Entrepreneurial Dynamics: Office of Entrepreneurial Development Resource Partners' Face-to-Face Counseling," September 2012, pp. 38, 50, 62, at https://www.sba.gov/sites/default/files/files/SBA_Converted_2012_d.pdf.

Notes: The survey's authors defined nascent clients as individuals who have taken one or more steps to start a business; startup clients as individuals who have been in business one year or less; and in-business clients as individuals who have been in business more than one year and their business was classified as small by the SBA.

Table 3. Percentage of Businesses That Changed Their Management Practices/Strategies As a Result of the SBA Management and Technical Assistance Training Received, by Client Business Development Stage, 2011 (percentage responding yes)

SBA Resource Partner	Startup	In-Business
Small Business Development Centers	56%	60%
SCORE	57%	61%
Women Business Centers	75%	59%

Source: U.S. Small Business Administration, Office of Entrepreneurial Development, "Impact Study of Entrepreneurial Dynamics: Office of Entrepreneurial Development Resource Partners' Face-to-Face Counseling," September 2012, pp. 40, 52, 64, at https://www.sba.gov/sites/default/files/files/SBA_Converted_2012_d.pdf.

Notes: The survey's authors defined startup clients as individuals who have been in business one year or less; and in-business clients as individuals who have been in business more than one year and their business was classified as small by the SBA.

The survey also asked SBA management and training assistance participants if they had changed their management practices or strategies as a result of the SBA management and technical assistance training they received. As shown in Table 3, more than half of SBDC and SCORE startup clients that responded to the survey reported that they had changed their management practices or strategies as a result of the SBA management and technical assistance training they received, slightly less than the percentages reported by in-business clients. In comparison, three-quarters of WBC startup clients that responded to the survey reported that they changed their management practices or strategies as a result of the assistance they received, somewhat higher than the percentage reported by in-business clients.

As shown in Table 4, 14% of SBDC startup clients, 11% of SCORE startup clients, and 12% of WBC startup clients of survey respondents reported that they agreed or strongly agreed with the statement that the management and technical assistance training they received enabled them to retain current staff, somewhat less than the percentages reported by in-business clients.

Table 4. Percentage of Businesses That Retained Current Staff As a Result of the SBA Management and Training Technical Assistance Received, by Client Business Development Stage, 2011 (percentage responding agree or strongly agree)

SBA Resource Partner	Startup	In-Business
Small Business Development Centers	14%	26%
SCORE	11%	19%
Women Business Centers	12%	22%

Source: U.S. Small Business Administration, Office of Entrepreneurial Development, "Impact Study of Entrepreneurial Dynamics: Office of Entrepreneurial Development Resource Partners' Face-to-Face Counseling," September 2012, pp. 42, 54, 66, at https://www.sba.gov/sites/default/files/files/SBA_Converted_2012_d.pdf.

Notes: The survey's authors defined startup clients as individuals who have been in business one year or less; and in-business clients as individuals who have been in business more than one year and their business was classified as small by the SBA.

As shown in Table 5, 13% of SBDC startup clients, 10% of SCORE startup clients, and 10% of WBC startup clients that responded to the survey reported that they either agreed or strongly agreed with the statement that the SBA management and technical assistance training they received enabled them to hire new staff, somewhat less than the percentages reported by in-business clients.

Table 5. Percentage of Businesses That Hired New Staff As a Result of the SBA Management and Training Technical Assistance Received, by Client Business Development Stage, 2011 (percentage responding agree or strongly agree)

SBA Resource Partner	Startup	In-Business
Small Business Development Centers	13%	20%
SCORE	10%	16%
Women Business Centers	10%	15%

Source: U.S. Small Business Administration, Office of Entrepreneurial Development, "Impact Study of Entrepreneurial Dynamics: Office of Entrepreneurial Development Resource Partners' Face-to-Face Counseling," September 2012, pp. 42, 54, 66, at https://www.sba.gov/sites/default/files/files/SBA_Converted_2012_d.pdf.

Notes: The survey's authors defined startup clients as individuals who have been in business one year or less; and in-business clients as individuals who have been in business more than one year and their business was classified as small by the SBA.

Table 6. Percentage of Businesses That Experienced an Increase in Their Profit Margin As a Result of the SBA Management and Training Technical Assistance Received, by Client Business Development Stage, 2011 (percentage responding agree or strongly agree)

SBA Resource Partner	Startup	In-Business
Small Business Development Centers	30%	32%
SCORE	24%	28%
Women Business Centers	31%	34%

Source: U.S. Small Business Administration, Office of Entrepreneurial Development, "Impact Study of Entrepreneurial Dynamics: Office of Entrepreneurial Development Resource Partners' Face-to-Face Counseling," September 2012, pp. 42, 54, 66, at https://www.sba.gov/sites/default/files/files/SBA_Converted_2012_d.pdf.

Notes: The survey's authors defined startup clients as individuals who have been in business one year or less; and in-business clients as individuals who have been in business more than one year and their business was classified as small by the SBA.

As shown in Table 6, 30% of SBDC startup clients, 24% of SCORE startup clients, and 31% of WBC startup clients that responded to the survey reported that they either agreed or strongly agreed with the statement that the SBA management and technical assistance training they received had a positive impact on their profit margin, somewhat less than the percentages reported by in-business clients.

The SBA's Growth Accelerators Initiative

Growth accelerators are organizations that help entrepreneurs start and scale their business. Accelerators are typically run by experienced entrepreneurs and help small businesses, especially startups, "access seed capital, mentors, and networking opportunities" and provide "targeted advice on revenue growth, job growth, and sourcing outside funding."[33] In 2012, the SBA hosted four regional events (Northeast, Midwest, South,

---

[33] SBA, *FY2016 Congressional Budget Justification and FY2014 Annual Performance Report*, p. 81, at https://www.sba.gov/sites/default/files/1-FY%202016%20CBJ%20FY%202014%20APR.PDF.

and Mid-Atlantic), which were attended by representatives "from over 100 universities and accelerators to discuss working with high-growth entrepreneurs."[34] These meetings "culminated in a White House event co-hosted by the SBA and the Department of Commerce which will help formalize the network of universities and accelerators, provide a series of 'train the trainer' events on various government programs that benefit high-growth entrepreneurs, and provide a playbook of best practices on engaging universities on innovation and entrepreneurship."[35]

The Obama Administration requested $5.0 million, and Congress recommended an appropriation of $2.5 million, for the SBA's growth accelerator initiative for FY2014. The SBA proposed to use the funding to provide matching grants to universities and private-sector accelerators "to start a new accelerator program (based on successful models) or scale an existing program."[36] The SBA also indicated that it planned to request funding for five years ($25 million in total funding) and feature a required 4:1 private-sector match.[37] However, because it received half of its budget request ($2.5 million), the SBA decided to reconsider the program's requirements. As part of that reconsideration, the SBA dropped the 4:1 private-sector match in an effort to enable the program to have a larger effect.[38]

On May 12, 2014, the SBA announced the availability of 50 growth accelerator grants of $50,000 each. It received more than 800 applications by the August 2, 2014, deadline. The 50 awards were announced in September 2014.[39]

---

[34] SBA, *FY2014 Congressional Budget Justification and FY2012 Annual Performance Report*, p. 59, at http://www.sba.gov/sites/default/files/files/1-FY%202014%20CBJ%20FY%202012%20APR.PDF.
[35] Ibid., pp. 59-60.
[36] Ibid., p. 60.
[37] Ibid.
[38] SBA, Office of Congressional and Legislative Affairs, "Correspondence with the author," May 6, 2014.
[39] SBA, "SBA Launches Accelerator Competition to Award $2.5 million for Small Business Startups," May 12, 2014, at https://www.sba.gov/content/sba-launches-accelerator-competition-award-25-million-small-business-startups-0; SBA, "More than 800 Small Business Startups Compete for 50 Cash Prizes in SBA's Growth Accelerator Competition," August 4, 2014, at https://www.sba.gov/content/more-800-small-business-startups-compete-50-cashprizes-sbas-growth-accelerator-competition; and SBA, "SBA Spurs Economic

Congress recommended that the program receive $4.0 million in FY2015, and $1.0 million in FY2016, FY2017, and FY2018.[40] Congress also directed the SBA in its explanatory statements accompanying P.L. 113-235 and P.L. 114-113 to "require $4 of matching funds for every $1 awarded under the growth accelerators program."[41]

The SBA announced the award of 80 growth accelerator grants of $50,000 each on August 4, 2015 ($4.0 million), 68 growth accelerator grants of $50,000 each on August 31, 2016 ($3.4 million), and 20 growth accelerator grants of $50,000 each on October 30, 2017 ($1 million).[42]

Reports from the first round of awardees indicated that more than 1,000 small businesses graduated from the accelerators initiative, with each accelerator graduating about 10 small businesses per year. Award

---

Growth, Announces 50 Awards to Accelerators," September 4, 2014, at https://www.sba.gov/content/sba-spurs-economic-growth-announces-50-awardsaccelerators.

[40] Rep. Harold Rogers, "Explanatory Statement Submitted by Mr. Rogers of Kentucky, Chairman of the House Committee on Appropriations Regarding the House Amendment to the Senate Amendment on H.R. 83," *Congressional Record*, vol. 160, part 151 (December 11, 2014), p. H9740; Rep. Harold Rogers, "Explanatory Statement Submitted By Mr. Rogers of Kentucky, Chairman of the House Committee on Appropriations Regarding House Amendment No. 1 to the Senate Amendment on H.R. 2029 Consolidated Appropriations Act," *Congressional Record*, vol. 161, no. 184- Book II (December 17, 2015), p. H10139; Rep. Rodney Frelinghuysen, "Explanatory Statement Submitted By Mr. Frelinghuysen of New Jersey, Chairman of the House Committee on Appropriations Regarding the House Amendment to the Senate Amendments on H.R. 244 [the Consolidated Appropriations Act, 2017]," *Congressional Record*, vol. 163, no. 76-Book II (May 3, 2017), p. H3786; and "Explanatory Statement Submitted by Mr. Frelinghuysen, Chairman of the House Committee on Appropriations Regarding the House Amendment to the Senate Amendments on H.R. 1625 [the Consolidated Appropriations Act, 2018] (Division E – Financial Services and General Government Appropriations Act, 2018)," p. 87, at http://docs.house.gov/billsthisweek/20180319/DIV%20E%20FSGG%20SOM%20FY18%20OMNI.OCR.pdf.

[41] Rep. Harold Rogers, "Explanatory Statement Submitted by Mr. Rogers of Kentucky, Chairman of the House Committee on Appropriations Regarding the House Amendment to the Senate Amendment on H.R. 83," *Congressional Record*, vol. 160, part 151 (December 11, 2014), p. H9741; and Rep. Harold Rogers, "Explanatory Statement Submitted By Mr. Rogers of Kentucky, Chairman of the House Committee on Appropriations Regarding House Amendment No. 1 to the Senate Amendment on H.R. 2029 Consolidated Appropriations Act," *Congressional Record*, vol. 161, no. 184-Book II (December 17, 2015), p. H10140.

[42] SBA, "SBA Boosts Economic Impact of Accelerators with $4.4 Million in Prizes," August 4, 2015, at https://www.sba.gov/content/sba-boosts-economic-impact-accelerators-44-million-prizes-0; SBA, "SBA Announces $3.4 Million for Small Business Startups," August 31, 2016, at https://www.sba.gov/content/sba-announces-34-millionsmall-business-startups; and SBA, "SBA Announces 20 Growth Accelerator Fund Competition Recipients," October 30, 2017, at https://www.sba.gov/node/1594788.

recipients also reported supporting the creation or retention of nearly 4,800 jobs.[43]

The Trump Administration requested that the initiative receive no funding in FY2018 and FY2019.[44]

SBA LENDING PROGRAMS

The SBA's business lending programs are designed to encourage lenders to provide loans to small businesses "that might not otherwise obtain financing on reasonable terms and conditions."[45] Historically, the SBA's lending programs have been justified on the grounds that small businesses can be at a disadvantage, compared with other businesses, when trying to obtain access to sufficient capital and credit.[46] As an economist explained,

> Growing firms need resources, but many small firms may have a hard time obtaining loans because they are young and have little credit history. Lenders may also be reluctant to lend to small firms with innovative products because it might be difficult to collect enough reliable information to correctly estimate the risk for such products. If it's true that the lending process leaves worthy projects unfunded, some suggest that it would be good to fix this "market failure" with

---

[43] SBA, *FY2017 Congressional Budget Justification and FY2015 Annual Performance Report*, p. 85, at https://www.sba.gov/sites/default/files/FY17-CBJ_FY15-APR.pdf.

[44] SBA, *FY2018 Congressional Budget Justification and FY2016 Annual Performance Report*, p. 12, at https://www.sba.gov/sites/default/files/aboutsbaarticle/FINAL_SBA_FY_2018_CBJ_May_22_2017c.pdf; and SBA, *FY2019 Congressional Budget Justification and FY2017 Annual Performance Report*, p. 13, at https://www.sba.gov/ sites/default/files/aboutsbaarticle/SBA_FY_2019_CBJ_APR_2_12_post.pdf.

[45] SBA, *Fiscal Year 2010 Congressional Budget Justification*, p. 30, at https://www.sba.gov/sites/default/files/aboutsbaarticle/Congressional_Budget_Justification_2010.pdf.

[46] Proponents of providing federal funding for the SBA's loan guarantee programs also argue that small business can promote competitive markets. See P.L. 83-163, §2(a), as amended; and 15 U.S.C. §631a.

government programs aimed at improving small businesses' access to credit.[47]

In FY2018, the SBA enhanced small business access to capital by approving about $30.2 billion in loans to small businesses. The SBA's two largest loan guaranty programs are the 7(a) loan guaranty program (nearly $25.4 billion approved in FY2018) and the 504/CDC loan guaranty program (nearly $4.8 billion approved in FY2018). In addition, the SBA's Microloan program, which includes startups among its targeted audiences, provides direct loans to 144 active nonprofit intermediary Microloan lenders to provide "microloans" of up to $50,000 to small business owners, entrepreneurs, and nonprofit child care centers. The Microloan program provided $76.8 million in loans to small businesses in FY2018.[48]

The SBA's 7(a), 504/CDC, and Microloan Programs

7(a) Loan Guaranty Program[49]

The SBA's 7(a) loan guaranty program is considered the agency's flagship loan guaranty program.[50] It is named from Section 7(a) of the Small Business Act of 1953 (P.L. 83-163, as amended), which authorizes the SBA to provide business loans to American small businesses. The SBA provides participating, certified lenders a guaranty of repayment in the case

---

[47] Veronique de Rugy, *Why the Small Business Administration's Loan Programs Should Be Abolished*, American Enterprise Institute for Public Policy Research, AEI Working Paper #126, April 13, 2006, at http://www.aei.org/wpcontent/uploads/2011/10/20060414_wp126.pdf. Also, see U.S. Government Accountability Office, *Small Business Administration: 7(a) Loan Program Needs Additional Performance Measures*, GAO-08-226T, November 1, 2007, pp. 3, 9-11, at http://www.gao.gov/new.items/d08226t.pdf.

[48] SBA, "Microloan Nationwide Loan Report, October 1, 2017 through September 30, 2018," October 26, 2018.

[49] For further information and analysis concerning the SBA's 7(a) program, see CRS Report R41146, *Small Business Administration 7(a) Loan Guaranty Program*, by Robert Jay Dilger.

[50] U.S. Congress, House Committee on Small Business, Subcommittee on Finance and Tax, *Subcommittee Hearing on Improving the SBA's Access to Capital Programs for Our Nation's Small Business*, 110th Cong., 2nd sess., March 5, 2008, H.Hrg. 110-76 (Washington: GPO, 2008), p. 2.

of a default of up to 85% of qualified loan amounts of $150,000 or less and up to 75% of qualified loan amounts exceeding $150,000 to the program's loan limit of $5 million.

Proceeds from 7(a) loans may be used to establish a new business or to assist in the operation, acquisition, or expansion of an existing business. Specific uses include to acquire land (by purchase or lease); improve a site (e.g., grading, streets, parking lots, and landscaping); purchase, convert, expand, or renovate one or more existing buildings; construct one or more new buildings; acquire (by purchase or lease) and install fixed assets; purchase inventory, supplies, and raw materials; finance working capital; and refinance certain outstanding debts.[51]

504 Certified Development Company Loan Guaranty Program[52]

The SBA's 504 Certified Development Company (504/CDC) loan guaranty program provides long-term fixed rate financing for major fixed assets, such as land, buildings, equipment, and machinery. A 504/CDC loan cannot be used for working capital or inventory. It is named from Section 504 of the Small Business Investment Act of 1958 (P.L. 85-699, as amended), which authorized the sale of debentures pursuant to Section 503 of the act, which previously authorized the program.[53]

The 504/CDC program is administered through nonprofit CDCs. Of the total project costs, a third-party lender must provide at least 50% of the financing, the CDC provides up to 40% of the financing backed by a 100% SBA-guaranteed debenture, and the applicant provides at least 10% of the financing.

The SBA's debenture is backed with the full faith and credit of the United States and is sold to underwriters who form debenture pools.

---

[51] 13 C.F.R. §120.120.
[52] For further information and analysis of the SBA's 504/CDC program, see CRS Report R41184, *Small Business Administration 504/CDC Loan Guaranty Program*, by Robert Jay Dilger.
[53] The 504/CDC program was preceded by a 501 state development company program (1958-1982), a 502 local development company program (1958-1995), and a 503/CDC program (1980-1986). The 504/CDC program started in 1986. There are a small number of for-profit CDCs that participated in these predecessor programs that have been grandfathered into the current 504/CDC program. See SBA, "SOP 50 10 5(G): Lender and Development Company Loan Programs," (effective October 1, 2014), p. 43, at https://www.sba.gov/sites/default/files/sops/

Investors purchase interests in the debenture pools and receive certificates representing ownership of all or part of the pool. The SBA and CDCs use various agents to facilitate the sale and service of the certificates and the orderly flow of funds among the parties.[54] After a 504/CDC loan is approved and disbursed, accounting for the loan is set up at the Central Servicing Agent (CSA, currently PricewaterhouseCoopers Public Sector LLP), not the SBA. The SBA guarantees the timely payment of the debenture. If the small business is behind in its loan payments, the SBA pays the difference to the investor on every semiannual due date.

The 504/CDC program is somewhat unique in that borrowers must meet one of two specified economic development objectives. First, borrowers, other than small manufacturers, must create or retain at least one job for every $75,000 of project debenture. Borrowers who are small manufacturers must create or retain one job per $120,000 of project debenture. The jobs created do not have to be at the project facility, but 75% of the jobs must be created in the community where the project is located. Using job retention to satisfy this requirement is allowed only if the CDC "can reasonably show that jobs would be lost to the community if the project was not done."[55]

Second, if the borrower does not meet the job creation or retention requirement, the borrower can retain eligibility by meeting any one of 5 community development goals or 10 public policy goals, provided the CDC's overall portfolio of outstanding debentures meets or exceeds the job creation or retention criteria of at least one job opportunity created or retained for every $75,000 in project debenture (or for every $85,000 in project debenture for projects located in special geographic areas such as Alaska, Hawaii, state-designated enterprise zones, empowerment zones,

---

[54] 13 C.F.R. §120.801. 504/CDC debentures are normally sold and proceeds disbursed on the Wednesday after the second Sunday of each month. See SBA, "SOP 50 10 5(I): Lender and Development Company Loan Programs," (effective January 1, 2017), pp. 295-297, at https://www.sba.gov/sites/default/files/sops/SOP_50_10_5_I_FINAL_Clean_Highlighted_Changes.pdf.

[55] SBA, "SOP 50 10 5(J): Lender and Development Company Loan Programs," (effective January 1, 2018), p. 297, at https://www.sba.gov/sites/default/files/2017-12/SOP%2050%2010%205%28J%29_Technical%20Corrections%20%28FINAL%29_1.pdf.

enterprise communities, labor surplus areas, or opportunity zones).[56] Loans to small manufacturers are excluded from the calculation of this average.[57]

The Microloan Program[58]

The SBA's Microloan program was authorized in 1991 (P.L. 102-140, the Departments of Commerce, Justice, and State, the Judiciary, and Related Agencies Appropriations Act, 1992) as a five-year demonstration program to address the perceived disadvantages faced by very small businesses in gaining access to capital. The program became operational in 1992, and it was made permanent, subject to reauthorization, in 1997 (P.L. 105-135, the Small Business Reauthorization Act of 1997). Its stated purpose is

> to assist women, low-income, veteran ... and minority entrepreneurs and business owners and other individuals possessing the capability to operate successful business concerns; to assist small business concerns in those areas suffering from a lack of credit due to economic downturns; ... to make loans to eligible intermediaries to enable such intermediaries to provide small-scale loans, particularly loans in amounts averaging not more than $10,000, to start-up, newly established, or growing small business concerns for working capital or the acquisition of materials, supplies, or equipment; [and] to make grants to eligible intermediaries that, together with non-Federal matching funds, will enable such

---

[56] SBA, "Development Company Loan Program - Job Creation and Retention Requirements; Additional Areas for Higher Portfolio Average," 83 *Federal Register* 55225-55226, November 2, 2018. Previously, P.L. 108-447, the Small Business Reauthorization and Manufacturing Assistance Act of 2004, had set these thresholds as: at least one job opportunity per every $50,000 guaranteed by the Administration and per every $75,000 guaranteed by the Administration for small manufactures. P.L. 111-5, the American Recovery and Reinvestment Act of 2009, increased the $50,000 threshold to every $65,000 guaranteed by the Administration.

[57] A job opportunity is defined as a full-time (or equivalent) permanent, or contracted, job created within two years of receipt of 504/CDC funds or retained in the community because of a 504/CDC loan. See SBA, "SOP 50 10 5(J): Lender and Development Company Loan Programs," effective January 1, 2018, p. 256, at https://www.sba.gov/ document/sop-50-10-5-lender-development-company-loan-programs.

[58] For further information and analysis concerning the SBA's Microloan program, see CRS Report R41057, *Small Business Administration Microloan Program*, by Robert Jay Dilger.

intermediaries to provide intensive marketing, management, and technical assistance to microloan borrowers.[59]

The maximum Microloan amount is $50,000 and no borrower may owe an intermediary more than $50,000 at any one time.[60] Microloan proceeds may be used only for working capital and acquisition of materials, supplies, furniture, fixtures, and equipment. Loans cannot be made to acquire land or property, and must be repaid within six years.[61] Within these parameters, loan terms vary depending on the loan's size, the planned use of funds, the requirements of the intermediary lender, and the needs of the small business borrower. Interest rates are negotiated between the borrower and the intermediary (within statutory limits), and typically range from 7% to 9%.[62] Each intermediary establishes its own lending and credit requirements. However, borrowers are generally required to provide some type of collateral, and a personal guarantee to repay the loan. The SBA does not review the loan for creditworthiness.[63]

Program Performance

The SBA maintains a relatively extensive output database for its business lending programs (e.g., number and amount of loans approved and disbursed by program and by year; number and amount of loans approved and disbursed by program and by year to various demographic groups, including startups; number and amount of loans approved and disbursed by program by state; amount of loan purchases and recoveries by program and by year). It also asks borrowers to report information concerning the impact the loans have on job creation and retention.

---

[59] 15 U.S.C. §636 7(m)(1)(A).
[60] 13 C.F.R §120.707. P.L. 111-240, the Small Business Jobs Act of 2010, increased the loan limit for borrowers from $35,000 to $50,000.
[61] Ibid.
[62] In FY2018, Microloan borrowers were charged, on average, an interest rate of 7.604%. See SBA, "Microloan Nationwide Loan Report, October 1, 2017 through September 30, 2018," October 26, 2018.
[63] SBA, "Microloan Program," at https://www.sba.gov/content/microloan-program.

As will be shown, these data suggest that the SBA provides lending support to small businesses at all stages of development, but to varying degrees, with the Microloan program providing a relatively higher share of its lending to startups than the 7(a) and 504/CDC programs. The data also suggest that these programs have a generally positive impact on job creation and retention, but, as will be discussed, the data are self-reported and subject to methodological limitations.

Extent of SBA Lending Assistance, By Developmental Stage

As expected given their missions, the Microloan program provides a greater percentage of its loan proceeds to startups (38.0% of total loan disbursements in FY2018) than does the 7(a) program (16.6% of total loan approvals to date in FY2019) and the 504/CDC program (16.8% of total loan approvals to date in FY2019).[64]

SBA VENTURE CAPITAL PROGRAMS

The SBA has two venture capital programs. The SBIC program, authorized by P.L. 85-699, the Small Business Investment Act of 1958, as amended, is the SBA's flagship venture capital program.[65] It is designed to "improve and stimulate the national economy in general and the small business segment thereof in particular" by stimulating and supplementing "the flow of private equity capital and long-term loan funds which small business concerns need for the sound financing of their business operations and for their growth, expansion, and modernization, and which are not available in adequate supply."[66] The SBA also sponsors the much smaller New Markets Venture Capital Program, which is not discussed here given

---

[64] SBA, "Microloan Nationwide Loan Report, October 1, 2017 through September 30, 2018," October 26, 2018; and SBA, "SBA Lending Statistics for Major Programs as of (12-14-2018) at https://www.sba.gov/about-sba/sbanewsroom/weekly-lending-reports/2018/sba-lending-statistics-major-programs-12-14-2018.

[65] For further information and analysis of the SBA's SBIC program, see CRS Report R41456, *SBA Small Business Investment Company Program*, by Robert Jay Dilger.

[66] 15 U.S.C. §661.

its relatively small size ($1.65 million in financing to four small businesses in FY2015, and no new financing since then). It is designed to promote economic development and the creation of wealth and job opportunities in low-income geographic areas by addressing the unmet equity investment needs of small businesses located in those areas.[67]

The SBIC Program

The SBA does not make direct investments in small businesses. It partners with privately owned and managed SBICs licensed by the SBA to provide financing to small businesses with private capital the SBIC has raised (called regulatory capital) and with funds (called leverage) the SBIC borrows at favorable rates because the SBA guarantees the debenture (loan obligation). As of September 30, 2018, there were 305 licensed SBICs participating in the SBIC program.[68]

A licensed debenture SBIC in good standing, with a demonstrated need for funds, may apply to the SBA for financial assistance (leverage) of up to 300% of its private capital. However, the SBA has traditionally approved debenture SBICs for a maximum of 200% of their private capital and no fund management team may exceed the allowable maximum amount of leverage of $175 million per SBIC and $350 million for two or more licenses under common control.[69]

SBICs pursue investments in a broad range of industries, geographic areas, and stages of investment. Some SBICs specialize in a particular field or industry, while others invest more generally. Most SBICs concentrate on

---

[67] For further information and analysis of the SBA's New Markets Venture Capital program, see CRS Report R42565, *SBA New Markets Venture Capital Program*, by Robert Jay Dilger.
[68] SBA, "SBIC Program: Fiscal Year Data for the period ending September 30, 2018," at https://www.sba.gov/article/ 2018/nov/16/fiscal-year-data-period-ending-september-30-2018.
[69] 13 C.F.R. §107.1120; 13 C.F.R. §107.1150; P.L. 114-113, the Consolidated Appropriations Act, 2016, which increased the multiple licenses/family of funds limit to $350 million from $225 million; and P.L. 115-187, the Small Business Investment Opportunity Act of 2017, which increased the maximum amount of leverage for individual SBICs to $175 million from $150 million.

a particular stage of investment (i.e., startup, expansion, or turnaround) and geographic area.

SBICs provide equity capital to small businesses in various ways, including by

- purchasing small business equity securities (e.g., stock, stock options, warrants, limited partnership interests, membership interests in a limited liability company, or joint venture interests);[70]
- making loans to small businesses, either independently or in cooperation with other private or public lenders, that have a maturity of no more than 20 years;[71]
- purchasing debt securities from small businesses;[72] and
- providing small businesses (subject to limitations) a guarantee of their monetary obligations to creditors not associated with the SBIC.[73]

The SBIC program currently has invested or committed about $30.1 billion in small businesses, with the SBA's share of capital at risk about $14.3 billion. In FY2018, the SBA committed to guarantee $2.52 billion in SBIC small business investments. SBICs invested another $2.98 billion from private capital for a total of $5.50 billion in financing for 1,151 small businesses.[74]

---

[70] 13 C.F.R. §107.800. A SBIC is not allowed to become a general partner in any unincorporated business or become jointly or severally liable for any obligations of an unincorporated business.

[71] 13 C.F.R. §107.810; and 13 C.F.R. §107.840.

[72] 13 C.F.R. §107.815. Debt securities are instruments evidencing a loan with an option or any other right to acquire equity securities in a small business or its affiliates, or a loan which by its terms is convertible into an equity position, or a loan with a right to receive royalties that are excluded from the cost of money.

[73] 13 C.F.R. §107.820.

[74] SBA, "SBIC Program: Fiscal Year Data for the period ending September 30, 2018," at https://www.sba.gov/article/2018/nov/16/fiscal-year-data-period-ending-september-30-2018.

Extent of SBIC Financial Assistance, by Developmental Stage

The SBIC program provides financing to small businesses at all developmental stages, with most of its financing provided to businesses that have been in operation for at least five years. The amount of SBIC financing provided to startups (defined as being in operation for one year or less) as a share of SBIC financing has increased somewhat since FY2014 (16.5% in FY2014, 17.9% in FY2015, 15.3% in FY2016, 19.3% in FY2017, and 23.0% in FY2018).[75]

Early Stage Debenture SBIC Initiative

In 2012, the Obama Administration established the early stage debenture SBIC initiative to encourage additional SBIC investments in startups (up to $150 million in SBIC leverage in FY2012, and up to $200 million in SBIC leverage per fiscal year thereafter until the initiative's $1 billion limit was reached).[76] Early stage debenture SBICs are required to invest at least 50% of their financings in early stage small businesses, defined as small businesses that have never achieved positive cash flow from operations in any fiscal year.[77]

In recognition of the higher risk associated with investments in early stage small businesses, the initiative includes "several new regulatory provisions intended to reduce the risk that an early stage SBIC would default on its leverage and to improve SBA's recovery prospects should a default occur."[78] For example, early stage debenture SBICs are required to raise more regulatory capital (at least $20 million) than debenture SBICs (at least $5 million). They are also subject to special distribution rules to require pro rata repayment of SBA leverage when making distributions of profits to their investors. In addition, early stage debenture SBICs are also provided less leverage (up to 100% of regulatory capital, $50 million maximum) than debenture SBICs (up to 200% of regulatory capital, $150

---

[75] SBA Office of Congressional and Legislative Affairs, "Correspondence with the author," December 20, 2018.
[76] SBA, "Small Business Investment Companies - Early Stage SBICs," 77 *Federal Register* 25043, 25050, April 27, 2012.
[77] Ibid., pp. 25051-25053.
[78] Ibid., p. 25043.

million maximum per SBIC and $225 million for two or more SBICs under common control).

On May 1, 2012, the SBA announced its first annual call for venture capital fund managers to submit an application to become a licensed early stage debenture SBIC.[79] Thirty-three venture capital funds submitted preliminary application materials. After these materials were examined and interviews held, the SBA announced on October 23, 2012, that it had issued Green Light letters to six funds, formally inviting them to file license applications.[80]

The SBA's second, third, fourth, and fifth annual calls for venture capital fund managers to submit an application to become a licensed early stage debenture SBIC took place on December 18, 2012, February 4, 2014, January 12, 2015, and February 2, 2016, respectively.[81]

To date, 5 of the 63 investment funds that have applied to participate in the program have been granted an early stage SBIC license.[82] As of September 30, 2016, the 5 early stage SBICs had raised $246.9 million in private capital, received $78.0 million in SBA-guaranteed leverage, had

---

[79] The deadline for completing the four-step application process for applicants with signed commitments for at least $15 million in regulatory capital and evidence of their ability to raise the remaining $5 million in regulatory capital was July 30, 2012. The deadline for all other applicants was May 15, 2013. Applicants must first complete a Management Assessment Questionnaire (MAQ), then, if invited, complete an interview process, then receive a Green Light letter, and, finally, submit the SBIC license application, consisting of SBA Form 2181 and SBA Form 2182. See SBA, "Small Business Investment Companies—Early Stage SBICs," 77 *Federal Register* 25775-25779, May 1, 2012.

[80] SBA, "SBA's Growth Capital Program Sets Record For Third Year in a Row $2.95 Billion in Financing for Small Businesses in FY12," at https://www.sba.gov/content/sbas-growth-capital-program-sets-record-third-year-row; and SBA, "The Small Business Investment Company (SBIC) Program: Annual Report FY2012," p. 20, at https://www.sba.gov/sites/default/files/files/SBIC%20Program%20FY%202012%20Annual%20Report.pdf.

[81] SBA, "Small Business Investment Companies—Early Stage SBICs," 77 *Federal Register* 74908-74913, December 18, 2012; SBA, "Small Business Investment Companies—Early Stage SBICs," 79 *Federal Register* 6665, February 4, 2014; SBA, "Small Business Investment Companies—Early Stage SBICs," 79 *Federal Register 18750*, April 3, 2014; SBA, "Small Business Investment Companies—Early Stage SBICs," 80 *Federal Register 1575-1579*, January 12, 2015; and SBA, "Small Business Investment Companies—Early Stage SBICs," 81 *Federal Register 5508-5511*, February 2, 2016.

[82] SBA, "Small Business Investment Companies–Early Stage," 80 *Federal Register* 14034, March 18, 2015; and SBA, Office of Innovation and Investment, slides, "SBIC Early Stage Innovation Program," at https://www.sba.gov/sites/ default/files/articles/OII Early Stage Slide Deck January_2016.pdf.

$105.3 million in outstanding commitments, and invested $160.7 million in 62 small businesses. In FY2016, early stage SBICs invested $66.2 million in 45 small businesses.[83]

On September 19, 2016, the SBA published a notice of proposed rulemaking in the *Federal Register*, which included proposed changes to the early stage SBIC initiative to "make material improvements to the program" and "attract more qualified early stage fund managers."[84] The SBA, at that time, indicated its intention to continue the initiative beyond its initial five-year term.[85] However, the SBA, now under the Trump Administration, stopped accepting new applications for the early stage SBIC initiative in 2017. In addition, on June 11, 2018, the SBA withdrew the September 19, 2016, proposed rule that included provisions designed to encourage qualified SBICs to participate in the initiative.[86] The SBA indicated that it took this action "because very few qualified funds applied to the Early Stage SBIC initiative, the costs were not commensurate with the results, and the comments to the proposed rule did not demonstrate broad support for a permanent Early Stage SBIC program."[87]

It is too early to determine the extent to which the SBA's decision to stop accepting new applications for the early stage debenture initiative may affect the share and amount of total SBA financing provided to startups.

---

[83] SBA, Office of Congressional and Legislative Affairs, "Correspondence with the author," November 15, 2016.

[84] SBA, "Small Business Investment Companies (SBIC); Early Stage Initiative," 81 *Federal Register* 64075-64080, September 19, 2016. The proposed changes were based in part on feedback received on an earlier, advance notice of proposed rulemaking. See SBA, "Small Business Investment Companies–Early Stage," 80 *Federal Register* 14034, March 18, 2015. The proposed changes would have allowed early stage applicants to apply at any time, similar to other SBIC applicants, instead of only during limited time frames identified in the *Federal Register* (which the SBA has published on an annual basis since 2012); allowed early stage SBICs to obtain an unsecured line of credit without SBA approval under specified conditions; allowed an application from an applicant under common control with an existing early stage SBIC that has outstanding debentures or debenture commitments; and increased the initiative's maximum leverage commitment of 100% of regulatory capital or $50 million, whichever is less, to 100% of regulatory capital or $75 million, whichever is less.

[85] SBA, "Small Business Investment Companies (SBIC); Early Stage Initiative," 81 *Federal Register* 64075, September 19, 2016.

[86] SBA, "Small Business Investment Companies (SBIC); Early Stage Initiative," 83 *Federal Register* 26875, June 11, 2018.

[87] Ibid., p. 26875.

CONCLUDING OBSERVATIONS

The SBA has indicated, from the very start of the agency, that assisting small businesses to create and retain jobs is part of its mission. However, the SBA also has a long-established tradition of providing assistance to all qualifying small businesses. With some exceptions, the SBA has generally not taken actions or requested authorization to focus its assistance solely onto those businesses, such as startups, that are judged to be the ones most likely to contribute to job growth or wealth creation. The tradition of providing SBA assistance to all qualified small businesses without regard to their potential for job growth or wealth creation is perhaps understandable given that the tradition aligns with one of the SBA's primary missions, which is to promote free markets—by limiting monopoly and oligarchy formation within all industries. In addition, the tradition of providing assistance to all qualified small businesses has, for the most part, never been challenged by Congress or interested small business organizations.

The SBA's recent initiatives to focus increased attention to assisting startups (e.g., the Growth Accelerators initiative and the recently sunset early stage debenture SBIC initiative) are less of a challenge to the SBA's tradition of assisting all qualified small businesses than a recognition of the potential role of startups in job creation and concerns about the pace of job growth during the current economic recovery.[88] For example, the SBA has offered the initiatives as supplements to, rather than replacements of, existing programs.

As mentioned previously, the relatively "high risk-high reward" of targeting SBA assistance to startups makes it tempting for some and controversial for others. Most who have participated in these programs report in surveys sponsored by the SBA that the programs were useful. However, determining if the risk of financial losses associated with

---

[88] For additional information concerning the recently sunset early stage debenture SBIC initiative see SBA, "Small Business Investment Companies - Early Stage SBICs," 76 *Federal Register* 76907-76917, December 9, 2011; SBA, "Small Business Investment Companies - Early Stage SBICs," 77 *Federal Register* 25042-25055, April 27, 2012; and CRS Report R41456, *SBA Small Business Investment Company Program*, by Robert Jay Dilger.

targeting SBA assistance to startups outweighs the startups' potential for job growth is difficult because the data collected by the SBA concerning these programs' impact on economic activity and job creation are somewhat limited and subject to methodological challenges concerning their validity as reliable performance measures.

In: Small Business
Editor: Angel Becker
ISBN: 978-1-53615-969-1
© 2019 Nova Science Publishers, Inc.

Chapter 5

SMALL BUSINESS MANAGEMENT AND TECHNICAL ASSISTANCE TRAINING PROGRAMS (UPDATED)[*]

Robert Jay Dilger

SUMMARY

The Small Business Administration (SBA) has provided technical and managerial assistance to small businesses since it began operations in 1953. Initially, the SBA provided its own small business management and technical assistance training programs. Over time, the SBA has relied increasingly on third parties to provide that training.

Congressional interest in the SBA's management and technical assistance training programs ($226.7 million in FY2019) has increased in recent years, primarily because these programs are viewed as a means to assist small businesses create and retain jobs. These programs fund about "14,000 resource partners," including 63 lead small business development centers (SBDCs) and more than 900 SBDC local outreach locations, 121 women's business centers (WBCs), and 320 chapters of the mentoring

---

[*] This is an edited, reformatted and augmented version of a Congressional Research Service publication R41352, prepared for Members and Committees of Congress dated February 21, 2019.

program, SCORE. The SBA reports that more than 1 million aspiring entrepreneurs and small business owners receive training from an SBA-supported resource partner each year.

The Department of Commerce also provides management and technical assistance training for small businesses. For example, its Minority Business Development Agency provides training to minority business owners to assist them in obtaining contracts and financial awards.

Some have argued that the SBA could improve program efficiency by eliminating duplication of services across federal agencies and improving cooperation and coordination among the SBA's resource partners. Congress has also explored ways to improve the SBA's measurement of these programs' effectiveness.

This chapter examines the historical development of federal small business management and technical assistance training programs; describes their current structures, operations, and budgets; and assesses their administration and oversight and the measures used to determine their effectiveness. It also discusses legislation to improve program performance, including

P.L. 114-88, the Recovery Improvements for Small Entities After Disaster Act of 2015 (RISE After Disaster Act of 2015), which, among other things, authorizes the SBA to provide up to two years of additional funding to its resource partners to assist small businesses located in a presidentially declared major disaster area and authorizes SBDCs to provide assistance outside the SBDC's state, without regard to geographical proximity to the SBDC, if the small business is in a presidentially declared major disaster area. This assistance can be provided "for a period of not more than two years after the date on which the President" has declared the area a major disaster; and

P.L. 115-141, the Consolidated Appropriations Act of 2018, among other provisions, relaxed requirements that Microloan intermediaries may spend no more than 25% of Microloan technical assistance grant funds on prospective borrowers and no more than 25% of those funds on contracts with third parties to provide that technical assistance by increasing those percentages to no more than 50%.

FEDERAL MANAGEMENT AND TECHNICAL ASSISTANCE TRAINING PROGRAMS

The Small Business Administration (SBA) administers several programs to support small businesses, including loan guaranty programs to enhance small business access to capital; programs to increase small business opportunities in federal contracting; direct loans for businesses, homeowners, and renters to assist their recovery from natural disasters; and access to entrepreneurial education to assist with business formation and expansion. The SBA has provided "technical and managerial aides to small-business concerns, by advising and counseling on matters in connection with government procurement and on policies, principles and practices of good management" since it began operations in 1953.[1]

Initially, the SBA provided its own management and technical assistance training programs. Over time, the SBA has relied increasingly on third parties to provide that training. More than 1 million aspiring entrepreneurs and small business owners receive training from an SBA-supported resource partner each year.[2]

The SBA has argued that its support of management and technical assistance training for small businesses has contributed "to the long-term success of these businesses and their ability to grow and create jobs."[3] It currently provides financial support to about 14,000 resource partners, including 63 small business development centers (SBDCs) and more than 900 SBDC local outreach locations, 121 women's business centers (WBCs), and 320 chapters of the mentoring program, SCORE (Service Corps of Retired Executives).[4]

The SBA receives an annual appropriation for entrepreneurial development/noncredit programs collectively (currently $247.7 million).[5]

---

[1] U.S. Congress, Senate Committee on Banking and Currency, *Extension of the Small Business Act of 1953*, report to accompany S. 2127, 84th Cong., 1st sess., July 22, 1955, S.Rept. 84-1350 (Washington: GPO, 1955), p. 17.

[2] U.S. Small Business Administration (SBA), *FY2019 Congressional Budget Justification and FY2017 Annual Performance Report*, p. 20, at https://www.sba.gov/sites/default/files/aboutsbaarticle/SBA_FY_2019_CBJ_APR_2_12_post.pdf.

[3] SBA, *Fiscal Year 2011 Congressional Budget Justification and FY2009 Annual Performance Report*, p. 4, at https://www.sba.gov/sites/default/files/ aboutsbaarticle/Congressional_Budget_Justification.pdf.

[4] SBA, *FY2019 Congressional Budget Justification and FY2017 Annual Performance Report*, p. 3, at https://www.sba.gov/sites/default/files/aboutsbaarticle/ SBA_FY_2019_CBJ_APR_2_12_post.pdf; SBA, "Women's Business Centers Directory," at http://www.sba.gov/about-offices-content/1/2895/resources/13729; and SCORE, "About SCORE," at https://www.score.org/about-score.

[5] P.L. 116-6, the Consolidated Appropriations Act, 2019.

The SBA uses these funds for its management and training programs ($226.7 million in FY2019), administration of the HUBZone program ($3.0 million), and the State Trade and Export Promotion program ($18.0 million).[6] Congress specifies the appropriation amount for SBDCs (currently $131.0 million) and the Microloan Technical Assistance Program (currently $31.0 million) in its annual appropriation act and includes recommended appropriation amounts for the SBA's other management and training programs in either the explanatory statement or the committee report accompanying the appropriations act. The SBA is not legally required to adhere to the recommended amounts but has traditionally done so in the past.

Table 1 shows the appropriation amounts Congress specified for SBDCs and the Microloan Technical Assistance Program and the appropriation amounts Congress recommended for the SBA's other management and training programs in FY2015 ($198.6 million), FY2016 ($210.1 million), FY2017 ($224.1 million), FY2018 ($226.1 million), and FY2019 ($226.7 million).

The Department of Commerce also provides management and technical assistance training for small businesses. For example, the Department of Commerce's Minority Business Development Agency (MBDA) provides training to minority business owners to assist them in obtaining contracts and financial awards.[7] In addition, the Department of Commerce's Economic Development Administration's Local Technical Assistance Program promotes efforts to build and expand local organizational capacity in economically distressed areas. As part of that effort, it funds projects that focus on technical or market feasibility studies of economic development projects or programs, which often include consultation with small businesses.[8]

---

[6] For additional information and analysis of the SBA's HUBZone program, see CRS Report R41268, *Small Business Administration HUBZone Program*, by Robert Jay Dilger. For additional information and analysis concerning the STEP program see CRS Report R43155, *Small Business Administration Trade and Export Promotion Programs*, by Sean Lowry.

[7] U.S. Department of Commerce, Minority Business Development Agency (MBDA), "Annual Performance Report, Fiscal Year 2015," pp. 1, 2, at https://www.mbda.gov/sites/mbda.gov/files/migrated/files-attachments/2015AnnualPerformanceReport.pdf.

[8] 13 C.F.R. §306.

Table 1. SBA Management and Technical Assistance Training Programs, Specified and Recommended Appropriations, FY2015-FY2019 ($ in millions)

Training Program	FY2015	FY2016	FY2017	FY2018	FY2019
Small Business Development Center Grants Program	$115.0	$117.0	$125.0	$130.0	$131.0
Microloan Technical Assistance Program	$22.3	$25.0	$31.0	$31.0	$31.0
Women's Business Center Grants Program	$15.0	$17.0	$18.0	$18.0	$18.5
Veterans Outreach (Veterans Business Outreach Centers, Boots to Business Initiative, Boots to Business Reboot Initiative, Veteran-Women Igniting the Spirit of Entrepreneurship [V-Wise], and Entrepreneurship Bootcamp for Veterans with Disabilities [EBV])	$10.5a	$12.3	$12.3	$12.3	$12.7
SCORE (Service Corps of Retired Executives)	$8.0	$10.5	$10.5	$11.5	$11.7
Entrepreneurial Education Initiative	$7.0	$10.0	$10.0	$6.0	$3.5
Entrepreneurial Development Initiative (Regional Innovation Clusters)	$6.0	$6.0	$5.0	$5.0	$5.0
PRIME Technical Assistance Program	$5.0	$5.0	$5.0	$5.0	$5.0
7(j) Technical Assistance Program	$2.8	$2.8	$2.8	$2.8	$2.8
Native American Outreach Program	$2.0	$2.0	$2.0	$2.0	$2.0
National Women's Business Council	$1.0	$1.5	$1.5	$1.5	$1.5
Growth Accelerators Initiative	$4.0	$1.0	$1.0	$1.0	$2.0
Total	**$198.6**	**$210.1**	**$224.1**	**$226.1**	**$226.7**

Sources: P.L. 113-235, the Consolidated and Further Continuing Appropriations Act, 2015; Rep. Harold Rogers, "Explanatory Statement Submitted by Mr. Rogers of Kentucky, Chairman of the House Committee on Appropriations Regarding the House Amendment to the Senate Amendment on H.R. 83," *Congressional Record*, vol. 160, part 151 (December 11, 2014), p. H9740; P.L. 114-113, Consolidated Appropriations Act, 2016; Rep. Harold Rogers, "Explanatory Statement Submitted By Mr. Rogers of Kentucky, Chairman of the House Committee on Appropriations Regarding House Amendment No. 1 to the Senate Amendment on H.R. 2029 Consolidated Appropriations Act," *Congressional Record*, vol. 161, no. 184-Book II (December 17, 2015), p. H10139; P.L. 115-31, the Consolidated Appropriations Act, 2017, Rep. Rodney Frelinghuysen, "Explanatory Statement Submitted By Mr. Frelinghuysen of New Jersey, Chairman of the House Committee on Appropriations Regarding the House Amendment to the Senate Amendments on H.R. 244 [the Consolidated Appropriations Act, 2017]," *Congressional Record*, vol. 163, no. 76-Book II (May 3, 2017), p. H3786; "Explanatory Statement Submitted by Mr. Frelinghuysen, Chairman of the House Committee on Appropriations Regarding the House Amendment to the Senate Amendments on H.R. 1625 [the Consolidated Appropriations Act, 2018] (Division E – Financial Services and General Government Appropriations Act, 2018)," p. 87, at http://docs.house.gov/billsthisweek/20180319/DIV%20E%20FSGG%20SOM%20FY18%20OMNI.OCR.pdf; P.L. 116-6, the Consolidated Appropriations Act, 2019, and H.Rept. 116-9, conference report accompanying the Consolidated Appropriations Act, 2019.

a. Includes $3.0 million for Veterans Business Outreach Centers and $7.5 million for the Boots to Business Initiative. Funding for other veterans outreach activities was provided through the SBA's salaries and expenses account.

For many years, a recurring theme at congressional hearings concerning the SBA's management and technical assistance training programs has been the perceived need to improve program efficiency by eliminating duplication of services and increasing cooperation and coordination both within and among its training resource partners. For example, the Obama Administration recommended in its FY2012-FY2017 budget recommendations that funding for the PRIME technical assistance program end. The Administration argued that PRIME overlaps and duplicates "the technical assistance provided by SBA's microlending intermediaries."[9] The Trump Administration has also requested the program's elimination.[10]

The House Committee on Small Business has argued that the SBA's various management and technical assistance training programs should be "folded into the mission of the SBDC program or their responsibilities should be taken over by other agencies" because they "overlap each other and duplicate the educational services provided by other agencies."[11]

---

[9] SBA, *FY2012 Congressional Budget Justification and FY2010 Annual Performance Report*, p. 4, at https://www.sba.gov/sites/default/files/aboutsbaarticle/ FINAL%20FY%202012%20 CBJ%20FY%202010%20APR_0.pdf. Also, see SBA, *FY2014 Congressional Budget Justification and FY2012 Annual Performance Report*, p. 22, at https://www.sba.gov/ sites/default/files/files/1-508- Compliant-FY-2014-CBJ%20FY%202012%20APR.pdf; and SBA, *FY2017 Congressional Budget Justification and FY2015 Annual Performance Report*, p. 19, at https://www.sba.gov/sites/default/files/FY17-CBJ_FY15-APR.pdf.

[10] SBA, *FY2018 Congressional Budget Justification and FY2016 Annual Performance Report*, p. 12, at https://www.sba.gov/sites/default/files/aboutsbaarticle/ FINAL_SBA_FY_2018_ CBJ_May_22_2017c.pdf; and SBA, *FY2019 Congressional Budget Justification and FY2017 Annual Performance Report*, p. 13, at https://www.sba.gov/sites/default/files/ aboutsbaarticle/SBA_FY_2019_CBJ_APR_2_12_post.pdf.

[11] U.S. Congress, House Committee on Small Business, "Views and Estimates of the Committee on Small Business on Matters to be set forth in the Concurrent Resolution on the Budget for FY2014," communication to the Chairman, House Committee on the Budget, 113th Cong., 1st sess., February 27, 2013, at http://smallbusiness.house.gov/ uploadedfiles/revised_ 2014_views_and_estimates_document.pdf. Previously, the House Committee on Small Business had recommended that funding for Women Business Centers, PRIME technical assistance, HUBZone outreach, and the Offices of Native American Affairs and International Trade be eliminated; and funding for 7(j) technical assistance, Microloan technical assistance, and the National Women's Business Council be reduced. See U.S. Congress, House Committee on Small Business, "Views and Estimates of the Committee on Small Business on Matters to be set forth in the Concurrent Resolution on the Budget for FY2013," communication to the Chairman, House Committee on the Budget, 112th Cong., 2nd sess., March 7, 2012, at http://smallbusiness.house.gov/uploadedfiles/ views_ and_estimates_fy_2013.pdf.

Congress has also explored ways to improve the SBA's measurement of these programs' effectiveness.

This chapter examines the historical development of federal small business management and technical assistance training programs; describes their current structures, operations, and budgets; and assesses their administration and oversight, including measures used to determine their effectiveness.

This chapter also examines legislation to improve SBA program performance and oversight, including

- P.L. 114-88, the Recovery Improvements for Small Entities After Disaster Act of 2015 (RISE After Disaster Act of 2015), which, among other things, authorizes the SBA to provide up to two years of additional financial assistance, on a competitive basis, to SBDCs, WBCs, SCORE, or any proposed consortium of such individuals or entities to assist small businesses located in a presidentially declared major disaster area and authorizes SBDCs to provide assistance to small businesses **outside the SBDC's state**, without regard to geographical proximity to the SBDC, if the small business is in a presidentially declared major disaster area. This assistance can be provided "for a period of not more than two years after the date on which the President" has declared the area a major disaster;[12] and
- P.L. 115-141, the Consolidated Appropriations Act of 2018, among other provisions, relaxed requirements that Microloan intermediaries may spend no more than 25% of Microloan technical assistance grant funds on prospective borrowers and no more than 25% of those funds on contracts with third parties to provide that technical assistance by increasing those percentages to

---

[12] P.L. 114-88 also, among other things, increases, for three years, the minimum disaster loan amount for which the SBA may require collateral, from $14,000 to $25,000 (or, as under existing law, any higher amount the SBA determines appropriate in the event of a disaster); provides a contracting preference for small businesses located in a disaster area if the small business concern will perform the work required under the contract in the disaster area; and doubles the value of the contract for purposes of determining agency compliance with federal small business procurement goals.

no more than 50% (originally in H.R. 2056, the Microloan Modernization Act of 2017, and S. 526, the Microloan Modernization Act of 2018).

In addition, it discusses H.R. 1774, the Developing the Next Generation of Small Businesses Act of 2017, which was introduced during the 115th Congress. The bill would have required the SBA to only use authorized entrepreneurial development programs (SCORE, WBCs, SBDCs, etc.) to deliver specified entrepreneurial development services; added data collection and reporting requirements for SBDCs; authorized to be appropriated $21.75 million for WBCs for each of FY2018-FY2021 (WBCs were appropriated $18.0 million in FY2018); increased the WBC annual grant award from not more than $150,000 to not more than $185,000 (adjusted annually to reflect change in inflation); authorized the award of an additional $65,000 to WBCs under specified circumstances; authorized the SBA to waive, in whole or in part, the WBC nonfederal matching requirement for up to two consecutive fiscal years under specified circumstances; modified SCORE program requirements with respect to the role of participating volunteers, program plans and goals, and reporting; and added language concerning the provision and reporting of online counseling by SCORE.

SBA MANAGEMENT AND TECHNICAL ASSISTANCE TRAINING PROGRAMS

The SBA supports a number of management and technical assistance training programs, including the following:

- Small Business Development Center Grants Program,
- Microloan Technical Assistance Program,
- Women's Business Center Grants Program,
- Veterans Business Development Programs,

- SCORE (Service Corps of Retired Executives),
- PRIME Technical Assistance Program,
- 7(j) Technical Assistance Program,
- Native American Outreach Program, and
- Several initiatives, including the Entrepreneurial Development Initiative (Regional Innovation Clusters), Boots to Business, Entrepreneurial Education, and Growth Accelerators.

The legislative history and current operating structures, functions, and budget for each of these programs is presented in this chapter. In addition, if the data are available, the program's performance based on outcome-based measures, such as their effect on small business formation, survivability, and expansion, and on job creation and retention, is also presented. Also, a brief description of each of these programs is provided in the Appendix.

Small Business Development Centers

In 1976, the SBA created the University Business Development Center pilot program to establish small business centers within universities to provide counseling and training for small businesses. The first center was founded at California State Polytechnic University at Pomona in December 1976. Seven more centers were funded over the next six months at universities in seven different states. By 1979, 16 SBDCs received SBA funding and were providing management and technical training assistance to small businesses.[13]

The SBDC program was provided statutory authorization by P.L. 96-302, the Small Business Development Center Act of 1980.[14] SBDCs were

---

[13] Association of Small Business Development Centers, "A Brief History of America's Small Business Development Center Network," Burke, VA, at http://www.asbdc-us.org/About_Us/aboutus_history.html.

[14] Ibid.; and U.S. Congress, Senate Committee on Small Business, *Oversight of the Small Business Administration's Small Business Development Center Program*, 98th Cong., 1st sess., February 8, 1983, S.Hrg. 98-31 (Washington: GPO, 1983), p. 2.

to "rely on the private sector primarily, and the university community, in partnership with the SBA and its other programs, to fill gaps in making quality management assistance available to the small business owner."[15] Although most SBDCs continued to be affiliated with universities, the legislation authorized the SBA to provide funding

> to any State government or any agency thereof, any regional entity, any State-chartered development, credit or finance corporation, any public or private institution of higher education, including but not limited to any land-grant college or university, any college or school of business, engineering, commerce, or agriculture, community college or junior college, or to any entity formed by two or more of the above entities.[16]

SBDC funding is allocated on a pro rata basis among the states (defined to include the District of Columbia, the Commonwealth of Puerto Rico, the U.S. Virgin Islands, Guam, and American Samoa) by a statutory formula "based on the percentage of the population of each State, as compared to the population of the United States."[17] If, as is currently the case, SBDC funding exceeds $90 million, the minimum funding level is "the sum of $500,000, plus a percentage of $500,000 equal to the percentage amount by which the amount made available exceeds $90 million."[18]

In 1984, P.L. 98-395, the Small Business Development Center Improvement Act of 1984, required SBDCs, as a condition of receiving SBA funding, to contribute a matching amount equal to the grant amount, and that the match must be provided by nonfederal sources and be comprised of not less than 50% cash and not more than 50% of indirect costs and in-kind contributions.[19] It also required SBDCs to have an

---

[15] U.S. Congress, Senate Committee on Small Business, *Oversight of the Small Business Administration's Small Business Development Center Program*, 98th Cong., 1st sess., February 8, 1983, S.Hrg. 98-31 (Washington: GPO, 1983), p. 2.
[16] Ibid., p. 4.
[17] 15 U.S.C. 648(a)(4)(C).
[18] Ibid., and P.L. 106-554, the Consolidated Appropriations Act, 2001.
[19] For American Samoa, Guam, and the U.S. Virgin Islands, the SBA is required to waive the matching requirements on awards less than $200,000 and has discretion to waive the match for awards exceeding $200,000. See 48 U.S.C. Section 1469a. Also, there is one exception

advisory board and a full-time director who has authority to make expenditures under the center's budget. It also required the SBA to implement a program of onsite evaluations for each SBDC and to make those evaluations at least once every two years.

Today, the SBA provides grants to SBDCs that are "hosted by leading universities, colleges, and state economic development agencies" to deliver management and technical assistance training "to small businesses and nascent entrepreneurs (pre-venture) in order to promote growth, expansion, innovation, increased productivity and management improvement."[20] These services are delivered, in most instances, on a nonfee, one-on-one confidential counseling basis and are administered by 63 lead service centers, one located in each state (four in Texas and six in California), the District of Columbia, Puerto Rico, the U.S. Virgin Islands, Guam, and American Samoa.[21]

These lead centers manage more than 900 service centers located throughout the United States and the territories.[22]

As shown in Table 2, SBDCs provided technical assistance training services to 433,554 clients in FY2017 (245,329 clients received training and 188,225 clients were advised), and assisted in forming 14,491 new businesses.

---

to the disallowance of federal funds as a cash match. Community Development Block Grant (CDBG) funds received from the Department of Housing and Urban Development are allowed when: (1) the SBDC activities are consistent with the authorized CDBG activities for which the funds were granted; and (2) the CDBG activities are identified in the Consolidated Plan of the CDBG grantee or in the agreement between the CDBG grantee and the subrecipient of the funds.

[20] SBA, "Small Business Development Center Fy/Cy 2011 Program Announcement for Renewal of the Cooperative Agreement for Current Recipient Organizations," p. 3, at https://www.sba.gov/sites/default/files/files/2011%20Program%20Announcement.pdf.

[21] Ibid.

[22] Association of Small Business Development Centers, "Welcome," Burke, Virginia, at http://www.asbdc-us.org/.

Table 2. Small Business Development Center Assistance, FY2014-FY2017

FY	# of Clients Trained or Advised	# of Businesses Created with SBDC Assistance
2017	433,554	14,491
2016	453,427	14,419
2015	454,898	13,123
2014	485,487	13,415

Source: U.S. Small Business Administration, *FY2019 Congressional Budget Justification and FY2017 Annual Performance Report*, p. 83, at https://www.sba.gov/sites/default/files/aboutsbaarticle/ SBA_FY_2019_CBJ_APR_2_12_post.pdf.

SBDCs received an appropriation of $115.0 million in FY2015, $117.0 million in FY2016, $125.0 million in FY2017, $130.0 million in FY2018, and $131.0 million in FY2019 (see Table 1). The Trump Administration requested $110.0 million for the program in FY2018 and $110.0 million in FY2019.[23]

In addition, as mentioned earlier, P.L. 114-88 expanded the role of SBDCs by, among other things

- authorizing the SBA to provide up to two years of additional financial assistance, on a competitive basis, to SBDCs, WBCs, SCORE, or any proposed consortium of such individuals or entities to assist small businesses located in a presidentially declared major disaster area;[24] and
- authorizing SBDCs to provide assistance to small businesses outside the SBDC's state, without regard to geographical proximity to the SBDC, if the small business is located in a presidentially declared major disaster area. This assistance can be

---

[23] SBA, *FY2018 Congressional Budget Justification and FY2016 Annual Performance Report*, p. 12, at https://www.sba.gov/sites/default/files/aboutsbaarticle/FINAL_SBA_FY_ 2018_ CBJ_May_22_2017c.pdf; and SBA, *FY2019 Congressional Budget Justification and FY2017 Annual Performance Report*, p. 13, at https://www.sba.gov/sites/default/files/ aboutsbaarticle/SBA_FY_2019_CBJ_APR_2_12_post.pdf.

[24] P.L. 114-88, §2101. The SBA administrator may make one extension of a grant, contract, or cooperative agreement under this paragraph for a period of not more than one year, upon a showing of good cause and need for the extension.

provided "for a period of not more than two years after the date on which the President" has declared the area a major disaster.[25]

As part of its legislative mandate to evaluate each SBDC, in 2003, the SBA's Office of Entrepreneurial Development designed "a multi-year time series study to assess the impact of the programs it offers to small businesses."[26] The survey has been administered annually in partnership with a private firm.

The 2014 survey was sent to 70,262 SBDC clients who had received five or more hours of counseling assistance in calendar year 2012. The survey was administered in the spring and summer of 2013.[27] A total of 10,407 surveys (14.8% return rate) were completed either by mail, email, or the internet.[28]

The 2014 survey indicated that, of the SBDC clients

- 90.7% reported that the services they received from SBDC counselors were beneficial;[29]
- 87.8% reported that the knowledge and expertise of their SBDC counselor was excellent (66.0%) or above average (21.8%);[30]
- 86.2% reported that their overall working relationship with their SBDC counselor was excellent (68.9%) or above average (17.3%);[31] and

---

[25] P.L. 114-88, §2103. The SBA administrator is authorized to extend the two-year limitation.
[26] SBA, Office of Entrepreneurial Development, "Impact Study of Entrepreneurial Development Resources," September 10, 2009, p. 2.
[27] SBA, Office of Entrepreneurial Development, "Correspondence with the author," November 4, 2015.
[28] Ibid.
[29] Ibid.
[30] Ibid. 8.7% of SBDC clients reported that the knowledge and expertise of their SBDC counselor was average, 1.5% of SBDC clients reported that the knowledge and expertise of their SBDC counselor was below average, and 1.9% of SBDC clients reported that the knowledge and expertise of their SBDC counselor was poor.
[31] Ibid. 9.3% of SBDC clients reported that their overall working relationship with their SBDC counselor was average, 2.0% of SBDC clients reported that their overall working relationship with their SBDC counselor was below average, and 2.4% of SBDC clients reported that their overall working relationship with their SBDC counselor was poor.

- 94.4% reported that they would recommend that other businesspersons contact the SBDC.[32]

Legislation

As mentioned previously, P.L. 114-88, among other things, authorizes the SBA to provide up to two years of additional funding to its management and training resource partners to assist small businesses located in a presidentially declared major disaster area and authorizes SBDCs to provide assistance outside the SBDC's state, without regard to geographical proximity to the SBDC, if the small business is in a presidentially declared major disaster area. This assistance can be provided "for a period of not more than two years after the date on which the President" has declared the area a major disaster.

Also, H.R. 1774, the Developing the Next Generation of Small Businesses Act of 2017, introduced during the 115th Congress, among other provisions, would have required the SBA to only use authorized entrepreneurial development programs (SCORE, WBCs, SBDCs, etc.) "to deliver entrepreneurial development services, entrepreneurial education, support for the development and maintenance of clusters, or business training" and would have added SBDC data collection and reporting requirements. Similar legislation was introduced during the 114th Congress (H.R. 207 and S. 999).[33]

Microloan Technical Assistance Program

Congress authorized the SBA's Microloan lending program in 1991 (P.L. 102-140, the Departments of Commerce, Justice, and State, the

---
[32] Ibid.
[33] The House-passed version of H.R. 2810, the National Defense Authorization Act for Fiscal Year 2018, included provisions similar to those concerning WBCs, SBDCs, and SCORE in H.R. 1774. These provisions were not included in the Senate-passed version of H.R. 2810 or in the bill's final version (P.L. 115-91, the National Defense Authorization Act for Fiscal Year 2018).

Judiciary, and Related Agencies Appropriations Act, 1992) to address the perceived disadvantages faced by women, low-income, veteran, and minority entrepreneurs and business owners gaining access to capital for starting or expanding their business. The program became operational in 1992. Its stated purpose is

> to assist women, low-income, veteran ... and minority entrepreneurs and business owners and other individuals possessing the capability to operate successful business concerns; to assist small business concerns in those areas suffering from a lack of credit due to economic downturns; ... to make loans to eligible intermediaries to enable such intermediaries to provide small-scale loans, particularly loans in amounts averaging not more than $10,000, to start-up, newly established, or growing small business concerns for working capital or the acquisition of materials, supplies, or equipment; [and] to make grants to eligible intermediaries that, together with non-Federal matching funds, will enable such intermediaries to provide intensive marketing, management, and technical assistance to microloan borrowers.[34]

Initially, the SBA's Microloan program was authorized as a five-year demonstration project. It was made permanent, subject to reauthorization, by P.L. 105-135, the Small Business Reauthorization Act of 1997.

The SBA's Microloan Technical Assistance Program, which is affiliated with the SBA's Microloan lending program but receives a separate appropriation, provides grants to Microloan intermediaries to provide management and technical training assistance to Microloan program borrowers and prospective borrowers.[35] There are currently 144 active Microloan intermediaries serving 49 states, the District of Columbia, and Puerto Rico.[36]

---

[34] 15 U.S.C. §636 7(m)(1)(A).
[35] For further analysis of the SBA's Microloan program, see CRS Report R41057, *Small Business Administration Microloan Program*, by Robert Jay Dilger.
[36] SBA, *Fiscal Year 2019 Congressional Budget Justification and FY2017 Annual Performance Report*, p. 37, at https://www.sba.gov/sites/default/files/aboutsbaarticle/ SBA_FY_ 19_508Final5_1.pdf. For a list of all Microloan intermediaries, regardless of lending volume, see SBA, *Microloan Program: Partner Identification & Management System*

Intermediaries are eligible to receive a Microloan technical assistance grant "of not more than 25% of the total outstanding balance of loans made to it" under the Microloan program.[37] Grant funds may be used only to provide marketing, management, and technical assistance to Microloan borrowers, except that no more than 50% of the funds may be used to provide such assistance to prospective Microloan borrowers and no more than 50% of the funds may be awarded to third parties to provide that technical assistance. Grant funds also may be used to attend required training.[38]

In most instances, intermediaries must contribute, solely from nonfederal sources, an amount equal to 25% of the grant amount.[39] In addition to cash or other direct funding, the contribution may include indirect costs or in-kind contributions paid for under nonfederal programs.[40]

The SBA does not require Microloan borrowers to participate in the Microloan Technical Assistance Program. However, intermediaries typically require Microloan borrowers to participate in the training program as a condition of the receipt of a microloan. Combining loan and intensive management and technical assistance training is one of the Microloan program's distinguishing features.[41]

As shown in Table 3, the Microloan Technical Assistance Program provided counseling services to 19,600 small businesses in FY2017.

The program was appropriated $22.3 million in FY2015, $25.0 million in FY2016, and $31.0 million in FY2017, FY2018, and FY2019 (see Table

---

Participating Intermediary Microlenders Report, June 21, 2017, at https://www.sba.gov/sites/default/files/articles/microlenderrpt5_20170621.pdf.
[37] 15 U.S.C. §636(m)(4)(A).
[38] 13 C.F.R. §120.712.
[39] Ibid.
[40] Ibid. Intermediaries may not borrow their contribution.
[41] Intermediaries that make at least 25% of their loans to small businesses located in or owned by residents of an Economically Distressed Area (defined as having 40% or more of its residents with an annual income that is at or below the poverty level), or have a portfolio of loans made under the program that averages not more than $10,000 during the period of the intermediary's participation in the program are eligible to receive an additional training grant equal to 5% of the total outstanding balance of loans made to the intermediary. Intermediaries are not required to make a matching contribution as a condition of receiving these additional grant funds. See 13 C.F.R. §120.712; and 15 U.S.C. §636(m)(4)(C)(i).

1). The Trump Administration requested $25.0 million for the program in FY2018 and $25.0 million in FY2019.[42]

Table 3. Microloan Technical Assistance, FY2014-FY2017

FY	# of Clients Advised	# of Grant Eligible Microlenders
2017	19,600	144
2016	17,948	140
2015	17,200	137
2014	15,668	137

Source: U.S. Small Business Administration *FY2019 Congressional Budget Justification and FY2017 Annual Performance Report*, pp. 37, 38, at https://www.sba.gov/sites/default/files/aboutsbaarticle/ SBA_FY_2019_CBJ_APR_2_12_post.pdf.

Legislation

As mentioned previously, P.L. 115-141, among other provisions, relaxed requirements that Microloan intermediaries may spend no more than 25% of Microloan technical assistance grant funds on prospective borrowers and no more than 25% of those funds on contracts with third parties to provide that technical assistance by increasing those percentages to no more than 50%. These provisions were originally in H.R. 2056 and S. 526.[43]

During the 114th Congress, H.R. 2670 and S. 1857 (its Senate companion bill) would have required the SBA administrator to establish a rule enabling intermediaries to apply for a waiver to the requirement that no more than 25% of Microloan technical assistance grant funds may be used to provide technical assistance to prospective borrowers.[44]

---

[42] SBA, *FY2018 Congressional Budget Justification and FY2016 Annual Performance Report*, p. 12, at https://www.sba.gov/sites/default/files/aboutsbaarticle/ FINAL_SBA_ FY_2018_ CBJ_May_22_2017c.pdf; and SBA, *FY2019 Congressional Budget Justification and FY2017 Annual Performance Report*, p. 13, at https://www.sba.gov/sites/default/files/ aboutsbaarticle/SBA_FY_2019_CBJ_APR_2_12_post.pdf.

[43] The bills would also increase the Microloan program's aggregate loan limit for intermediaries after their first year of participation in the program from $5 million to $6 million.

[44] H.R. 2670 was passed by the House on July 13, 2015. S. 1857 was ordered to be reported by the Senate Committee on Small Business and Entrepreneurship on July 29, 2015, and subsequently reported and placed on the Senate Legislative Calendar under General Orders on September 15, 2015. The bills would have also increased the Microloan program's aggregate loan limit for intermediaries after their first year of participation in the program from $5 million to $6 million and the program's repayment terms from not more than 6

Women's Business Centers

The Women's Business Center (WBC) Renewable Grant Program was initially established by P.L. 100-533, the Women's Business Ownership Act of 1988, as the Women's Business Demonstration Pilot Program. The act directed the SBA to provide financial assistance to private, nonprofit organizations to conduct demonstration projects giving financial, management, and marketing assistance to small businesses, including start-up businesses, owned and controlled by women. Since its inception, the program has targeted the needs of socially and economically disadvantaged women.[45] The WBC program was expanded and provided permanent legislative status by P.L. 109-108, the Science, State, Justice, Commerce, and Related Agencies Appropriations Act, 2006.

Since the program's inception, the SBA has awarded WBCs a grant of up to $150,000 per year. Initially, the grant was awarded for one year, with the possibility of being renewed twice, for a total of up to three years. As a condition of the receipt of funds, the WBC was required to raise at least one nonfederal dollar for each two federal dollars during the grant's first year (1:2), one nonfederal dollar for each federal dollar during year two (1:1), and two nonfederal dollars for each federal dollar during year three (2:1).[46] Over the years, Congress has extended the length of the WBC program's grant award and reduced the program's matching requirement.

Today, WBC initial grants are awarded for up to five years, consisting of a base period of 12 months from the date of the award and four 12-

---

years to not more than 10 years for loans greater than $10,000. For additional information, see CRS Report R41057, *Small Business Administration Microloan Program*, by Robert Jay Dilger.

[45] U.S. Congress, House Committee on Small Business, *Review of Women's Business Center Program*, 106th Cong., February 11, 1999, Serial No. 106-2 (Washington: GPO, 1999), p. 4.

[46] Matching contributions must come from nonfederal sources such as state and local governments, private individuals, corporations and foundations, and program income. Community Development Block Grant funds, when permissible under the terms of that program, may also be used as a match. At least half of the nonfederal match must be in the form of cash. SBA, "Women's Business Center (Initial Grant), FY2011" at http://www.sba.gov/sites/default/files/files/ Program%20Announcement%20OWBO-2011-01-1%20-%20New%20WBC%20in%20Idaho.pdf.

month option periods.[47] The SBA determines if the option periods are exercised and makes that determination subject to the continuation of program authority, the availability of funds, and the recipient organization's compliance with federal law, SBA regulations, and the terms and conditions specified in a cooperative agreement. WBCs that successfully complete the initial five-year grant period may apply for an unlimited number of three-year funding intervals.[48]

During their initial five-year grant period, WBCs are now required to provide a nonfederal match of one nonfederal dollar for each two federal dollars in years one and two (1:2), and one nonfederal dollar for each federal dollar in years three, four and five (1:1).[49] After the initial five-year grant period, the matching requirement in subsequent three-year funding intervals is not more than 50% of federal funding (1:1).[50] The nonfederal match may consist of cash, in-kind, and program income.[51]

---

[47] P.L. 105-135, the Small Business Reauthorization Act of 1997, authorized the SBA to award grants to WBCs for up to five years—one base year and four option years. P.L. 106-165, the Women's Business Centers Sustainability Act of 1999, provided WBCs that had completed the initial five-year grant an opportunity to apply for an additional five-year sustainability grant. Thus, the act allowed successful WBCs to receive SBA funding for a total of 10 years. Because the program has permitted permanent three-year funding intervals since 2007, the sustainability grants would be phased out by FY2012, leaving the initial five-year grants with the continuous three-year option. See SBA, *FY2012 Congressional Budget Justification and FY2010 Annual Performance Report*, p. 49, at https://www.sba.gov/sites/default/files/aboutsbaarticle/FINAL%20FY%202012%20CBJ%20FY%202010%20APR_0.pdf.

[48] P.L. 110-28, the U.S. Troop Readiness, Veterans' Care, Katrina Recovery, and Iraq Accountability Appropriations Act, 2007, allowed WBCs that successfully completed the initial five-year grant to apply for an unlimited number of three-year funding renewals.

[49] P.L. 105-135 reduced the program's matching to one nonfederal dollar for each two federal dollars in years one through three rather than just during the first year (1:2), one nonfederal dollar for each federal dollar in year four rather than during year two (1:1), and two nonfederal dollars for each federal dollar in year five rather than in year three (2:1). P.L. 106-17, the Women's Business Center Amendments Act of 1999, reduced the program's matching requirement to one nonfederal dollar for each two federal dollars in years one and two (1:2), and one nonfederal dollar for each federal dollar in years three, four and five (1:1).

[50] P.L. 110-28 reduced the federal share to not more than 50% for all grant years (1:1) following the initial five-year grant.

[51] P.L. 105-135 specified that not more than one-half of the nonfederal sector matching assistance may be in the form of in-kind contributions that are budget line items only, including office equipment and office space.

Today, there are 121 WBCs located throughout most of the United States and the territories.[52] As shown in Table 4, WBCs provided assistance to 140,628 clients in FY2017 (114,310 clients received technical assistance training services and 26,318 clients were advised), and assisted in the formation of 17,438 new businesses.[53]

Congress recommended that the WBC program receive $15.0 million in FY2015, $17.0 million in FY2016, $18.0 million in FY2017, $18.0 million in FY2018, and $18.5 million in FY2019 (see Table 1). The Trump Administration requested $16.0 million for the program for FY2018 and $16.0 million for FY2019.[54]

P.L. 105-135 required the SBA to "develop and implement an annual programmatic and financial examination of each" WBC.[55] As part of its legislative mandate to implement an annual programmatic and financial examination of each WBC, the SBA's Office of Entrepreneurial Development includes WBCs in its previously mentioned multiyear time series study of its programs.

Data from the SBA's 2014 client survey concerning WBCs are not yet available. The firm administering the 2013 survey of SBA management and training clients contacted 2,997 WBC clients and received 529 completed surveys (17.7% return rate).[56] The survey indicated that

---

[52] SBA, "Women's Business Centers Directory," at https://www.sba.gov/tools/local-assistance/wbc.

[53] SBA, *FY2018 Congressional Budget Justification and FY2016 Annual Performance Report*, pp. 52, 53, at https://www.sba.gov/sites/default/files/aboutsbaarticle/ FINAL_SBA_FY_2018_CBJ_May_22_2017c.pdf.

[54] SBA, *FY2018 Congressional Budget Justification and FY2016 Annual Performance Report*, p. 12, at https://www.sba.gov/sites/default/files/aboutsbaarticle/ FINAL_SBA_FY_2018_CBJ_May_22_2017c.pdf; and SBA, *FY2019 Congressional Budget Justification and FY2017 Annual Performance Report*, p. 13, at https://www.sba.gov/sites/default/files/aboutsbaarticle/SBA_FY_2019_CBJ_APR_2_12_post.pdf.

[55] P.L. 105-135, §29. Women's Business Center Program.

[56] SBA, Office of Entrepreneurial Development, "Impact Study of Entrepreneurial Dynamics: Office of Entrepreneurial Development Resource Partners' Face-to-Face Counseling," September 2013, p. 8, at https://www.sba.gov/sites/ default/files/files/OED_Impact Report_09302013_Final.pdf.

Table 4. Women Business Center Assistance, FY2014-FY2017

FY	# of Clients Trained or Advised	# of Businesses Created with WBC Assistance
2017	140,628	17,438
2016	145,415	17,435
2015	140,716	NA
2014	140,037	NA

Source: U.S. Small Business Administration *FY2019 Congressional Budget Justification and FY2017 Annual Performance Report*, p. 85, at https://www.sba.gov/sites/default/files/aboutsbaarticle/SBA_FY_2019_CBJ_APR_2_12_post.pdf.

Notes: The number of businesses created with WBC assistance in FY2014 and FY2015 was determined using a different methodology than what was used for FY2016 and FY2017. The data for FY2014 and FY2015 (708 and 766 new business starts, respectively) are omitted from the table because the data are not comparable to the FY2016 and FY2017 data.

- 80% of WBC clients reported that the services they received from counselors were useful or very useful, 2% had no opinion, and 18% reported that the services they received from counselors were somewhat useful or not useful;[57]
- 61% of WBC clients reported that they changed their management practices/strategies as a result of the assistance they received;[58] and
- the top five changes to management practices involved their business plan (56%), marketing plan (46%), general management (36%), cash flow analysis (31%), and financial strategy (30%).[59]

Legislation

As mentioned earlier, P.L. 114-88 expanded the role of WBCs by authorizing the SBA to provide up to two years of additional financial assistance, on a competitive basis, to SBDCs, WBCs, SCORE, or any proposed consortium of such individuals or entities to assist small businesses located in a presidentially declared major disaster area.[60]

In addition, H.R. 1774, introduced during the 115th Congress, would have required the SBA to use only authorized entrepreneurial development

---

[57] Ibid., p. 19.
[58] Ibid., p. 20.
[59] Ibid., p. 21.
[60] P.L. 114-88, §2101. The SBA administrator may make one extension of a grant, contract, or cooperative agreement under this paragraph for a period of not more than one year, upon a showing of good cause and need for the extension.

programs (SCORE, WBCs, SBDCs, etc.) to deliver specified entrepreneurial development services; authorized to be appropriated $21.75 million for WBCs for each of FY2018-FY2021 (WBCs received $18.0 million in FY2018); increased the WBC annual grant award from not more than $150,000 to not more than $185,000 (adjusted annually to reflect change in inflation); authorized the award of an additional $65,000 to WBCs under specified circumstances; and authorized the SBA to waive, in whole or in part, the WBC nonfederal matching requirement for up to two consecutive fiscal years under specified circumstances.[61] Similar legislation was introduced during the 114th Congress (H.R. 207 and S. 2126).

Veterans Business Development Programs

The SBA has supported management and technical assistance training for veteran-owned small businesses since its formation as an agency. However, during the 1990s, some in Congress noted that a direct loan program for veterans was eliminated by the SBA in 1995 and that the "training and counseling for veterans dropped from 38,775 total counseling sessions for veterans in 1993 to 29,821 sessions in 1998."[62] Concerned that "the needs of veterans have been diminished systematically at the SBA," Congress adopted P.L. 106-50, the Veterans Entrepreneurship and Small Business Development Act of 1999.[63]

The act reemphasized the SBA's responsibility "to reach out to and include veterans in its programs providing financial and technical

---

[61] The specified circumstances include the consideration of the economic conditions affecting the recipient organization; the waiver's impact on the women's business center program's credibility; the recipient organization's demonstrated ability to raise nonfederal funds; and the recipient organization's performance. The House-passed version of H.R. 2810, the National Defense Authorization Act for Fiscal Year 2018, included provisions similar to those concerning WBCs, SBDCs, and SCORE in H.R. 1774. These provisions were not included in the Senate-passed version of H.R. 2810 or in the bill's final version (P.L. 115-91, the National Defense Authorization Act for Fiscal Year 2018).

[62] U.S. Congress, House Committee on Small Business, *Veterans Entrepreneurship and Small Business Development Act of 1999*, report to accompany H.R. 1568, 106th Cong., 1st sess., June 29, 1999, H.Rept. 106-206 (Washington: GPO, 1999), pp. 14, 15.

[63] Ibid.

assistance."[64] It also included veterans as a target group for the SBA's 7(a), 504/CDC, and Microloan programs. In addition, it required the SBA to enter into a memorandum of understanding with SCORE to, among other things, establish "a program to coordinate counseling and training regarding entrepreneurship to veterans through the chapters of SCORE throughout the United States."[65] The act also directed the SBA to enter into a memorandum of understanding with SBDCs, the Department of Veteran Affairs, and the National Veterans Business Development Corporation "with respect to entrepreneurial assistance to veterans, including service-disabled veterans."[66] It specified, among other things, that the SBA conduct and distribute studies on the formation, management, financing, marketing, and operation of small business concerns by veterans; provide training and counseling on these topics to veterans; assist veterans regarding procurement opportunities with federal, state, and local agencies, especially agencies funded in whole or in part with federal funds; and provide internet or other distance-learning academic instruction for veterans in business subjects, including accounting, marketing, and business fundamentals.[67]

The SBA's Office of Veterans Business Development (OVBD) was established to address these statutory requirements.[68] The OVBD currently administers several management and training programs to assist veteran-owned businesses, including the following:

- The Entrepreneurship Bootcamp for Veterans with Disabilities Consortium of Universities provides "experiential training in

---

[64] U.S. Congress, House Committee on Small Business, *Veterans Entrepreneurship and Small Business Development Act of 1999*, report to accompany H.R. 1568, 106th Cong., 1st sess., June 29, 1999, H.Rept. 106-206 (Washington: GPO, 1999), p. 14.
[65] P.L. 106-50, §301. Score Program.
[66] Ibid., §302. Entrepreneurial Assistance.
[67] Ibid.
[68] SBA, *FY2016 Congressional Budget Justification and FY2014 Annual Performance Report*, p. 97, at https://www.sba.gov/sites/default/files/1-FY%202016%20CBJ%20FY%202014%20APR.PDF.

entrepreneurship and small business management to post-9/11 veterans with disabilities" at eight universities.[69]

- The Veteran Women Igniting the Spirit of Entrepreneurship (V-WISE) program, administered through a cooperative agreement with Syracuse University, offers women veterans a 15-day, online course on entrepreneurship skills and the "language of business," followed by a 3-day conference (offered twice a year at varying locations) in which participants "are exposed to successful entrepreneurs and CEOs of Fortune 500 companies and leaders in government" and participate in courses on business planning, marketing, accounting and finance, operations and production, human resources, and work-life balance.[70]

- The Operation Endure and Grow Program, administered through a cooperative agreement with Syracuse University, offers an eight-week online training program on "the fundamentals of launching and/or growing a small business" and is available to National Guard and reservists and their family members.[71]

- The Boots to Business program (started in 2012), which is "an elective track within the Department of Defense's revised Training Assistance Program called Transition Goals, Plans, Success (Transition GPS) and has three parts: the Entrepreneurship Track Overview—a 10-minute introductory video shown during the mandatory five-day Transition GPS course which introduces entrepreneurship as a post-service career option; Introduction to Entrepreneurship—a two-day classroom course on entrepreneurship and business fundamentals offered as one of the three

---

[69] Syracuse University, "About the EBV," Syracuse, NY, at http://ebv.vets.syr.edu/; and SBA, "SBA Expands Entrepreneurship Boot Camp for Vets: Announces Two New Programs for Women Vets, Guard, Reservists and Families," November 10, 2010, at https://www.sba.gov/sites/default/files/news_release_10-63.pdf.

[70] Syracuse University, "Women Veterans Igniting the Spirit of Entrepreneurship (V-WISE)," Syracuse, NY, at http://vwise.vets.syr.edu/; and SBA, "SBA Expands Entrepreneurship Boot Camp for Vets: Announces Two New Programs for Women Vets, Guard, Reservists and Families," November 10, 2010, at https://www.sba.gov/sites/default/ files/news_ release_10-63.pdf.

[71] Syracuse University, "About Operation Endure and Grow," Syracuse, NY, at http://vets.syr.edu/education/endure- grow/.

Transition GPS elective tracks; and Foundations of Entrepreneurship—an eight-week, instructor-led online course that offers in-depth instruction on the elements of a business plan and tips and techniques for starting a business."[72]

- The Boots to Business Reboot program (started in 2014) assists veterans who have already transitioned to civilian life.[73]
- The Veterans Business Outreach Centers (VBOC) program provides veterans and their spouses management and technical assistance training at 22 locations, including assistance with the Boots to Business program, the development and maintenance of a five-year business plan, and referrals to other SBA resource partners when appropriate for additional training or mentoring services.[74]

Prior to FY2016, Congress recommended appropriations for VBOCs and the Boots to Business initiative. Funding for the OVBD's other veterans assistance programs was provided through the SBA's salaries and expenses account.

Starting in FY2016, Congress has recommended a single amount for all OVBD programs (currently $12.7 million) (see Table 1). The Trump

---

[72] SBA, "Operation Boots to Business: From Service to Startup," at https://www.sba.gov/offices/ headquarters/ovbd/ resources/160511; and SBA, "Operation Boots to Business: Fact Sheet," at https://www.sba.gov/sites/default/files/files/ B2B_Fact%20Sheet.pdf.

[73] Ibid., pp. 90, 99 .

[74] SBA, "Veterans Business Outreach Centers," at https://www.sba.gov/offices/ head quarters/ovbd/resources/1548576. There were 14 VBOCs in 2015 and 20 in 2017. VBOC grants, starting at $180,000, "are made for up to a three-year period of performance, consisting of a base period of 12 months from the date of award and up to two renewal option periods of 12 months each. Exercise of the option periods will be solely at SBA's discretion and is subject to continuing program authority, the availability of funds, and the recipient's continued satisfactory performance and compliance." Also, "funding per VBOC will vary based on proposed Boots to Business (B2B) program delivery and associated outreach." See SBA, Office of Veterans Business Development, "FY 2015 Program Announcement No. VBOC-2015-02," pp. 6-7, at https://www.sba.gov/offices/ headquarters/ ovbd/spotlight. In FY2013, the Veterans Business Outreach Centers Program conducted its ninth annual "Customer Satisfaction Survey." The FY2013 survey found that 91% of the clients using the centers were satisfied or highly satisfied with the quality, relevance, and timeliness of the assistance provided. See SBA, *FY2015 Congressional Budget Justification and FY2013 Annual Performance Report*, p. 81, at https://www.sba.gov/sites/default/ files/files/ FY%202015%20CBJ%20FY% 202013% 20APR%20FINAL%20508(1).pdf.

Administration requested $11.25 million for these programs in FY2018 and $11.25 million in FY2019.[75]

As shown in Table 5, VBOCs trained or advised 48,839 veterans in FY2016 and 17,320 veterans participated in the Boots to Business Initiative.

SCORE (Service Corps of Retired Executives)

The SBA has partnered with various voluntary business and professional service organizations to provide management and technical assistance training to small businesses since the 1950s. On October 5, 1964, using authority under the Small Business Act to provide "technical and managerial aids to small business concerns" in cooperation with "educational and other nonprofit organizations, associations, and institutions," then-SBA Administrator Eugene P. Foley officially launched SCORE (Service Corps of Retired Executives) as a national, volunteer organization with 2,000 members, uniting more than 50 independent nonprofit organizations into a single, national nonprofit organization.[76] Since then, the SBA has provided financial assistance to SCORE to provide training to small business owners and prospective owners.[77]

---

[75] SBA, *FY2018 Congressional Budget Justification and FY2016 Annual Performance Report*, p. 12, at https://www.sba.gov/sites/default/files/aboutsbaarticle/ FINAL_SBA_FY_2018_ CBJ_May_22_2017c.pdf; and SBA, *FY2019 Congressional Budget Justification and FY2017 Annual Performance Report*, p. 13, at https://www.sba.gov/sites/default/files/aboutsbaarticle/SBA_FY_2019_CBJ_APR_2_12_post.pdf.

[76] P.L. 83-163, the Small Business Act of 1953; and U.S. Congress, Senate Select Committee on Small Business, *Small Business Administration - 1965*, 89th Cong., 1st sess., May 19, 1965 (Washington: GPO, 1965), pp. 21, 45; and SCORE (Service Corps of Retired Executives), "Milestones in SCORE History," Washington, DC, at https://www.score.org/ node/147953.

[77] U.S. Congress, Senate Select Committee on Small Business and House Select Committee on Small Business, *1966 Federal Handbook for Small Business: A Survey of Small Business Programs in the Federal Government Agencies*, committee print, 89th Cong., 3rd sess., January 31, 1966 (Washington: GPO, 1966), p. 5; and U.S. Congress, House Committee on Small Business, Subcommittee on Rural Development, Entrepreneurship, and Trade, *Subcommittee Hearing on Legislative Initiatives to Modernize SBA's Entrepreneurial Development Programs*, 111th Cong., 1st sess., April 2, 2009 (Washington: GPO, 2009), p. 6.

Table 5. Office of Veterans Business Development Assistance, By Program, FY2014-FY2017

FY	Veterans Business Outreach Centers	Boots to Business Initiative
2017	48,839	17,320
2016	47,342	17,966
2015	62,117	14,457
2014	78,124	14,684

Source: U.S. Small Business Administration *FY2019 Congressional Budget Justification and FY2017 Annual Performance Report*, p. 92, at https://www.sba.gov/sites/default/files/aboutsbaarticle/SBA_FY_2019_CBJ_APR_2_12_post.pdf.

Table 6. SCORE Assistance, FY2014-FY2017

FY	# of Clients Trained or Counseled	# of Businesses Created with SCORE Assistance
2017	646,260	NA
2016	433,394	54,027
2015	349,539	39,495
2014	442,374	NA

Source: U.S. Small Business Administration *FY2019 Congressional Budget Justification and FY2017 Annual Performance Report*, pp. 86, 87, at https://www.sba.gov/sites/default/files/aboutsbaarticle/SBA_FY_2019_CBJ_APR_2_12_post.pdf.

Notes: The number of businesses created with SCORE assistance in FY2014 was determined using a different methodology than what was used for FY2015 and FY2016. The data for FY2014 (628 new business starts) are omitted from the table because the data are not comparable to the FY2015 and FY2016 data.

Over the years, Congress has authorized the SBA to take certain actions relating to SCORE. For example, P.L. 89-754, the Demonstration Cities and Metropolitan Development Act of 1966, authorized the SBA to permit members of nonprofit organizations use of the SBA's office facilities and services. P.L. 90-104, the Small Business Act Amendments of 1967, added the authority to pay travel and subsistence expenses "incurred at the request of the Administration in connection with travel to a point more than fifty miles distant from the home of that individual in providing gratuitous services to small businessmen" or "in connection with attendance at meetings sponsored by the Administration."[78] P.L. 93-113, the Domestic Volunteer Service Act of 1973, was the first statute to

---

[78] U.S. Congress, Senate Select Committee on Small Business, *Small Business Act*, 90th Cong., 1st sess., November 22, 1967 (Washington: GPO, 1967), pp. 13, 14.

mention SCORE directly, providing the Director of ACTION authority to work with SCORE to "expand the application of their expertise beyond Small Business Administration clients."[79] P.L. 95-510, a bill to amend the Small Business Act, provided the SBA explicit statutory authorization to work with SCORE (Section 8(b)(1)(B)). P.L. 106-554, the Consolidated Appropriations Act, 2001 (Section 1(a)(9)—the Small Business Reauthorization Act of 2000) authorized SCORE to solicit cash and in-kind contributions from the private sector to be used to carry out its functions.

The SBA currently provides grants to SCORE to provide in-person mentoring, online training, and "nearly 9,000 local training workshops annually" to small businesses.[80] SCORE's 320 chapters and more than 800 branch offices are located throughout the United States and partner with more than 11,000 volunteer counselors, who are working or retired business owners, executives and corporate leaders, to provide management and training assistance to small businesses "at no charge or at very low cost."[81]

As shown in Table 6, SCORE's volunteer network of business professionals provided assistance to 646,260 clients in FY2017 (519,368 clients received technical assistance training services and 126,892 client received counseling services).

Congress recommended that SCORE receive $8.0 million in FY2015, $10.5 million in FY2016 and FY2017, $11.5 million in FY2018, and $11.7

---

[79] P.L. 93-113, the Domestic Volunteer Service Act of 1973, §302. Authority to Establish, Coordinate, and Operate Programs. ACTION was created on July 1, 1971, by President Richard M. Nixon (Reorganization Plan Number One and Executive Order 11603) to oversee several federal volunteer agencies, including the Peace Corps, VISTA (Volunteers in Service to America); and SCORE. P.L. 103-82, the National and Community Service Trust Act of 1993, directed that ACTION be merged with the Commission on National and Community Service to form the Corporation for National and Community Service, which became operational in 1994. See Corporation for National and Community Service, "National Service Timeline," Washington, DC, at http://www.nationalservice.gov/about/role_impact/ history_timeline.asp.

[80] SBA, *FY2013 Congressional Budget Justification and FY2011 Annual Performance Report*, p. 45, at https://www.sba.gov/sites/default/files/files/1-508%20Compliant%20FY%202013 %20CBJ%20FY%202011%20APR(1).pdf.

[81] SCORE (Service Corps of Retired Executives), "About SCORE," Washington, DC, at https://www.score.org/about- score.

million in FY2019 (see Table 1). The Trump Administration requested $9.9 million for the program in FY2018 and FY2019.[82]

The SBA Office of Entrepreneurial Development includes SCORE in its multiyear time series study to assess its programs' effectiveness. The 2014 survey was sent to 124,612 SCORE clients who had a valid email address and received at least one mentoring session in any form (telephone, online/email, in-person, or other form) during FY2013 (October 2012-September 2013). The survey was initially distributed by email, and telephone calls were used as a follow-up to ensure at least 30 responses were received from each responding SCORE chapter. The survey was administered between October 2013 and December 2013.[83] A total of 13,548 surveys (10.9% return rate) were completed either by email or telephone, representing 318 of SCORE's then-330 chapters.[84]

The 2014 survey indicated that, of the SCORE clients

- 60.9% reported that they strongly agreed (32.2%) or agreed (28.7%) with the following statement: SCORE is important to my success;[85]
- 44.8% reported that they strongly agreed (18.4%) or agreed (26.4%) with the following statement: As a result of working with SCORE, I have changed my business strategies or practices;[86]
- 32.6% reported that they strongly agreed (12.1%) or agreed (20.5%) with the following statement: Working with SCORE helped me add employees in the past year;[87] and

---

[82] SBA, *FY2018 Congressional Budget Justification and FY2016 Annual Performance Report*, p. 12, at https://www.sba.gov/sites/default/files/aboutsbaarticle/ FINAL_SBA_FY_2018_ CBJ _May_22_2017c.pdf; and SBA, *FY2019 Congressional Budget Justification and FY2017 Annual Performance Report*, p. 13, at https://www.sba.gov/sites/ default/ files/ aboutsba article/SBA_FY_2019_CBJ_APR_2_12_post.pdf.

[83] SBA, Office of Entrepreneurial Development, "Correspondence with the author," November 4, 2015.

[84] Ibid.

[85] Ibid. 23.8% reported that they were neutral in response to the following statement: SCORE is important to my success; 7.2% disagreed, and 8.1% strongly disagreed.

[86] Ibid. 20.9% reported that they were neutral in response to the following statement: As a result of working with SCORE, I have changed my business strategies or practices; 8.2% disagreed, 9.8% strongly disagreed, and 6.4% did not reply or indicated they don't know.

- 51.8% reported that they strongly agreed (17.0%) or agreed (34.8%) with the following statement: Working with SCORE helped me grow my business revenue.[88]

Legislation

As mentioned earlier, P.L. 114-88 expanded SCORE's role by authorizing the SBA to provide up to two years of additional financial assistance, on a competitive basis, to SBDCs, WBCs, SCORE, or any proposed consortium of such individuals or entities to assist small businesses located in a presidentially declared major disaster area.[89]

In addition, H.R. 1774, introduced during the 115th Congress, would have required the SBA to use only authorized entrepreneurial development programs (SCORE, WBCs, SBDCs, etc.) to deliver specified entrepreneurial development services; modified SCORE program requirements with respect to the role of participating volunteers, program plans and goals, and reporting; and added language concerning the provision and reporting of online counseling by SCORE. Similar legislation was introduced during the 114th Congress (H.R. 207, H.R. 4788, and S. 1000).[90]

---

[87] Ibid. 27.0% reported that they were neutral in response to the following statement: Working with SCORE helped me add employees in the past year; 17.4% disagreed, and 13.6% strongly disagreed.

[88] Ibid. 26.9% reported that they were neutral in response to the following statement: Working with SCORE helped me grow my business revenue; 10.1% disagreed, and 11.2% strongly disagreed.

[89] P.L. 114-88, §2101. The SBA administrator may make one extension of a grant, contract, or cooperative agreement under this paragraph for a period of not more than one year, upon a showing of good cause and need for the extension.

[90] The House-passed version of H.R. 2810, the National Defense Authorization Act for Fiscal Year 2018, included provisions similar to those concerning WBCs, SBDCs, and SCORE in H.R. 1774. These provisions were not included in the Senate-passed version of H.R. 2810 or in the bill's final version (P.L. 115-91, the National Defense Authorization Act for Fiscal Year 2018).

Program for Investment in Micro-Entrepreneurs (PRIME)

P.L. 106-102, the Gramm-Leach-Bliley Act (of 1999) (Subtitle C—Microenterprise Technical Assistance and Capacity Building Program), amended P.L. 103-325, the Riegle Community Development and Regulatory Improvement Act of 1994, to authorize the SBA to "establish a microenterprise technical assistance and capacity building grant program."[91] The program was to "provide assistance from the Administration in the form of grants" to

> nonprofit microenterprise development organizations or programs (or a group or collaborative thereof) that has a demonstrated record of delivering microenterprise services to disadvantaged entrepreneurs; an intermediary; a microenterprise development organization or program that is accountable to a local community, working in conjunction with a state or local government or Indian tribe; or an Indian tribe acting on its own, if the Indian tribe can certify that no private organization or program referred to in this paragraph exists within its jurisdiction."[92]

The SBA was directed "to ensure that not less than 50% of the grants ... are used to benefit very low-income persons, including those residing on Indian reservations."[93] It was also directed to

> (1) provide training and technical assistance to disadvantaged entrepreneurs; (2) provide training and capacity building services to microenterprise development organizations and programs and groups of such organizations to assist such organizations and programs in developing microenterprise training and services; (3) aid in researching and developing the best practices in the field of microenterprise and technical assistance programs for disadvantaged entrepreneurs; and (4) for such other activities as the Administrator determines are consistent with the purposes of this subtitle.[94]

---

[91] P.L. 106-102, the Gramm-Leach-Bliley Act, §173. Establishment of Program.
[92] P.L. 106-102, §173. Establishment of Program and §175. Qualified Organizations.
[93] P.L. 106-102, §176. Allocation of Assistance; Subgrants.
[94] P.L. 106-102, §174. Uses of Assistance.

The SBA's PRIME program was designed to meet these legislative requirements by providing assistance to organizations that "help low-income entrepreneurs who lack sufficient training and education to gain access to capital to establish and expand their small businesses."[95] The program offers four types of grants:

- *Technical Assistance Grants* support training and technical assistance to disadvantaged microentrepreneurs,
- *Capacity Building Grants* support training and capacity building services to microenterprise development organizations and programs to assist them in developing microenterprise training and services,
- *Research and Development Grants* support the development and sharing of best practices in the field of microenterprise development and technical assistance programs for disadvantaged microentrepreneurs, and
- *Discretionary Grants* support other activities determined to be consistent with these purposes.[96]

Grants are awarded on an annual basis. Applicants may be approved for option year funding for up to four subsequent years. Award amounts vary depending on the availability of funds. However, no single grantee may receive more than $250,000 or 10% of the total funds made available for the program in a single fiscal year, whichever is less. The minimum grant award for technical assistance and capacity building grants is $50,000. There is no minimum grant award amount for research and development or discretionary grants.[97] The SBA typically awards at least 75% of the grant funds for technical assistance, at least 15% for capacity building, and the remainder for research and development or discretionary activities.[98]

---

[95] SBA, "What is PRIME?" at https://www.sba.gov/offices/headquarters/oca/resources/11416.
[96] Ibid.
[97] Ibid.
[98] Ibid. For Technical Assistance and Capacity Building Grants, after the initial grant, funding for additional year(s) must be no more than 67% of the initial grant amount. For Research and

Recipients must match 50% of the funding from nonfederal sources. Revenue from fees, grants, and gifts; income from loan sources; and in-kind resources from nonfederal public or private sources may be used to comply with the matching requirement.[99] SBA regulations indicate that "applicants or grantees with severe constraints on available sources of matching funds may request that the Administrator or designee reduce or eliminate the matching requirements."[100] Any reductions or eliminations must not exceed 10% of the aggregate of all PRIME grant funds made available by SBA in any fiscal year.[101]

Table 7. PRIME Grant Funding, FY2014-FY2018 ($ in millions)

FY	# of Grants	$ Awarded	Range of Awards
2018	32	$5.0	$75,000 to $250,000
2017	34	$5.0	$55,000 to $250,000
2016	37	$5.0	$75,000 to $230,000
2015	39	$5.0	$35,000 to $200,000
2014	24	$3.5	$94,000 to $250,000

Source: U.S. Small Business Administration, "SBA PRIME Grantees (by State), Fiscal Year 2014," at https://www.sba.gov/sites/default/files/prime_grantees_2014.pdf; U.S. Small Business Administration, "SBA Awards $5 Million in PRIME Grants," September 18, 2015, at https://www.sba.gov/content/sba-awards-5-million- prime-grants; U.S. Small Business Administration, "SBA Awards $5 Million in PRIME Grants," September 16, 2016, at https://www.sba.gov/content/ sba-awards-5-million-prime-grants-5; U.S. Small Business Administration, "SBA Awards $5 Million in PRIME Grants to Help Emerging Micro-entrepreneurs Gain Access to Capital," September 7, 2017, at https://www.sba.gov/about-sba/sba-newsroom/press-releases-media-advisories/sba-awards-5-million-prime-grants-help-emerging-micro-entrepreneurs-gain-access-capital; and U.S. Small Business Administration, "SBA Awards $5 Million in PRIME Grants to Help Emerging Micro-entrepreneurs Gain Access to Capital," September 28, 2018, at https:// www.sba.gov/about-sba/sba-newsroom/press-releases-media-advisories/sba-awards-5-million-prime-grants-help-emerging-micro-entrepreneurs-gain-access-capital-0.

Development and Discretionary Grants, after the initial grant, funding for additional year(s) will be approved at the SBA's discretion.

[99] SBA, "Program for Investment in Microentrepreneurs Act ("PRIME"): Microenterprise and Technical Assistance Programs to Disadvantaged Entrepreneurs, Fiscal Year 2010," June 2010, pp. 2, 8, at https://www.sba.gov/sites/default/files/files/ serv_fa_2010_primetrack 123.pdf.
[100] 13 C.F.R. §119.8.
[101] Ibid.

Table 7 provides the number and amount of PRIME awards from FY2014 to FY2018.

Congress has recommended that the PRIME program receive $5.0 million in each fiscal year since FY2015 (see Table 1).

As mentioned previously, the Obama Administration recommended in its FY2012-FY2017 budget requests that funding for the PRIME program be eliminated. It argued that the PRIME program overlaps and duplicates the SBA's Microloan Technical Assistance Program.[102] The Trump Administration requested that the program receive no funding in FY2018 and FY2019.[103]

7(j) Management and Technical Assistance Program

Using what it viewed as broad statutory powers granted under Section 8(a) of the Small Business Act of 1958, as amended, the SBA issued regulations in 1970 creating the 8(a) contracting program to "assist small concerns owned by disadvantaged persons to become self-sufficient, viable businesses capable of competing effectively in the market place."[104]

---

[102] SBA, *FY2012 Congressional Budget Justification and FY2010 Annual Performance Report*, p. 4, at https://www.sba.gov/sites/default/files/aboutsbaarticle/ FINAL%20FY%202012%20 CBJ%20FY%202010%20APR_0.pdf; SBA, *FY2013 Congressional Budget Justification and FY2011 Annual Performance Report*, pp. 8, 15, at https://www.sba.gov/sites/ default/ files/files/1-508%20Compliant%20FY%202013%20CBJ%20FY%202011%20APR(1).pdf; SBA, *FY2014 Congressional Budget Justification and FY2012 Annual Performance Report*, p. 22, 27, at https://www.sba.gov/sites/default/files/files/1-508- Compliant-FY-2014- CBJ%20FY%202012%20APR.pdf; and SBA, *FY2017 Congressional Budget Justification and FY2015 Annual Performance Report*, p. 19, at https://www.sba.gov/sites/default/files/ FY17-CBJ_FY15-APR.pdf.

[103] SBA, *FY2018 Congressional Budget Justification and FY2016 Annual Performance Report*, p. 12, at https://www.sba.gov/sites/default/files/aboutsbaarticle/ FINAL_SBA_FY_2018_ CBJ _May_22_2017c.pdf; and SBA, *FY2019 Congressional Budget Justification and FY2017 Annual Performance Report*, p. 13, at https://www.sba.gov/sites/ default/files/ aboutsbaarticle/SBA_FY_2019_CBJ_APR_2_12_post.pdf.

[104] 13 C.F.R. §124.8-1(b) (1970); and Notes, "Minority Enterprise, Federal Contracting, and the SBA's 8(a) Program: A New Approach to an Old Problem," *Michigan Law Review*, vol. 71, no. 2 (December 1972), pp. 377, 378. For further analysis of the Minority Small Business and Capital Ownership Development Program, also known as the 8(a) program, see CRS Report R44844, *SBA's "8(a) Program": Overview, History, and Current Issues*, by Robert Jay Dilger.

Using its statutory authority under Section 7(j) of the Small Business Act to provide management and technical assistance through contracts, grants, and cooperative agreement to qualified service providers, the regulations specified that "the SBA may provide technical and management assistance to assist in the performance of the subcontracts."[105]

On October 24, 1978, P.L. 95-507, to amend the Small Business Act and the Small Business Investment Act of 1958, provided the SBA explicit statutory authority to extend financial, management, technical, and other services to socially and economically disadvantaged small businesses. The SBA's current regulations indicate that the 7(j) Management and Technical Assistance Program, named after the section of the Small Business Act of 1958, as amended, authorizing the SBA to provide management and technical assistance training, will, "through its private sector service providers" deliver "a wide variety of management and technical assistance to eligible individuals or concerns to meet their specific needs, including: (a) counseling and training in the areas of financing, management, accounting, bookkeeping, marketing, and operation of small business concerns; and (b) the identification and development of new business opportunities."[106] Eligible individuals and businesses include "8(a) certified firms, small disadvantaged businesses, businesses operating in areas of high unemployment, or low income or firms owned by low income individuals."[107]

As shown on Table 8, the 7(j) program assisted 4,100 small business owners in FY2017.

Congress has recommended that the 7(j) program receive $2.8 million in each fiscal year since FY2015 (see Table 1).

The Trump Administration requested $2.8 million for the program in FY2018 and FY2019.[108]

---

[105] 13 C.F.R. §124.8-1(d) (1970).
[106] 13 C.F.R. §124.702.
[107] SBA, *FY2012 Congressional Budget Justification and FY2010 Annual Performance Report*, p. 75, at https://www.sba.gov/sites/default/files/aboutsbaarticle/ FINAL%20FY%202012% 20CBJ%20FY%202010%20APR_0.pdf.
[108] SBA, *FY2018 Congressional Budget Justification and FY2016 Annual Performance Report*, p. 12, at https://www.sba.gov/sites/default/files/aboutsbaarticle/ FINAL_SBA_FY_ 2018_CBJ_May_22_2017c.pdf; and SBA, *FY2019 Congressional Budget Justification and*

Table 8. 7(j) Assistance, FY2014-FY2017

FY	# of Clients Trained or Counseled
2017	4,100
2016	5,245
2015	5,360
2014	4,104

Source: U.S. Small Business Administration *FY2019 Congressional Budget Justification and FY2017 Annual Performance Report*, p. 74, at https://www.sba.gov/sites/default/files/aboutsbaarticle/ SBA_FY_2019_CBJ_APR_2_12_post.pdf.

Native American Outreach Program

The SBA established the Office of Native American Affairs in 1994 to "address the unique needs of America's First people."[109] It oversees the Native American Outreach Program, which provides management and technical educational assistance to American Indians, Alaska Natives, Native Hawaiians, and "the indigenous people of Guam and American Samoa ... to promote entity-owned and individual 8(a) certification, government contracting, entrepreneurial education, and capital access."[110] The program's management and technical assistance services are available to members of these groups living in most areas of the nation.[111] However, "for Native Americans living in much of Indian Country, actual reservations communities where the land is held in trust by the U.S. federal government, SBA loan guarantees and technical assistance services are not available."[112]

FY2017 Annual Performance Report, p. 13, at https://www.sba.gov/sites/default/ files/aboutsbaarticle/SBA_FY_2019_CBJ_APR_2_12_post.pdf.

[109] U.S. Congress, House Committee on Small Business, Subcommittee on Workforce, Empowerment, and Government Programs, *Oversight of the Small Business Administration's Entrepreneurial Development Programs*, 109th Cong., 2nd sess., March 2, 2006, Serial No. 109-40 (Washington: GPO, 2006), pp. 5, 37. H.R. 2352, the Job Creation Through Entrepreneurship Act of 2009, would have provided statutory authorization for the Office of Native American Affairs. It was passed by the House on May 20, 2009.

[110] SBA, *FY2011 Congressional Budget Justification and FY2009 Annual Performance Report*, p. 65, at https://www.sba.gov/sites/default/files/aboutsbaarticle/ Congressional_Budget_ Justification.pdf.

[111] Ibid.

[112] Ibid.

In FY2017, the SBA's Office of Native American Affairs assisted 3,192 small businesses. It provided workshops on business development and financial literacy, training webinars, incubator training, and online classes for Native American entrepreneurs.[113]

Congress has recommended that the Native American Outreach Program receive $2.0 million in each fiscal year since FY2015 (see Table 1). The Trump Administration requested $1.5 million for the program in FY2018 and FY2019.[114]

SBA Initiatives

In addition to the Boots to Business initiative discussed under "Veterans Business Development Programs," Congress has recommended appropriations for the following three Obama Administration management and training initiatives: the Entrepreneurial Development Initiative (Regional Innovation Clusters), Entrepreneurial Education, and Growth Accelerators.

Entrepreneurial Development Initiative (Regional Innovation Clusters)

The SBA has supported regional innovation clusters since FY2009, when it partnered with small business suppliers working in the field of robotics in Michigan. In FY2010, the SBA was involved in the rollouts of two additional clusters: another robotics cluster in southeast Virginia and a cluster involving a partnership with the Department of Energy and several other federal agencies with the goal of developing a regional cluster in

---

[113] SBA, *FY2019 Congressional Budget Justification and FY2017 Annual Performance Report*, p. 96, at https://www.sba.gov/sites/default/files/aboutsbaarticle/ SBA_FY_2019_ CBJ_APR _2_12_post.pdf.

[114] SBA, *FY2018 Congressional Budget Justification and FY2016 Annual Performance Report*, p. 12, at https://www.sba.gov/sites/default/files/aboutsbaarticle/ FINAL_SBA_FY_2018_ CBJ_May_22_2017c.pdf; and SBA, *FY2019 Congressional Budget Justification and FY2017 Annual Performance Report*, p. 13, at https://www.sba.gov/sites/default/about sbaarticle/SBA_FY_2019_CBJ_APR_2_12_post.pdf.

energy efficiency homes and businesses.[115] In FY2011, SBA awarded funds to 10 regional innovation clusters. In FY2012, these clusters "spurred $48 million in private capital raised through venture and angel capital sources, $6.5 million in early stage investment from SBIR [Small Business Innovation Research program] and STTR [Small Business Technology Transfer program] awards, and over $217 million in contracts or subcontracts from the federal government."[116]

President Obama requested, and Congress recommended, an appropriation of $5.0 million for the SBA's Entrepreneurial Development Initiative (Regional Innovation Clusters) in FY2014. Congress recommended that the program receive $6.0 million in FY2015, $6.0 million in FY2016, and $5.0 million in each fiscal year since FY2017 (see Table 1). The Trump Administration requested that the program receive no funds in FY2018 and in FY2019.[117] The SBA reports that there are currently 56 federally supported regional innovation clusters, with the SBA directly involved in 40 of them.[118]

---

[115] SBA, *FY2011 Congressional Budget Justification and FY2009 Annual Performance Report*, p. 59, at https://www.sba.gov/sites/default/files/ aboutsbaarticle/ Congressional_ Budget_ Justification.pdf.

[116] SBA, *FY2014 Congressional Budget Justification and FY2012 Annual Performance Report*, p. 60, at https://www.sba.gov/sites/default/files/1-FY%202016%20CBJ%20FY%202014%20APR.PDF. The Small Business Innovation Research (SBIR) program is a competitive program that encourages domestic small businesses to engage in federal research and development that has the potential for commercialization. For additional information and analysis concerning the SBIR program, see CRS Report R43695, *Small Business Innovation Research and Small Business Technology Transfer Programs*, by John F. Sargent Jr. The Small Business Technology Transfer (STTR) program is a competitive program that reserves a specific percentage of federal research and development funding for awards to small business and nonprofit research institutions. For additional information and analysis concerning the STTR program, see CRS Report RL33527, *Technology Transfer: Use of Federally Funded Research and Development*, by Wendy H. Schacht.

[117] SBA, *FY2018 Congressional Budget Justification and FY2016 Annual Performance Report*, p. 12, at https://www.sba.gov/sites/default/files/aboutsbaarticle/ FINAL_SBA_FY_2018_CBJ_May_22_2017c.pdf; and SBA, *FY2019 Congressional Budget Justification and FY2017 Annual Performance Report*, p. 13, at https://www.sba.gov/sites/default/files/aboutsbaarticle/SBA_FY_2019_CBJ_APR_2_12_post.pdf.

[118] The SBA is the lead agency supporting 10 SBA Pilot Contract-Based clusters; partners with the Economic Development Agency, Employment and Training Agency, National Institute of Standards and Technology, and Department of Energy to support 10 Jobs Accelerator Advanced Manufacturing clusters; and partners with the Economic Development Agency and Employment and Training Agency to support 20 Jobs Accelerator Collaboration Clusters. See SBA, "SBA Supports 56 Federally Funded Cluster Initiatives," at https://www.sba.gov/sba-clusters; and SBA, "56 Federally Supported Cluster Initiatives," at

The SBA describes regional innovation clusters as "on-the-ground collaborations between business, research, education, financing and government institutions that work to develop and grow a particular industry or related set of industries in a particular geographic region."[119] Targeted activities for the 40 clusters currently being supported by the SBA include "business development, intellectual property matters, export and import development, finance, marketing, commercialization of new technology and federal and private-sector supply chain opportunities."[120]

Entrepreneurial Education

The SBA started its Entrepreneurship Education initiative in 2008. At that time, it was called the Emerging 200 Underserved initiative (E200), reflecting the initiative's provision of assistance to 200 inner city small businesses. In FY2009, it was renamed the Emerging Leaders initiative to reflect the SBA's decision to increase the number of small businesses participating in the initiative. It was renamed the Entrepreneurial Education initiative in FY2013, and it is funded under that name in appropriation acts, but the SBA, and others, often still call it the Emerging Leaders Initiative. The initiative currently

> offers high-growth small businesses in underserved communities a seven-month executive leader education series that elevates their growth trajectory, creates jobs, and contributes to the economic well-being of their local communities. Participants receive more than 100 hours of specialized training, technical resources, a professional networking system, and other resources to strengthen their business model and promote economic development within urban communities. At the conclusion of the training, participants produce a three-year strategic growth action plan with benchmarks and performance targets that help

---

https://www.google.com/url?q=https://www.sba.gov/sites/default/files/SBA%2520 Supports%252056%2520Federally%2520Funded%2520Cluster%2520Initiatives_1. pdf&sa=U&ved=0CBMQFjAHahUKEwjinvOB9rXIAhULPD4KHZ_ODFA&client= internal-uds-cse&usg= AFQjCNEcVUjShZkcIYqlUrIn7ma3IZBRQg.

[119] SBA, *FY2016 Congressional Budget Justification and FY2014 Annual Performance Report*, p. 63, at https://www.sba.gov/sites/default/files/1-FY%202016%20CBJ%20FY%202014% 20 APR.PDF.

[120] Ibid., p. 64.

them access the necessary support and resources to move forward for the next stage of business growth.[121]

The Entrepreneurial Education initiative was initially offered in 10 communities (Albuquerque, Atlanta, Baltimore, Boston, Chicago, Des Moines, Memphis, Milwaukee, New Orleans, and Philadelphia) and provided training to 200 inner city small businesses. The program was funded through the SBA's Office of Entrepreneurship Education.[122] Since the initiative's inception, the SBA has requested separate appropriations to fund and expand the initiative. In FY2012, the initiative offered training in 27 communities, with more than 450 small businesses participating.[123]

The Obama Administration requested $40.0 million in its FY2014 budget request to sponsor entrepreneur training in 40 locations and to create an online entrepreneurship training program.[124] Congress included the Entrepreneurship Education initiative in its list of SBA entrepreneurial development/noncredit programs to be funded in FY2014. This was the first time that the initiative was included in the list. In the explanatory statement accompanying the Consolidated Appropriations Act, 2014, Congress recommended that the initiative receive $5.0 million in FY2014.[125] Congress recommended that the program receive $7.0 million in FY2015, $10.0 million in FY2016 and FY2017, $6.0 million in FY2018, and $3.5 million in FY2019 (see Table 1). The Trump Administration requested $2.0 million for the program in FY2018 and FY2019.[126]

---

[121] SBA, *FY2014 Congressional Budget Justification and FY2012 Annual Performance Report*, p.71, at https://www.sba.gov/sites/default/files/1-FY%202016%20CBJ%20FY%202014%20APR.PDF.

[122] SBA, *FY2010 Congressional Budget Justification*, p.67, at https://www.sba.gov/sites/default/files/aboutsbaarticle/ Congressional_Budget_Justification_2010.pdf.

[123] SBA, *FY2014 Congressional Budget Justification and FY2012 Annual Performance Report*, p. 71, at https://www.sba.gov/sites/default/files/1-FY%202016%20CBJ%20FY%202014%20APR.PDF.

[124] Ibid., p. 10.

[125] Recommended funding levels for the SBA's noncredit programs in FY2014 are provided in the "Explanatory Statement" accompanying the Consolidated Appropriations Act, 2014 (Division E - Financial Services and General Government Appropriations Act, 2014), pp. 37-39, at http://docs.house.gov/billsthisweek/20140113/113-HR3547- JSOM-D-F.pdf.

[126] SBA, *FY2018 Congressional Budget Justification and FY2016 Annual Performance Report*, p. 12, at https://www.sba.gov/sites/default/files/aboutsbaarticle/ FINAL_SBA_FY_2018_ CBJ_May_22_2017c.pdf; and SBA, *FY2019 Congressional Budget Justification and*

The Entrepreneurship Education initiative was offered in 57 cities in FY2017 and served more than 900 small business owners.[127] These owners are required to have been in business for at least three years, have annual revenue of at least $400,000, and have at least one employee, other than the owner, to participate in the initiative. There is no cost to the participants.[128]

Growth Accelerators

The SBA describes growth accelerators as "organizations that help entrepreneurs start and scale their businesses."[129] Growth accelerators are typically run by experienced entrepreneurs and help small businesses access seed capital and mentors. The SBA claims that growth accelerators "help accelerate a startup company's path towards success with targeted advice on revenue growth, job, and sourcing outside funding."[130]

In FY2012, the SBA sponsored several meetings with university officials and faculty, entrepreneurs, and representatives of growth accelerators to discuss mentoring and how to best assist "high-growth" entrepreneurs. These meetings "culminated with a White House event co-hosted by the SBA and the Department of Commerce to help formalize the network of universities and accelerators, provide a series of 'train the trainers' events on various government programs that benefit high-growth entrepreneurs, and provide a playbook of best practices on engaging universities on innovation and entrepreneurship."[131]

FY2017 Annual Performance Report, p. 13, at https://www.sba.gov/sites/default/files/aboutsbaarticle/ SBA_FY_2019_CBJ_APR_2_12_post.pdf.

[127] SBA, *FY2019 Congressional Budget Justification and FY2017 Annual Performance Report*, p. 89, at https://www.sba.gov/sites/default/files/aboutsbaarticle/ SBA_FY_2019_CBJ_APR_2_12_post.pdf.

[128] SBA, "SBA Emerging Leaders Initiative," at https://www.sba.gov/about-sba/sba_initiatives/sba_emerging_leaders_initiative.

[129] SBA, *FY2018 Congressional Budget Justification and FY2016 Annual Performance Report*, p. 75, at https://www.sba.gov/sites/default/files/aboutsbaarticle/ FINAL_SBA_FY_2018_CBJ_May_22_2017c.pdf.

[130] Ibid.

[131] SBA, *FY2014 Congressional Budget Justification and FY2012 Annual Performance Report*, p. 60, at https://www.sba.gov/sites/default/files/1-FY%202016%20CBJ%20FY%202014%20APR.PDF.

In FY2014, the Obama Administration requested $5.0 million, and Congress recommended an appropriation of $2.5 million, for the growth accelerator initiative. The Obama Administration proposed to use the funding to provide matching grants to universities and private sector accelerators "to start a new accelerator program (based on successful models) or scale an existing program."[132] The Obama Administration also indicated that it planned to request funding for five years ($25 million in total funding) and feature a required 4:1 private-sector match.[133] However, because it received half of its budget request ($2.5 million), the SBA decided to reconsider the program's requirements. As part of that reconsideration, the SBA decided to drop the 4:1 private- sector match in an effort to enable the program to have a larger effect.[134]

The SBA announced the availability of 50 growth accelerator grants of $50,000 each on May 12, 2014, and received more than 800 applications by the August 2, 2014, deadline. The 50 awards were announced in September 2014.[135]

Congress recommended that the program receive $4.0 million in FY2015, $1.0 million in FY2016, FY2017, and FY2018, and $2 million in FY2019 (see Table 1). Congress also directed the SBA in its explanatory statements accompanying P.L. 113-235 and P.L. 114-113 to "require $4 of matching funds for every $1 awarded under the growth accelerators program."[136] The Trump Administration requested that the program receive no funding in FY2018 and FY2019.[137]

---

[132] Ibid.
[133] Ibid.
[134] SBA, Office of Congressional and Legislative Affairs, "Correspondence with the author," May 6, 2014.
[135] SBA, "SBA Launches Accelerator Competition to Award $2.5 million for Small Business Startups," May 12, 2014, at https://www.sba.gov/content/sba-launches-accelerator-competition-award-25-million-small-business-startups-0; SBA, "More than 800 Small Business Startups Compete for 50 Cash Prizes in SBA's Growth Accelerator Competition," August 4, 2014, at https://www.sba.gov/content/more-800-small-business-startups-compete-50-cash- prizes-sbas-growth-accelerator-competition; and SBA, "SBA Spurs Economic Growth, Announces 50 Awards to Accelerators," September 4, 2014, at https://www.sba. gov/content/sba-spurs-economic-growth-announces-50-awards- accelerators.
[136] Rep. Harold Rogers, "Explanatory Statement Submitted by Mr. Rogers of Kentucky, Chairman of the House Committee on Appropriations Regarding the House Amendment to the Senate Amendment on H.R. 83," *Congressional Record*, vol. 160, part 151 (December 11, 2014), p. H9741; and Rep. Harold Rogers, "Explanatory Statement Submitted By Mr.

The SBA announced the award of 80 growth accelerator grants of $50,000 each on August 4, 2015 ($4.0 million), 68 growth accelerator grants of $50,000 each on August 31, 2016 ($3.4 million), and 20 growth accelerator grants of $50,000 each on October 30, 2017 ($1 million).[138]

DEPARTMENT OF COMMERCE SMALL BUSINESS MANAGEMENT AND TECHNICAL ASSISTANCE TRAINING PROGRAMS

As mentioned previously, the Department of Commerce's Minority Business Development Agency (MBDA) provides training to minority business owners to assist them in obtaining contracts and financial awards.[139] In addition, the Department of Commerce's Economic Development Administration's Local Technical Assistance Program promotes efforts to build and expand local organizational capacity in distressed areas. As part of that effort, it funds projects that focus on technical or market feasibility studies of economic development projects or programs, which often include consultation with small businesses.[140]

Rogers of Kentucky, Chairman of the House Committee on Appropriations Regarding House Amendment No. 1 to the Senate Amendment on H.R. 2029 Consolidated Appropriations Act," *Congressional Record*, vol. 161, no. 184-Book II (December 17, 2015), p. H10140.

[137] SBA, *FY2018 Congressional Budget Justification and FY2016 Annual Performance Report*, p. 12, at https://www.sba.gov/sites/default/files/aboutsbaarticle/ FINAL_SBA_FY_ 2018_ CBJ_May_22_2017c.pdf; and SBA, *FY2019 Congressional Budget Justification and FY2017 Annual Performance Report*, p. 13, at https://www.sba.gov/sites/ default/ files/ aboutsbaarticle/SBA_FY_2019_CBJ_APR_2_12_post.pdf.

[138] SBA, "SBA Boosts Economic Impact of Accelerators with $4.4 Million in Prizes," August 4, 2015, at https://www.sba.gov/content/sba-boosts-economic-impact-accelerators-44-million-prizes-0; SBA, "SBA Announces $3.4 Million for Small Business Startups," August 31, 2016, at https://www.sba.gov/content/sba-announces-34-million- small-business-startups; and SBA, "SBA Announces 20 Growth Accelerator Fund Competition Recipients," October 30, 2017, at https://www.sba.gov/node/1594788.

[139] U.S. Department of Commerce, MBDA, "Annual Performance Report, Fiscal Year 2011; America: Built to Last," p. 76, at https://www.mbda.gov/sites/mbda.gov/files/apr2011.pdf.

[140] 13 C.F.R. §306.

The Minority Business Development Agency

The MBDA was established by President Richard M. Nixon by Executive Order 11625, issued on October 13, 1971, and published in the *Federal Register* the next day. It clarified the authority of the Secretary of Commerce to

- implement federal policy in support of the minority business enterprise program,
- provide additional technical and management assistance to disadvantaged businesses,
- assist in demonstration projects, and
- coordinate the participation of all federal departments and agencies in an increased minority enterprise effort.[141]

The MBDA received an appropriation of $30.0 million in FY2015, $32.0 million in FY2016, $34.0 million in FY2017, $39.0 million in FY2018, and $40 million in FY2019.[142] The Trump Administration requested $6.0 million to close the agency in FY2018 and a reduction to $10.0 million in FY2019.[143]

As part of its mission, the MBDA seeks to train minority business owners to become first- or second-tier suppliers to private corporations and the federal government. Progress is measured in the business's increased gross receipts, number of employees, and size and scale of the firms associated with minority business enterprises.

---

[141] The Executive Office of the President, "Executive Order 11625," 36 *Federal Register* 11625, October 14, 1971; and 3 C.F.R., 1971-1975 Comp. 9. 616. The MBDA superseded the Office of Minority Business Enterprise, which was established by Executive Order 11458 signed by President Richard Nixon on March 5, 1969.

[142] P.L. 113-235; P.L. 114-113, P.L. 115-31; P.L. 115-56, P.L. 115-141; and P.L. 116-6.

[143] U.S. Office of Management and Budget (OMB), "Appendix: Budget of the U.S. Government, Fiscal Year 2018," p. 190, at https://www.whitehouse.gov/sites/whitehouse.gov/ files/omb/ budget/fy2018/appendix.pdf; and OMB, "Appendix: Budget of the U.S. Government, Fiscal Year 2019," p. 189, at https://www.gpo.gov/fdsys/pkg/BUDGET-2019-APP/pdf/BUDGET-2019-APP.pdf.

The MBDA reported that in FY2015 it helped to create and retain 36,896 jobs and assisted minority-owned and operated businesses in obtaining more than $5.9 billion in contracts and capital awards.[144]

The EDA Local Technical Assistance Program

P.L. 89-186, the Public Works and Economic Development Act of 1965, authorized the Department of Commerce's Economic Development Administration (EDA) to provide financial assistance to economically distressed areas in the United States that are characterized by high levels of unemployment and low per-capita income. The EDA currently administers seven Economic Development Assistance Programs (EDAPs) that award matching grants for public works, economic adjustment, planning, technical assistance, research and evaluation, trade adjustment assistance, and global climate change mitigation.[145]

Grants awarded under the EDA's Local Technical Assistance Program are designed to help solve specific economic development problems, respond to development opportunities, and build and expand local organizational capacity in distressed areas.[146] The majority of local technical assistance projects focus on technical or market feasibility studies of economic development projects or programs, including consultation with small businesses. The EDA's Local Technical Assistance Program

---

[144] U.S. Department of Commerce, MBDA, "Annual Performance Report, Fiscal Year 2015," pp. 1, 2, at https://www.mbda.gov/sites/mbda.gov/files/migrated/files-attachments/2015Annual PerformanceReport.pdf.

[145] In addition, since 1970, Congress has periodically allocated supplemental funds for the Economic Development Administration (EDA) to assist with disaster mitigation and economic recovery. Also, EDA grant applicants must be designated by EDA as part of an EDD—a multijurisdictional consortium of county and local governments—to be eligible for EDA funding and grants. To be designated as an EDD, an area must meet the definition of economic distress, under 13 C.F.R. 303.3: "(i) An unemployment rate that is, for the most recent twenty-four (24) month period for which data are available, at least one (1) percentage point greater than the national average unemployment rate; (ii) Per capita income that is, for the most recent period for which data are available, eighty (80) percent or less of the national average per capita income; or (iii) A Special Need, as determined by Economic Development Administration (EDA)."

[146] 13 C.F.R. §306.

received an appropriation of $11.0 million in FY2015, $10.5 million in FY2016, $9.0 million in FY2017, and $9.5 million in FY2018 and FY2019. [147] The Trump Administration requested $30.0 million to close the EDA in FY2018 and $14.9 million to close it in FY2019.[148]

CONGRESSIONAL ISSUES

For many years, a recurring theme at congressional hearings concerning the SBA's management and technical assistance training programs has been the perceived need to improve program efficiency by eliminating duplication of services or increasing cooperation and coordination both within and among SCORE, WBCs, and SBDCs.[149] For

---

[147] Rep. Harold Rogers, "Explanatory Statement Submitted by Mr. Rogers of Kentucky, Chairman of the House Committee on Appropriations Regarding the House Amendment to the Senate Amendment on H.R. 83," *Congressional Record*, vol. 160, part 151 (December 11, 2014), p. H9342; Rep. Harold Rogers, "Explanatory Statement Submitted By Mr. Rogers of Kentucky, Chairman of the House Committee on Appropriations Regarding House Amendment No. 1 to the Senate Amendment on H.R. 2029 Consolidated Appropriations Act," *Congressional Record*, vol. 161, no. 184- Book II (December 17, 2015), p. H9732; Rep. Rodney Frelinghuysen, "Explanatory Statement Submitted By Mr. Frelinghuysen of New Jersey, Chairman of the House Committee on Appropriations Regarding the House Amendment to the Senate Amendments on H.R. 244 [the Consolidated Appropriations Act, 2017]," *Congressional Record*, vol. 163, no. 76-Book II (May 3, 2017), p. H3365; "Explanatory Statement Submitted by Mr. Frelinghuysen, Chairman of the House Committee on Appropriations Regarding the House Amendment to the Senate Amendments on H.R. 1625 [the Consolidated Appropriations Act, 2018] (Division B – Commerce, Justice, Science, and Related Agencies Appropriations Act, 2018]," p. 2, at http://docs.house.gov/billsthisweek/20180319/DIV%20B%20CJS%20SOM-%20FY18-OMNI.OCR.pdf; and H.Rept. 116-9, conference report to accompany the Consolidated Appropriations Act, 2019.

[148] OMB, "Appendix: Budget of the U.S. Government, Fiscal Year 2018," pp. 181-183, at https://www.govinfo.gov/ content/pkg/BUDGET-2018-APP/pdf/BUDGET-2018-APP.pdf; and OMB, "Appendix: Budget of the U.S. Government, Fiscal Year 2019," pp. 182, 183, at https://www.gpo.gov/fdsys/pkg/BUDGET-2019-APP/pdf/BUDGET-2019-APP-1-6.pdf.

[149] U.S. Congress, House Committee on Small Business, *Full Committee Markup of H.R. 2352 The Job Creation Through Entrepreneurship Act of 2009*, 111th Cong., 1st sess., May 13, 2009, Doc. No. 111-022 (Washington: GPO, 2009), pp. 2, 14; U.S. Congress, Senate Committee on Small Business, *SBA's Management and Assistance Programs*, Roundtable before the Committee on Small Business United States Senate, 106th Cong., 1st sess., May 20, 1999, S. Hrg. 106-337 (Washington: GPO, 1999), pp. 69, 74, 82, 92; U.S. Congress, House Committee on Small Business, *To Investigate the Legislation That Would Increase the Extent and Scope of the Services Provided By Small Business Development Centers*, 107th Cong., 1st sess., July 19, 2001, Serial No. 107-20 (Washington: GPO, 2001), pp. 13,

example, the House Committee on Small Business has argued that the SBA's various management and technical assistance training programs should be "folded into the mission of the SBDC program or their responsibilities should be taken over by other agencies" because they "overlap each other and duplicate the educational services provided by other agencies."[150]

In addition, as mentioned previously, the Obama Administration recommended that the PRIME program be eliminated, arguing that it overlaps and duplicates the SBA's Microloan Technical Assistance Program. The Trump Administration has also recommended that the PRIME program, the Growth Accelerators Initiative, and the Entrepreneurial Development Initiative (Regional Innovation Clusters) be eliminated because they overlap private-sector "mechanisms to foster local business development and investment" or are "duplicative of other federal programs."[151]

In contrast, Congress has approved continued funding for these programs and the Boots to Business and Boots to Business: Reboot initiatives. In recent years, Congress has also explored ways to improve the

---

59, 60; and U.S. Congress, Senate Committee on Small Business, *Oversight on the Small Business Administration's Small Business Development Center Program*, 100th Cong., 1st sess., October 15, 1987, S. Hrg. 100-339 (Washington: GPO, 1987), pp. 6, 165, 168, 230.

[150] U.S. Congress, House Committee on Small Business, "Views and Estimates of the Committee on Small Business on Matters to be set forth in the Concurrent Resolution on the Budget for FY2014," communication to the Chairman, House Committee on the Budget, 113th Cong., 1st sess., February 27, 2013, at http://smallbusiness.house.gov/ uploadedfiles/revised_2014_views_and_estimates_document.pdf. Previously, the House Committee on Small Business had recommended that funding for Women Business Centers, PRIME technical assistance, HUBZone outreach, and the Offices of Native American Affairs and International Trade be eliminated; and funding for 7(j) technical assistance, Microloan technical assistance, and the National Women's Business Council be reduced. See U.S. Congress, House Committee on Small Business, "Views and Estimates of the Committee on Small Business on Matters to be set forth in the Concurrent Resolution on the Budget for FY2013," communication to the Chairman, House Committee on the Budget, 112th Cong., 2nd sess., March 7, 2012, at http://smallbusiness.house.gov/uploadedfiles/ views_and_estimates_fy_2013.pdf.

[151] OMB, "America First: A Budget Blueprint to Make America Great Again: Small Business Administration," p. 47, at https://www.whitehouse.gov/sites/whitehouse.gov/files/omb/ budget/fy2018/2018_blueprint.pdf; and SBA, *FY2018 Congressional Budget Justification and FY2016 Annual Performance Report*, p. 58, at https://www.sba.gov/sites/default/files/aboutsbaarticle/ FINAL_SBA_FY_2018_CBJ_May_22_2017c.pdf.

SBA's measurement of its management and training programs' effectiveness.

Program Administration

In 2007, the U.S. Government Accountability Office (GAO) was asked to assess the SBA's oversight of WBCs and the coordination and duplication of services among the SBA's management and technical training assistance programs. GAO found that

> As described in the terms of the SBA award, WBCs are required to coordinate with local SBDCs and SCORE chapters. In addition, SBA officials told us that they expected district offices to ensure that the programs did not duplicate each other. However, based on our review, WBCs lacked guidance and information from SBA on how to successfully carry out their coordination efforts. Most of the WBCs that we spoke with explained that in some situations they referred clients to an SBDC or SCORE counselor, and some WBCs also took steps to more actively coordinate with local SBDCs and SCORE chapters to avoid duplication and leverage resources. We learned that WBCs used a variety of approaches to facilitate coordination, such as memorandums of understanding, information-sharing meetings, and co-locating staff and services. However, some WBCs told us that they faced challenges in coordinating services with SBDC and SCORE, in part because the programs have similar performance measures, and this could result in competition among the service providers in some locations. We also found that on some occasions SBA encouraged WBCs to provide services that were similar to services already provided by SBDCs in their district. Such challenges thwart coordination efforts and could increase the risk of duplication in some geographic areas.[152]

---

[152] U.S. Government Accountability Office, *Small Business Administration: Opportunities Exist to Improve Oversight of Women's Business Centers and Coordination among SBA's Business Assistance Programs*, GAO-08-49, November 2007, pp. 6, 24-31, at http://www.gao.gov/new.items/d0849.pdf.

Some organizations have argued that the SBA's management and technical assistance training programs should be merged. For example, the U.S. Women's Chamber of Commerce argued that

> over the last 50 years, the SBA entrepreneurial development system has grown into a fragmented array of programs, which has resulted in a disorganized, overlapping, and [in] efficient delivery of service through a system that is ill-prepared to effectively address the challenges of our economy....
>
> if we are to serve the needs of American entrepreneurs, we must commit to a top to bottom restructuring of the delivery of the entrepreneurial services of the SBA. The myriad of entrepreneurial development programs should be unified into one centrally managed organization that has the flexibility to provide services when and where they are needed.[153]

These organizations argue that merging the SBA's management and technical assistance training programs would provide greater coordination of services and "one clear channel for assistance" that "is paramount to the average business owner seeking help."[154] Advocates of merging the SBA's management and technical assistance training programs often mention merging them into the SBDC Program because, in their view, it has the advantage of having a broader connection to mainstream resources and its locations are "greater and more diverse" than other SBA management and technical assistance training programs.[155]

---

[153] U.S. Congress, House Committee on Small Business, *Full Committee Hearing on the State of the SBA's Entrepreneurial Development Programs and Their Role in Promoting an Economic Recovery*, 111th Cong., 1st sess., February 11, 2009, Small Business Comm. Doc. No. 111-005 (Washington: GPO, 2009), p. 4.

[154] U.S. Congress, House Committee on Small Business, Subcommittee on Rural Development, Entrepreneurship, and Trade, *Subcommittee Hearing on Legislative Initiatives to Modernize SBA's Entrepreneurial Development Programs*, 111th Cong., 1st sess., April 2, 2009 (Washington: GPO, 2009), p. 29.

[155] U.S. Congress, House Committee on Small Business, *Full Committee Hearing on the State of the SBA's Entrepreneurial Development Programs and Their Role in Promoting an Economic Recovery*, 111th Cong., 1st sess., February 11, 2009, Small Business Committee Doc. No. 111-005 (Washington: GPO, 2009), p. 26.

Others argue that providing separate management and training assistance programs for specific groups is the best means to ensure that those groups' unique challenges are recognized and their unique needs are met.[156] For example, when asked at a congressional hearing about the rationale for having separate management and technical assistance training programs for specific groups, a representative of the Association of Women's Business Centers stated,

> I think that there is tremendous rationale for having different programs.... The women's business center programs really target a very different kind of population than the SBDCs.... We serve very different clientele.... We create a very different culture at the women's business center. We really have made it a welcoming place where ... they feel comfortable.... And it's very important to me that the woman have a place where they feel comfortable ... and where they see other women like themselves who are aspiring to reach their dreams.[157]

At another congressional hearing, the Association of Women's Business Centers' executive director argued that "the new three-year funding arrangement" for WBCs had enabled them to "concentrate on better serving their clients and growing their programs" and that WBCs should be provided continued and expanded funding because they provide effective services:

> We know that when our program performance is measured against any other enterprise assistance program, we will meet or exceed any performance measures. Indeed, the SBA's own client-based performance reviews have shown our clients to be just as satisfied or in some cases

---

[156] Ibid., pp. 15, 17, 26, 29, 58-65, 72; and U.S. Congress, House Committee on Small Business, *Women's Business Ownership Act of 1988*, report to accompany H.R. 5050, 100th Cong., 2nd sess., September 22, 1988, H.Rept. 100-955 (Washington: GPO, 1988), pp. 9, 10, 13, 14.

[157] U.S. Congress, House Committee on Small Business, *Full Committee Legislative Hearing on Energy, Veterans Entrepreneurship, and the SBA's Entrepreneurial Development Programs*, 110th Cong., 1st sess., May 16, 2007, Serial Number 110-22 (Washington: GPO, 2007), p. 20.

more satisfied with the services they have received compared to the SBA's other entrepreneurial development efforts.[158]

Instead of merging programs, some argue that improved communication among the SBA's management and technical assistance training resource partners and enhanced SBA program oversight is needed. For example, during the 111th Congress, the House passed H.R. 2352, the Job Creation Through Entrepreneurship Act of 2009, on May 20, 2009, by a vote of 406-15. The Senate did not take action on the bill. In its committee report accompanying the bill, the House Committee on Small Business concluded that

> Each ED [Entrepreneurial Development] program has a unique mandate and service delivery approach that is customized to its particular clients. However, as a network, the programs have established local connections and resources that benefit entrepreneurs within a region. Enhanced coordination among this network is critical to make the most of scarce resources available for small firms. It can also ensure that best practices are shared amongst providers that have similar goals but work within different contexts.[159]

In an effort to enhance the oversight and coordination of the SBA's management and technical assistance training programs, the Job Creation Through Entrepreneurship Act of 2009 would have required the SBA to

- create a new online, multilingual distance training and education program that was fully integrated into the SBA's existing management and technical assistance training programs and "allows entrepreneurs and small business owners the opportunity

---

[158] U.S. Congress, House Committee on Small Business, Full Committee Hearing on the State of the SBA's Entrepreneurial Development Programs and Their Role in Promoting an Economic Recovery, 111th Cong., 1st sess., February 11, 2009, Small Business Committee Doc. No. 111-005 (Washington: GPO, 2009), pp. 45, 47.

[159] U.S. Congress, House Committee on Small Business, *Job Creation Through Entrepreneurship Act of 2009*, report to accompany H.R. 2352, 111th Cong., 1st sess., May 15, 2009, H.Rept. 111-112 (Washington: GPO, 2009), pp. 17, 18.

to exchange technical assistance through the sharing of information."[160]
- coordinate its management and technical assistance training programs "with State and local economic development agencies and other federal agencies as appropriate."[161]
- "report annually to Congress, in consultation with other federal departments and agencies as appropriate, on opportunities to foster coordination, limit duplication, and improve program delivery for federal entrepreneurial development activities."[162]

During the 112th Congress, S. 3442, the SUCCESS Act of 2012, and S. 3572, the Restoring Tax and Regulatory Certainty to Small Businesses Act of 2012, sought to address the coordination issue by requiring the SBA, in consultation with other federal departments and agencies, to submit an annual report to Congress "describing opportunities to foster coordination of, limit duplication among, and improve program delivery for federal entrepreneurial development programs."[163] The SUCCESS Act of 2012 was referred to the Senate Committee on Small Business and Entrepreneurship, which held hearings on the bill.[164] The Restoring Tax and Regulatory Certainty to Small Businesses Act of 2012 was referred to the Senate Committee on Finance.

There has also been some discussion of merging SBA's small business management and training programs with business management and training programs offered by other federal agencies, both as a means to improve program performance and to achieve savings. For example, P.L. 111-139, Increasing the Statutory Limit on the Public Debt, requires GAO to "conduct routine investigations to identify programs, agencies, offices,

---

[160] H.R. 2352, the Job Creation Through Entrepreneurship Act of 2009, §201. Educating Entrepreneurs Through Technology; and H.R. 2352, §601. Expanding Entrepreneurship.
[161] H.R. 2352, §601. Expanding Entrepreneurship.
[162] Ibid.
[163] S. 3442, the SUCCESS Act of 2012, §411. Expanding Entrepreneurship; and S. 3572, the Restoring Tax and Regulatory Certainty to Small Businesses Act of 2012, §411. Expanding Entrepreneurship.
[164] U.S. Senate, Committee on Small Business and Entrepreneurship, "Creating Jobs and Growing the Economy: Legislative Proposals to Strengthen the Entrepreneurial Ecosystem," November 29, 2012, at http://www.sbc.senate.gov/public/index.cfm?p=Hearings.

and initiatives with duplicative goals and activities within Departments and governmentwide and report annually to Congress on the findings."[165] GAO identified 51 programmatic areas in its 2012 annual report on federal duplication "where programs may be able to achieve greater efficiencies or become more effective in providing government services."[166] GAO identified management and training assistance provided to businesses by the SBA and the Departments of Commerce, Housing and Urban Development, and Agriculture as one of these areas.[167] GAO identified 53 business management and technical assistance programs sponsored by the SBA and these three departments. GAO reported that "the number of programs that support entrepreneurs—53—and the overlap among these programs raise questions about whether a fragmented system is the most effective way to support entrepreneurs. By exploring alternatives, agencies may be able to determine whether there are more efficient ways to continue to serve the unique needs of entrepreneurs, including consolidating various programs."[168]

As mentioned previously, the House Committee on Small Business has argued that "given tight budgetary constraints" the SBA's various management and technical assistance training programs "should be folded into the mission of the SBDC program or their responsibilities should be taken over by other agencies."[169] The House Committee on Small Business has also indicated its opposition to the Obama Administration's increased use of, and requests for increased funding for, management and training initiatives. For example, Representative Sam Graves, then-chair of the

---

[165] P.L. 111-139, Increasing the statutory limit on the public debt, §21. Identification, Consolidation, and Elimination of Duplicative Government Programs.
[166] U.S. Government Accountability Office, *2012 Annual Report: Opportunities to Reduce Duplication, Overlap and Fragmentation, Achieve Savings, and Enhance Results*, GAO-12-342SP, February 28, 2012, p. 1, http://www.gao.gov/ assets/590/588818.pdf.
[167] Ibid., pp. 52-61.
[168] Ibid., p. 55.
[169] U.S. Congress, House Committee on Small Business, "Views and Estimates of the Committee on Small Business on Matters to be set forth in the Concurrent Resolution on the Budget for FY2014," communication to the Chairman, House Committee on the Budget, 113th Cong., 1st sess., February 27, 2013, at http://smallbusiness.house.gov/uploadedfiles/revised_2014_views_and_estimates_document.pdf.

House Committee on Small Business, indicated in his opening remarks at a congressional hearing in April 2014 that

> Despite reports that the federal government is riddled with redundant [management and training] programs for entrepreneurs, the SBA has increasingly spawned its own entrepreneurial development initiatives. In doing so, the SBA has repeatedly requested increased funding for its own initiatives while allowing funding for statutorily authorized programs, such as SBDCs, to remain static.... I continue to question the necessity of these initiatives given the potential overlap with both private and public sector efforts already in existence.[170]

In addition, as mentioned previously, H.R. 1774 would, among other provisions, require the SBA to only use authorized entrepreneurial development programs (SCORE, WBCs, SBDCs, etc.) to deliver specified entrepreneurial development services.

Program Evaluation

GAO noted in its 2007 assessment of the SBA's management and technical assistance training programs that, in addition to its annual survey of WBC, SBDC, and SCORE participants, the SBA requires WBCs to provide quarterly performance reports that include "the WBCs' actual accomplishments, compared with their performance goals for the reporting period; actual budget expenditures, compared with an estimated budget; cost of client fees; success stories; and names of WBC personnel and board members."[171] GAO also noted that WBCs are also required to issue fourth quarter performance reports that "also include a summary of the year's

---

[170] Rep. Sam Graves, "Opening Statement of Chairman Sam Graves, Committee on Small Business Hearing: 'SBA- created Initiatives: Necessary or Redundant Spending," April 30, 214, at http://smallbusiness.house.gov/uploadedfiles/ opening_statement-press_4-30-2014.pdf.

[171] U.S. Government Accountability Office, *Small Business Administration: Opportunities Exist to Improve Oversight of Women's Business Centers and Coordination among SBA's Business Assistance Programs*, GAO-08-49, November 2007, p. 15, at http://www.gao.gov/new.items/d0849.pdf.

activities and economic impact data that the WBCs collect from their clients, such as number of business start- ups, number of jobs created, and gross receipts."[172] SBDCs have similar reporting requirements.[173]

In recent years, Congress has considered requiring the SBA to expand its use of outcome-based measures to determine the effectiveness of its management and technical training assistance programs. For example, during the 111th Congress, the previously mentioned Job Creation Through Entrepreneurship Act of 2009 would have required the SBA to create "outcome-based measures of the amount of job creation or economic activity generated in the local community as a result of efforts made and services provided by each women's business center."[174] It would also have required the SBA to "develop and implement a consistent data collection process to cover all entrepreneurial development programs" including "data relating to job creation, performance, and any other data determined appropriate by the Administrator with respect to the Administration's entrepreneurial development programs."[175]

During the 112th Congress, the SUCCESS Act of 2012 and Restoring Tax and Regulatory Certainty to Small Businesses Act of 2012 would have required the SBA to "promulgate a rule to develop and implement a consistent data collection process for the entrepreneurial development programs" that included data "relating to job creation and performance and any other data determined appropriate by the Administrator."[176]

During the 114th Congress, H.R. 207 would have required the SBA to issue an annual report concerning "all entrepreneurial development activities undertaken in the current fiscal year." This chapter would include a description and operating details for each program and activity; operating circulars, manuals, and standard operating procedures for each program and activity; a description of the process used to award grants under each program and activity; a list of all awardees, contractors, and vendors and

---

[172] Ibid.
[173] SBA, "Small Business Development Center Fy/Cy 2011 Program Announcement for Renewal of the Cooperative Agreement for Current Recipient Organizations," pp. 27-38, at https://www.sba.gov/sites/default/files/files/2011%20Program%20Announcement.pdf.
[174] H.R. 2352, §404. Performance and Planning.
[175] H.R. 2352, §601. Expanding Entrepreneurship.
[176] S. 3442, §411. Expanding Entrepreneurship; and S. 3572, §411. Expanding Entrepreneurship.

the amount of awards provided for the current fiscal year for each program and activity; the amount of funding obligated for the current fiscal year for each program and activity; and the names and titles for those individuals responsible for each program and activity. This legislative language was reintroduced during the 115th Congress in H.R. 1774, the Developing the Next Generation of Small Businesses Act of 2017.

CONCLUDING OBSERVATIONS

Congressional interest in the federal government's small business management and technical assistance training programs has increased in recent years. One of the reasons for the heightened level of interest in these programs is that small business has led job formation and retention during previous economic recoveries.[177] It has been argued that effective small business management and technical assistance training programs are needed if small businesses are to lead job creation and retention during the current economic recovery. As then-Representative Heath Shuler stated during a congressional hearing in 2009:

> We often talk about the role that small business plays in the creation of jobs and with good reason. Small firms generate between 60 and 80 percent of new positions. Following the recession in the mid-1990s, they created 3.8 million jobs.... we could use that growth today. But unfortunately, many firms are struggling to make ends meet. Let's allow them to hire new workers. In the face of historic economic challenges, we should be investing in America's job creators. SBA's Entrepreneurial Development Programs, or ED, do just that. Of all the tools in the small

---

[177] SBA, Office of Advocacy, *Small Business Economic Indicators for 2003*, August 2004, p. 3; Brian Headd, "Small Businesses Most Likely to Lead Economic Recovery," *The Small Business Advocate*, vol. 28, no. 6 (July 2009), pp. 1, 2; and SBA, "Fiscal Year 2010 Congressional Budget Justification," p. 1, at https://www.sba.gov/sites/default/files/aboutsbaarticle/Congressional_Budget_Justification_2010.pdf.

business toolbox, these are some of the most critical. They help small firms do everything from draft business plans to access capital.[178]

The general consensus is that federal management and technical assistance training programs serve an important purpose and, for the most part, are providing needed services that are not available elsewhere. As Karen Mills, then-SBA administrator, stated during a press interview in 2010:

> We find that our counseling operations are equally important as our credit operations because small businesses really need help and advice, and when they get it, they tend to have more sales and more profits and more longevity, and they hire more people. So we have looked forward and said, "How do we get all the tools small businesses need into their hands?" Maybe they want to export. Maybe they want to know how to use broadband. Maybe they are veterans who are coming back and want to start a business or grow their business. Our job is to make sure all that information and opportunity is accessible for small businesses so they can do what they do, which is keep our economy strong.[179]

There is also a general consensus that making federal management and technical assistance training programs more effective and responsive to the needs of small business would assist the national economic recovery. However, there are disagreements over how to achieve that goal.

Some advocate (1) increasing funding for existing programs to enable them to provide additional training opportunities for small businesses while, at the same time, maintaining separate training programs for specific demographic groups as a means to ensure that those groups' specific needs are met; (2) requiring the SBA to make more extensive use of outcome-based measures to better determine the programs' effect on small business

---

[178] U.S. Congress, House Committee on Small Business, Subcommittee on Rural Development, Entrepreneurship and Trade, *Subcommittee On Rural Development, Entrepreneurship And Trade Markup On Entrepreneurial Development Programs Legislation*, 111th Cong., 1st sess., April 30, 2009, Small Business Committee Document No. 111-118 [ERRATA – printing error, should be 111-018] (Washington: GPO, 2009), p. 1.

[179] David Port, "But Where Is the Money?" *Entrepreneur Magazine*, August 2010, at http://www.entrepreneur.com/magazine/entrepreneur/2010/august/207500.html.

formation and retention, job creation and retention, and the generation of wealth; and (3) temporarily reducing or eliminating federal matching requirements to enable SBA's management and technical assistance training resource partners to focus greater attention to service delivery and less to fund raising. Others argue for a merger of existing programs to reduce costs and improve program efficiency, to focus available resources on augmenting the capacity of SBDCs to meet the needs of all small business groups, and require the SBA to make more extensive use of outcome-based performance measures to determine program effectiveness.

No case studies or empirical data are available concerning the efficiencies that might be gained by merging the SBA's management and technical assistance training programs. Advocates argue that merging the programs would improve communications, reduce confusion by business owners seeking assistance by ensuring that all small business management and technical assistance training centers serve all small business owners and aspiring entrepreneurs, lead to more sustainable and predictable funding for the programs from nonfederal sources, and result in more consistent and standard operating procedures throughout the country.[180] Opponents argue that any gains in program efficiency that might be realized would be more than offset by the loss of targeted services for constituencies that often require different information and training to meet their unique challenges and needs.[181]

---

[180] U.S. Congress, House Committee on Small Business, *Full Committee Hearing on the State of the SBA's Entrepreneurial Development Programs and Their Role in Promoting an Economic Recovery*, 111th Cong., 1st sess., February 11, 2009, Small Business Committee Doc. No. 111-005 (Washington: GPO, 2009), pp. 3-5, 24-27, 29; and U.S. Congress, House Committee on Small Business, *Full Committee Hearing on Legislation to Reauthorize and Modernize SBA's Entrepreneurial Development Programs*, 111th Cong., 1st sess., May 6, 2009 (Washington: GPO, 2009), pp. 3-5, 15, 27-34.

[181] U.S. Congress, House Committee on Small Business, Full Committee Hearing on the State of the SBA's Entrepreneurial Development Programs and Their Role in Promoting an Economic Recovery, 111th Cong., 1st sess., February 11, 2009, Small Business Committee Doc. No. 111-005 (Washington: GPO, 2009), pp. 44-49; U.S. Congress, House Committee on Small Business, Job Creation Through Entrepreneurship Act of 2009, report to accompany H.R. 2352, 111th Cong., 1st sess., May 15, 2009, H.Rept. 111-112 (Washington: GPO, 2009), pp. 16-31; and U.S. Congress, House Committee on Small Business, Women's Business Ownership Act of 1988, report to accompany H.R. 5050, 100th Cong., 2nd sess., September 22, 1988, H.Rept. 100-955 (Washington: GPO, 1988), pp. 9, 10, 13, 14.

APPENDIX. BRIEF DESCRIPTIONS OF SBA MANAGEMENT AND TECHNICAL ASSISTANCE TRAINING PROGRAMS

Table A-1. Brief Descriptions of SBA Management and Technical Assistance Training Programs

Program Name	Authority	Brief Description	Number	Federal Matching Requirement
Small Business Development Center Grant Program	P.L. 96-302, 1980	Provides management and technical assistance training to small businesses through centers located in leading universities, colleges, and state economic development agencies.	63 lead centers and 900+ local centers	50% match from nonfederal sources comprised of not less than 50% cash and not more than 50% of indirect costs.
Women Business Center Grant Program	P.L. 100-533, 1988	Provides long-term training, counseling, networking, and mentoring to women entrepreneurs, especially those who are socially and economically disadvantaged.	121	50% match from nonfederal sources; not more than one-half of the nonfederal matching assistance may be in the form of in-kind contributions, including office equipment and office space.
SCORE (Service Corps of Retired Executives)	Section 8(b) of the Small Business Act; P.L. 89-754, 1966	Provides technical, managerial, and informational assistance to small business concerns through in-person mentoring by volunteer counselors who are working or, in most instances, retired business owners.	320 chapters and 800+ branch offices	None
7(j) Technical Assistance Program	Section 7(j) of the Small Business Act; Section 8(a) of the Small Business Act; P.L. 95-507, 1978	Provides management and technical assistance training to 8(a) certified firms, small disadvantaged businesses, businesses operating in areas of high unemployment or low-income and firms owned by low-income individuals.	10 service providers in FY2018	None

Table A-1. (Continued)

Program Name	Authority	Brief Description	Number	Federal Matching Requirement
Microloan Technical Assistance Program	P.L. 102-140, 1992	Provides management and technical assistance training to Microloan borrowers and, within specified limits, to prospective Microloan borrowers.	144 actively lending intermediaries	25% from nonfederal sources; no matching requirement if the intermediary makes at least 50% of its loans in an Economically Distressed Area.
Native American Outreach Program	Section 7(j) of the Small Business Act; SBA regulations, 1994	Provides management and technical assistance training to American Indians, Alaska Natives, Native Hawaiians and "the indigenous people of Guam and American Samoa ... to promote entity-owned and individual 8(a) certification, government contracting, entrepreneurial education, and capital access."	7 service providers in FY2017	None
PRIME Technical Assistance Program	P.L. 106-102, 1999	Provides assistance in the form of grants to nonprofit microenterprise development organizations or programs that have a demonstrated record of delivering microenterprise services to disadvantaged entrepreneurs.	32 service providers in FY2018	50% from nonfederal sources; sources such as fees, grants, gifts, income from loan sources, and in-kind resources from nonfederal public or private sources may be used to comply with the matching funds requirement
Veterans Business Development Programs	P.L. 106-50, 1999	The SBA's Office of Veterans Business Development mission is to (1) expand the provision of and improve access to technical assistance regarding entrepreneurship for	22 Veterans Business Office Centers and other providers	None

Program Name	Authority	Brief Description	Number	Federal Matching Requirement
		the Nation's veterans; and (2) to assist veterans, including service-disabled veterans, with the formation and expansion of small business concerns by working with and organizing public and private resources, including those of the SBA.		

Sources: Federal statutes cited in table.

In: Small Business
Editor: Angel Becker

ISBN: 978-1-53615-969-1
© 2019 Nova Science Publishers, Inc.

Chapter 6

SMALL BUSINESS MENTOR-PROTÉGÉ PROGRAMS (UPDATED)[*]

Robert Jay Dilger

SUMMARY

Mentor-protégé programs typically seek to pair new businesses with more experienced businesses in mutually beneficial relationships. Protégés may receive financial, technical, or management assistance from mentors in obtaining and performing federal contracts or subcontracts, or serving as suppliers under such contracts or subcontracts. Mentors may receive credit toward subcontracting goals, reimbursement of certain expenses, or other incentives.

The federal government currently has several mentor-protégé programs to assist small businesses in various ways. For example, the 8(a) Mentor-Protégé Program is a government-wide program designed to assist small businesses "owned and controlled by socially and economically disadvantaged individuals" participating in the Small Business Administration's (SBA's) Minority Small Business and Capital Ownership Development Program (commonly known as the 8(a)

---

[*] This is an edited, reformatted and augmented version of Congressional Research Service, Publication No. R41722, dated January 7, 2019.

program) in obtaining and performing federal contracts. Toward that end, mentors may (1) form joint ventures with protégés that are eligible to perform federal contracts set aside for small businesses; (2) make certain equity investments in protégé firms; (3) lend or subcontract to protégé firms; and (4) provide technical or management assistance to their protégés. The Department of Defense (DOD) Mentor-Protégé Program, in contrast, is agency-specific. It is designed to assist various types of small businesses and other entities in obtaining and performing DOD subcontracts and serving as suppliers on DOD contracts. Mentors may (1) make advance or progress payments to their protégés that DOD reimburses; (2) award subcontracts to their protégés on a noncompetitive basis when they would not otherwise be able to do so; (3) lend money to or make investments in protégé firms; and (4) provide or arrange for other assistance.

Other agencies also have agency-specific mentor-protégé programs designed to assist various types of small businesses or other entities in obtaining and performing subcontracts under agency prime contracts. The Department of Homeland Security (DHS), for example, has a mentor-protégé program wherein mentors may provide protégés with rent-free use of facilities or equipment, temporary personnel for training, property, loans, or other assistance. Because these programs are not based in statute, unlike the SBA and DOD programs, they generally rely upon preexisting authorities (e.g., authorizing use of evaluation factors) or publicity to incentivize mentor participation. See Table A.1 for a summary comparison.

P.L. 111-240, the Small Business Jobs Act of 2010, authorized the SBA to establish mentor-protégé programs for small businesses owned and controlled by service-disabled veterans, small businesses owned and controlled by women, and small businesses located in a HUBZone. P.L. 112-239, the National Defense Authorization Act for Fiscal Year 2013, authorized the SBA to establish a mentor-protégé program for all small businesses, and generally prohibits agencies from carrying out mentor-protégé programs that have not been approved by the SBA.

Based on the authority provided by these two laws, the SBA published a final rule in the *Federal Register* on July 25, 2016, modifying the 8(a) Mentor-Protégé Program and establishing, effective August 24, 2016, "a government-wide mentor-protégé program for all small business concerns, consistent with the SBA's mentor-protégé program for participants in the SBA's 8(a) Business Development program." The all small business Mentor-Protégé Program began accepting applications on October 1, 2016.

The SBA noted in the final rule that because the new all small business mentor-protégé program applies to all federal small business contracts and federal agencies, "conceivably other agency-specific mentor-protégé programs would not be needed." Since then, several federal agencies have ended their mentor-protégé programs and encouraged interested parties to consider the SBA's all small business Mentor-Protégé program.

INTRODUCTION

Mentor-protégé programs are designed to assist small business development, focusing on enhancing the protégé's capacity to serve as either a prime contractor or a subcontractor in federal contracts. These programs typically seek to pair new businesses and more experienced businesses in mutually beneficial relationships. Protégés may receive financial, technical, or management assistance from mentors in obtaining and performing federal contracts or subcontracts, or serving as suppliers under such contracts or subcontracts, whereas mentors may receive credit toward subcontracting goals, reimbursement of certain expenses,[1] or other incentives for assisting protégés.

Four federal agencies have SBA-approved mentor-protégé programs:

- Department of Energy,
- Department of Homeland Security (DHS),
- National Aeronautics and Space Administration, and
- U.S. Small Business Administration (SBA).[2]

Two federal agencies have mentor-protégé programs that do not require SBA's approval because their programs are not covered by the Small Business Act:

---

[1] Three federal departments and agencies provide mentors reimbursement for certain expenses related to providing assistance to protégés: the Department of Defense (DOD), Department of Energy, and Federal Aviation Administration.

[2] U.S. Small Business Administration (SBA), "Report to Congress on Mentor-Protégé Programs for Fiscal Year 2016," May 17, 2017, at https://www.sba.gov/sites/default/files/resources_articles/Report_to_Congress_on_FY16Mentor_Protege_Programs_2017_05_03.pdf.

- Department of Defense (DOD) and
- Federal Aviation Administration.

Three federal agencies have mentor-protégé programs that, in 2018, were awaiting SBA's approval:

- Department of Health and Human Services,
- Department of Transportation, and
- Department of the Treasury.[3]

Mentor-protégé programs seek to assist small businesses in various ways.[4] For example,

- the 8(a) Mentor-Protégé Program assists "small businesses owned and controlled by socially and economically disadvantaged individuals" participating in the SBA's Minority Small Business and Capital Ownership Development Program (commonly known as the 8(a) program) in obtaining and performing contracts with executive-branch agencies;
- the SBA's all small business Mentor-Protégé Program is "a government-wide mentor-protégé program for all small business concerns, consistent with the SBA's mentor-protégé program for participants in the SBA's 8(a) Business Development program."[5]

---

[3] Three federal agencies (Department of Education, Department of Housing and Urban Development, and Department of Veterans Affairs) do not have active mentor-protégé programs. Also, four federal agencies are retiring their mentor-protégé programs, largely due to the implementation of the new all small business program (Department of State, Environmental Protection Agency, General Services Administration, and United States Agency for International Development). See SBA, "The Federal Mentor-Protégé Program Landscape."

[4] For purposes of federal procurement law, a business is "small" if it is independently owned and operated; is not dominant in its field of operations; and meets any definitions or standards established by the SBA. 15 U.S.C. §632(a)(1)-(2)(A). These standards focus primarily upon the size of the business as measured by the number of employees or its gross income, but they also take into account the size of other businesses within the same industry. 13 C.F.R. §§121.101-121.108.

[5] SBA, "Small Business Mentor Protégé Program; Small Business Size Regulations; Government Contracting Programs; 8(a) Business Development/Small Disadvantaged Business Status

- the DOD Mentor-Protégé Program assists various types of small businesses and other entities in performing as subcontractors or suppliers on DOD contracts; and
- other agency-specific mentor-protégé programs, such as that of the DHS, provide mentor firms incentives to subcontract agency prime contracts with small businesses.

Congressional interest in small business mentor-protégé programs has increased in recent years, in part because of reports that large businesses serving as mentors have improperly received federal contracting assistance intended for small businesses.[6] The SBA's suspension (and later reinstatement) of a mentor in the 8(a) Mentor-Protégé Program for possible fraud, as well as reports of other fraud in several of the SBA's contracting programs, has also contributed to congressional interest.

During the 111th Congress, P.L. 111-240, the Small Business Jobs Act of 2010, authorized the SBA to establish mentor-protégé programs for small businesses owned and controlled by service-disabled veterans, small businesses owned and controlled by women, and small businesses located in a HUBZone "modeled" on the 8(a) Mentor-Protégé Program.[7] P.L. 111-

---

Determinations; HUBZone Program; Women-Owned Small Business Federal Contract Program; Rules of Procedure Governing Cases Before the Office of Hearings and Appeals," 80 *Federal Register* 6618, February 5, 2015.

[6] For example, in one notable instance, in October 2010, the SBA suspended a mentor participating in the 8(a) Mentor-Protégé Program from government contracting because of allegations that the firm used "front companies" to obtain the majority of the work and revenue under contracts set aside for small businesses. See, e.g., SBA, "Statement from Administrator Mills on the Suspension of GTSI from Federal Contracting Program," October 1, 2010, at https://www.sba.gov/content/statement-administrator-mills-suspension-gtsi-federal-contracting-program; and SBA, "Administrative Agreement, between GTSI Corp. ("GTSI") and the United States Small Business Administration ("SBA")," October 19, 2010, at https://www.sba.gov/content/gtsi-administrative-agreement-10-19-2010. Also see GAO, *Small Business Administration: Undercover Tests Show HUBZone Program Remains Vulnerable to Fraud and Abuse*, GAO-10-920T, July 28, 2010, pp. 2-4, at http://www.gao.gov/new.items/d10920t.pdf; GAO, *8(a) Program: Fourteen Ineligible Firms Received $325 Million in Sole-Source and Set-Aside Contracts*, GAO-10-425, March 30, 2010, pp. 7-22, 29, at http://www.gao.gov/new.items/d10425.pdf; GAO, *Service-Disabled Veteran-Owned Small Business Program: Case Studies Show Fraud and Abuse Allowed Ineligible Firms to Obtain Millions of Dollars in Contracts*, GAO-10-108, October 23, 2009, pp. 4-13, at http://www.gao.gov/new.items/d10108.pdf.

[7] SBA, "Small Business Jobs Act: Small Business Mentor-Protégé Programs," 75 *Federal Register* 79869, December 20, 2010; SBA, "Semiannual Regulatory Agenda, Small

240 also required the Government Accountability Office (GAO) to assess the effectiveness of mentor-protégé programs generally.[8] GAO's findings were reported on June 15, 2011.[9]

During the 112th Congress, P.L. 112-239, the National Defense Authorization Act for Fiscal Year 2013, authorized the SBA to establish a mentor-protégé program for "all" small businesses that is generally "identical" to the 8(a) Mentor-Protégé Program. In an effort to promote uniformity, the act, with some exceptions, prohibits agencies from carrying out mentor-protégé programs that have not been approved by the SBA.[10]

Based on the authority provided by these two laws, the SBA published a proposed rule in the *Federal Register* on February 5, 2015, "to establish a government-wide mentor-protégé program for all small business concerns, consistent with SBA's mentor-protégé program for participants in the SBA's 8(a) Business Development program in order to make the mentor-protégé rules for each of the programs as consistent as possible."[11] The SBA decided that it would not implement additional mentor-protégé programs for service-disabled veteran-owned and -controlled small businesses, women-owned and -controlled small businesses, and HUBZone small businesses because they "would be necessarily included

---

Business Jobs Act: Small Business Mentor-Protégé Programs," 76 *Federal Register* 40140, July 7, 2011; SBA, "Small Business Jobs Act: Small Business Mentor-Protégé Programs," 78 *Federal Register* 1492, January 8, 2013; SBA, "Small Business Mentor-Protégé Programs," 78 *Federal Register* 44334, July 23, 2013; and SBA, "Small Business Mentor-Protégé Programs," 79 *Federal Register* 1089, January 7, 2014.

[8] Small Business Jobs Act of 2010, P.L. 111-240, §§1345 & 1347, 124 Stat. 2546-47 (September 27, 2010).

[9] GAO, *Mentor-Protégé Programs Have Policies That Aim to Benefit Participants But Do Not Require Postagreement Tracking*, GAO-11-548R, June 15, 2011, p. 1, at http://www.gao.gov/new.items/d11548r.pdf. The statute required that the report be submitted by March 26, 2011—180 days after the act's date of enactment, which was September 27, 2010. P.L. 111-240, §1345(c), 124 Stat. 2546.

[10] The Senate version of the bill (S. 3254) did not include these provisions, but the conference report to H.R. 4310, which was agreed to by the House on December 20, 2012, and by the Senate on December 21, 2012, included them. The program under P.L. 112-239 need not be identical to the 8(a) Mentor-Protégé Program insofar as differences may be "necessary" given the types of small businesses included in the program as protégés.

[11] SBA, "Small Business Mentor Protégé Program; Small Business Size Regulations; Government Contracting Programs; 8(a) Business Development/Small Disadvantaged Business Status Determinations; HUBZone Program; Women-Owned Small Business Federal Contract Program; Rules of Procedure Governing Cases Before the Office of Hearings and Appeals," 80 *Federal Register* 6618, February 5, 2015.

within any mentor-protégé program targeting all small business concerns."[12] The SBA also announced that "having five separate small business mentor-protégé programs could become confusing to the public and procuring agencies and hard to implement by the SBA."[13] The SBA estimated at that time that approximately 2,000 small businesses could become active in the proposed mentor-protégé program for small businesses.[14]

On July 25, 2016, the SBA published a final rule in the *Federal Register* establishing, effective August 24, 2016, the new, government-wide mentor-protégé program for all small businesses. The final rule also modified the SBA's 8(a) Mentor-Protégé Program in an effort to make the two programs as consistent as possible.[15] As a result, 8(a) small businesses may participate in either program.

The SBA began to accept applications for the all small business Mentor-Protégé Program on October 1, 2016.

The SBA noted in the final rule that because its new small business mentor-protégé program will apply to all federal small business contracts and federal agencies, "conceivably other agency-specific mentor-protégé programs would not be needed."[16] In recognition that one or more agency-specific mentor-protégé programs may be discontinued and that several of these programs provide incentives in the contract evaluation process to mentor firms that provide significant subcontracting work to their protégés, the SBA allows procuring agencies, in appropriate circumstances, to provide subcontracting incentives to mentor firms participating in its mentor-protégé programs as well.[17]

This chapter provides an overview of the federal government's various small business mentor-protégé programs. As is discussed below, while all these programs are intended to assist small businesses in performing as

---

[12] Ibid., pp. 6618-6619.
[13] Ibid., p. 6619.
[14] Ibid., p. 6628; and SBA, "Small Business Mentor Protégé Program," 81 *Federal Register* 48574, July 25, 2016.
[15] SBA, "Small Business Mentor Protégé Program," 81 *Federal Register* 48558-48595, July 25, 2016.
[16] Ibid., p. 48565.
[17] Ibid., p. 48566.

contractors, subcontractors, or suppliers on federal or federally funded contracts, the programs differ in their scope and operations. Table A.1 in the Appendix provides an overview of key differences among the programs.

MENTOR-PROTÉGÉ PROGRAMS ADMINISTERED BY THE SBA

The SBA administers three mentor-protégé programs, one for firms participating in the 8(a) program, another for firms in its Small Business Innovation Research (SBIR) and Small Business Technology Transfer (STTR) programs,[18] and one for all small businesses.

8(a) Mentor-Protégé Program

Amendments made to the Small Business Act in 1978 directed the SBA to develop a program to "assist" small businesses owned and controlled by socially and economically disadvantaged individuals that are eligible to receive contracts under Section 8(a) of the act ("8(a) small businesses") in performing these contracts.[19] The SBA implemented this direction, in part, by establishing a mentor-protégé program on July 30, 1998,[20] wherein mentors "enhance the capabilities" of 8(a) firms and "improve [their] ability to successfully compete for contracts" by

---

[18] For additional information and analysis concerning the Small Business Innovation Research (SBIR) and Small Business Technology Transfer (STTR) programs, see CRS Report R43695, *Small Business Innovation Research and Small Business Technology Transfer Programs*, by John F. Sargent Jr.
[19] An Act to Amend the Small Business Act and the Small Business Investment Act of 1958, P.L. 95-507, §204, 92 Stat. 1766 (codified, as amended, at 15 U.S.C. §636(j)(10)).
[20] SBA, "Small Business Size Regulations; 8(a) Business Development/Small Disadvantaged Business Status Determinations; Rules of Procedure Governing Cases Before the Office of Hearings and Appeals: Final Rule," 63 *Federal Register* 35739, June 30, 1998.

providing various forms of assistance.[21] Such assistance may include technical or management assistance; financial assistance in the form of equity investments or loans; subcontracts; trade education; and assistance in performing prime contracts with the government through joint venture agreements.[22]

Although the SBA was directed to establish this mentor-protégé program and SBA rules govern participation in the program, as discussed below, the 8(a) Mentor-Protégé Program is government-wide in the sense that firms in the program may enjoy the benefits of participation in it while performing the contracts of any federal agency.[23]

In fact, when agencies that do not have their own mentor-protégé programs, such as those discussed below, are involved, the 8(a) Mentor-Protégé Program may be referred to as if it were that agency's program.[24]

The SBA's 8(a) Mentor-Protégé Program is administered by the SBA's Office of Business Development. This makes it somewhat different from the agency-specific mentor-protégé programs, discussed later, which generally are the responsibility of the agency's Office of Small and

---

[21] 13 C.F.R. §124.520(a). See also GAO, *Small Business: SBA Could Better Focus Its 8(a) Program to Help Firms Obtain Contracts*, GAO/RCED-00-196, July 20, 2000, p. 14, at http://www.gao.gov/new.items/rc00196.pdf.

[22] 13 C.F.R. §124.520(a).

[23] For example, mentor-protégé joint ventures may qualify as "small" for purposes of contracts set aside for small businesses by any executive branch agency, not just by the SBA. The same is not necessarily true for joint ventures involving mentors and protégés in agency-specific programs. See, e.g., SBA, "Small Business Size Regulations; 8(a) Business Development/Small Disadvantaged Business Status Determinations," 74 *Federal Register* 55694, October 28, 2009 ("[A]n exception to affiliation for protégés in other Federal mentor/protégé programs will be recognized by SBA only where specifically authorized by statute (e.g., DOD's mentor/protégé program) or where SBA has authorized an exception to affiliation for a mentor/protégé program of another Federal agency under the procedures set forth in §121.903."). This requirement was incorporated in the final rule. See SBA, "Small Business Size Regulations; 8(a) Business Development/Small Disadvantaged Business Status Determinations," 76 *Federal Register* 8222-8223, February 11, 2011.

[24] See, e.g., Listing of Mentor Protégé Programs, at http://www.eds-gov.com/mentorprotege/links.asp (characterizing the Department of Agriculture as having a "mentor-protégé office"). This is a reference to the Department of Agriculture's Office of Small and Disadvantaged Business Utilization, which provides information about the 8(a) Mentor-Protégé Program and other federal mentor-protégé programs. The department does not have its own mentor-protégé program.

Disadvantaged Business Utilization (OSDBU) and may involve coordination with agency contracting offices.[25]

As of February 27, 2018, there were 493 active 8(a) mentor-protégé agreements.[26]

"Socially and economically disadvantaged individuals," for purposes of the 8(a) program

Individuals who belong to one of the following racial or ethnic groups, or who can prove that they are personally socially disadvantaged, and who have a personal net worth of $250,000 or less at the time of application to the program ($750,000 for continuing eligibility) may be approved by the SBA to participate in the 8(a) program for up to nine years:

Black Americans; Hispanic Americans; Native Americans (American Indians, Eskimos, Aleuts, or Native Hawaiians); Asian Pacific Americans (persons with origins from Burma, Thailand, Malaysia, Indonesia, Singapore, Brunei, Japan, China [including Hong Kong], Taiwan, Laos, Cambodia [Kampuchea], Vietnam, Korea, The Philippines, U.S. Trust Territory of the Pacific Islands [Republic of Palau], Republic of the Marshall Islands, Federated States of Micronesia, the Commonwealth of the Northern Mariana Islands, Guam, Samoa, Macao, Fiji, Tonga, Kiribati, Tuvalu, or Nauru); Subcontinent Asian Americans (persons with origins from India, Pakistan, Bangladesh, Sri Lanka, Bhutan, the Maldives Islands, or Nepal); and members of other groups designated from time to time by SBA.

Source: 13 C.F.R. §§124.103-124.104.

Regulations Governing the 8(a) Mentor-Protégé Program

SBA regulations govern various aspects of the 8(a) Mentor-Protégé Program, including who may qualify as a mentor or protégé, the content of written agreements between mentors and protégés, and the SBA's evaluation of the mentor-protégé relationship. Under these regulations, "Any [for profit] concern that demonstrates a commitment and the ability

---

[25] GAO, *Mentor-Protégé Programs Have Policies That Aim to Benefit Participants But Do Not Require Postagreement Tracking*, GAO-11-548R, June 15, 2011, p. 3, at http://www.gao.gov/new.items/d11548r.pdf.

[26] SBA, "All Small Mentor Protégé Program," February 27, 2018.

to assist developing 8(a) Participants may act as a mentor," including large firms, other small businesses, firms that have graduated from the 8(a) program, and other 8(a) firms that are in the "transitional stage," or final five years of the 8(a) program.[27] Only firms approved by the SBA may serve as mentors, and SBA regulations require that each mentor (1) demonstrate that it "is capable of carrying out its responsibilities to assist the protégé firm under the proposed mentor-protégé agreement";[28] (2) possess "good character";[29] (3) not be debarred or suspended from government contracting; and (4) be able to "impart value to a protégé firm due to lessons learned and practical experienced gained because of the [8(a) program], or through its knowledge of general business operations and government contracting."[30]

Protégés, in turn, are required by SBA regulations to be small businesses "owned and controlled by socially and economically disadvantaged individuals" that are in good standing in the 8(a) program. Protégés must also qualify as small for the size standard corresponding to their primary (or, under specified circumstances, their secondary) North American Industry code and demonstrate how the business development assistance to be received through the mentor-protégé relationship would advance the goals and objectives set forth in their business plans.[31]

---

[27] 13 C.F.R. §124.520(b). Previously, nonprofit entities were eligible to serve as mentors. For discussion concerning restricting eligibility to for profit entities, see SBA, "Small Business Mentor Protégé Program," 81 *Federal Register* 48562, 48563, July 25, 2016.

[28] Previously, SBA regulations required that prospective mentors submit their federal tax returns for the past two years to the SBA for review to demonstrate their "favorable financial health." 13 C.F.R. §124.520(b)(3) (2010). This requirement changed effective March 14, 2011, to authorize the submission of audited financial statements and Securities and Exchange Commission filings, as well as tax returns. See SBA, "Small Business Size Regulations; 8(a) Business Development/Small Disadvantaged Business Status Determinations," 76 *Federal Register* 8243, February 11, 2011. Approved mentors are also required to certify annually that they continue to possess good character and a favorable financial position. 13 C.F.R. §124.520(b)(4). For discussion concerning the change from "favorable financial health" to "capable of carrying out its responsibilities," see SBA, "Small Business Mentor Protégé Program," 81 *Federal Register* 48563, July 25, 2016.

[29] *Good character* is not defined for purposes of this provision, although SBA regulations otherwise address what it means for individuals applying to the 8(a) program to possess good character. See 13 C.F.R. §124.108(a).

[30] 13 C.F.R. §124.520(b)(1)(i)-(iv).

[31] Previously, protégés were required to (1) be in the "developmental stage," or the first four years of the 8(a) program; (2) have never received an 8(a) contract; or (3) have a size that is

Initially, mentors could only have one protégé, and protégés could have only one mentor.[32] However, these restrictions were removed effective March 14, 2011.[33] SBA's regulations now provide that mentors are generally expected to have no more than one protégé at a time. However, mentors may have up to three protégés at one time provided that they can demonstrate that "the additional mentor/protégé relationship[s] will not adversely affect the development of either protégé firm."[34] Protégés are also generally expected to have no more than one mentor at a time. However, protégés may, under specified circumstances, have two mentors.[35]

The SBA requires that mentors and protégés enter a written agreement, approved by the SBA's Associate Administrator for Business Development, which sets forth the protégé's needs and describes the assistance the mentor will provide.[36] This agreement generally obligates the mentor to furnish assistance to the protégé for at least one year,[37] although it does allow either mentor or protégé to terminate the agreement with 30 days' advance notice to the other party and the SBA.[38] In addition,

---

less than half the size standard corresponding to their primary North American Industry code. For discussion of the change in these requirements, see SBA, "Small Business Mentor Protégé Program," 81 *Federal Register* 48564, 48565, July 25, 2016.

[32] 13 C.F.R. §124.520(b)(2) & (c)(3) (2010).

[33] See SBA, "Small Business Size Regulations; 8(a) Business Development/Small Disadvantaged Business Status Determinations," 76 *Federal Register* 8243, February 11, 2011.

[34] 13 C.F.R. §124.520(b)(2).

[35] 13 C.F.R. §124.520(c)(3). The specified circumstances are that the AA/BD [Associate Administrator for Business Development] may approve a second mentor for a particular protégé firm in which the second relationship will not compete or otherwise conflict with the business development assistance set forth in the first mentor/protégé relationship and either (1) the second relationship pertains to a secondary NAICS code or (2) the protégé firm is seeking to acquire a specific expertise that the first mentor does not possess. Note: ...the AA/BD may authorize a participant to be both a protégé and a mentor at the same time where the participant can demonstrate that the second relationship will not compete or otherwise conflict with the first mentor-protégé relationship. See SBA, "Small Business Mentor Protégé Program," 81 *Federal Register* 48584, July 25, 2016.

[36] 13 C.F.R. §124.520(e)(1). Pursuant to these regulations, the SBA will not approve the agreement if it determines that the assistance to be provided is insufficient to promote any developmental gains by the protégé, or if the SBA determines that the agreement is merely a vehicle to enable a non-8(a) firm to receive 8(a) contracts. 13 C.F.R. §124.520(e)(2). The regulations also provide that the SBA must approve all changes to the agreement in advance. 13 C.F.R. §124.520(e)(5).

[37] 13 C.F.R. §124.520(e)(1)(iii).

[38] 13 C.F.R. §124.520(e)(3).

the agreement provides that the SBA will review the mentor-protégé agreement annually to determine whether to approve its continuation.[39] The SBA's evaluation is based, in part, on the protégé's annual reports regarding its contacts with its mentor and the benefits it has received from the mentor-protégé relationship, including (1) all technical or management assistance the mentor has provided to the protégé; (2) all loans to or equity investments made by the mentor in the protégé; (3) all subcontracts awarded to the protégé by the mentor; and (4) all federal contracts awarded to a joint venture of the mentor and protégé.[40]

Unless rescinded in writing, the mentor-protégé agreement will automatically renew for another year. The term of a mentor-protégé agreement is limited to three years but may be extended for a second three-year period.[41] Protégés may have two three-year mentor-protégé agreements with different mentors, and each agreement may be extended an additional three years provided the protégé has received, and will continue to receive, the agreed-upon business development assistance.[42] The SBA may terminate the mentor-protégé agreement at any time if it determines that the protégé is not adequately benefiting from the relationship or that the parties are not complying with any of the agreement's terms or conditions.[43]

Participant Benefits

Participation in the 8(a) Mentor-Protégé Program is intended to benefit both mentors and protégés. Serving as a mentor to an 8(a) firm counts toward any subcontracting requirements to which the mentor firm may be subject under Section 8(d) of the Small Business Act.[44] Section 8(d) requires that all federal contractors awarded a contract valued in excess of $700,000 ($1.5 million for construction contracts) that offers subcontracting possibilities agree to a "subcontracting plan" which ensures

---

[39] 13 C.F.R. §124.520(e)(4).
[40] 13 C.F.R. §124.112(b)(6); 13 C.F.R. §124.520(g)(1)(i)-(v).
[41] SBA, "Small Business Mentor Protégé Program," 81 *Federal Register* 48585, July 25, 2016.
[42] Ibid.
[43] Ibid.
[44] 13 C.F.R. §125.3(b)(3)(ix).

that small businesses have "the maximum practicable opportunity to participate in [contract] performance."[45] In addition, in certain circumstances, mentors may form joint ventures with their protégés that are eligible to be awarded an 8(a) contract or another contract set aside for small businesses.[46] Mentor firms and joint ventures involving mentor firms would otherwise generally be ineligible for such contracts because they would not qualify as "small" under the SBA regulations.[47] Mentor firms may also acquire an equity interest of up to 40% in the protégé firm in order to help the protégé firm raise capital.[48] Because mentor firms are not 8(a) participants, they would generally be prohibited from owning more than 10%-20% of an 8(a) firm.[49] However, their participation in the 8(a) Mentor-Protégé Program permits them to acquire a larger ownership share.

Protégés not only receive various forms of assistance from their mentors, but also may generally retain their status as "small businesses" while doing so.[50] If they received similar assistance from entities other than their mentors, they could risk being found to be other than "small" because of how the SBA determines size. The SBA combines the gross income of the firm, or the number of its employees, with those of its "affiliates" when determining whether the firm is small,[51] and the SBA could potentially find

---

[45] 15 U.S.C. §637(d)(3)(A).
[46] 13 C.F.R. §124.513(b)(3); 13 C.F.R. §124.520(d)(1). For the joint venture to be eligible for the award, the protégé must qualify as small for the size standard corresponding to the NAICS code assigned to the procurement, and, in the case of sole-source 8(a) procurements, has not "reached the dollar limit set forth in §124.519." 13 C.F.R. §124.520(d)(1). Section 124.519 generally prohibits 8(a) firms from receiving additional sole-source awards once they have received a combined total of competitive and sole-source awards in excess of $100 million, in the case of firms whose size is based on their number of employees, or in excess of an amount equivalent to the lesser of (1) $100 million or (2) five times the size standard for the industry, in the case of firms whose size is based on their revenues.
[47] See generally 13 C.F.R. §121.103.
[48] 13 C.F.R. §124.520(d)(2).
[49] 13 C.F.R. §124.105(h)(1)-(2). Ownership is limited to 10% when the 8(a) firm in is the "developmental stage" of the 8(a) program and 20% when it is in the "transitional stage." Ibid. The developmental stage consists of the first four years of the 8(a) program, while the transitional stage consists of the last five years.
[50] 13 C.F.R. §124.520(d)(3). But see 13 C.F.R. §121.103(b)(6) (noting that, while a protégé is not an affiliate of its mentor because it receives assistance from its mentor under the mentor-protégé program, "[a]ffiliation may be found ... for other reasons").
[51] 13 C.F.R. §§121.101-121.108. Firms are "affiliates" when "one controls or has the power to control the other, or a third party or parties controls or has the power to control both." 13 C.F.R. §121.103(a)(1).

that firms are affiliates because of assistance such as that which mentors provide to protégés.[52] However, SBA regulations provide that "[n]o determination of affiliation or control may be found between a protégé firm and its mentor based on the mentor-protégé agreement or any assistance provided pursuant to the agreement."[53]

GAO's Reports, SBA Regulations, and Recent Legislative Action

The 8(a) Mentor-Protégé Program has been the subject of congressional and agency attention for a number of reasons, including reports of fraud in the program.[54] In addition, in 2010, GAO reported that the "SBA did not maintain an accurate inventory of 8(a) Mentor-Protégé Program participant data, which limited the agency's ability to monitor these firms,"[55] and concluded that the "SBA has not been able to properly oversee this program."[56]

Legislation adopted during the 111th Congress (P.L. 111-240) required GAO to conduct a study of the 8(a) program and "other relationships and strategic alliances pairing a larger business and a small business concern" to gain access to federal contracts.[57] The study's purpose was "to determine whether the programs and relationships are effectively supporting the goal of increasing the participation of small business concerns in government contracting."[58] GAO's report was submitted to the House and Senate Committees on Small Business on June 15, 2011.[59]

In this chapter, GAO examined mentor-protégé programs in 13 federal agencies it identified as having a mentor-protégé program, including the SBA. It reported that most federal mentor-protégé programs had "similar

---

[52] See generally 13 C.F.R. §121.103.
[53] 13 C.F.R. §124.520(d)(4).
[54] For additional information and analysis of the 8(a) program, see CRS Report R44844, *SBA's "8(a) Program": Overview, History, and Current Issues*, by Robert Jay Dilger.
[55] GAO, *Small Business Administration: Steps Have Been Taken to Improve Administration of the 8(a) Program, but Key Controls for Continued Eligibility Need Strengthening*, GAO-10-353, March 30, 2010, preface, at http://www.gao.gov/new.items/d10353.pdf.
[56] Ibid., p. 24.
[57] P.L. 111-240, §1345(a), 124 Stat. 2546.
[58] Ibid.
[59] See GAO, *Mentor-Protégé Programs Have Policies That Aim to Benefit Participants But Do Not Require Postagreement Tracking*, GAO-11-548R, June 15, 2011, p. 1, at http://www.gao.gov/new.items/d11548r.pdf.

policies and procedures," but that some differences exist.[60] For example, GAO noted that "different agencies have varying guidance regarding the length of mentor-protégé agreements and whether protégés are allowed to have more than one mentor," and the "DOD mentor-protégé program is the only mentor-protégé program mandated by law and receiving appropriated funding."[61] GAO also reported that "most agencies have policies and reporting requirements to help ensure that protégés are benefiting from participation in their mentor-protégé programs."[62] However, it found that only DOD, the National Aeronautics and Space Administration, and the U.S. Agency for International Development "have policies in place to collect information on protégé progress after the mentor-protégé agreements have terminated."[63] GAO recommended that all of the agencies it examined "consider collecting and maintaining protégé post-completion information" because that information "could be used to help [the agencies] further assess the success of their programs and help ensure that small businesses are benefiting from participation in the programs as intended."[64]

Prior to the release of GAO's report, the SBA announced, on February 11, 2011, revisions to its regulations pertaining to the 8(a) program.[65] Among the changes, which took effect on March 14, 2011, are some pertaining to the 8(a) Mentor-Protégé Program. These changes

- required that assistance provided through the mentor-protégé relationship be tied to the protégé's SBA-approved business plan;
- allowed mentors to have up to three protégés;
- allowed firms seeking to become mentors to submit audited financial statements or other evidence to demonstrate their "favorable financial health" (this provision was revised in 2016);

---

[60] Ibid., p. 4.
[61] Ibid., pp. 4-5.
[62] Ibid., p. 9.
[63] Ibid.
[64] Ibid.
[65] SBA, "Small Business Size Regulations; 8(a) Business Development/Small Disadvantaged Business Status Determinations," 76 *Federal Register* 8222-8223, February 11, 2011.

- explicitly recognized nonprofits as potential mentors (this provision was eliminated in 2016);
- permitted protégés to have a second mentor in certain circumstances;[66]
- prohibited SBA from approving a mentor-protégé agreement if the proposed protégé has less than six months remaining in its term in the 8(a) program (this provision was eliminated in 2016);
- permitted firms to request reconsideration of SBA's denial of a proposed mentor-protégé agreement;
- required firms whose proposed mentor-protégé agreement is rejected to wait at least 60 calendar days before submitting a new mentor-protégé agreement with the same proposed mentor;
- authorized SBA to recommend the issuance of a "stop work" order on any executive branch contract performed by a mentor-protégé joint venture when it determines that the mentor has not provided the protégé with the development assistance set forth in the mentor-protégé agreement; and
- prohibited mentors who are terminated for failure to provide assistance under their mentor-protégé agreement from serving as a mentor for two years.[67]

The SBA also made several changes to the regulations governing joint ventures between 8(a) mentors and protégés to ensure that "non-sophisticated 8(a) firms" are not "taken advantage of by certain non-8(a) joint venture partners."[68] Specifically, the SBA now requires that (1) the 8(a) firm receive profits from the joint venture commensurate with the work it performs; (2) the 8(a) firm perform at least 40% of the work done by the joint venture; and (3) each 8(a) firm that performs an 8(a) contract

---

[66] To obtain a second mentor, a protégé would have to demonstrate that (1) the second relationship pertains to an unrelated secondary NAICS code; (2) the first mentor does not possess the specific expertise that is the subject of the mentor-protégé agreement with the second mentor; and (3) the two relationships will not compete or otherwise conflict with each other.

[67] SBA, "Small Business Size Regulations; 8(a) Business Development/Small Disadvantaged Business Status Determinations," 76 *Federal Register* 8244-8247, February 11, 2011.

[68] Ibid., p. 8243.

through a joint venture report to the SBA how it performed the required percentages of the work (i.e., how the joint venture performed at least 50% of the work of the contract, as well as how the 8(a) participant to the joint venture performed at least 40% of the work done by the joint venture).[69] Further, under the amended regulations, non-8(a) firms that form joint ventures with 8(a) firms to perform sole-source contracts in excess of $4 million ($7.0 million for manufacturing contracts) are generally prohibited from serving as subcontractors (at any tier) on the contract.[70] However, this latter provision is arguably most relevant to joint ventures involving 8(a) firms owned by Alaska Native Corporations or other entities which, until recently, were eligible for sole-source awards of any amount without any justifications or approvals required from the procuring agency.

In addition, the final rule establishing the new SBA small business mentor-protégé program amended the current joint venture provisions to clarify the conditions for creating and operating joint venture partnerships.[71]

P.L. 112-239 also sought to reduce the variation that GAO found among agency-specific mentor-protégé programs by requiring that any such programs be approved by the SBA pursuant to regulations, "which shall ensure that such programs improve the ability of protégés to compete for Federal prime contracts and subcontracts."[72] The SBA administrator was required to issue regulations with respect to mentor-protégé programs not later than 270 days after the bill's enactment, which was January 2,

---

[69] Ibid., pp. 8242-8243. Under the revised regulations, joint ventures established and approved by SBA would also be eligible to receive additional contracts if an addendum to the joint venture agreement setting forth the performance requirements on such contracts is provided to and approved by the SBA prior to the contract award.

[70] Ibid., p. 8241. The non-8(a) firm may serve as a subcontractor only if the SBA's Associate Administrator for Business Development determines that other potential subcontractors are not available.

[71] SBA, "Small Business Mentor Protégé Program," 81 *Federal Register* 48559-48562, 48583-48584, July 25, 2016.

[72] Any federal mentor-protégé program in effect at the date of the bill's enactment must submit plans to the SBA for approval within 6 months of the SBA's promulgation of rules with respect to mentor-protégé programs and receive final approval or denial within 180 days after receipt. In addition, DOD's Mentor-Protégé Program and mentoring assistance under the Small Business Innovation Research Program and the Small Business Technology Transfer Program were made exempt from the approval process.

2013 (the regulations were issued on July 25, 2016). At a minimum, these regulations must address 10 criteria, including (1) eligibility for program participants, (2) the types of developmental assistance provided to protégés, (3) the length of mentor-protégé relationships, (4) the benefits that may accrue to the mentor as a result of program participation, and (5) the reporting requirements during and following program participation.[73] DOD's Mentor-Protégé Program and mentoring assistance under the Small Business Innovation Research Program and the Small Business Technology Transfer Program are exempt from the approval process.

Effective August 24, 2016, federal agencies (other than DOD and the two exempt programs) were provided a year to submit a plan to the SBA Administrator for approval to continue a previously existing mentor-protégé program. Approval is contingent on whether the proposed program will assist protégés to compete for federal prime contracts and subcontracts and whether it complies with the rules and regulations of the SBA's mentor-protégé programs (as set forth in 13 C.F.R. §§125.9 and 124.520).[74]

As mentioned previously, four federal agencies currently have SBA-approved mentor-protégé programs (Department of Energy, Department of Homeland Security, National Aeronautics and Space Administration, and the SBA); two federal agencies have mentor-protégé programs that do not require SBA's approval because their programs are not covered by the Small Business Act (DOD and the Federal Aviation Administration); and three federal agencies have mentor-protégé programs that, in 2018, were awaiting the SBA's approval (Department of Health and Human Services, Department of Transportation, and Department of the Treasury).

In addition, before starting a new mentor-protégé program, agency heads must submit a plan and receive the SBA Administrator's approval.[75] Agencies sponsoring an agency-specific mentor-protégé program must

---

[73] These provisions originated with H.R. 3985, the Building Better Business Partnerships Act of 2012. The Senate version of the bill (S. 3254) did not include these provisions, but they were included in the bill's conference report, which was agreed to by the House on December 20, 2012, and by the Senate on December 21, 2012. The bill was signed by President Obama on January 2, 2013.
[74] SBA, "Small Business Mentor Protégé Program," 81 *Federal Register* 48589, July 25, 2016.
[75] Ibid.

report annually to the SBA specific information, such as the number and type of small business participants, the assistance provided, and the protégés' progress in competing for federal contracts.[76]

Mentoring Networks under the Federal and State Technology Partnership Program

In 2000, Congress amended the Small Business Act by directing the SBA Administrator to establish the Federal and State Technology (FAST) Partnership Program in order to "strengthen the technological competitiveness of small business concerns in the States"[77] by providing a wide range of assistance, including mentoring. Congress further authorized SBA to make grants and enter cooperative agreements with states and state-endorsed nonprofit organizations as part of the FAST program so as to enhance

> outreach, financial support, and technical assistance to technology-based small business concerns participating in or interested in participating in an SBIR program, including initiatives ... to establish or operate a Mentoring Network within the FAST program to provide business advice and counseling that will assist small business concerns that have been identified by FAST program participants, program managers of participating SBIR agencies, the [SBA], or other entities that are knowledgeable about the SBIR and STTR program as good candidates for the SBIR and STTR programs, and that would benefit from mentoring.[78]

---

[76] Ibid., p. 48590.
[77] Consolidated Appropriations Act, 2001, P.L. 106-554, §111, 114 Stat. 2764A-674 to 2764A-680 (December 21, 2000) (codified at 15 U.S.C. §657d(b)). The program expired on September 30, 2005, and was reauthorized under the Consolidated Appropriations Act, 2010, P.L. 111-117, "Small Business Administration"—"Salaries and Expenses," 123 Stat. 3198 (December 16, 2009) (codified at 15 U.S.C. §657d(b)).
[78] 15 U.S.C. §657d(c)(1)(E)(ii).

Such mentoring networks are to (1) provide business advice and counseling; (2) identify volunteer mentors to guide small businesses in proposal writing, marketing, etc.; (3) have experience working with small businesses participating in the SBIR and STTR programs; and (4) agree to reimburse volunteer mentors for out-of-pocket expenses related to service as a mentor.[79]

In FY2018, the SBA awarded 24 FAST partnership awards of $125,000 each to state and local economic development entities, small business technology development centers, women's business centers, incubators, accelerators, colleges, and universities.[80] The program received an appropriation of $2 million each year from FY2010 to FY2015 and $3 million each year from FY2016 to FY2018.[81]

Recent Developments

During the 114th Congress, P.L. 114-88, the Recovery Improvements for Small Entities After Disaster Act of 2015 (RISE After Disaster Act), directed the SBA Administrator to provide special consideration to a FAST applicant that is located in an area affected by a catastrophic incident.

During the 115th Congress, the Trump Administration recommended that funding for the FAST program be eliminated.[82]

---

[79] 15 U.S.C. §657e(c)(1)-(5).
[80] SBA, "SBA Awards Grants to 24 State and Local Economic Development Entities, SBTDCs, and Universities to Support Small Business Innovation and R&D Commercialization," August 29, 2018, at https://www.sba.gov/about-sba/ sba-newsroom/press-releases-media-advisories/sba-awards-grants-24-state-and-local-economic-development-entitiessbtdcs-and-universities-support.
[81] P.L. 111-117; P.L. 112-8; P.L. 112-74, "Small Business Administration"—"Salaries and Expenses"; P.L. 112-175; P.L. 113-76; P.L. 113-235, P.L. 114-113, P.L. 115-31, and P.L. 115-141.
[82] SBA, "FY2018 Congressional Budget Justification and FY2016 Annual Performance Report," pp. 11, 75, at https://www.sba.gov/sites/default/files/aboutsbaarticle/FINAL_SBA_FY_2018_CBJ_May_22_2017c.pdf; and SBA, "FY2019 Congressional Budget Justification and FY2017 Annual Performance Report," pp. 68, 69, at https://www.sba.gov/sites/default/files/aboutsbaarticle/SBA_FY_19_508-Final-FINAL.PDF.

SBA's All Small Business Mentor-Protégé Program

The SBA's all small business mentor-protégé program is generally required to be "identical" to the SBA's 8(a) Mentor-Protégé Program, except that the SBA may make modifications to the extent necessary given the types of small businesses included in the program as protégés. For example, among other things, the small businesses mentor-protégé program requires a protégé to qualify as small for the size standard corresponding to its primary (or, under specified circumstances, its secondary) NAICS code. The 8(a) Mentor-Protégé Program also requires protégés to be small businesses unconditionally owned and controlled by socially and economically disadvantaged individuals, to demonstrate potential for success, and to be eligible to receive contracts under Section 8(a) of the Small Business Act.

The SBA initially proposed to permit only firms that have been affirmatively determined by the SBA to be small to qualify as protégés for the small business mentor-protégé program because small businesses in the 8(a) program are certified as being small by the SBA.[83] However, given the expected volume of applications for the small business mentor-protégé program, the SBA decided in the final rule to allow applicants to the new program to self-certify as small. The SBA will rely on size protest procedures to prevent ineligible businesses from unduly benefitting from its mentor-protégé relationship under the new program.[84]

In addition, the SBA's Office of Business Development administers the 8(a) Mentor-Protégé Program. Given that "the volume of firms seeking mentor-protégé relationships [under the new small business mentor-protégé program] could excessively delay SBA's processing of applications," the SBA decided, after considering various options, "to establish a separate unit within the Office of Business Development whose sole function [is] to process mentor-protégé applications and review the MPAs [mentor-protégé agreements] and the assistance provided under

---

[83] SBA, "Small Business Mentor Protégé Program," 81 *Federal Register* 48564-48565, July 25, 2016.
[84] Ibid., p. 48565.

them once approved."[85] The SBA indicated that "the efficiencies gained by having a dedicated staff for the small business mentor-protégé program will allow SBA to timely process applications ... and [reduce] the need for open and closed enrollment periods."[86]

As of December 1, 2018, there were 644 active all small business mentor-protégé agreements.[87]

DOD MENTOR-PROTÉGÉ PROGRAM

Congress authorized a pilot mentor-protégé program for DOD in 1990. The program's purposes are to

(1) enhance the capabilities of disadvantaged small business concerns to perform as subcontractors and suppliers under Department of Defense contracts and other contracts and subcontracts; and (2) increase the participation of such business concerns as subcontractors and suppliers under Department of Defense contracts, other Federal Government contracts, and commercial contracts.[88]

DOD's Mentor-Protégé Program began on October 1, 1991, and was the first federal mentor-protégé program to become operational. Originally

---

[85] Ibid., p. 48562.
[86] Ibid.
[87] SBA, "Active mentor-protégé agreements," at https://www.sba.gov/document/support—active-mentor-protegeagreements. There were 102 active all small business mentor-protégé agreements on March 2, 2017, 377 on January 1, 2018, 443 on February 27, 2018, and 473 on April 5, 2018. See SBA, "All Small Mentor-Protégé Program Resources: Active Mentor-Protégé Agreements," at https://www.sba.gov/sites/default/files/articles/ASMPP_MPA_Approval_List_as_of_01.01.18.xlsx; and SBA, "All Small Mentor-Protégé Program," February 27, 2018.
[88] P.L. 114-92, the National Defense Authorization Act for Fiscal Year 2016, §861 (codified, as amended, at 10 U.S.C. §2302 note). See P.L. 101-510, An Act to Authorize Appropriations for Fiscal Year 1991 for Military Activities of the Department of Defense, for Military Construction, and for Defense Activities of the Department of Energy, to Prescribe Personnel Strengths for the Armed Forces and for Other Purposes, §831, 104 Stat. 1607-08 (November 5, 1990) for earlier language. The wording of the program's purpose was modified somewhat by P.L. 114-92 in an effort to better reflect the goals of the mentor-protégé programs sponsored by the SBA and other civilian agencies.

scheduled to expire in 1994,[89] it has been repeatedly extended, most recently through FY2018 for the formation of new agreements, and FY2021 for the reimbursement of incurred costs under existing agreements.[90]

DOD's Mentor-Protégé Program differs from the SBA's 8(a) Mentor-Protégé Program and all small business Mentor-Protégé Program in that its primary focus is upon small businesses performing subcontracts and as suppliers on federal contracts, not upon small businesses performing federal contracts. In addition, mentors in the DOD program may provide assistance to their protégés that is somewhat different than that which mentors may provide to protégés in the 8(a) and new small business mentor-protégé programs. Notably, such assistance may include advance payments, which federal agencies are generally prohibited from making, and progress payments, which are generally discouraged under federal procurement law.[91]

---

[89] P.L. 101-510, An Act to Authorize Appropriations for Fiscal Year 1991 for Military Activities of the Department of Defense, for Military Construction, and for Defense Activities of the Department of Energy, to Prescribe Personnel Strengths for the Armed Forces and for Other Purposes, at §831(j)(1), 104 Stat. 1610 (providing that firms eligible to participate in the program may enter mentor-protégé agreements during the period commencing on October 1, 1991, and ending on September 30, 1994). Under this provision, firms could incur costs for reimbursement through September 30, 1996, and could receive credit for unreimbursed costs through September 30, 1999. Ibid. at §831(j)(2)- (3). See also U.S. General Accounting Office, *Defense Contracting: Interim Report on Mentor-Protégé Program for Small Disadvantaged Firms*, GAO/NSIAD-92-135, March 30, 1992, pp. 1-3, at http://www.gao.gov/assets/220/215849.pdf.

[90] See, e.g., P.L. 112-81, the National Defense Authorization Act for FY2012, §867, 125 Stat. 1526; and P.L. 114-92, the National Defense Authorization Act for FY2016, §861.

[91] Advance payments are payments made to a contractor before any costs have been incurred on a contract, while progress payments are payments made during the performance of work, but before completion of the contract, on the basis of either a percentage of completion of the work or the incurrence of costs. Advance payments are generally only authorized when (1) the contractor gives adequate security; (2) the payments do not exceed the contract price; and (3) the agency head or a designee determines that advance payment is in the public interest or facilitates the national defense. See, e.g., 48 C.F.R. §32.402(b)-(c). Progress payments made on the basis of percentage of completion under construction or certain other contracts are considered invoice payments and are permissible. *See* 48 C.F.R. §32.500(b). Progress payments made on the basis of performance milestones are considered financing payments and are likewise permissible. Other progress payments based on costs are generally considered "unusual progress payments" and may be used only when authorized in "exceptional cases." See 48 C.F.R. §§32.501, 32.501-2.

Mentors may also (1) award subcontracts on a noncompetitive basis to their protégés even if they are otherwise subject to "competition in subcontracting" requirements;[92] (2) make investments in protégé firms in exchange for an ownership interest in the firm (not to exceed 10% of the total ownership interest): (3) lend money; and (4) provide assistance in general business management, engineering and technical matters, etc.[93]

**"Socially and economically disadvantaged individuals,"
for purposes of the DOD Mentor-Protégé Program**

Individuals who belong to one of the following racial or ethnic groups, or who can prove that they are personally socially disadvantaged, and who have a personal net worth of $750,000 or less may qualify as socially and economically disadvantaged without being certified as such by SBA:

Black Americans; Hispanic Americans; Native Americans (American Indians, Eskimos, Aleuts, or Native Hawaiians); Asian Pacific Americans (persons with origins from Burma, Thailand, Malaysia, Indonesia, Singapore, Brunei, Japan, China [including Hong Kong], Taiwan, Laos, Cambodia [Kampuchea], Vietnam, Korea, The Philippines, U.S. Trust Territory of the Pacific Islands [Republic of Palau], Republic of the Marshall Islands, Federated States of Micronesia, the Commonwealth of the Northern Mariana Islands, Guam, Samoa, Macao, Fiji, Tonga, Kiribati, Tuvalu, or Nauru); Subcontinent Asian Americans (persons with origins from India, Pakistan, Bangladesh, Sri Lanka, Bhutan, the Maldives Islands, or Nepal); and members of other groups designated from time to time by SBA.

Source: 13 C.F.R. §124.1002.

Regulations Governing the DOD Mentor-Protégé Program

Mentor firms are prime contractors with at least one active subcontracting plan negotiated as required under Section 8(d) of the Small Business Act, or under the DOD Comprehensive Subcontracting Test

---

[92] 48 C.F.R. §52.244-5(a)-(b). Some contracts provide that the contractor "shall select subcontractors (including suppliers) on a competitive basis to the maximum practicable extent consistent with the objectives and requirements of the contract." See generally 48 C.F.R. §44.204(c).
[93] 48 C.F.R. Ch. 2, Appendix I, I-106(d)(1)-(7).

Program.[94] Initially, only small businesses owned and controlled by socially and economically disadvantaged individuals could qualify as protégés.[95] However, the listing of eligible protégés was later expanded[96] to include (1) businesses owned and controlled by Indian tribes or Alaska Native Corporations; (2) businesses owned and controlled by Native Hawaiian Organizations; (3) qualified organizations employing "severely disabled individuals"; (4) women-owned small businesses; (5) service-disabled veteran-owned small businesses; and (6) Historically Underutilized Business Zone (HUBZone) small businesses.[97] Mentors generally may rely in good faith on their protégés' written representations that they are eligible.[98]

Under DOD regulations, mentors' participation in the program must be approved by DOD.[99] While protégés are selected by the mentor,[100] the SBA may, at any time, determine that a protégé is ineligible.[101] Each mentor is allowed to have multiple protégés, but each protégé may have only one mentor at any time.[102]

---

[94] 48 C.F.R. §219.7102(a). Mentors generally may not be small businesses. See 48 C.F.R. Ch. 2, Appendix I, I-102(a)(1).

[95] See P.L. 101-510, §831(m)(2), 104 Stat. 1611.

[96] See, e.g., An Act to Authorize Appropriations for Fiscal Year 2001 for Military Activities of the Department of Defense, for Military Construction, and for Defense Activities of the Department of Energy, to Prescribe Personnel Strengths for Such Fiscal Year for the Armed Forces, and for Other Purposes, P.L. 106-398, §807, 114 Stat. 1654A-208 (October 30, 2000).

[97] 48 C.F.R. §219.7102(b)(1)(i)-(vii). A severely disabled individual is an individual who is blind (as defined in 41 U.S.C. §8501) or a severely diasbled individaul (as defined in such section).

[98] 48 C.F.R. Ch. 2, Appendix I, I-102(c).

[99] New mentor applications may be submitted to the Office of Small Business Programs (OSBP) of the cognizant military service or defense agency (if concurrently submitting a reimbursable agreement) or to the DOD OSBP office (prior to the submission of an agreement).

[100] 48 C.F.R. §219.7102(b)(3). Selection of protégé firms by mentor firms may not be protested other than as to the size or disadvantaged status of the protégé. See 48 C.F.R. Ch. 2, Appendix I, I-104(b)-(c).

[101] 48 C.F.R. Ch. 2, Appendix I, I-102(d). When the protégé is determined to be ineligible, any assistance provided to the protégé after the date of that determination may not be considered assistance furnished under the program.

[102] 48 C.F.R. Ch. 2, Appendix I, I-104(e).

As of January 1, 2018, there were 63 active mentor-protégé agreements involving 39 mentors and 63 protégés.[103] One mentor had seven protégés, 1 mentor had 6 protégés, 1 mentor had 5 protégés, 2 mentors had 3 protégés, 5 mentors had 2 protégés, and 29 mentors had one protégé.[104]

Mentors and protégés are required, by regulation, to enter into an agreement establishing a developmental assistance program for the protégé.[105] The agreement is to include (1) the type(s) of assistance the mentor will provide and how the protégé will benefit; (2) factors for assessing the protégé's progress; (3) an estimate of the dollar value and types of subcontracts to be awarded to the protégé; (4) a program participation term of up to three years; (5) procedures whereby the mentor or protégé may withdraw from the program on 30 days' advance notice; and (6) procedures for the mentor firm to terminate the mentor-protégé agreement for cause.[106] DOD generally requires that this agreement be approved before the mentor incurs any costs.[107] The mentor firm is responsible for making semiannual reports on progress during the term of the agreement, while the protégé is required to provide data on its progress at the end of each fiscal year during the term of the agreement, and for each of the two fiscal years following the agreement's expiration.[108] In addition, the Defense Contract Management Agency (DCMA) is to conduct annual performance reviews of all mentor-protégé agreements, and determinations made in these reviews "should" be a major factor in determining the amount, if any, of reimbursement the mentor firm is eligible to receive in the remaining years of the program participation term under the agreement.[109]

---

[103] DOD, "Active MPP [Mentor-Protégé Program] Agreements," at http://business.defense.gov/Programs/MentorProtege-Program/Protege-Eligibility-Requirementsi.
[104] Ibid.
[105] 48 C.F.R. Ch. 2, Appendix I, I-106.
[106] 48 C.F.R. Ch. 2, Appendix I, I-107.
[107] 48 C.F.R. Ch. 2, Appendix I, I-108(c).
[108] 48 C.F.R. Ch. 2, Appendix I, I-112.2(a) & (e).
[109] 48 C.F.R. §219.7106; 48 C.F.R. Ch. 2, Appendix I, I-113. The DCMA is an independent organization within DOD that performs contract administration functions for DOD and other agencies.

Participant Benefits

Among the benefits that the DOD program provides for mentors are (1) reimbursement of specified assistance costs and (2) credit for unreimbursed costs toward applicable subcontracting goals.[110] DOD and the mentor firm may agree that DOD will reimburse the mentor for certain advance payments or progress payments made to assist protégé firms in performing a subcontract or supplying goods or services under a contract.[111] Alternatively, DOD may credit toward the mentor's subcontracting plan an amount equivalent to the amount of unreimbursed assistance that the mentor provides to its protégé(s).[112] For example, if a contractor provides $10,000 in developmental assistance to its protégé, this $10,000 could count as if it were a $10,000 subcontract awarded to a small business.

---

[110] 48 C.F.R. §219.7102(d)(1)-(2); 48 C.F.R. §19.702(d). When a mentor receives credit toward its subcontracting goals because of developmental assistance provided to its protégé, it is ineligible for monetary incentives for subcontracting with small disadvantaged businesses. 48 C.F.R. §219.1203. Otherwise, under Subpart 19.12 of the Federal Acquisition Regulation, agencies have authority to incorporate in their prime contracts "monetary incentives" for subcontracting with small businesses owned and controlled by socially and economically disadvantaged individuals. Such incentives reward prime contractors by paying them up to 10% of the amount by which their performance in subcontracting with such businesses exceeds their targets for subcontracting with them. See 48 C.F.R. §§19.1201-19.1202-4. On September 9, 2011, the Obama Administration proposed relocating the regulations governing monetary incentives to Subpart 19.17 of the Federal Acquisition Regulation. See DOD, GSA, and National Aeronautics and Space Administration, "Federal Acquisition Regulation: Constitutionality of Federal Contracting Programs for Minority-Owned and Other Small Businesses," 76 *Federal Register* 55849, September 9, 2011. However, no such change has been made to date.

[111] 48 C.F.R. §219.7103-2(b) & (f); 48 C.F.R. §252.232-7005. The amount of such payments generally may not exceed $1 million per year. But see 48 C.F.R. Ch. 2, Appendix I, I-108(a)(6) (permitting developmental costs in excess of $1 million when a specific justification for such costs has been presented). When the mentor will be reimbursed for developmental assistance provided to the protégé, the mentor must establish the accounting treatment of developmental assistance costs before incurring such costs. 48 C.F.R. §219.7104(b). Additionally, under DOD regulations, the subcontract between the mentor and protégé must include provisions substantially the same as the provisions in the Federal Acquisition Regulation (FAR) regarding advance payments; the contractor must have administered the advance payments in accordance with FAR Subpart 32.4; and the contractor must agree that any financial loss resulting from the protégé's failure or inability to repay any unliquidated advance payments is the sole financial responsibility of the contractor. 48 C.F.R. §252.232-7005.

[112] 48 C.F.R. Ch. 2, Appendix I, I-110. Subcontracts awarded to certain current or former protégés also count toward these goals. See 48 C.F.R. §252.219-7003(c).

Recent Developments

P.L. 114-92, the National Defense Authorization Act for FY2016, extended the DOD Mentor-Protégé Program through FY2018 for the formation of new agreements and through FY2021 for the reimbursement of incurred costs under existing agreements.[113] The act also changed eligibility requirements so that protégés

- can participate in the program only during the five-year period beginning on the date they enter into their first DOD mentor-protégé agreement;
- must be less than half the SBA size standard assigned to its corresponding NAICS code; and
- must either be a nontraditional defense contractor or currently provide goods or services in the private sector that are critical to enhancing the capabilities of the defense supplier base and fulfilling key DOD needs.

These changes were designed to better align DOD's Mentor-Protégé Program's eligibility requirements with those of the SBA's 8(a) Mentor-Protégé Program (as they were at that time) and to further ensure that DOD's program focused on providing assistance to mentors and protégés that were meeting key DOD needs.

The act also

- specified that the mentor must not be affiliated with the protégé firm prior to the approval of the mentor-protégé agreement;[114]
- disallowed reimbursement for business-development activities and explicitly stated that DOD "may not reimburse any fee assessed by the mentor firm for services provided to the protégé firm pursuant to subsection (f)(6) [assistance from small business development

---

[113] See National Defense Authorization Act for FY2016, P.L. 114-92, §861.
[114] P.L. 114-328, the National Defense Authorization Act for Fiscal Year 2017, requires the SBA to determine whether a prospective protégé firm is affiliated with its proposed mentor prior to approval of a DOD mentor-protégé agreement.

centers, entities providing procurement technical assistance or a historically black college or university or a minority institution of higher education] or for business development expenses incurred by the mentor firm under a contract awarded to the mentor firm while participating in a joint venture with the protégé firm"; and
- added reporting requirements for mentor firms and review requirements for DOD's Office of Small Business Programs.

These changes were designed to ensure that DOD "was not paying mentors to help protégés bid on contracts the protégé would have bid on in any case ... and to stop reimbursing mentors for sending their protégés to obtain assistance from other federal funded resources."[115]

Previously, in 2007, GAO conducted an analysis of this program. As part of its analysis, GAO administered a web-based survey of former DOD protégé firms and received responses from 48 of the 76 protégé firms that completed or left the program during FY2004 and FY2005. GAO concluded that most former protégé firms valued their experience in the DOD program, with 93% of respondents reporting that their participation enhanced, at least to some degree, their firm's overall capabilities; 87% of respondents reporting that support from their mentors helped their business development; and about 84% of respondents reporting that mentor support helped their engineering or technical expertise.[116] In addition, 71% of protégés responding to the survey reported that they "were at least generally satisfied with their experience with the program, with their reasons ranging from enhanced capabilities and heightened exposure in the marketplace, to quantifiable business growth."[117] However, about 15% of protégés reported dissatisfaction with their participation in the program,

---

[115] U.S. Congress, House Committee on Small Business, Subcommittee on Contracting and Workforce, *Maximizing Mentoring: How are the SBA and DOD Mentor-Protégé Programs Serving Small Businesses?*, Hearing Memorandum, prepared by House Committee on Small Business Staff, 114th Cong., 1st sess., October 26, 2015, p. 9, at http://smbiz.house.gov/uploadedfiles/10-27-2015_hearing_memo.pdf.

[116] GAO, *Contract Management: Protégés Value DOD's Mentor-Protégé Program, but Annual Reporting to Congress Needs Improvement*, GAO-07-151, January 31, 2007, p. 6, at http://www.gao.gov/new.items/d07151.pdf.

[117] Ibid., p. 7.

and about 21% reported that they did not receive the level of mentoring that they had anticipated.[118]

DOD has provided $401.4 million to mentor firms since the program's inception through FY2017. DOD provided $28.3 million to mentor firms in FY2016 and $23.2 million in FY2017. It anticipated that it would provide $33.5 million in FY2018, and it expects to provide $29.8 million in FY2019.[119]

OTHER AGENCY-SPECIFIC MENTOR-PROTÉGÉ PROGRAMS

Other agencies, like DHS, have established independent mentor-protégé programs to encourage their large prime contractors to work with small business subcontractors when performing agency contracts. Because these programs are not based in statute, unlike the SBA and DOD programs discussed above, they generally rely upon existing authorities (e.g., authorizing use of evaluation factors) or publicity to incentivize mentor participation. Such programs generally supplement the 8(a) Mentor-Protégé Program, in that firms in the 8(a) program may also

---

[118] Ibid.
[119] DOD, Office of the Secretary of Defense, "Fiscal Year (FY) 2018 Budget Submission: Defense Wide Justification Book Volume 1 of 2," February 2017, Exhibit P-40, Budget Line Item Justification: PB 2017 Office of the Secretary of Defense, at http://comptroller.defense.gov/Portals/45/Documents/defbudget/FY2018/budget_justificatio n/pdfs/ 02_Procurement/OSD_0300D_FY18_PB_FINAL.pdf; and DOD, Office of the Secretary of Defense, "Fiscal Year (FY) 2019 Budget Submission: Defense Wide Justification Book Volume 1 of 2," February 2018, Exhibit P-40, Budget Line Item Justification: PB 2019 Office of the Secretary of Defense, at http://comptroller. defense.gov/Portals/45/Documents/defbudget/fy2019/budget_justification/pdfs/02_Procure ment/U_PROCUREMENT_MasterJustificationBook_DefenseWide_PB_2019.pdf. P.L. 115-245, the Department of Defense and Labor, Health and Human Services, and Education Appropriations Act, 2019, and Continuing Appropriations Act, 2019, authorizes DOD to transfer funds from its FY2019 procurement appropriations to the DOD Mentor-Protégé Program.

participate in agency-specific programs.[120] However, small businesses that are not 8(a) firms and other entities may also be eligible to participate.[121]

DHS's Mentor-Protégé Program is discussed here as a representative example of such programs. Several other agencies have similar programs, which are described in Table 1. Note that while this chapter describes these programs as they presently exist, certain changes may be made to these programs in light of the requirements of the National Defense Authorization Act for FY2013 (P.L. 112-239). This legislation generally requires that agency-specific mentor-protégé programs be approved by the SBA pursuant to regulations that would require such programs to address, among other things, (1) eligibility for program participants, (2) the types of developmental assistance provided to protégés, (3) the length of mentor-protégé relationships, (4) the benefits that may accrue to the mentor as a result of program participation, and (5) the reporting requirements during and following program participation.

DHS Mentor-Protégé Program

DHS established its mentor-protégé program in 2003 to "motivate and encourage large business prime contractor firms to provide mutually beneficial developmental assistance" to small businesses.[122] Mentor firms may provide various types of assistance to their protégés, including

---

[120] See, e.g., 48 C.F.R. §519.7007(c) ("A protégé firm [in GSA's Mentor-Protégé Program] must not have another formal, active mentor-protégé relationship under GSA's Mentor-Protégé Program but may have an active mentor-protégé relationship under another agency's program.").

[121] See, e.g., 48 C.F.R. §619.202-70 (small disadvantaged businesses; women-owned small businesses; Historically Underutilized Business Zone small businesses; veteran-owned small businesses; and service-disabled veteran-owned small businesses eligible for the Department of State Mentor-Protégé Program); 48 C.F.R. §919.7007 (8(a) firms and other small disadvantaged businesses; historically black colleges and universities and other minority institutions of higher education; women-owned small businesses; and service-disabled veteran-owned small businesses eligible for the Department of Energy Mentor-Protégé Program).

[122] DHS, "Mentor-Protégé Program," at https://www.dhs.gov/mentor-prot%C3%A9g%C3%A9-program; DHS, "Department of Homeland Security Acquisition Regulation," 68 *Federal Register* 67868-67870, December 4, 2003.

temporary assignment of personnel to the protégé firm for the purpose of training, rent-free use of facilities or equipment, overall business management/planning, financial and organizational management, business development, technical assistance, property, loans, and other types of assistance.[123]

As of August 1, 2018, DHS had 44 active mentor-protégé agreements involving 36 mentors and 43 protégés.[124] One mentor had 3 protégés, 6 mentors had 2 protégés, and 29 mentors had 1 protégé.[125] The DHS program does not receive a separate funding appropriation.

Regulations Governing the DHS Mentor-Protégé Program

Mentors are "large prime contractors capable of providing developmental assistance."[126] Protégé firms can be small businesses, veteran-owned small businesses, service-disabled veteran-owned small businesses, HUBZone small businesses, "small disadvantaged businesses,"[127] and women-owned small businesses.[128] Although mentors and protégés apparently do not need to be approved by DHS, they are required, by regulation, to have their mentor-protégé agreement approved by the DHS Office of Small and Disadvantaged Business Utilization (OSDBU).[129] This mentor-protégé agreement is evaluated on the extent to which the mentor plans to provide developmental assistance. If accepted into the program, the mentor-protégé relationship generally lasts for 36 months. The mentor and protégé are required to submit a jointly written mid-term progress report at 18 months, and, at the end of the 36 months, the mentor and protégé are required to submit a final report and complete a

---

[123] DHS, "Mentor-Protégé Program," at http://www.dhs.gov/xopnbiz/smallbusiness/editorial_0716.shtm.
[124] DHS, "Mentor-Protégé Companies," at https://www.dhs.gov/mentor-protege-companies.
[125] Ibid. One protégé had 2 mentors and 42 protégés had 1 mentor.
[126] 48 C.F.R. §3052.219-71(b)(1).
[127] "Small disadvantaged businesses" (SDBs) are those owned and controlled by socially and economically disadvantaged individuals. All 8(a) firms are SDBs. However, firms that are not participating in the 8(a) program may, depending upon the program, also be certified or self-certify as SDBs.
[128] 48 C.F.R. §3052.219-71(b)(2).
[129] 48 C.F.R. §3052.219-71(b)(3).

"lessons learned" evaluation separately. Protégés are also required to submit a post-award report annually for two years.[130]

Participant Benefits

Participation as a mentor in the DHS Mentor-Protégé Program may serve as a source selection factor or subfactor in certain negotiated procurements,[131] potentially giving mentor firms an advantage over nonmentors and, thereby, encouraging firms to become mentors.

Table 1. Other Agencies with Agency-Specific Mentor-Protégé Programs

Agency	Eligible Protégés	Incentives for Mentors
Department of Energy 48 C.F.R. Subpart 919.70 (active, SBA approved)	8(a) firms and other small disadvantaged businesses; historically black colleges and universities and other minority institutions of higher learning; women-owned small businesses; service-disabled veteran-owned small businesses	Eligibility for award fees based on their performance as mentors Subcontracts awarded to protégés count toward subcontracting goals
Department of Health and Human Services 48 C.F.R. §352.219-70 (not active)	Small businesses; veteran-owned small businesses; service-disabled veteran-owned small businesses; small disadvantaged businesses; Historically Underutilized Business Zone (HUBZone) small businesses; woman-owned small businesses	Certain assistance provided to protégés credited toward subcontracting plans
Department of State 48 C.F.R. §619.202-70 (retiring the program)	Small businesses; small disadvantaged businesses; women-owned small businesses; HUBZone small businesses; veteran-owned small businesses;	Mentor-protégé agreement may be considered in evaluating adequacy of proposed subcontracting plan and in responsibility determinations Agency mentoring award (nonmonetary)

---

[130] DHS, "Mentor-Protégé Program Details," at http://www.dhs.gov/xlibrary/assets/opnbiz/osdbu-mentor-protegedetails.pdf.
[131] 48 C.F.R. §3052.219-72.

Small Business Mentor-Protégé Programs (Updated)

Agency	Eligible Protégés	Incentives for Mentors
	service-disabled veteran-owned small businesses	
Department of the Treasury 48 C.F.R. Subpart 1019.202-70 (not active)	Small businesses; women-owned small businesses; 8(a) firms and other small disadvantaged businesses; veteran-owned small businesses; service-disabled veteran-owned small businesses; HUBZone small businesses	Bonus (not to exceed 5% of the relative importance assigned to technical/management factors) credited to mentor in negotiated procurements Mentor-protégé agreement may be considered in evaluating adequacy of proposed subcontracting plan and in responsibility determinations Agency mentoring award (nonmonetary)
Department of Veterans Affairs 48 C.F.R. Subpart 819.71 (not active)	Veteran-owned small businesses; service-disabled veteran-owned small businesses	Costs incurred in providing developmental assistance to protégés may be considered in determining indirect costs rates for reimbursement Evaluation credits during source selection Factor in evaluating past performance and determining contractor responsibility Agency mentoring award (nonmonetary) Invitation to mentor-protégé annual conference
Environmental Protection Agency 48 C.F.R. §§1552.219-70 to 1552.219-71 (retiring the program)	Small disadvantaged businesses (women deemed to be socially disadvantaged pursuant to P.L. 102-389); historically black colleges and universities	Subcontracts of $1 million or less awarded to protégés are exempt from the competition requirements in 48 C.F.R. §44.202-2(a)(5), 52.244-2(b)(2)(iii), and 52.244-5 Costs incurred in providing developmental assistance to protégés may be considered in determining indirect costs rates for reimbursement
Federal Aviation Administration FAA Mentor-Protégé Program available at http://www.sbo.faa.gov/MentorProtege.cfm (active, SBA approval not required)	Small businesses; small socially and economically disadvantaged businesses; small disadvantaged businesses; service-disabled veteran-owned small businesses; historically black colleges and universities; minority institutions; women-owned small businesses	Evaluation credits during source selection Subcontracts awarded to protégés count toward subcontracting goals Costs incurred in providing developmental assistance to protégés may be considered in determining indirect costs rates for reimbursement Procurements set aside for firms that are "participants in the FAA Mentor-Protégé Program"[a]
General Services Administration 48 C.F.R. Subpart 519.70 (retiring the program)	Small businesses; small disadvantaged businesses; veteran-owned small businesses; service-disabled	Costs incurred in providing developmental assistance to protégés may be considered in determining indirect costs rates for reimbursement

Table 1. (Continued)

Agency	Eligible Protégés	Incentives for Mentors
	veteran-owned small businesses; HUBZone small businesses; woman-owned small businesses	Evaluation credits during source selection Factor in evaluating past performance and determining contractor responsibility Agency mentoring award (nonmonetary) Invitation to mentor-protégé annual conference
National Aeronautics and Space Administration 48 C.F.R. Subpart 1819.72 (active, SBA approved)	Small disadvantaged businesses; women-owned small businesses; HUBZone small businesses; veteran-owned small businesses; service-disabled veteran-owned small businesses; historically black colleges and universities; minority institutions; nonprofit agencies employing persons who are "blind or severely disabled"	May count costs of development assistance provided to protégés toward subcontracting plan Costs incurred in providing developmental assistance to protégés may be considered in determining indirect costs rates for reimbursement Eligible to earn separate award fees associated with the provision of developmental assistance to NASA SBIR Phase II protégés
U.S. Agency for International Development 48 C.F.R. Subpart 719.273 (retiring the program)	Small businesses; small disadvantaged small businesses; veteran-owned small businesses; service-disabled veteran-owned small businesses; HUBZone small businesses; woman-owned small businesses	Costs incurred in providing developmental assistance to protégés may be considered in determining indirect costs rates for reimbursement Evaluation credits during source selection Factor in evaluating past performance and determining contractor responsibility Agency mentoring award (nonmonetary) Invitation to mentor-protégé annual conference

Source: Congressional Research Service, based on various sources cited in Table 1.

[a.] It is unclear whether "participant" here refers to mentors, protégés, or joint ventures involving mentors and protégés. Because agencies generally may not restrict competition absent express statutory authorization, such set-asides may be limited to small business protégés, as opposed to mentor firms.

In addition, mentors may credit costs incurred in providing assistance to their protégés toward their goals for subcontracting with small businesses.[132] Mentors are also eligible for an annual award presented by DHS to the firm providing the most effective developmental support to a protégé.[133]

DOT Funding Recipients' Mentor-Protégé Programs

Department of Transportation (DOT) regulations authorize recipients of certain federal transportation funding to establish mentor-protégé programs "in which another [disadvantaged business enterprise (DBE)] or non-DBE firm is the principal source of business development assistance to a DBE firm."[134] These programs are designed "to further the development of DBEs, including but not limited to assisting them to move into nontraditional areas of work or compete in the marketplace outside the DBE program, via the provision of training and assistance."[135] For example, mentors in the Ohio Department of Transportation Mentor/Protégé Program may assist protégés by (1) setting targets for improvement; (2) setting time tables for meeting those targets; (3) assisting with the protégé's business strategies; (4) assisting in evaluating outcomes; (5) assisting in developing protégés' business plans; (6) regularly reviewing protégés' business and action plans; and (7) monitoring protégés' key business indicators, including their cash flow, work in progress, and recent bids.[136] Those in the Illinois Department of Transportation Mentor-Protégé Program similarly may provide training

---

[132] 48 C.F.R. §3052.219-71(d). ("For example, a mentor/large business prime contractor would report a $10,000 subcontract to the protégé/small business subcontractor and $5,000 of developmental assistance to the protégé/small business subcontractor as $15,000").

[133] DHS, "Mentor-Protégé Program Details," at http://www.dhs.gov/xlibrary/assets/opnbiz/ OSDBU_MentorProtegeDetails.pdf.

[134] 49 C.F.R. §26.35(b).

[135] U.S. Department of Transportation, "DBE Final Rule, Appendix D to Part 26 - Mentor-Protégé Program Guidelines," at http://www.osdbu.dot.gov/DBEProgram/final/final60.cfm. Recipients of DOT funding are particularly encouraged to use mentor-protégé programs to assist DBEs in performing work outside of specific fields in which DBEs are "overconcentrated." 49 C.F.R. §26.33(b).

[136] Ohio Department of Transportation Mentor/Protégé Program, p. 5, at https://www.fhwa.dot.gov/resourcecenter/teams/civilrights/odot_mentor.pdf.

and development, technical and management assistance, personnel, financial assistance, and equipment to their protégés.[137]

According to DOT, data concerning the number and performance of DBE mentor-protégé agreements are retained at the state level and are not reported to the DOT.[138]

"Disadvantaged business enterprises," for purposes of DOT funding programs

Individuals who belong to one of the following racial or ethnic groups, or who can prove that they are personally socially disadvantaged, and who have a personal net worth of $1.32 million may qualify as "disadvantaged business enterprises" upon certification by a state funding recipient:

(i) "Black Americans," which includes persons having origins in any of the Black racial groups of Africa; (ii) "Hispanic Americans," which includes persons of Mexican, Puerto Rican, Cuban, Dominican, Central or South American, or other Spanish or Portuguese culture or origin, regardless of race; (iii) "Native Americans," which includes persons who are American Indians, Eskimos, Aleuts, or Native Hawaiians; (iv) "Asian-Pacific Americans," which includes persons whose origins are from Japan, China, Taiwan, Korea, Burma (Myanmar), Vietnam, Laos, Cambodia (Kampuchea), Thailand, Malaysia, Indonesia, the Philippines, Brunei, Samoa, Guam, the U.S. Trust Territories of the Pacific Islands (Republic of Palau), the Commonwealth of the Northern Marianas Islands, Macao, Fiji, Tonga, Kiribati, [T]uvalu, Nauru, Federated States of Micronesia, or Hong Kong; (v) "Subcontinent Asian Americans," which includes persons whose origins are from India, Pakistan, Bangladesh, Bhutan, the Maldives Islands, Nepal or Sri Lanka; (vi) Women; (vii) [a]ny additional groups whose members are designated as socially and economically disadvantaged by the SBA, at such time as the SBA designation becomes effective.

Source: 49 C.F.R. §26.5; 49 C.F.R. §26.67.

---

[137] Illinois Department of Transportation, Mentor-Protégé Program Sample Development Plan, at http://www.dot.state.il.us/obwd/Mentor%20Protege%20Sample%20Development%20Plan.pdf.

[138] DOT, Office of Small and Disadvantaged Business Utilization, telephone consultation, March 1, 2011.

The DOT program does not receive a separate funding appropriation. DOT is seeking SBA-approval for its mentor-protégé programs.

Regulations Governing DOT Mentor-Protégé Programs

DBEs may participate in DOT mentor-protégé programs as either mentors or protégés. However, under DOT regulations, all DBEs involved in a mentor-protégé agreement must be independent business entities that meet the requirements for certification as a DBE. These regulations also require that firms be certified before participating as a protégé in a mentor-protégé arrangement.[139]

The relationship between mentor and protégé is based on a written development plan, approved by the recipient of the DOT funding, "which clearly sets forth the objectives of the parties and their respective roles, the duration of the arrangement and the services and resources to be provided by the mentor to the protégé."[140] The formal mentor-protégé agreement may establish a fee schedule to cover the direct and indirect cost of services provided by the mentor to the protégé. Services provided by the mentor may be reimbursable if these services and any associated costs are "directly attributable and properly allowable."[141]

Participant Benefits

Mentor firms may generally count the amount of assistance they provide to their protégés toward their goals for contracting or subcontracting with DBEs. However, under DOT regulations, a non-DBE mentor firm cannot receive credit for meeting more than half of its goal on any contract by using its own protégé.[142] These regulations also prohibit a non-DBE mentor firm from receiving DBE credit for using its own protégé on more than every other contract performed by the protégé.[143] For example, if Mentor Firm X uses Protégé Firm Y to perform a subcontract, Mentor Firm X cannot get DBE credit for using Protégé Firm Y on another

---

[139] 49 C.F.R. Part 26, App'x D, at C.
[140] 49 C.F.R. Part 26, App'x D, at (B)(1).
[141] 49 C.F.R. Part 26, App'x D, at (B)(2).
[142] 49 C.F.R. §26.35(b)(2)(i).
[143] 49 C.F.R. §26.35(b)(2)(ii).

subcontract until Protégé Firm Y first works on an intervening prime contract or subcontract with a different prime contractor.[144] There are no comparable restrictions for other mentor-protégé programs.

CONCLUSION

Congressional interest in small business mentor-protégé programs has increased in recent years for a variety of reasons, including reports that these programs are being used by large businesses to perform federal contracts, in violation of small business procurement laws and regulations and contrary to the intent of the mentor-protégé programs.[145] The SBA's suspension (and later reinstatement) of a mentor in the 8(a) Mentor-Protégé Program for fraud,[146] as well as reports of fraud in several of the SBA's contracting programs, has also contributed to congressional interest.[147] In addition, GAO found in 2011 that the SBA "has not been able to properly oversee [the 8(a) mentor-protégé] program,"[148] and the SBA issued new regulations for the 8(a) program generally, and for the 8(a) Mentor-Protégé Program in particular, to better ensure that its benefits "flow to the intended recipients" and "help prevent waste, fraud and abuse."[149] GAO has also recommended that federal agencies collect and maintain protégé post-completion information "to help ensure that small businesses are benefiting from participation in the programs as intended."[150] Given these

---

[144] DOT, "DBE Final Rule, Section 26.35 - What Role do Business Development and Mentor-Protégé Programs Have in the DBE Program?" at http://www.osdbu.dot.gov/DBEProgram/final/final19.cfm.

[145] For additional information and analysis concerning the 8(a) Program, see CRS Report R44844, *SBA's "8(a) Program": Overview, History, and Current Issues*, by Robert Jay Dilger.

[146] Ibid.

[147] Ibid.

[148] Ibid., p. 24.

[149] SBA, "Final Regulations Will Strengthen 8(a) Business Development Program for Small Businesses," February 11, 2011, at http://www.sba.gov/content/final-regulations-will-strengthen-8a-business-development-program-smallbusinesses.

[150] GAO, *Mentor-Protégé Programs Have Policies That Aim to Benefit Participants But Do Not Require Postagreement Tracking*, GAO-11-548R, June 15, 2011, p. 9, at http://www.gao.gov/new.items/d11548r.pdf.

developments, and SBA's recent addition of a mentor-protégé program for non-8(a) small businesses, it seems likely that mentor-protégé programs will remain subject to congressional oversight or proposed legislation during the 115th Congress.

Effective August 24, 2016, federal agencies sponsoring an agency-specific mentor-protégé program must report annually to the SBA specific information, such as the number and type of small business participants, the assistance provided, and the protégés' progress in competing for federal contracts.[151] This information could prove useful to Congress as it conducts oversight of these programs.

In addition, Congress could specify additional information that the SBA, and other federal agencies, must maintain and report annually to Congress concerning their mentor-protégé programs. For example, DOD has historically been required to report the following information regarding its mentor-protégé program: (1) the number of mentor-protégé agreements entered into during the fiscal year; (2) the number of mentor-protégé agreements in effect during the fiscal year; (3) the total amount reimbursed to mentor firms during the fiscal year; (4) each mentor-protégé agreement, if any, approved during the fiscal year that provided a program participation term in excess of three years, together with the justification for the approval; (5) each reimbursement of a mentor firm in excess of the program's limits made during the fiscal year, together with the justification for the approval; and (6) trends in the progress made in employment, revenues, and participation in agency contracts by protégé firms participating in the program during the fiscal year and protégé firms that completed or otherwise terminated participation in the program during the preceding two fiscal years.[152]

---

[151] SBA, "Small Business Mentor Protégé Program," 81 *Federal Register* 48590, July 25, 2016.
[152] See, e.g., National Defense Authorization Act for Fiscal Year 2000, P.L. 106-65, §811, 113 Stat. 706-10 (October 5, 1999).

APPENDIX. COMPARISON OF SELECTED AGENCIES' MENTOR-PROTÉGÉ PROGRAMS

Table A.1. Tabular Comparison of Selected Agencies' Mentor-Protégé Programs

	SBA 8(a)	DOD	DHS	DOT
Primary focus	Contracts	Subcontracts; suppliers	Subcontracts	Federally funded contracts
Eligible mentors	Large firms; small firms; 8(a) graduates; other 8(a) firms in the transitional stage	Prime contractors with at least one active subcontracting plan (small businesses generally ineligible)	Large prime contractors	Another disadvantaged business enterprise (DBE) or a non-DBE firm
Eligible protégés	Small disadvantaged businesses participating in the 8(a) Program	Small disadvantaged businesses; businesses owned and controlled by Indian tribes, Alaska Native Corporations or Native Hawaiian Organizations; qualified organizations employing the "severely disabled"; women-owned and service-disabled veteran-owned small businesses; HUBZone small businesses	Small businesses; veteran-owned small businesses; service-disabled veteran-owned small businesses; HUBZone small businesses, small disadvantaged businesses; women-owned small businesses	Small disadvantaged businesses; women-owned small businesses
Notable types of assistance	Assistance in performing prime contracts with the government in the form of joint ventures Financial assistance in the form of equity investments or loans Subcontracts Technical or management assistance	Advance and progress payments Award of subcontracts on a noncompetitive basis Investments in protégé firm in exchange for ownership interests Loans Assistance in general business management, engineering and technical matters, etc.	Rent-free use of facilities or equipment; property Temporary assignment of personnel to protégé for training Financial and organizational management Overall business management, planning, and development Technical assistance	Varies by program, but can include: training and development; technical and management assistance; personnel; financial assistance; and equipment

	SBA 8(a)	DOD	DHS	DOT
Incentives for mentor firms	Assistance counts toward subcontracting goals Can form joint venture with protégé that may be eligible for 8(a) and other small business contracts May acquire ownership of up to 40% in protégé firm Can receive incentives in contract evaluations	Reimbursement of certain developmental assistance costs Unreimbursed development costs credited toward subcontracting goals Can award subcontracts on a noncompetitive basis to the protégé	Participation in mentor-protégé program can serve as an evaluation factor in negotiated procurements Costs incurred in providing assistance to protégé count toward subcontracting goals Agency award for best mentor	Can generally count the amount of assistance provided to protégés toward goals for contracting or subcontracting with DBEs Certain assistance costs may be reimbursed

Source: Congressional Research Service, based on various sources cited in this chapter.

INDEX

#

504/CDC, vii, viii, xiii, 13, 14, 162, 172, 173, 174, 177, 190, 191, 192, 193, 195, 225

7(a) loans, vii, x, 4, 13, 58, 60, 61, 62, 63, 64, 66, 67, 68, 69, 70, 71, 77, 85, 88, 89, 92, 94, 95, 98, 191

A

access, vii, viii, x, xi, xii, xiii, 1, 2, 3, 4, 5, 15, 20, 24, 39, 47, 64, 65, 66, 103, 104, 105, 106, 107, 110, 111, 114, 115, 120, 125, 132, 133, 144, 171, 172, 173, 177, 186, 189, 190, 193, 205, 217, 234, 235, 238, 242, 243, 259, 262, 279

accountability, 137

accounting, 29, 120, 121, 141, 143, 144, 146, 147, 148, 149, 150, 153, 192, 225, 226, 237, 292

adjustment, 32, 40, 150, 247

agencies, xiv, xv, xvi, 28, 77, 90, 127, 130, 134, 135, 153, 179, 204, 208, 213, 225, 230, 239, 246, 249, 254, 255, 261, 266, 267, 268, 270, 271, 273, 279, 283, 284, 287, 288, 291, 292, 295, 296, 300, 304, 305

Alaska, xi, 104, 107, 122, 123, 192, 238, 262, 282, 290, 306

Alaska Natives, 238, 262

American Samoa, xi, 104, 107, 119, 122, 123, 126, 138, 157, 158, 180, 212, 213, 238, 262

Appropriations Act, 13, 188, 193, 207, 217, 220, 221, 242, 248, 284, 295

assets, viii, 2, 5, 11, 15, 16, 17, 20, 22, 29, 30, 46, 48, 49, 51, 52, 54, 66, 106, 110, 122, 126, 130, 135, 191, 255, 288, 298, 301

audit(s), 10, 38, 41, 42, 62, 95, 104, 109, 119, 125, 126, 128, 130, 131, 132, 134, 135, 138, 143, 144, 145, 146, 147, 148, 149, 150, 151, 157, 158, 161, 162, 164, 165, 166, 167, 168

authority, ix, xv, xvi, 2, 6, 13, 14, 15, 16, 39, 41, 46, 47, 48, 54, 58, 60, 62, 63, 64, 65, 76, 81, 88, 89, 130, 131, 132, 146, 213, 221, 227, 228, 229, 246, 266, 270, 292, 295

average revenue, 179

B

balance sheet, 23
bank financing, 114
bank holding companies, 16, 28, 44, 52
banking, 19, 20, 26, 28, 29, 30, 50, 51
banks, viii, 2, 5, 17, 18, 19, 21, 22, 23, 24, 25, 26, 29, 30, 31, 33, 36, 37, 39, 44, 46, 47, 49, 50, 51, 62, 64, 85, 86, 95, 106, 110, 111, 133, 134, 135
base year, 221
benefits, 273, 277, 283, 292, 296, 304
Bhutan, 274, 289, 302
borrowers, x, xiv, 10, 15, 21, 57, 58, 59, 60, 61, 62, 63, 64, 65, 67, 71, 72, 81, 83, 84, 86, 88, 92, 93, 94, 99, 100, 116, 117, 120, 129, 133, 135, 137, 142, 192, 194, 204, 209, 217, 218, 219, 262
budget line, 221
bureaucracy, 25
business management, xii, xiii, 171, 173, 203, 254, 258, 289, 297, 306
business model, 241
business startups, vii, viii, xii, 171, 172, 173, 175, 187, 244
business strategy, 19, 50
businesses, viii, ix, x, xii, xiv, xv, 1, 2, 3, 4, 5, 10, 12, 14, 15, 20, 21, 25, 29, 32, 37, 46, 48, 60, 61, 62, 64, 66, 67, 68, 69, 70, 72, 84, 85, 103, 105, 106, 108, 109, 111, 114, 116, 118, 121, 151, 168, 171, 172, 173, 175, 177, 178, 179, 180, 181, 182, 183, 188, 189, 190, 196, 197, 198, 200, 201, 205, 206, 209, 211, 213, 220, 222, 223, 225, 229, 230, 236, 237, 240, 241, 242, 243, 246, 247, 255, 259, 261, 265, 266, 267, 268, 269, 270, 271, 272, 278, 285, 286, 288, 290, 292, 296, 297, 298, 299, 300, 304, 306
buyer, 151

C

Cambodia, 274, 289, 302
capacity building, 233, 234
capital programs, 118, 160
Capital Purchase Program (CPP), 17, 24, 31, 49
cash, 16, 20, 26, 49, 83, 116, 117, 160, 198, 212, 213, 218, 220, 221, 223, 230, 244, 261, 301
cash flow, 83, 198, 223, 301
certification, 64, 134, 139, 146, 149, 155, 157, 238, 262, 302, 303
challenges, xiii, 21, 132, 133, 172, 177, 202, 250, 251, 252, 258, 260
clients, 174, 179, 180, 181, 182, 183, 184, 185, 186, 213, 215, 222, 223, 227, 230, 231, 250, 252, 253, 257
collateral, xi, 10, 60, 64, 85, 104, 106, 113, 114, 116, 117, 120, 124, 125, 135, 161, 162, 194, 209
colleges, 179, 213, 261, 285, 296, 298, 299, 300
commercial, 7, 9, 14, 17, 21, 32, 43, 52, 60, 62, 108, 287
community, viii, 2, 5, 6, 16, 20, 22, 23, 25, 31, 36, 46, 47, 50, 51, 52, 54, 60, 66, 106, 110, 192, 193, 212
compensation, 46
competition, 63, 187, 244, 250, 289, 299, 300
competitive markets, 189
compliance, vii, x, xi, 43, 58, 59, 61, 63, 73, 74, 75, 76, 77, 78, 80, 82, 83, 88, 89, 90, 92, 94, 104, 109, 137, 138, 140, 141, 143, 144, 145, 146, 147, 149, 153, 154, 155, 156, 157, 158, 159, 160, 161, 162, 163, 164, 167, 168, 209, 221, 227
conference, 87, 130, 131, 165, 207, 226, 248, 270, 283, 299, 300
conflict, 149, 163, 164, 276, 281

Congress, viii, ix, x, xi, xiv, 1, 2, 4, 6, 13, 14, 22, 27, 31, 37, 39, 41, 42, 45, 46, 47, 60, 103, 104, 105, 107, 109, 110, 131, 134, 135, 136, 173, 176, 178, 180, 187, 188, 190, 201, 203, 204, 205, 206, 208, 209, 210, 211, 212, 216, 219, 220, 222, 223, 224,225, 227, 228, 229, 230, 232, 236, 237, 238, 239, 240, 242, 244, 247, 248, 249, 251, 252, 253, 254, 255, 257, 259, 260, 267, 269, 270, 279, 284, 285, 287, 294, 305
congressional hearings, 208, 248
consensus, 175, 259
consent, 115, 165
Consolidated Appropriations Act, x, xiv, 58, 61, 188, 196, 204, 205, 207, 209, 212, 230, 242, 245, 248, 284
construction, 3, 12, 52, 115, 162, 174, 277, 288
cooperation, xiv, 197, 204, 208, 228, 248
cooperative agreements, 284
coordination, xiv, 204, 208, 248, 250, 251, 253, 254, 274
cost, xiii, 13, 20, 24, 26, 41, 42, 43, 44, 51, 65, 66, 116, 119, 150, 152, 153, 159, 160, 168, 172, 177, 197, 230, 243, 256, 303
cost effectiveness, xiii, 172, 177
counsel, 173
counseling, 178, 179, 180, 181, 182, 205, 210, 211, 213, 215, 218, 224, 225, 230, 232, 237, 259, 261, 284, 285
credit history, 189
credit market, viii, x, 1, 4, 7, 46, 92, 103, 105
creditors, 197
creditworthiness, 10, 99, 194
customers, xiii, 172, 177

D

data collection, 210, 216, 257
database, 194
debentures, 30, 176, 191, 192, 200
debt service, 78
debts, 191
deficit, viii, x, 1, 4, 46, 103, 105
Department of Agriculture, 273
Department of Commerce, xiii, 158, 187, 204, 206, 243, 245, 247
Department of Defense, xv, 13, 226, 266, 267, 268, 287, 288, 290, 295
Department of Education, 268
Department of Energy, 239, 240, 267, 283, 287, 288, 290, 296, 298
Department of Health and Human Services, 268, 283, 298
Department of Homeland Security, xv, 266, 267, 283, 296
Department of the Treasury, ix, 3, 6, 22, 27, 41, 42, 43, 46, 106, 109, 119, 268, 283, 299
Department of Transportation, 268, 283, 301, 302
depository institutions, 16, 28, 44, 52
deposits, 114
direct investment, 196
disaster, xiv, 62, 113, 173, 204, 209, 214, 216, 223, 232, 247
disaster area, xiv, 204, 209, 214, 216, 223, 232
disbursement, 121, 127, 130, 131, 133, 145, 146, 154, 157, 160, 167
disclosure, 70
District of Columbia, xi, 31, 66, 104, 106, 107, 119, 122, 123, 179, 212, 213, 217

E

economic development, 179, 192, 196, 206, 213, 241, 245, 247, 254, 261, 285
economic downturn, 86, 193, 217
economic growth, 10, 107, 111
economic problem, 107, 111
economic theory, xii, 172
education, 205, 216, 226, 234, 238, 241, 253, 262, 273
educational services, 208, 249
employees, xii, 3, 12, 66, 108, 115, 116, 117, 118, 120, 135, 168, 172, 175, 179, 231, 232, 246, 268, 278
employment, xii, 3, 4, 12, 172, 175, 179, 305
energy efficiency, 240
engineering, 212, 289, 294, 306
enrollment, 144, 145, 147, 161, 287
entrepreneurs, xiii, 66, 172, 177, 178, 179, 186, 190, 193, 204, 205, 213, 217, 226, 233, 234, 235, 239, 243, 251, 253, 255, 256, 260, 261, 262
entrepreneurship, 66, 187, 225, 226, 242, 243, 262

F

families, 37
family members, 87, 226
farmers, 17, 32, 52
farmland, 17, 32, 52
federal agency, 273
federal assistance, xii, 40, 172, 174
federal banking regulators, 29
federal deficit, viii, x, 1, 4, 46, 103, 105
federal funds, 23, 77, 109, 120, 130, 163, 213, 225
federal government, viii, x, xiv, 1, 4, 25, 46, 103, 105, 238, 240, 246, 256, 258, 265, 271
federal law, 221
Federal Register, xvi, 193, 198, 199, 200, 201, 246, 266, 269, 270, 271, 272, 273, 275, 276, 277, 280, 281, 282, 283, 286, 292, 296, 305
Federal Reserve, 6, 8, 21, 44, 66, 67, 92, 134
Federal Reserve Board, 6, 8, 44
financial, viii, x, xiii, xiv, 1, 4, 6, 10, 15, 16, 20, 22, 23, 28, 29, 30, 37, 38, 40, 46, 48, 49, 50, 51, 52, 53, 54, 64, 83, 85, 87, 103, 105, 145, 151, 178, 180, 182, 196, 201, 204, 205, 206, 209, 214, 220, 222, 223, 224, 228, 232, 237, 239, 245, 247, 265, 267,273, 275, 280, 284, 292, 297, 302, 306
financial condition, 40
financial crisis, 15, 48
financial institutions, 6, 16, 23, 28, 29, 38, 46, 48, 105
financial markets, 10
financial performance, 10
financial support, 178, 205, 284
financial system, 23, 46
firm size, xii, 63, 172, 175
fiscal year, x, 15, 54, 58, 59, 60, 61, 62, 65, 66, 67, 68, 69, 70, 71, 72, 73, 74, 75, 76, 77, 78, 79, 80, 82, 92, 94, 96, 98, 100, 198, 210, 224, 234, 235, 236, 237, 239, 240, 257, 291, 305
formation, xii, 171, 173, 176, 180, 181, 201, 205, 211, 222, 224, 225, 258, 260, 263, 288, 293
formula, xi, 104, 106, 109, 119, 121, 122, 212
fraud, 269, 279, 304
funding, viii, ix, x, xi, xiv, 2, 5, 13, 15, 18, 23, 30, 31, 36, 38, 104, 105, 106, 108, 113, 114, 115, 119, 120, 121, 122, 125, 128, 129, 133, 140, 141, 142, 150, 154, 158, 162, 163, 166, 169, 186, 187, 189, 204, 208, 211, 212, 216, 218, 221, 227,

234, 235, 236,240, 242, 243, 244, 247, 249, 252, 255, 256, 258, 259, 260, 280, 285, 297, 301, 302, 303
funds, ix, xi, xiv, 2, 6, 10, 13, 14, 16, 20, 23, 30, 32, 36, 37, 38, 40, 41, 42, 46, 51, 52, 63, 104, 106, 107, 108, 109, 114, 115, 118, 120, 121, 125, 126, 127, 129, 130, 131, 132, 133, 135, 136, 138, 139, 140, 141, 142, 143, 145, 146, 147, 148, 149, 150, 151, 152, 153, 155, 156, 157, 158, 159, 160, 163, 164, 165, 166, 167, 168, 169, 188, 192, 193, 194, 195, 196, 199, 200, 204, 206, 209, 213, 217, 218, 219, 220, 221, 224, 227, 234, 235, 240, 244, 245, 247, 262, 295

G

global climate change, 247
government procurement, 178, 205
grants, 15, 142, 187, 188, 193, 213, 217, 220, 221, 227, 230, 233, 234, 235, 237, 244, 245, 247, 257, 262, 284, 285
growth, xiii, 3, 9, 35, 37, 60, 63, 107, 172, 177, 179, 186, 187, 188, 195, 199, 201, 202, 213, 241, 243, 244, 245, 258, 294
Guam, xi, 104, 107, 119, 122, 123, 179, 212, 213, 238, 262, 274, 289, 302
guidance, x, 58, 60, 61, 63, 85, 86, 87, 92, 94, 127, 130, 131, 134, 135, 136, 139, 140, 141, 142, 143, 144, 145, 151, 153, 156, 158, 161, 166, 250, 280
guidelines, 43, 78, 126, 127, 133, 136, 137, 140, 144, 149, 151, 152, 153, 160, 161, 162, 163, 165, 166

H

higher education, 212, 294, 296
history, 15, 92, 211, 230
holding company, 16, 44, 52

homeowners, xii, 171, 173, 205
human resources, 226

I

income, 18, 28, 63, 109, 113, 120, 125, 141, 144, 145, 146, 193, 196, 217, 218, 220, 221, 233, 234, 235, 237, 247, 261, 262, 268, 278
income tax, 18, 28, 63, 113, 146
individuals, xv, 121, 181, 182, 183, 184, 185, 186, 193, 209, 214, 217, 220, 223, 232, 237, 258, 261, 265, 268, 272, 274, 275, 286, 289, 290, 292, 297
industrial sectors, 98
industry, 3, 61, 63, 64, 76, 82, 84, 85, 88, 93, 95, 196, 241, 268, 278
institutions, 15, 16, 17, 18, 28, 29, 30, 31, 32, 33, 35, 36, 38, 39, 40, 41, 44, 48, 49, 52, 53, 228, 241, 296, 298, 299, 300
intellectual property, 241
interest rates, 26, 43, 116
intermediaries, xiv, 15, 62, 193, 204, 208, 209, 217, 218, 219, 262
internal controls, 79, 80
investment, ix, xi, 3, 6, 16, 18, 20, 22, 28, 30, 39, 40, 41, 42, 45, 48, 51, 53, 54, 66, 104, 106, 114, 115, 118, 122, 125, 126, 129, 148, 153, 159, 160, 163, 164, 166, 169, 175, 176, 196, 199, 240, 249
investment capital, 118
investors, 14, 40, 118, 136, 166, 198
issues, 20, 29, 43, 61, 74, 75, 76, 77, 78, 92, 95, 133, 139, 146, 149, 158, 162

J

job creation, xii, xiii, 4, 107, 111, 162, 172, 174, 175, 176, 177, 192, 194, 195, 201, 202, 211, 257, 258, 260

L

joint ventures, xv, 266, 273, 278, 281, 282, 300, 306
justification, xii, 74, 76, 78, 81, 172, 174, 292, 295, 305

labor force, xii, 172, 174
laws, viii, xvi, 1, 4, 266, 270, 304
laws and regulations, 304
learning, 133, 225, 298
legislation, xiv, 13, 23, 39, 44, 45, 47, 110, 111, 204, 209, 212, 216, 224, 232, 296, 305
legislative authority, 62
legislative proposals, 110
lender credit, vii, x, 58
lending, vii, viii, ix, x, xi, xiii, 2, 5, 6, 8, 10, 11, 14, 15, 16, 17, 18, 19, 20, 21, 22, 23, 24, 25, 26, 28, 29, 30, 31, 32, 33, 35, 36, 37, 38, 40, 41, 42, 45, 47, 48, 49, 50, 52, 53, 54, 58, 60, 61, 62, 65, 66, 68, 85, 86, 92, 98, 104, 105, 107, 108, 110, 112, 114, 115, 120, 129, 130, 168, 172, 173, 174, 177, 189, 194, 195, 216, 217, 262
lending process, 189
loan guarantees, 14
loan principal, 161
loans, vii, ix, x, xv, 2, 4, 5, 7, 9, 10, 11, 12, 13, 14, 15, 16, 17, 21, 22, 23, 25, 26, 32, 33, 37, 38, 39, 42, 43, 46, 49, 52, 53, 58, 60, 61, 62, 63, 64, 65, 66, 67, 68, 69, 70, 71, 72, 74, 76, 77, 78, 80, 81, 82, 85, 86, 87, 88, 89, 90, 92, 94, 95, 98, 99,100, 105, 108, 111, 114, 115, 116, 117, 120, 128, 129, 133, 134, 135, 136, 138, 139, 140, 141, 142, 144, 145, 146, 147, 148, 150, 151, 152, 154, 155, 156, 159, 161, 162, 165, 168, 177, 189, 190, 191, 193, 194, 197, 205, 217, 218, 220, 262, 266, 273, 277, 297, 306

local community, 233, 257
local government, 220, 233, 247

M

majority, 24, 28, 62, 67, 68, 69, 72, 139, 142, 152, 247, 269
management, vii, viii, xii, xiii, xiv, xv, 15, 59, 64, 74, 80, 82, 83, 118, 120, 142, 158, 172, 176, 178, 179, 180, 181, 183, 184, 185, 186, 194, 196, 203, 204, 205, 206, 208, 209, 210, 211, 212, 213, 216, 217, 218, 220, 222, 223, 224, 225, 227, 228, 230, 237, 238, 239, 246, 248, 250, 251, 252, 253, 254, 255, 256, 257, 258, 259, 260, 261, 262, 265, 266, 267, 273, 277, 297, 299, 302, 306
manufacturing, 3, 282
market failure, 189
market share, 11
marketing, 15, 180, 194, 217, 218, 220, 223, 225, 226, 237, 241, 285
marketplace, 294, 301
materials, 127, 136, 149, 193, 194, 199, 217
measurement, xiv, 128, 204, 209, 250
media, 175, 178, 235, 285
median, 74, 99, 100
memorandums of understanding, 250
mentoring, xiii, 178, 203, 205, 227, 230, 231, 243, 261, 282, 283, 284, 285, 295, 298, 299, 300
mentoring program, xiii, 178, 204, 205
microloan, 194, 217, 218
microloan lending programs, vii, viii, xiii, 172, 173, 177
mission, 64, 65, 174, 179, 201, 208, 246, 249, 255, 262
missions, 173, 195, 201
misuse, 138, 139, 140, 142, 145, 148, 156, 159, 163, 167

N

national debt, 24, 111, 112
National Defense Authorization Act, xv, 216, 224, 232, 266, 270, 287, 288, 293, 296, 305
Native Americans, 238, 274, 289, 302
natural disaster, xii, 171, 173, 205
networking, xiii, 172, 177, 186, 241, 261
nonprofit organizations, 180, 220, 228, 229, 284

O

Obama Administration, xi, 27, 47, 104, 108, 109, 110, 187, 198, 208, 236, 239, 242, 244, 249, 255, 292
Obama, President Barack, 27, 46, 47, 55, 110, 113, 240, 283
Office of Inspector General (OIG), vii, xi, 28, 30, 38, 41, 42, 43, 44, 45, 77, 94, 104, 109, 119, 125, 126, 136, 137, 138, 139, 140, 141, 142, 143, 144, 145, 146, 147, 148, 149, 150, 151, 152, 153, 154, 155, 156, 157, 158, 159, 160, 161, 162, 163, 164, 165, 166, 167, 168, 176
Office of Management and Budget, 27, 106, 109, 129, 246
Office of the Inspector General, 28, 30, 38, 42, 43, 44
officials, 30, 36, 61, 73, 75, 76, 81, 83, 92, 94, 95, 127, 130, 132, 133, 134, 135, 136, 139, 140, 144, 146, 150, 151, 153, 162, 165, 169, 243, 250
operations, vii, viii, x, xiii, xiv, 1, 3, 46, 103, 105, 178, 195, 198, 203, 204, 205, 209, 226, 259, 268, 272, 275
opportunities, xii, xiii, 171, 172, 173, 177, 186, 196, 205, 225, 237, 241, 247, 254, 259
outreach, xiii, 19, 50, 130, 178, 203, 205, 207, 208, 227, 249, 284
oversight, ix, xi, xiv, 2, 5, 22, 23, 24, 25, 40, 45, 58, 61, 63, 65, 73, 90, 94, 104, 109, 137, 147, 169, 204, 209, 250, 253, 305
ownership, 67, 68, 83, 87, 146, 155, 163, 192, 278, 289, 306, 307

P

participants, xi, xvi, 24, 30, 32, 33, 34, 35, 36, 37, 38, 42, 43, 45, 104, 107, 109, 125, 126, 130, 131, 132, 133, 134, 135, 137, 138, 160, 166, 183, 184, 226, 241, 243, 256, 266, 268, 270, 278, 283, 284, 296, 299, 305
per capita income, 247
percentile, 74
personnel costs, 140, 141
policy, 45, 63, 64, 74, 75, 78, 79, 94, 126, 127, 129, 130, 131, 136, 137, 140, 144, 149, 151, 153, 161, 162, 163, 173, 246
poor performance, 24
population, xii, 70, 80, 82, 84, 92, 93, 119, 172, 174, 212, 252
portfolio, 62, 68, 73, 74, 76, 99, 114, 152, 192, 218
poverty, 70, 71, 93, 218
poverty line, 71, 93
President, xiv, 4, 12, 27, 46, 47, 55, 106, 110, 113, 119, 204, 209, 215, 216, 230, 240, 246, 283
principles, 178, 205
private sector, 109, 129, 136, 212, 230, 237, 244, 293
procurement, 115, 116, 209, 225, 268, 278, 288, 294, 295, 304
profit, 22, 23, 28, 47, 62, 110, 182, 186, 191, 274, 275
profit margin, 182, 186
public debt, 20, 51, 255

public interest, 288
public investment, 120
public policy, 15, 192
public sector, 256

R

real estate, 10, 12, 17, 32, 52, 66, 113, 115, 139, 140, 162
recession, 3, 11, 12, 25, 83, 113, 258
recommendations, 28, 42, 58, 89, 134, 136, 137, 145, 148, 163, 208
recovery, xi, xii, 20, 104, 109, 111, 171, 173, 198, 201, 205, 247, 258, 259
regulations, 16, 27, 28, 29, 30, 49, 77, 94, 158, 169, 179, 221, 235, 236, 237, 262, 274, 275, 276, 278, 279, 280, 281, 282, 283, 290, 292, 296, 301, 303, 304
regulatory agencies, 29, 30
research institutions, 240
reserves, 10, 29, 30, 139, 148, 153, 240
resources, viii, x, 1, 4, 14, 46, 60, 63, 86, 87, 103, 105, 166, 189, 205, 227, 234, 235, 241, 250, 251, 253, 260, 262, 263, 267, 294, 303
response, vii, xi, 21, 47, 60, 75, 80, 89, 90, 104, 109, 112, 127, 128, 131, 132, 137, 145, 146, 181, 231, 232
restrictions, 25, 45, 47, 115, 116, 117, 118, 137, 138, 150, 152, 276, 304
revenue, 111, 113, 179, 186, 232, 243, 269
risk, 10, 14, 16, 17, 23, 24, 26, 29, 30, 32, 44, 48, 49, 59, 60, 65, 68, 73, 74, 76, 84, 85, 89, 99, 114, 116, 117, 138, 146, 152, 166, 176, 189, 197, 198, 201, 250, 278
risk management, 74
rules, 30, 77, 111, 164, 165, 169, 198, 270, 273, 282, 283

S

savings, 16, 17, 18, 28, 33, 43, 49, 52, 254
scarce resources, 253
scope, 62, 76, 86, 148, 272
SCORE (formerly the Service Corps of Retired Executives), vii, viii, xiii, 99, 172, 177, 178, 179, 180, 181, 182, 183, 184, 185, 186, 204, 205, 207, 209, 210, 211, 214, 216, 223, 224, 225, 228, 229, 230, 231, 232, 248, 250, 256, 261
Secretary of Commerce, 246
Secretary of Defense, 295
Secretary of the Treasury, viii, x, 2, 4, 12, 15, 16, 19, 20, 21, 36, 39, 41, 42, 48, 50, 51, 54, 104, 105, 107, 110
securities, 17, 36, 43, 44, 45, 46, 49, 50, 116, 176, 197, 288
Senate, 16, 25, 26, 27, 50, 51, 52, 53, 54, 91, 109, 112, 113, 114, 174, 178, 180, 188, 205, 207, 211, 212, 216, 219, 224, 228, 229, 232, 244, 248, 253, 254, 270, 279, 283
service organizations, 228
service provider, 237, 250, 261, 262
services, xiv, 10, 29, 173, 179, 180, 204, 208, 210, 213, 215, 216, 218, 222, 223, 224, 227, 229, 230, 232, 233, 234, 237, 238, 248, 250, 251, 252, 253, 255, 256, 257, 259, 260, 262, 292, 293, 303
Small Business Development Centers (SBDCs), vii, viii, xii, xiii, 172, 176, 178, 179, 180, 183, 184, 185, 186, 203, 204, 205, 206, 209, 210, 211, 212, 213, 214, 216, 223, 224, 225, 232, 248, 250, 252, 256, 257, 260
small business loans, v, vii, ix, 2, 5, 6, 7, 9, 10, 11, 12, 13, 14, 17, 22, 26, 42, 43, 49, 57, 67, 108, 138, 168
small business mentor-protégé programs, vi, viii, 265, 269, 271, 288, 304

Index

small firms, 7, 63, 189, 253, 259, 306
spending, viii, x, xii, 1, 4, 24, 46, 47, 103, 105, 111, 113, 132, 133, 135, 172, 174
State of the Union address, 47
state oversight, 137
State Small Business Credit Initiative (SSBCI), v, vii, viii, x, 2, 5, 15, 47, 103, 104, 106, 107, 108, 109, 110, 111, 112, 113, 114, 115, 116, 117, 118, 119, 120, 121, 122, 123, 124, 125, 126, 127, 128, 129, 130, 131, 132, 133, 134, 135, 136, 137, 138, 139, 140, 141, 142, 143, 144, 145, 146, 147, 148, 149, 150, 151, 152, 153, 154, 155, 156, 157, 158, 159, 160, 161, 162, 163, 164, 165, 166, 167, 168, 169
subsidy, 43, 141
suppliers, xiv, xv, 239, 246, 265, 266, 267, 269, 272, 287, 288, 289, 293, 306

T

target, 59, 60, 84, 88, 108, 116, 117, 118, 135, 177, 178, 225, 252
target population, 59, 84, 88
tax credits, 22, 111
tax incentive, 111
taxation, 29
taxes, 12, 18, 146
taxpayers, 23, 24, 39, 43
technical assistance, vii, viii, xii, xiii, xiv, 14, 15, 64, 171, 172, 173, 176, 178, 179, 180, 183, 184, 185, 186, 194, 203, 204, 205, 206, 208, 209, 210, 213, 217, 218, 219, 222, 224, 225, 227, 228, 230, 233, 234, 237, 238, 247, 248, 249, 251, 252, 253, 254, 255, 256, 258, 259, 260, 261, 262, 284, 294, 297
technical comments, 90
training programs, vii, viii, xii, xiii, xiv, 171, 172, 173, 176, 178, 203, 204, 205, 206, 208, 209, 210, 225, 248, 250, 251, 252, 253, 254, 255, 256, 258, 259, 260
transactions, 31, 33, 35, 80, 116, 135, 142, 143, 144, 145, 147, 148, 152, 155, 156, 159, 160, 162, 164
Treasury Secretary, 21, 27, 39, 40, 41

U

U.S. Department of Commerce, 206, 245, 247
U.S. Department of the Treasury, 17, 18, 19, 27, 28, 29, 30, 31, 32, 33, 35, 36, 37, 38, 42, 43, 44, 46, 106, 107, 108, 114, 115, 116, 117, 118, 119, 121, 125, 126, 127, 131, 132, 136, 137, 138, 139, 140, 141, 142, 143, 144, 145, 146, 147, 148, 150, 151, 152, 154, 155, 156, 157, 159, 161, 162, 164, 165, 166, 167, 168, 169
U.S. Treasury, 19, 27, 128
unemployment rate, 247
United States, v, 3, 15, 27, 46, 48, 57, 63, 66, 91, 109, 180, 191, 212, 213, 222, 225, 230, 247, 248, 268, 269
universities, 179, 187, 211, 212, 213, 225, 243, 244, 261, 285, 296, 298, 299, 300

V

venture capital, vii, viii, xi, xii, xiii, 104, 106, 114, 118, 120, 123, 124, 125, 127, 135, 143, 148, 150, 152, 153, 155, 159, 160, 161, 162, 164, 166, 167, 171, 172, 173, 175, 177, 195, 196, 199
vote, 24, 27, 110, 112, 149, 253
voting, 163, 167

W

wealth, 196, 201, 260

White House, 46, 47, 105, 110, 187, 243
Women Business Centers (WBCs), vii, viii, xii, xiii, 172, 176, 178, 179, 180, 182, 183, 184, 185, 186, 203, 205, 208, 209, 210, 214, 216, 220, 221, 222, 223, 224, 232, 248, 249, 250, 252, 256

workers, 3, 12, 258

workforce, xii, 172, 174

Related Nova Publications

SMALL BUSINESS CONSIDERATIONS, ECONOMICS AND RESEARCH. VOLUME 10

EDITORS: Peter R. Bennett and Margaret O. Myers

SERIES: Business Issues, Competition and Entrepreneurship

BOOK DESCRIPTION: This book is a compilation of CRS reports pertaining to small businesses. Some of the topics discussed herein include current mentor-protégé programs, the Small Business Administration's new budget authority, economic research on net job creation, and congressional interest in small business access to capital.

HARDCOVER ISBN: 978-1-53614-630-1
RETAIL PRICE: $150

BUSINESS TRENDS IN THE 21ST CENTURY: REGULATIONS AND LEGISLATION

AUTHOR: Cruz Omar Clemente Escamilla

SERIES: Business Issues, Competition and Entrepreneurship

BOOK DESCRIPTION: This book opens with an examination of the economic circumstances of veteran-owned business. It provides a brief overview of veterans' employment experiences, comparing unemployment and labor force participation rates for veterans, veterans who have left the military since September 2001 and nonveterans.

SOFTCOVER ISBN: 978-1-53614-260-0
RETAIL PRICE: $160

To see a complete list of Nova publications, please visit our website at www.novapublishers.com